FRAGMENTED MEMORIES

>>>>>>>>>>>>>>>>>>>>>>>>>>>>>>>>>

# FRAGMENTED MEMORIES

<<<<<<<<<<<<<<<<<<<<<<<<<<<<<<<

*Struggling to be Tai-Ahom in India*

>>>>>>>>>>>>>>>>>>>>>>>>>>>>>>>>>

## YASMIN SAIKIA

<<<<<<<<<<<<<<<<<<<<<<<<<<<<<<<

>>>>>>>

*Duke University Press    Durham & London    2004*

<<<<<<<

© 2004 Duke University Press
All rights reserved
Printed in the United States of America on acid-free paper ∞
Designed by Amy Ruth Buchanan
Typeset in Monotype Garamond by Keystone Typesetting, Inc.
Library of Congress Cataloging-in-Publication Data appear on the last
printed page of this book. Duke University Press gratefully acknowledges
the support of the University of North Carolina at Chapel Hill, which
provided a Scholarly Publications Grant toward
the production of this book.

*For my teachers*

*Irfan Habib and*

*Thongchai Winichakul*

>>>>>>>>>>>>>>>>>>>>>>>>>>>>>>>

# Contents

<<<<<<<<<<<<<<<<<<<<<<<<<<<<<<<

## *Acknowledgments*

Writing this book has been a journey to many known and unknown places and to different time periods, concepts of histories, memories, and pasts. Along the way I was fortunate to have the wonderful company of many friends, teachers, and family and community members. Our joint explorations and probings enabled me to conceptualize and write this volume, and I now want to thank everyone for their gracious generosity, kindness, assistance, encouragement, and humor in making it a memorable experience. My readers will meet many of my companions along the path of the narrative, and thus to avoid repetitious explanations and acknowledgments I will acknowledge here only those who do not appear in the text, or who appear only peripherally.

My parents, Jahanara and Anwar Saikia, have inspired and influenced me with their love for Assam. Their constant and critical engagement with issues and their deep concerns for the people and the place made me aware of the problems as well as wanting to learn more. Jyoti Prashad Agarwala's music provided a portal to a poetic text of Assam's history that became my entry point into the emotions and hopes of the people. I deeply thank my parents and the Assamese interlocutors, Agarwala and many others, who paved the way for me to pursue the study of Assam.

Chad Haines, my partner and friend of many years, has been a constant source of support at each and every stage of writing this book. As I was finishing the book Chad asked me to teach him colloquial Assamese, and his interest allowed me to articulate and remember the language of my heart and, in turn, made writing about Assam more real and immediate.

I would like to thank Margaret Weiner, Patricia Sawin, David Ludden, Cynthia Talbot, David Gilmartin, Sugata Bose, Sanjib Baruah, and the members of the Triangle South Asia Colloquium for their comments on various sections and chapters of the manuscript. I would especially like to thank the three anonymous readers from Duke University Press for their incisive comments and helpful suggestions for improvement.

Don Raleigh, Barbara Harris, Jerma Jackson, and the faculty and staff members of the History Department at the University of North Carolina at Chapel Hill have given me a lot of their time: many of them patiently listened to my ideas and some read sections of different chapters and shared their thoughts with me. It has been a wonderful experience to be part of the History Department community and to write my book surrounded by friends and well-wishers.

My sisters Shahnaz and Shabnam; my nephews Javed, Zoheb, and Shahveer; my brothers-in-law Guni and the late Masood (who passed away before the book was completed); and my friends James Lancaster, Abdulla Badshah, Nila Chatterjee, and Wilbert Van der Klauww kept me engaged in wonderful conversations outside and beyond the book. My research and writing was funded, at different stages, by the University of North Carolina, Chapel Hill, the University Research Council (Chapel Hill), Odum Research Institute, Carleton College, the American Institute of Indian Studies, the Social Science Research Council, and the graduate school at the University of Wisconsin at Madison. I thank them all for their support.

I wish to thank my editor Valerie Millholland for her continuous support and encouragement, beginning from the day I conceived of the idea of writing this book. Kathleen McNeil assisted in editing and indexing, and Karin Breiwitz and the staff at the Center for Teaching and Learning at the University of North Carolina, Chapel Hill did the painstaking work of preparing the maps. I am indebted to them.

I owe this book to the people and place of Assam. Although I have lived nearly half of my life outside Assam, every time I visited home I met people who encouraged me to pursue my interest in Assam's history and culture and who even offered me their assistance with my research. I have been very fortunate to be able to engage them at an intellectual level, and together we have investigated a small part of Assam's history through the lens of the Tai-Ahom identity movement. These extraordinary people live in small villages and towns and have no access to the arenas of international scholarship where they can present their knowledge, hopes, and demands. I invite my readers to travel with me to my home, encounter some of the people I have met, and engage in their history, politics, and struggles for identity.

# *Preface*

In December 1992, I traveled to Guwahati, in the state of Assam in India. Just two days before, the historic Baburi mosque at Ayodhya (built by the first Mughal king, Babur, in A.D. 1526) had been demolished by a group of Hindu fundamentalists working under the aegis of the Bharatiya Janata Party, the Shiva Sena, and the Vishwa Hindu Parishad. Their aim was to reclaim the site of the mosque as the birthplace of the Hindu god Rama. Since the incident at Ayodhya, politics throughout most of India have focused on religious identity issues, and tensions between the Hindu majority and the Muslim and Christian minority groups have increased dramatically, resulting in violent clashes and the brutal repression of minority voices and identity. While watching events unfold after Ayodhya, I realized that identity in India is, as elsewhere, neither stable nor fixed but rather fluid and changeable; it can be made and unmade in a flash, over and over again by various agents and agendas. I have also realized that the construction of identity serves vested interests and is controlled by people in power. These realizations have motivated me to examine the problem of identity and to explore the processes of identity construction in India. Indeed, this volume focuses on the activities and struggles for identity of an obscure minority community called Tai-Ahom in the northeast Indian state of Assam.[1]

However, during that fateful December of 1992, I had not yet developed these research interests. I was on my way to my homeland Assam not to investigate identity but to meet Domboru Deodhai Phukan. In a then recent article on Assam, the Thai anthropologist Barend Jan Terwiel had identified the *deodhai* as the last living Tai-Ahom priest and, as such, a repository of the ancient rituals and customs of Assam's Tai-Ahom religion and culture (Terwiel 1983).[2] Because I am an "ethnic Assamese," I was intrigued by Terwiel's article.[3] Who are the Tai-Ahoms? What is their history and culture? Are they related to the Assamese? How can I learn about their history? These and similar questions had motivated my travel.

This was not, however, my first encounter with Tai-Ahom. At Aligarh Muslim University, where I did my undergraduate studies, my history professors (particularly Irfan Habib) had been very curious about the history of Assam. Irfan Habib had expected that as an Assamese I would have been exposed to the historical materials, such as the *buranjis* (chronicles of Assam), and the history of the region, and that I would be able to talk about them. Vaguely, I knew that my last name, Saikia, was an "Ahom" title, but I did not know anything about the history of Assam because I had not studied it; in our history textbooks Assam's history was not included. My ignorance of the history of Assam thus motivated me to undertake a study of the buranjis, and I was able to pursue this study in graduate school at the University of Wisconsin at Madison. My trip to Assam in 1992 was focused on meeting Domboru Deodhai and making arrangements to learn the Tai-Ahom language so that I would be able to read Ahom buranjis.[4] I expected that these buranjis would reveal to me the history of Assam and the story of Tai-Ahom.

On arriving at Guwahati, I made several inquiries about the deodhai, but it was next to impossible to trace him. No one I spoke to seemed to know who he was, and all were perplexed that I was making such a fuss about him and the Tai-Ahom community. Finally, after two weeks of intense search, I found out that Domboru Deodhai lived in an obscure hamlet called Akhoyan within the Patsako village circle in Sibsagar district, three hundred miles northeast of Guwahati. On December 26, a freezing winter morning, I embarked on a journey to meet Domboru Deodhai. The road to his home and the Tai-Ahom community was not easy, as I found out during this initial trip and then over and over again in the years to follow. The challenges, however, made it more enticing and compelling. My visit to Patsako and Domboru Deodhai's home on December 26, 1992, was eventful in many ways. The journey was backbreaking in the most literal sense. Seated on the back seat of a small Maruti car, I was tossed about like a yo-yo as we inched along the Guwahati-Sibsagar road, which was littered with potholes all the way.[5] After more than eight hours on the road we saw the first sign for Patsako village. However, at this point the road nearly ceased to exist. All I could see was the ink-black night stretching in front of me, without a soul in sight. After several minutes on a zig-zagging track, we came to a small store. The owner was waiting, so it seemed, because as soon as I explained the purpose of my visit he offered to take me to the deodhai's house. After walking for nearly a mile on a dark, unpaved village road and through freshly harvested paddy fields, we came to a rickety old gate leading to Domboru Deodhai's house.

As soon as I stepped inside, a man spoke out from the darkness in Assamese: "I have been waiting for you all day. I thought you would never come." He did not give me time to ponder how it was that he knew I was coming to see him; I had sent no information in advance. In the same breath he continued, "Why do you want to study the Tai-Ahom language and history? You should study your own history and culture; you are a Muslim woman; you should study Islamic history." As my eyes adjusted to the darkness, I could make out the profile of an elderly man dressed in a long white shirt, a white sarong, and a large white turban. The hanging night mist made him look ephemeral; I expected him to vanish any moment. My initial uncertainty was quickly put to rest as I saw him approach me with a kind, warm smile on his face. He invited me into his home and, under the flickering light of an earthen lamp, pulled out from a metal trunk several handwritten manuscripts that he referred to as the original *puthis* of the Tai-Ahoms.[6] But before we settled down to read them, Domboru Deodhai asked me to explain my interest in Ahom history. I hesitatingly told him that buranjis were one of the few premodern sources of local history that were produced outside the writing culture of medieval Delhi, which made them unique and highly attractive for scholarly investigation. Domboru Deodhai was not impressed, however, with my academic answer. So he asked me about my parents, and then pushed me further to tell him about my roots. When I mentioned my paternal grandfather's name he jumped up and said, "Now I know why you are here. You are one of us." He went on to talk about my "clan," which he knew well, and he claimed that I had returned to reconnect with my heritage. In that moment all of our differences melted away and Domboru Deodhai made me part of his world. "Next time you visit me, we will read these sacred texts together," he said. Then he added, "I will teach you the Ahom language so that you can find out for yourself about the swargadeos [kings, the word translates as "spirit of Heaven"] and the history of the Tai-Ahom community. . . . I will let you read these sacred puthis because I believe you are a kindred soul."[7] With these very emotional words, Domboru Deodhai welcomed me to explore a new chapter of Assam's history and the community called Tai-Ahom.

That evening he sang for me Bihu songs and recited several Tai-Ahom prayers in Assamese.[8] His grandchildren joined him in these prayers. The chant was repetitive: "Saw nuru, saw kaw ai, pha tu sing phra hum, si ki ara ni pan, boi maw saw kaw ai." He did not translate the prayer, but he told me he was invoking the gods. Then he started chanting in Assamese a prayer to the thirteenth-century hero called Sukapha, who he claimed was the founder of the Ahom kingdom in Assam. As Domboru Deodhai explained, "the swargadeos are like gods. In the Tai-Ahom religious belief, god is a kind of Buddha. Since ancestors are primary to the Tai-Ahom belief system, Buddha and the ancestors are invited to reside in our presence."

Domboru Deodhai also openly talked about the contemporary Tai-Ahom identity struggle. He explained to me, "We have a long and arduous struggle ahead. The Hindus have totally crushed us. But we have to fight for our rights. This is the country of our forefathers, our swargadeos. We have to regain our lost glory and might. I will continue the struggle till my last breath." Throughout our conversation, his eighty-year-old wife sat by herself in a corner and listened. She was dressed in *mekhala sador* (Assamese female attire). She wore the Hindu mark of marriage—a phut (a vermillion dot sometimes called a bindi) on her forehead. She admitted to her lack of knowledge of the Tai-Ahom language, and she acknowledged that although she considered herself the wife of a Tai-Ahom deodhai she was also a Hindu. The women of the household—Domboru Deodhai's daughter, as well as his daughter-in-law—endorsed the same view. His son, Bidya Phukan, was less vocal about associating Ahom and Hinduism. I was quite confused. Domboru Deodhai, according to Terwiel, is an Ahom deodhai, a high priest of a religion that is different from Hinduism. But his family claimed that they were Tai-Ahom as well as Hindu. At the end of the prayers, Domboru Deodhai invited me to eat with the family. The food served was a normal Assamese meal—several rice preparations along with yogurt and sour cream, accompanied by tea. In the course of the meal, Domboru Deodhai told me stories about his visits to Thailand and Australia, which had been sponsored by Terwiel. He then asked me if I would invite him to the United States. Apparently, Domboru Deodhai enjoyed being in the limelight. He had a youthful energy and enthusiasm that was endearing. I left Domboru Deodhai's house well fed and confident that I could return to study the Ahom buranjis with him whenever I was ready. Back in Madison, in a room far away from Assam, I started the project by reading buranjis in Assamese, my native language. Earlier, I had translated several Assamese buranjis over a period of two years and used them in my master's thesis, later published as a book, titled *In the Meadows of Gold: Telling Tales of the Swargadeos at the Crossroads of Assam* (1997). Against my expectations, my book has become a text for the present Tai-Ahom movement. Even the Assamese use it to interpret their history and to support their self-determination movement.[9]

Unfortunately, after my initial trip in 1992 I never saw Domboru Deodhai again. Three months after my return from India, in March 1993, Domboru Deodhai passed away on his way to attend the annual meeting of the Ban Ok Publik Muang Tai (the Tai-Ahom Sahitya Sabha, or the Eastern Tai Literary Society) at Geleki, in the district of Golaghat, not too far from Sibsagar.[10] I received news of his death while in Madison. Bidya Phukan, Domboru Deodhai's son, was kind enough to write me a note inviting me to attend the performance of the ritual of *dampata* for his deceased father.[11] He added, "My father would have liked for you to come back and continue your research." This strengthened my determination to return to Assam, which I did in 1994. I stayed in several villages for a period of eighteen months. Bidya Phukan received me warmly in his father's home, although I never again saw the puthis that his father had offered to read with me. During my stay in the villages, I realized that it would be essential for me to understand the Tai-Ahom struggle for identity in the present if I hoped to understand their past, their history.

Thus my trip to India in 1992 was in more than one sense the beginning of my journey. It made me deeply aware that institutions of power create the presence or absence of communities. In other words, they construct and destroy identities. I also realized then that labels matter, if for nothing else then to bargain with those who control power. This knowledge and my interest in Tai-Ahom history compelled me to return in 1994 to pursue the story of the Tai-Ahoms and to investigate their struggle to overcome erasure in a national history that had declared them "dead." Those who claim to be Tai-Ahom want to be recognized as a distinct community with an identity and a history that are separate from those of the Assamese, and by extension, from the rest of India.

Here we might ask: Who are the Tai-Ahom? What is Tai-Ahom history and culture? There are no simple answers to these questions. But one thing is certain: Tai-Ahom is a powerful memory compelling some people in Assam to search for an alternative to the label of Assamese and/or Indian. One may assume that the present memory of Tai-Ahom is backed by history, a history that has been formed from a collective representation of the past in official and popular narratives. However, to become such a history, I would argue, a story has to be backed by power and institutions of power. Although a history and culture of the Ahom community exists in popular discourse and local narratives, it is curiously absent in national official records. Hence, the present attempt to make an identity of Tai-Ahom is not backed by a known and accepted past; rather it is a political enterprise that involves remembering and constructing a past in order to become a people with a history in the present. It is a contemporary enterprise that invokes collective memory as its foundation. Collective memory is constituted in this instance by things, stories, and narratives that are kept alive through oral traditions. Hence memory, like the history of Tai-Ahom, is not an unmediated, natural, organic reality. Memory is the product of processes that are selective and, to a large extent, motivated by the will to prepare a record or recollection for future use (Nora 1989; Fentress and Wickham 1992; LeGoff 1992). History and memory are thus intimately associated with the exercise of power. The attempt by Tai-Ahom to memorialize a past is an ongoing effort involving many agents and agendas that have constructed a multiplicity of representations from different perspectives. But these representations are elusive and not definitively determined because power is still being negotiated between various groups. In the meantime, to understand Tai-Ahom we have to turn to interpretative spaces such as museums and archives, popular and academic writings, and the everyday life and politics of marginal village communities in Assam. The task is made very difficult because although Tai-Ahom is a name, there is no distinct community called Tai-Ahom: it is a name without a clearly defined people. The abstract memory of Tai-Ahom is particularly provocative for this reason.

This book tells a story about identity construction and claims of memory concerning the so-called Tai-Ahoms of Assam. The people who call themselves Tai-Ahom today are from several disenfranchised and disempowered groups that are struggling to find a place, become recognized by the Indian state, and have an identity. In other words, their struggle is to possess a "history" that has been denied them. Tai-Ahom identity, in this sense, is an assertion of presence; it is the here and now seeking a place in the future. Strategies used in achieving this goal have been multidirectional and multivoiced.

I had traveled to Assam to read and translate buranjis in order to investigate the historical Ahom. However, once I started my work in Assam, I realized that the buranjis had become history books and thus were a site for identity formation of Ahom. In addition, I encountered a variety of events (public rallies, protest marches, festivals, and worship) that could be considered part of a Tai-Ahom revivalism movement. The questions that came to my mind were: Who is Ahom in Assam? Why at that time were so many people struggling to be Tai-Ahom when only a few years ago they had been struggling, along with several other groups, to create one distinctive Assamese identity? Why were they seeking a self-definition that discarded both Assamese and Indian identities? Who was orchestrating this new self-definition?

Since my decision to try to answer these questions I have observed that my role has changed in these enterprises—indeed, even as I was collecting data, observing and interviewing participants, and taking notes. By choosing to work on the Tai-Ahom movement and not that of the Bodo, Kachari, Chakma, or Naga that were also ongoing in the northeast, I recognized one movement and bypassed others. I could be seen as the native returning with the power endowed by "Western scholarship." In the course of my fieldwork, on several occasions, I found that Tai-Ahom performances were put on simply for my benefit. This was especially evident in the performance of rituals. The Tai-Ahom activists recognized that I was a researcher looking for Tai-Ahom materials. They felt obliged, I suppose, to provide me with data on Tai-Ahom culture and society. Many of the performances I observed had a very limited life and were mainly confined to the period of my stay in the village. Others outlived my presence to become a part of the village performance of being Tai-Ahom.

Furthermore, by visiting one village, staying in another, and bypassing a third, I made some villages more Tai-Ahom than others. Moreover, by learning the Tai-Ahom language, I sent a clear message to many that they too could do it, thereby adding strength to the ongoing debate as to whether or not the Tai-Ahom language was "dead," as had been earlier determined. In attending public functions, addressing political and cultural gatherings, and participating in religious rituals, I helped emblematize the revivalism of Tai-Ahom as an authentic endeavor, because these activities became my source of information on contemporary Tai-Ahom. In turn, the activists looked to me as their potential voice in the West. At the end of two years of research (1994–1996), when it was time for me to leave, various groups approached me to ask that I write their version of Tai-Ahom history. Different groups wanted different representations.

This book is written in a narrative style, but it does not follow a linear structure. In fact, the chronological order has been reversed in part 1. As a participating-observing researcher I am a voice in the narration, but it is not a family snapshot. Also, there is no single common thread in the story. The overarching theme is of various people seeking some sort of an identity that for the present is articulated as Tai-Ahom.

# Locating Tai-Ahom in Assam:

## The Place and People

Certain histories do not require lengthy introductions. For example, a general history of Europe or a history of the Holocaust would discuss familiar subjects even if their writers approached the representations of these subjects in new ways. Thus, a historian addressing these subjects would not have to inform her or his readers of Europe's location or explain to them the identity of the Jewish people. Indeed, most schoolchildren worldwide learn about these subjects from their textbooks; and Hollywood, novels, and other media help to keep them alive in peoples' memories long after their last history lessons have ended. Histories that can start without a preface are the histories of the known; they are the dominant stories in the narrative of world history.

But let us not forget that history is present in all communities. Even powerless and unknown groups have their histories. The story of the Tai-Ahom is one such little-known story. Thus, one could not start the narrative of Tai-Ahom history without first addressing the context within which the stories about this community have developed and are produced today. The physical and cultural spaces of Assam—the arena of the Tai-Ahom struggle—first must be understood before a narrative of identity construction can commence.

Assam is a northeastern state in modern India. The origin of the name Assam is variously interpreted; according to some, it derives from the Sanskrit word *asama*, which means "uneven" and "undulating" and refers to the area's hilly terrain. According to others, the word Assam comes from *cham*, which is a Sanskrit cognate for the verb "to eat." This second interpretation is based on the region's fabled reputation as a land of cannibals or a land inhabited by people who ate whatever they found. Thus, when the first group of Brahmins came to Assam and found that the people there were not cannibals, they called the area and the people

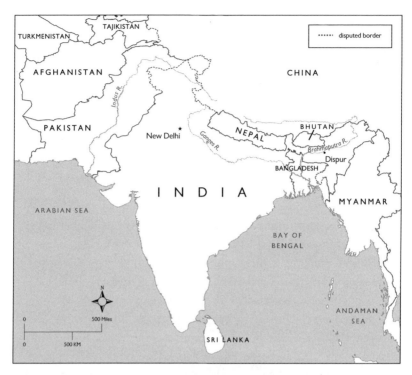

Map of India. (Courtesy of the Teaching and Learning Center, University of North Carolina, Chapel Hill)

A-cham, "not cannibal land and people." A third interpretation claims that the name derives from "Ahom," which was used to describe a group of warriors that came from the east (probably Upper Burma) and settled there after winning several battles against the local Barahi and Moran peoples. Modern historians who subscribe to this third interpretation believe that Ahom means "unequal" or "unparalleled" (although no such word has been found in local dialects).[1] Scholars of Assam tell us that the words Ahom, Asama, and Assam are the same, but are pronounced differently depending on the speaker. These interpretations inaugurate the story of the place, but the history of premodern Assam is unknown. According to the Greek traveler Periplus (who is fabled to have traveled to India with Alexander in 327 B.C.), because of extremes of storm, bitter cold, and difficult terrain and also "because of some divine power of the gods," the area east of the Gangetic delta has not been explored (1989, 234–36). Was he talking of the region we know today as Assam? We cannot be certain so many centuries later, but the eastern area he describes

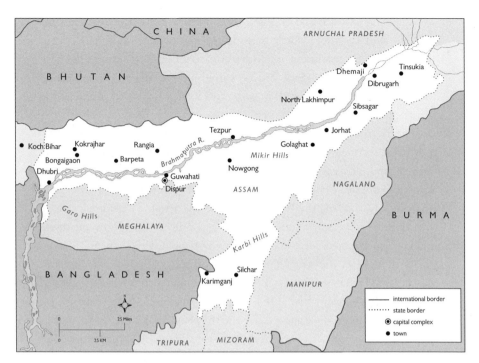

Map of Assam, showing the principal towns of Upper and Lower Assam. (Courtesy of
the Teaching and Learning Center, University of North Carolina, Chapel Hill)

is probably the northeast region of India, the greater region in which
Assam is located.

The term "northeast" is an administrative nomenclature coined in
postindependent India to denote the seven states of Assam, Nagaland,
Manipur, Mizoram, Tripura, Meghalaya, and Arunachal Pradesh. These
seven states are divided further into "plain" and "hill" states, depending
on their topography and the culture of the people living in them. Assam is
the dominant "plain" state; Tripura and Manipur straddle the classification as both hill and plain states; and the remaining five are strictly defined
as "hill" states. The separation of plain and hill is more than topographical. The Assam Valley has a majority Hindu population, while the hill
areas are dominated by a variety of Christian and non-Hindu animist
groups. Religious differences, however, have not created deep divisions
between the plain and hill areas. This may be because the "plain" state of
Assam that serves as a hinterland connects the northeast region to the rest
of India, and maintaining good relationships between the states is crucial

for enabling smooth and continuous economic exchanges through the narrow land corridor, which is no more than a mile wide in western Assam. Hence, the administrative division of hill and plain states has been relevant to the inhabitants only in some circumstances. Nevertheless, these divisions have persisted in some form since British colonial agents annexed Assam in 1826.

The Bengal East Frontier Regulation 1 of 1873, which created the northeast frontier, demarcated two distinct zones: the area of the inner line, or the hill areas; and the directly administered territory commonly known as the area of the outer line, or the plains. According to the work of Captain J. F. Mitchell, the "inner line is not the frontier; it is merely a line fixed by the government to guide the civil officers as to how far their jurisdiction extends, but it was not in any way intended to cancel [British] treaty rights with the tribe" (1883, iv).[2] The area of Assam was initially demarcated by the provisions of Act 23, caption 3, section 1, which classified it as a "backward tract." In 1874 it was made into a province to be administered by colonial agents. Beyond the plains of Assam, that is, in the hills, the "inner line" administration was in place. As a consequence, according to government records, "the plains [became] . . . increasingly identical in culture with India proper, with the result that the contrasts between the plains and the hills, instead of diminishing, have increased."[3] This colonial system continues to be maintained by the postcolonial Indian government, and it was exactly asserted in 1967 in the Reorganization of States. At that time of reorganization, the erstwhile Assam province was divided along ethnic lines into Assam proper, Meghalaya, and Arunachal Pradesh (the latter two being designated as hill states).

Ironically, while the division between plain and hill states is emphasized for administrative reasons, the Indian government's perception of the northeast is singular: it is seen as a region that is marginally connected to the Indian union, with a dubious loyalty to the nation. Christian missionary activities in the northeast are blamed for the lack of attachment to India. However, this is an external view: in Assam and in the rest of the northeast, Christian missionaries are not seen as outsiders. Missionaries were the pioneers in establishing schools, and they continue to offer important services in education. It is important to note here that in the hills of the northeast most of the communities that converted are the so-called tribal people, communities that were never included within the caste Hindu fold. Recently, however, with the rising trend of Hindu nationalism in the rest of India, some claims have been made that the Christian missionaries should be expelled from the northeast so that the mentality of the people might be Indianized through the introduction of "Indian education," to be supervised and controlled by Indian administrators. Advocates of expulsion claim that doing so would also discourage the continued conversion of the local tribal populace to Christianity. Such opinions are, however, particularly unpopular in Nagaland, Meghalaya, and Mizoram, which are Christian-majority states. Needless to say, such differences of opinion have led to added tensions between Delhi and the northeast.

The present-day plain state of Assam covers eighty-two thousand square kilometers of land that includes two rich alluvial valleys—Brahmaputra and Barak—along with the hills of Mikir, Garo, and Karbi. The twenty-six million people of Assam are divided into one hundred and ninety-two dialect groups (Barua 1996, 240). The continuous, ongoing migration of peoples and ideas into the region from both South and Southeast Asia has made the region a crossroads. At times, Indic elements and polities have played dominant roles, and at other times Southeast Asian cultures and regimes have influenced the region and its people. The multiple ethnic communities that have emerged in the crossroads of Assam live in a condition that can be described as "peaceful chaos."

The largest and most dominant group in Assam is the Assamese-speaking community of the Brahmaputra Valley,[4] which is comprised of a variety of ethnic and religious groups, including Hindus, Muslims, Christians, Buddhists, and animists.[5] This composite group is identified as "ethnic Assamese" by the government in Delhi. Until recently, the group that is now claiming to be Tai-Ahom had been assigned to the category of Assamese. The "ethnic Assamese" of the Brahmaputra Valley have a difficult relationship with the people of Barak Valley, the other constituent area of Assam, which is predominantly inhabited by Bengali-speaking Hindus and Muslims. Language marks these differences: Assamese in the Brahmaputra Valley versus Bengali in the Barak Valley. A short note here on the Assamese language is important in order to understand how it operates as an identity marker and creates a territory of "us" and "them" between the Assam and Barak valleys.

The Assamese language is an *aprombhasa,* which essentially means that it is a modified or a corrupt form of the original language from which it was derived. Some believe that the source of Assamese (or Ahamia, as it is locally referred to)[6] is a derivative of Sanskrit and an aprombhasa of Magadhi (of Bihar) or Gauda (of Bengal) (see Medhi 1988; Goswami

1988; B. Baruz 1941). Others say that Assamese combines elements of local dialects with the Bodo language of the Tibeto-Burman family, and, according to T. P. Verma, "with Sanskrit and many other languages that it has come in contact with" (1976, 30). This claim is based on a study of Assamese script, which, although very similar to Bengali, has some peculiar differences both in sound and alphabet. It is probably most likely that Assamese developed over a period of time, from the fifth century on, and absorbed a variety of influences from Sanskrit, Tibeto-Burman, and Tai (Medhi 1988, 42).

The early period of the development of Assamese can be traced to two main centers and two different scripts. One was the kingdom of Kamrupa in western Assam, which had close ties with north Bengal.[7] The Kamrupi Assamese follows a proto-Nagari script, and the language combines words from Magadhi and Maithali of Bihar with some modified Sanskrit words and terms (Neog 1974). The other center of writing was Sadiya, capital of the Chutia kingdom in eastern Assam, and the inscriptions are in a Tai script. One can assume that the spoken language also had affinity with Tai.

Between the seventeenth and the nineteenth centuries, four styles of Assamese writing developed in the Brahmaputra Valley: Gargaya (particularly practiced in eastern Assam for writing buranjis), Bamunia (for religious texts), Lakhari, and Kaithali (practiced in western Assam). All of these scripts merged into one when the printing press was developed in the nineteenth century and the American Baptist Mission created standardized Assamese letters. The first printed Assamese book is called *Dharmapustak*; it is a Christian Bible in translation that was printed at the mission press in Sreerampur, Bengal, in 1835. Although the written language of Assamese was then standardized, and the rules of Sanskrit grammar were then established as the norm, spoken Assamese continued to combine words from many different sources. Hence, people of eastern (Upper) Assam speak Assamese differently from people in western (Lower) Assam. The boundaries of difference between the two speech communities are maintained in marriage arrangements, and consequently the peoples of Lower and Upper Assam rarely interact with each other on personal or intimate terms. As a result, two distinct communities have emerged; and the cultures, politics, and concerns of Lower and Upper Assam continue to be markedly different.

While the internal divisions between Assamese speakers are considerable, they dislike and share a general sense of mistrust of the Bengali speakers of Barak Valley. This anti-Barak/anti-Bengali feeling of the Assamese has in recent years taken a new shape. As a result, Bengali speakers in Assam have been reduced to the status of illegal Bangladeshi immigrants, and local political demagogues in Assam, supported by the national Bharatiya Janata Party, are demanding their expulsion.[8] A clear division, however, is made on religious grounds, and thus only Bengali Muslims are targeted as illegal. This targeting of Muslims reflects national religious divisions more than any clear history of religious conflict internal to Assam, where language has been a more divisive issue. The politics of language and identity in Assam is very complicated, and I will discuss in some detail in chapter 1 linguistic issues as they have informed the rise of the Assamese identity movement.

In addition, both the lack of a shared historical past and the absence of a memory of association that can bridge the differences between the peoples of the Brahmaputra and Barak valleys contribute to their mutual animosity and distrust. The two valleys were combined into a single unit during the partition of India in 1947. Barak Valley was included in Assam, and thus made part of India, because it had a Hindu-majority population. Sylhet, another section of the erstwhile Surma (Barak) Valley, was made part of East Pakistan due to its Muslim-majority population. The language and historical differences between the two valleys of Assam have over time resulted in different political agendas. In the Brahmaputra Valley two political themes dominate: establishing Assamese as the principal language and a demand for autonomy. These issues became prominent in the 1960s, particularly after the reorganization of 1967. Assam's shared borders with both Bangladesh and Bhutan became crucial thereafter. When in 1979 the ethnic Assamese of the Brahmaputra Valley led the anti-Bangladeshi movement, the people in the Barak Valley refused to join. In fact, they resented the "ethnic" politics of the Brahmaputra Valley. Even today the people of Barak Valley long to be claimed by Bangladesh and West Bengal in India and thereby affirm their position as Bengalis living in Assam.

The history of Brahmaputra Valley before its annexation to the British Raj in the nineteenth century is independent of the rest of India. Also, this history is multiple for the period before the nineteenth century because different dynasties ruled several territorial pockets. Of these, the semi-mythical kingdom of Pragjotishpur (unknown date), which was later replaced by the kingdoms of Kamata (twelfth through fifteenth centuries) and Koch (sixteenth through seventeenth centuries), dominated the western sector. The proximity of the Koch kingdom to Bengal made it vulnerable to attacks from that end, and it was reduced to a vassal state over time. In eastern Assam, toward the area of modern-day Arunachal Pradesh, was the famed kingdom of Sadiya, ruled by the Chutias, who held power by regulating the easterly trade and migration of people to and from Tibet, southern China, and Assam. In the Brahmaputra Valley, extending to the Cachar hills of the Barak Valley, the Kacharis had their kingdom. South of the Barak Valley, at the margins of East Bengal (modern-day Bangladesh), the Jaiantia kingdom was powerful. In 1228, local tradition recounts that a group of warriors, later to be called Ahoms by their rivals, entered from the east (they claim that their homeland was in Upper Burma) and defeated the various ruling chiefs. After conquering the Chutias, Kacharis, and Jaiantias, they became the undisputed rulers of the upper Brahmaputra Valley. The migrant warrior community, under the rule of a swargadeo (from heaven, and hence a god), brought the various groups of the hills and plains together into one body politic. This polity is what we know as the Ahom kingdom of Assam. At its peak in the seventeenth century the Ahom kingdom stretched from Sadiya in the east to Guwahati in the west. The river Luit, also known as Brahmaputra, separated the Ahom kingdom from the territories of its rivals.[9] The river enabled the people of the Ahom kingdom to develop an agrarian system and culture that differentiated the subjects of the swargadeo from the people in the hills who did not have settled agriculture.

The rise of the Ahom kingdom in the east coincided with the emergence of Muslim power in Delhi. From the thirteenth century until the latter half of the seventeenth century, the rulers of Delhi made several attempts to annex the Assam kingdom in the hope of opening up a land route for trade with inner and southeast Asia. In the reign of Aurangzeb, the last great Mughal (1657–1707), a devastating attack reduced the ruling swargadeo, Jayadhvaj Singha (1648–1663), to a temporary vassal of the Mughal Badshah. He agreed to pay tribute to the Mughal emperor but repudiated the claim within a year. The rulers of Assam continued to maintain their independence for nearly a hundred and fifty years thereafter. Between 1792 and 1813 border skirmishes with the Burmese made Assam vulnerable to several levels of external interferences. The British became fearful that the Burmese might overrun the region and subsequently knock on their door in Bengal. Also, the British rivals, the French, who were reduced in power on the subcontinent after 1757, had shifted their attention to Burma and were gaining ground in the Burmese court.

Colonial interest in Assam developed as a consequence. After a few years of direct involvement in Assam, the British turned their attention to Manipur, which they feared was the more likely route for the Burmese to use to move into the region. As soon as the British turned their backs on Assam in 1813, the troops of the king of Burma moved in and brought Assam under Burmese political control. The British panic that followed resulted in the first Anglo-Burmese war, and in 1826 the defeated king of Burma was forced by the Treaty of Yandabo to cede the areas of Assam and Arakan to the British. The British then occupied Assam, but administration was left to the local king, swargadeo Purandar Singha (1818–1819; 1826–1838), on the condition that he pay fifty thousand rupees (a significant sum) as revenue to the British. Gradually, the swargadeo's powers were diminished through the constant interference of colonial agents. Under the pretext of bad administration, in 1838 after the second Anglo-Burmese war the kingdom of Assam was occupied and brought under direct colonial administration.

In 1947, when India became independent, after prolonged deliberations between the Indian National Congress organization and the British government, the British decided that the Assam Valley should be part of the Indian union, but it was truncated and a section, Sylhet, was relinquished to East Pakistan (present-day Bangladesh). The liminal position of Assam in Indian politics was inaugurated at this very moment; the problem of Assam's positionality within the union was confounded by the politics of location to which was added a religio-cultural complication. The population of Assam included diverse non-Aryan linguistic and cultural groups (also known as "uncivilized" by the rest of India) and multireligious communities. The geographical position of Assam—at the borders of South, Southeast, and Inner Asia, coupled with its unclear political and cultural position within the new nation-state, reaffirmed the peculiar "frontier" mentality that had come to be associated with the people and the place in postindependence India. The frontier mentality concerning Assam is evident even today in the media's representation of the state as an exotic place worthy of ecotourism but requiring caution because it is suggested that militancy is rampant. The frontierization has generated a state of restlessness within Assam that keeps the people anxious and the society in a fluid, transforming mode.

The lack of a "fixed" position for Assam within the Indian political imagination is countered locally by a seemingly permanent agrarian culture created by the unquestionable presence of the Brahmaputra River, which dominates life and the economy along its banks. The ebb and flow of the river channels the rhythm of agrarian life. Visitors, even today, find Assam a kind of "sleepy village," and the local people endorse this view with the homegrown dictum "laahe, laahe," meaning "go slow." But life is not always easy, slow paced, or quiet. Every year, from May until late July, the monsoon rains lash through the region and create havoc along the banks of the Brahmaputra. Annually, many people are dislocated and dispossessed of their meager personal belongings. When the rains cease, the alluvial plains of the Brahmaputra are replenished with fresh silt and agrarian life reconvenes until the next cycle of rain begins. In addition to these violent rains, militant activities, according to the Indian government, cause continuous instability in the region.

Notwithstanding that the use of the terms militant and militancy to describe a way of life in Assam is highly problematic, the root of political unrest in the region is entwined with the reality of economic marginalization. Economic disempowerment is not simply rhetoric for politicians but a lived experience for most Assamese. The Assamese people are very poor, even though Assam is rich in resources, including natural gas, petroleum, timber, wildlife, and lime. Assam is also India's largest producer of tea, one of the nation's main export items. In 1999–2000 the per capita income in Assam was around Rs. 9,162 (US$203), 41 percent below the national average of Rs. 16,567 (US$368).[10] This makes Assam one of the poorest states in the nation, and over 40 percent of the people live under the poverty line. Most of the natural resources are located in the heartland of the former Ahom kingdom, also known in colonial administrative parlance as Upper Assam and locally referred to as Ujani Aham. But the local people of this region are not the owners of the resources, nor are a significant number of young men and women employed in the oil and natural gas industries or at the tea plantations. The personal experiences of poverty coupled with rising public awareness of the disparity in the development of Assam vis-à-vis the rest of India are expressed in a growing public resentment that shapes political agendas and creates a state of restlessness. This situation is often viewed by outside observers as "militancy." Revolt movements are mushrooming in Assam: the Bodo movement (which has been demanding an autonomous Bodoland in the western sector [S. Baruah 1999]), the Dimasa and Karbi movements in the lower reaches of the Brahmaputra Valley, and the Tai-Ahom movement in the upper Brahmaputra Valley are strident anti-Assamese movements ongoing in Assam. In the surrounding states of the northeast, there are numerous movements claiming autonomy of territory and history (Haza-rika 1994). For example, the struggle of the Naga people for an autono-mous Nagaland has been in the headlines for several decades. Likewise, the People's Liberation Army of Manipur, the Khasi Students Union, the Achick Liberation Matgrik Army of Meghalaya, and the All Tripura Tribal Force in Tripura, to name a few of the resistance movements in the northeast, have been demanding autonomy from Delhi, a demand that they base on their unique cultures and histories. The Tai-Ahom identity movement is located within this paradigm of local identity assertions taking place in the northeast.

Disparate groups of people in the villages of Upper Assam are organiz-ing to express their inchoate and confused feelings of economic disem-powerment, social marginalization, and cultural peripheralization. Their struggles look longingly to the past—the glorious days of swargadeos rule—to imagine a better future as Tai-Ahom. The experiences and feel-ings of these people have led them to believe that they are different from the Assamese people of the towns and those living outside Upper Assam. They think and believe that they and their culture and society are distinc-tive. It is this distinction that they are now claiming and calling Tai-Ahom. For two years, from 1994 to 1996, I followed the trail of this movement in different parts of Assam. In 1996, when I left Assam, approximately six hundred thousand of the twenty-six million people of Assam were par-ticipating in the Tai-Ahom identity struggle.[11] As a statistical number this is a small group. But in the northeast region where a number of differ-ent linguistic and cultural movements are ongoing and raising probing questions about Assamese and Indian identity, the rise of the Tai-Ahom movement cannot be ignored. The Assamese as a group are a mix of people: the assertion of Ahoms as separate from the Assamese is a prob-lematic sign of the internal breakdown of the composite Assamese iden-tity. Potentially, this could unravel the Assamese community and create multiple fragmentary groups that, in turn, would benefit the "other" non-Assamese communities living in Assam. Hence, the Assamese are watch-ing the Tai-Ahom movement with interest and concern.

## BETWEEN HISTORY, MEMORY, AND IDENTITY

The current fascination with identity has generated an impressive body of literature on the subject. Identity today, in the twenty-first century, has become the "purest of cliches" (Gleason 1983, 913). While gaining in rhetorical power, as people become more conscious and confused about their identity, identity study as a phenomenon is losing its historical foundation. Instead of emphasizing the process of identity formation, recent scholarship has abstracted the process of identity formation and defined it as a process of negotiating the tensions and discourses of labels that occurs in the site of the globalized world. "Imagined communities," to borrow Benedict Anderson's term, are regularly emerging, thus making identity look like a "thing" that can be lost and found like checked baggage within sites of power and disempowerment. Scholars opine that "invention" and "imagination" are sustained through "exercises in social engineering" orchestrated by the powerful (Hobsbawm 1986). How is manipulation of identity accomplished? The dual lens of ethnicity and nationalism are premised as the powerful tools for such manipulation. I will not attempt here to summarize the vast body of knowledge on the subject of identity, but the sketch that I provide will be sufficient to show the broad trends and reveal the gaps that I aim to overcome in this book.

Since the end of World War II and the rising trend of national and ethnic movements that emerged in its wake, scholars of identity have identified two broad trends worldwide. Identity, according to a group called the "primordialists," championed by Clifford Geertz, is based on ethnicity; the components of which are a shared language, lineage, customs, rituals, and belief systems (Geertz 1963, 1973). Others, who adopt an "instrumentalist" approach, stress that it is not enough to examine the cultural content of ethnic groups to understand how identities are formed, but rather investigation must focus on how and why the boundaries of differences have been created and are maintained (Leach 1965; F. Barth 1969). The "instrumentalist" approach to ethnicity became dominant as studies began to appear that emphasized the language, culture, and community used by social groups to create and politicize collective identity (Keyes 1981; Brass 1985; Horowtiz 1985; A. Smith 1986; Connor 1992; Toland 1993). What these studies have emphasized is that once a community "realizes" its identity, it is there once and for all and can be presented by people in power as an absolute identity.

Another group emphasizes in its theory the nation-state as the foundation of identity. This group theorizes that nationalism, the instrument that invented nation-states in the first place, is at the heart of modern identity (Gellner 1983; Hobsbawm 1983; Anderson 1991). In support of their argument these scholars have emphasized the mechanisms through which national identity becomes possible. Print capitalism, according to Anderson, creates and helps to sustain a national imagination that allows people to "think" that they know each other, and even though they may never meet or even hear of each other, "in the minds of each lives the image of their communion" (1991, 6). Scholars of nationalism have asserted that in different parts of the world the construction of national identity happened in different time periods, but overall the effect was that people imagined that they belonged to a "nation." Elie Kedourie, who wrote his book *Nationalism* at a time when several excolonies in Africa were struggling for independence from European rulers, identified the nationalist aspirations of colonized people as "seen to satisfy a need, to fulfill a want . . . to belong together to a coherent and stable community" (1960, 101). Not unlike Anderson, Anthony Smith argues that nationalism is "a surrogate religion which aims to overcome the sense of futility . . . by linking communities whose generations form indissoluble links in a chain of memories and identities" (1986, 176). For Europe, Sola Baron (1960) has emphasized the role of the Christian religion in creating connection between people and institutions and facilitating nationalistic experiences. Partha Chatterjee differs somewhat in his presentation of third-world nationalism in India. He has argued that outside official nationalism, there are multiple imaginings of nonelite, subaltern sections of society that survived in the "inner domain." As such, "in this, its true and essential domain, the nation [was] sovereign, even when the nation [was] in the hands of the colonial power" (1993, 6). More recent scholarship on the nation-state and nationalist identity has emphasized that national identity is a trope that hides power; therefore an investigation of power is important in order to understand how such identities are created in the first place. Issues such as educational policies, legal systems, forms of administration and bureaucracy, and territoriality engendered through mapping have become new foci of investigation (Gillis 1994; Winichakul 1994).

The theory that nation informs identity, although quite dominant in scholarship and easily accepted by the public at large, no longer remains unchallenged. Increasingly, scholars are critiquing the plotting of national narratives of identity as false and self-serving, merely one among various kinds of imaginings and with no particular claim to authenticity in the twenty-first century. At the ground level, the nation as the site of imagination of identity is also losing much of its appeal to people because it is transforming into a fixed, monolithic identity that does not account for the multiplicities constituting nation-states. What I loosely term "between history and memory" is a paradigm that has been gaining ground since the

1980s in identity studies. The emergence of local identities worldwide that challenge the memory and history of the nation-state has caught the attention of many scholars. Since the 1990s, memory's role in the creation of identities has come to the fore. The study by Pierre Nora (1989) of memory and identity has proved particularly influential. Memory in France, according to Nora, is a vast typology of symbolics existing outside of the French state and it has since the nineteenth century subverted the history constructed and upheld by the state. Prasenjit Duara suggests that there is nothing new about this because "national history secures for the contested and contingent nation the false unity of a self-same, national subject evolving through time," enabling a relationship between linear historicity and the nation-state that is ultimately false (1995, 4).

At the core of new studies of identity is a deepening exploration of whether memory is a reliable tool for knowing the past. One group of historians contends that history is an expression of power and is limited to the triumphant. Hence, one has to turn to memory to retrieve the voices of the silenced and oppressed and to understand the lived experiences that make us aware of how communities construct their sense of past and belonging. Memory in this sense is a gateway to a past that history has closed. A second group, writing in the winter 2000 issue of *Representations,* warns that the growing emphasis on memory is likely to open the floodgates of a struggle that will undermine critical history. The relationship between history and memory is politicized as the tensions between them rise. At the core of the debate is the assumption that history has a claim to truth while memory does not. What is surprising is the reluctance of scholars to acknowledge that both history and memory are processes of creation: history, like memory, creates its subject—it does not simply recover it. It is worrisome that the debate hides the issue: Whose memory? Whose history is considered as a form of knowledge, and what gets disqualified as inadequate and hence not history? It is necessary to remember that memory, like history, is the site of the triumphant; the winner gets the memory as well as the history (Zertal 2000).

Undoubtedly, power is the problematic that needs emphasis, rather than the question of whether history and memory are complementary or opposing constructions. Michel-Rolph Trouillot (1995) emphasizes this when he asserts that some history becomes possible because of the power behind it; history is a story of those who have won. Memory, as Jacques Le Goff points out, is "not only an activity of organizing knowledge in a new way, but also an aspect of the organization of a new power" (1992, 62).

Both memory and history have motives. Collecting, preserving, remembering, memorizing, narrating, recounting, even forgetting are active processes aimed at achieving specific outcomes. The means and the goal of the labor are both constituted by power and put into the service of the powerful. Both history and memory operate at sociopolitical levels. Their internal structure and modes of transmission are not necessarily an establishment of some sort of "truth"; to become a discourse, episteme, or paradigm they have to be believed by the people to whom they are presented. How are they made believable? The assumption that history can be verified and corroborated through evidence and be believable as "true" does not convince me. Nor does the argument that memory is an intimate, personal thing of an individual or collective—something constructed in peoples' heads—make it an unbelievable and unreliable tool for understanding the past. Factors such as politics, economics, society, and culture that make some kind of historical narrative and social memory possible and believable are to me more important concerns.

This logic orders my study on the Tai-Ahom as I investigate the processes and agents that organize the production of memory-history in Assam to constitute both a community and a platform for making claims about identity. The memory-identity project I highlight is structured around particulars: events, actors, distinct genres of literature, spaces, and places. Together, they constitute a politics of identity as Tai-Ahom that outlines a contestation with Indian national history and identity. Neither the collective memory nor the collective identity of Tai-Ahom has anything to do with any sort of past as it might be "objectively" reconstructed from the evidence available to us. I argue here that a culture of memory is created and commemorated as an identity project that makes a Tai-Ahom history thinkable today. The history of Tai-Ahom does not exist by itself; it becomes possible only from recounting the stories. Tai-Ahom exists in narrative, not outside it. The memory of Tai-Ahom is historically and socially constituted; it is not "free floating" to be retrieved at will. The proponents of Tai-Ahom want to fix the past so that they can retrieve at will this history, but the project is not yet complete. Today the label and memories of Tai-Ahom at best serve as portals to access something that official history has erased and that can serve as the site of an ongoing identity movement.

I focus on three main issues in this book: the problem of competing identities in modern India; the impact of place and culture (the river and the development of the society and economy); and the outcomes of cur-

rent memory building concerning Tai-Ahom. I show that identity formation is a continuous process, involving various agents and agendas that
variously interpret the mechanisms and meanings of Tai-Ahom. To facilitate my project I have organized the book into two parts. Part 1 (chapters
1–3) is a narration of stories concerning Tai-Ahom told by different agents
in different time periods. I begin the narrative of Tai-Ahom in the present
and gradually move back in time to explore how and why the memory-
history of Tai-Ahom has gained the acceptance to become a dominant
story in present-day Assam. Tai-Ahom identity is flexible because it is
bound to memories that are constantly reshaped. By delineating different
time frames and actors, in part 1 I show how the memory-history of Tai-
Ahom has been constructed in a multiplicity of agendas and locations.
Some of the stories have been built over time, and some one upon another,
but they are not continuous. Fragmented narratives are at the core of what
was and is Tai-Ahom. By highlighting the "fragments" I develop an argument showing the multiple processes of identity and memory constructions. I argue that there is no single explanation that is definitive. Instead, a
variety of representations of Tai-Ahom, past and present, have enabled its
construction and recognition and, hopefully, will continue to do so in the
future. In part 1, I first investigate the postcolonial Indian government's
positions regarding, and construction of, the labels Indian, Assamese, and
Tai-Ahom. Some of New Delhi's images concerning Assam and the people are new, while others are recycled colonial assumptions. Next, I explore
the story of how an Ahom community was constructed and destroyed in
the colonial period. I examine the processes and reasons for colonial
construction that presented its finding of Ahom based on information in
the local chronicles of Assam, the buranjis. Finally, I explore what the
precolonial buranjis tell us about Ahom to show that it is variously described in this site. The story of Ahom in the first part of the book thus
begins in the present and ends in the thirteenth century. I have started the
story of Tai-Ahom identity with the twentieth-century developments in
India to make the reader aware that the process of history making is a
current enterprise. It is through the present remembering that an awareness of a separate identity as Ahom has emerged, which is written back in
time and claimed. Ahom history, like all other histories, is a presentist
project, and I urge readers to keep that in mind as they encounter the layers
of history making presented in part 1.

In part 2 (chapters 4–6) I highlight the performance and production of
Tai-Ahom society and culture in Assam and Thailand to show that iden-

tity construction is both a social and political process. In particular, I attend to the sites where the memories of Tai-Ahom are created and circulate as well as to the politicization of memory objects. I focus on the economic, social, and political conditions in the place called Ujani Aham to narrate a story of peripheralization that generates an emotion-laden language to qualify an "us" (Tai-Ahom) as different from others. Thus, Tai-Ahom self ("who-ness") and place ("where-ness") in Assam are intimately connected. Further, I investigate the discourses—local, national, and transnational—of the leaders, Tai-Ahom, Assamese, Indian, and Thai, to argue that Tai-Ahom identity involves a variety of imaginations and expectations but it is not yet a determined identity that is recognizable to "outsiders" like me. Following this, I investigate the question of why some people in Assam want to be Tai-Ahom. I argue that Tai-Ahom is a dissident space advocating a consciousness of the dispossessed and forgotten subjects in the margins, and a politics seeking social and economic justice and rights to land and resources. Although engaging a diverse and motley group, the promises of "real" benefits, many hope, will make them participatory citizens in the nation-state. This notion is very appealing because the practice of citizenship is not a lived experience in the margins of Assam.[12]

In the final analysis, this book concerns the specific problem of a community seeking identity in the present. In other words, my aim is to understand how the "dead" history of Ahom has been transferred into living memory to construct identity and to demand the rights of citizenship that are being denied.

### TRACKING TAI-AHOM IN ASSAM: MULTISITED HISTORIES AND METHODS

When I started my research by asking a basic question about who and what counts as Tai-Ahom, people in Assam could not provide a definite answer. The identity movement, nonetheless, was both visible and palpable. A historiographical and practical dilemma then arose: How and what do I write about Tai-Ahom if there is no community to represent? For me, the dilemma intensified when I realized I had accepted the task to tell their story. I believe interlocutors are also creators of narratives. Colonial agents wrote the first version of Ahom history, then local scholars like S. K. Bhuyan, Padmanath Gohain, Lila Gogoi, and others in Assam reinforced the colonial narrative and introduced some new elements in their new versions.[13] In Assam, the story about Ahom continues to be under construction. When I entered the field, many asked me to be the "voice" of Ahom people abroad; they saw me both as insider and outsider. For them my roots in Assam, particularly Upper Assam, and being a Saikia, which is considered an Ahom surname, made me one of them. But could a Muslim be an Ahom like them? They were not quite certain. Another troubling issue was class. If Ahom is made of the economically deprived, disempowered rural poor who are struggling for rights and some privileges, how could I, as a member of the urban professional class, be Ahom in that sense? Indeed, I was myself confused.

Like the majority in Assam, rich and poor, I have grown up as an Assamese; that is, I spoke Assamese as my first language; humanism was the religion in my home, although we participated in all religious festivities—Pujas, Christmas, and Eids; and Assamese culture was a priority. Assamese culture, as I understood it growing up, was anchored in the language, while religion and/or ethnicity played secondary or peripheral roles. Our civic status as Assamese citizens conferred on us rights and created responsibilities toward the community that gave us a structure of an identity. Assamese in this sense was quite flexible and was capable of accommodating differences rather than marking boundaries of separation between the people who considered themselves Assamese. Several years later when I returned to Assam to undertake research on the Ahoms I had to deal with questions that revealed several fractures in this identity. There were now different kinds of Assamese: Assamese Hindus, Tai-Ahoms, Bodos (who claim they are not Assamese although they live in Assam), Assamese Muslims, Assamese Christians, and many more groups. I was placed in the category called Assamese Muslim. What did it mean? Was language my primary identity marker and religion a new device to construct a secondary identity label? Were the Assamese Muslims an excluded group, outsiders in Assam? With these questions arose another: Who is an Assamese? Are the Ahoms the original community or the Assamese the primary group in Assam? I encountered these questions time and again in the course of my research. Like my Ahom friends, I do not have a clear notion of my identity in Assam anymore, nor do I know who should have the right to represent such an identity. But I do know that identity construction is a process, and different groups claim to speak on behalf of the Assamese as well as on the behalf of others seeking new identities in Assam.

Without arriving at an answer concerning my place within the Ahom enterprise and their understanding of self and other, the Tai-Ahom leaders who represented different groups within the movement asked me to write the history of Ahom to further their quest for identity. Some asked me to write the history of the Tai-Ahom people beginning in China; another group wanted a Thai ancestry. Others rejected the idea of "foreign" origin and wanted to be accepted and respected by caste Hindus; some wanted Tai-Ahom within the umbrella of Assamese but as a separate community from Hindu and Indian; many wanted Tai-Ahom to be represented as a tribal community with a royal past, and on and on. These groups, with their myriad ideas and expectations, were all seeking to become something, and they saw me as a possible interlocutor to facilitate that happening. Many of them had significantly assisted me in my research project: they hosted me in their homes and fed me while I worked on site, and some even accompanied me to remote sites, arranged clandestine meetings with militants, shared with me their knowledge and resources, and even presented me with copies of their family buranjis. They were remarkable people, but I could not choose one telling over another.

To tell a certain story fulfills specific purposes and affects readers' perceptions, thus influencing them to think fundamentally the same way as the narrator of the story. As a member of a minority community and, more so, as a woman (both of which make me deeply conscious of the experiences of marginality and disempowerment), I am keenly aware that an interlocutor in my position cannot speak for the subordinated, invisible subaltern; indeed, I can only represent them. The ideological and intellectual burden of being an interlocutor, in this case, along with the paradox of my own sense of identity, repeatedly created doubts about how and where to start the story of Tai-Ahom. After much deliberation, I decided that the story line had to begin with an initial explanation of my subjective position so that readers could be made aware of the influences that color my reading and interpretation of the Tai-Ahom past. This would enable them to interact with the narrative as a viewpoint, as one of the many narratives that can be told on the subject. Hence, I decided that my section on method and analysis must be part of a chapter rather than tucked away in a "preface" that many readers tend to skip. This is a deliberate, epistemological act.

Every beginning is contingent (Foucault 1972). Because there is no empirical evidence of a historical Tai-Ahom community before colonialism, and because the inhabitants of Assam are not sure if they can point to a specific community today as Tai-Ahom, I had at my disposal several possibilities—ideological, political, historical, and philosophical—for beginning my narrative. I could start with the politics of colonialism in the nineteenth century and the colonial invention that people in Assam lacked history. It appears that the more that British merchants and administrators penetrated the interiors of Assam to expand the reach of colonialism, the more British scholars wrote about the lack of history of the natives in these margins. In the beginning of the nineteenth century, colonial practice had already established a neat category to classify natives of India—Aryans or non-Aryans—and within these broad classifications were several subgroups of castes and religions. Subjected groups had to fit within these categories. In the margins of Assam, colonials "found" Tai-Ahoms but could not fit them into the established categories of known castes and religious groups. Thus they dismissed them as an "unknowable" community and soon declared them "dead." For convenience, a new category, "Assamese," was devised, and everyone in the region of Assam was christened with this new name. The vast majority of "Assamese," the colonials found, were some sort of caste Hindus. They also found that within Assam there were Assamese- and Bengali-speaking Muslims. The Assamese Muslims became Assamese by colonial estimation and the Bengalis were deemed an immigrant community. Beyond this the late colonial administrators did not explain what "Assamese" meant or signified. In light of this I asked myself if the colonial representation of Ahom as a "dead" community would be the best starting point of my narrative. However, this appeared to me to be highly problematic: a community is not dead or alive because others think or say so.

As an alternative, I reasoned that I could adopt a traditional historical position and begin the story in the so-called period of genesis of Ahom in the thirteenth century; in the process of migration and war that legend says made the group into Ahoms—the "unique," "unparalleled" community—in the eyes of their rivals and adversaries. This framework did not appeal to me, however, because the historical itinerary would have to endorse a linear model of narrative history. In that case, the history of Tai-Ahom would become a series of progressive events dominated by key players moving the community forward from the thirteenth century to the present. In the precolonial period of the buranji literature we learn that Ahom was not a specific group. Ahom, in the buranjis (as I will show in chapter 3), is a term used to qualify a class position and not a specific community. Needless to say, I was deeply concerned: How could I write the history of an absent community and put it in the framework of linear time moving forward in a self-conscious manner?

A third option was to begin in the present, with the struggle for Tai-Ahom identity. This approach, while it underscores contemporary events and those actors involved in the construction of identity, I believe ultimately draws attention to the foundational site of Tai-Ahom identity production, that is, the construction of history and memory. It makes us deeply aware that the past is available to us only from the standpoint of the present, and the Tai-Ahom example explicitly enumerates this point. The Tai-Ahom past does not exist beyond those remembering it, and hence it is to the people—their knowledge, emotions, and images—that we ultimately have to refer in order to understand what Tai-Ahom identity and history are for them. Such a narrative lets us directly encounter the web of Tai-Ahom memories. Like Matt Matsuda (1996), I believe that "memory has a history." It is produced in a series of "locations" as a collaboration that is motivated by certain explicit purposes. In the Tai-Ahom case, as I found out, the narrative of the community begins in the struggle between contemporary competing agents, who suggest various interpretations engaging various time frames and places in order to construct Tai-Ahom memory within and beyond Assam. By engaging the various representations we interact with a complex and rich historical process that is continuously constructing the meaning of Ahom. The process is ongoing, even now. I believe that this exercise—the investigation of the interaction of the past with the present, of people and history—will allow us to explore the ways in which the past is put to "use" in a contemporary identity movement. It also historicizes memory rather than simply pursuing it as a methodological tool to construct the past. Hence, I tell the story of Tai-Ahom as a series of memory constructions both because this approach has meaning for the group that is remembering and because it allows us to enter into a dialogue with them, examine their arguments, and test their claims for making a Tai-Ahom identity.

To understand what these images mean to Tai-Ahom people, I had to situate the present-day community within its oral traditions and the written history of Assam. Moreover, I had to ask how they interpret these accounts and use them as a source of knowledge about their past. This meant adopting a multifaceted methodology. I combined archival research with oral history and fieldwork, and I did close readings of the buranjis with the aim of exploring various facets of "local" memory-history among a wide cross-section of people, including political activists, intellectuals, militant leaders, shamans, students, and those with more ordinary lives.

I started my research on Tai-Ahom memory-history by reading several buranjis.[14] For this work I undertook Thai language training because the Ahom language is "dead" and there was no way to receive formal training in it. Thai provided vocabulary and an understanding of grammatical structure, although the scripts for Ahom and Thai bear no resemblance. For a few months I also studied Lao, which closely matches the Tai-Ahom script. In present-day Assam, the Tai-Ahom language is used by a small group of deodhais for "sacred" purposes such as officiating in religious rituals. Being a woman and, more so, being Muslim, made some deodhais (all of whom are male) not very keen to teach me the language of their gods. Hence, it was with great difficulty, and only by invoking my connection with the late Domboru Deodhai, that I could engage a teacher from a related language group called Aiton to teach me the Tai-Ahom language and script. Many in Assam, when they learned that I was studying Tai, were quite amazed. Curiously, however, the Tai-Ahom leaders were most delighted that I was making an effort to understand their past. With the help of my language teacher, Nabin Syam, I read the *Ahom Buranji*,[15] and on my own I read the Assamese buranjis and translated several of these chronicles to document the history of Ahom. Although these works were deemed by colonial and local scholars of Assam to be ancient texts of the Tai-Ahom community (believed to date from the thirteenth century), I found that buranjis are artifacts of much more recent times, probably the seventeenth century and onward, and today are commemorated as the "source" of Tai-Ahom identity. I also found that buranjis rarely mentioned the term Ahom, and on the rare occasions when it occurred it was not used to denote a community. The term identity never occurs in the buranjis. I realized that to document Tai-Ahom history I had to interact with the people and investigate their notions of past and present, of memory and identity. For this I had to travel to Assam and live in Tai-Ahom villages.

I was able to undertake this project due to the several advantages I have as an Assamese. My family is based in Assam, and thus I had access to people, documents, and places normally not available to "outsiders." Until 1996, Assam and the rest of the northeast were under the government's Restricted Areas Policy (RAP), which meant that, except for limited guided tourism, no "non-Indians" could visit the area. The government of India has been very strict about maintaining RAP, and thus Western academic interest on the northeast had never developed. As a consequence, another fellow Assamese and I are the only two scholars in the United States of America who, as far as I know, are actively involved in Assam studies outside of Assam. My Assamese origin privileged me to return to Assam without much difficulty. Once there, I was able to follow the Tai-Ahom movement very closely, in public and private exchanges, within homes and offices, in male and female spaces, in sacred and mundane activities, and in towns and villages.

What was the reaction of Tai-Ahom leaders to me, a Muslim woman, trying to understand their quest for identity? And what did the Muslim community in Assam think about my interest in Tai-Ahom? Curiously, my religion was not a matter of concern to anyone, and in fact, I did not expect it would be. In the public realm in Assam everyone was an Assamese and that civic status had not yet eroded, and the people were not insecure about sharing and interacting with each other. Now as I write, however, with incredible sadness after the genocide of Muslims in Godhra, Gujarat, in February 2002,[16] I am astounded that the organization of community based on shared language and culture still survives in Assam and is able to transcend religious differences. Perhaps because the majority of people in Assam are poor and disempowered, random violence based on religion is not as likely as elsewhere in India where people have more to gain and lose in consequence. All communities in Assam are codependent, and they have to maintain amity and share their scarce resources or else the majority would die of starvation. I offer here an economic explanation of why people in Assam have learned to exist together and religious identities are not used for generating violence. On the other hand, my mother, a professor of philosophy, believes that Assam is an example for the rest of India to follow because the Assamese people have consciously adopted a path of nonviolence and peaceful coexistence since historic times.

Whatever the explanation, it is true that those centuries-old associations and communications are not yet obliterated in Assam. Even today, post-Godhra, when I go back to Assam I feel I have returned home, and the sense of insecurity that I feel as a Muslim in the rest of India disappears. Is it because Assam is a familiar place and I know what to expect? Maybe so. But one cannot discount the fact that orthodoxy has no place in Assam, be it Hindu or Muslim, and as a consequence people do not approach religion, theirs and others, with fear and resentment. The grand narrative of Hindu and Muslim strife that is part of Indian history cannot be applied to Assam, at least not yet. While I was in Assam undertaking research, my relationships with my Tai-Ahom friends and others were not muddied by banal presuppositions of religious difference. Hence, I could embark on my research without religious and social obstacles.

In the course of my stay in Assam (1994–1996), I met several people who claimed that they were Tai-Ahom and thus different from other Assamese groups. I was bewildered. On the one hand, written sources such as the buranjis are silent about an ethnic community called Ahom, but here a group in Assam was claiming such a history and invoking the buranjis as the repositories of their original culture and identity as Tai-Ahom! How was this possible? What was going on? These questions kept coming back to my mind. I made a breakthrough, however, when I met Phatik and Kiran Gogoi, both active executive members of the Ban Ok. Phatik Gogoi invited me to meet the members of the Guwahati unit, and soon I found myself invited to their homes by each of them in turn. I was received warmly and openly, and everyone showed a great deal of interest in my project and freely discussed with me the Tai-Ahom identity movement. However, although they answered my questions honestly, they were unable to answer specific questions concerning the history of Tai-Ahom. With great tact, confidence, and hope, the Guwahati unit directed me to the village of Patsako, to meet with members of the Upper Assam units of the Ban Ok, who they believed could answer all my questions concerning Ahom history.

After meeting with all of the important members of the Sibsagar group, with their blessings and introductions I traveled to Patsako, which I previously had visited on December 26, 1992. Patsako is a small village composed of a few hundred households and is located thirty miles northeast of Sibsagar town. Within Patsako is the deodhai enclave of Akhoyan, where Domboru Deodhai's family lived. I was hoping that during this visit, my second, I would have the opportunity to meet the "authentic" deodhai families who would educate me on Tai-Ahom history. But my initial visit to Patsako was a disaster. People were not certain why I was in their village and became suspicious of my intentions. Gossip traveled quickly, and soon I was represented as a government agent sent to collect information about the activities of the Tai-Ahom and the United Liberation Front of Assam, both of which are considered anti-Indian movements. Needless to say, the story got more distorted as it was passed along: no one was certain if I was an agent for the American or Indian government, and the people of the village refused to interact with me. In the end I stayed in the government resthouse at Sibsagar, and during this time I consulted the archive in the Tai-Ahom Jadughar (museum). The archive has a rich collection of Tai-Ahom manuscripts, although the majority of them are religious texts. While I was visiting, Domboru Deodhai's son, who worked in the museum, took me under his wing. He also invited me, once again, to Patsako to meet his family, and in his home I met several other key members of the Tai-Ahom movement. After these events I found I was accepted, and the village adopted me. I then moved to a place near the village, where I lived for several months.

In the end, my visit to Patsako was rewarding. I was able to freely roam around the village visiting families and I often had meals with them. Here I need to mention that India's religious and caste taboos of interdining are not maintained in Assam, and Hindus and Muslims eat together in public and private spaces. Rice binds the Assamese Hindus, Muslims, and others into one community, as I will discuss in chapter 4. Hence, when I was in the villages I ate whatever my hosts offered without hesitation. It was in the family mealtime gatherings that I learned a great deal about Tai-Ahoms because conversations were free and unhampered. I participated as much as I could, but mostly I listened. I wanted to hear "Tai-Ahom" people talk about themselves, their stories, history, culture, and society, as well as learn about their hopes and expectations for the future. During the time I stayed there, I had access to several manuscripts in the village. Most were religious texts, manuals of oracles, divination, and astrology not immediately useful for studying the history of Ahom. Until recently, I was told, deodhai families took no interest in these chronicles. However, since the onset of the Tai-Ahom movement, scholars and activists had visited Patsako to study the chronicles, and the village on the whole had renewed its interest in the documents. Nonetheless, in many homes I found manuscripts perched on the bamboo ledge above the stove in the kitchen, where they were covered with soot from years of neglect. These chronicles were not being read because even though the Patsako Tai-Ahom Academy occasionally offered Tai language classes, the language was not known by most in the village.

Patsako, being a deodhai village, is observant in religious rituals and practices, but they are not exclusionary. During my stay, I was able to observe as well as participate in several religious activities and festivals, even though I am a Muslim woman. At the cost of repetition I find these assumptions about religious divisions puzzling, even as I note that it is the lack of religious division, at least at a public and cultural level, that is unique to Assam. During these occasions of religious celebrations, my Tai-Ahom hosts welcomed me to participate, and I did so without hesitation. I became an Ahom-Muslim, whatever that is, while I lived in the villages. I cannot claim that I became one of the community members, but throughout my stay I was treated as an "honorary member." The women were especially social and interacted warmly. Male and female spaces in Patsako were not usually demarcated except during political discussions. On such occasions, I was always the only woman in the company of several men, old and young, listening, talking, and deliberating issues that concerned the Tai-Ahom. After three months, I found, I had spoken to each member of the village several times. I had visited all of the households and had seen all of the Tai-Ahom artifacts in the village. I had come to Patsako with the intention of learning the original history of the Tai-Ahoms from the "authentic" deodhais and their oldest and most valuable buranjis. However, I was not more knowledgeable about Tai-Ahom history, even though after three months I did learn a lot about the activities and agenda of the identity movement. The stories of the past began and ended with Sukapha, the thirteenth-century hero who, the present group claimed, migrated from the east, beyond Assam. Although they have several versions of this migration story, that is the extent of the history. Ahom, according to them, originated with Sukapha, and they are his progeny: thus, they are Tai-Ahom. For them, this is their history, and no other version is available or suitable.

After this encounter in Patsako, I moved on to visit over ten other villages. Some I chose and several others were recommended to me. Not all of them were Tai-Ahom, but they all claimed to be Tai people and all shared a common linguistic background. In particular, Rohan Syam Gaon in Sapekhati; Khamyang Gaon in Salapathar; Tai-Turung Gaon in Titabar; and Phakey Gaon in Jeypore proved very helpful, even though they were non-Ahom, Buddhist villages. They all shared openly with me their definite opinions about Tai-Ahom history, culture, and struggle for recognition. I lived for short periods in each of these villages, and, as in Patsako, I had several rewarding experiences. Although villagers were doubtful about the "Tai-ness" of Ahom, they recognized the Assam kingdom as an Ahom administration—meaning that the Ahom nobility ruled it. For them the Ahom were a mix of people, some immigrants and others indigenous to the Assam valley. The villagers were not certain if the immigrants were of Tai ancestry, but they identified them as people who came from beyond Assam, possibly from Upper Burma. Further, they all agreed that it was time that the Tai communities in Assam were acknowledged by the Indian government. Toward this end the Tai communities supported the Tai-Ahom movement, which they perceived as the only hope for the Tais in Assam. No one in these villages tried to discourage me from studying Tai-Ahom history and language, but on several occasions they asked me not to include them—the Tai groups—in my story. Their concern was that if I were to do so, I would lump the Ahom people with the "real" Tai communities of Assam, like them, and they were uncertain about it. They qualified the difference in a very subtle way, "Ahoms were rulers; we are only *Tai* peasants who migrated to Assam in the eighteenth century. It is not desirable that rulers and subjects should be put in the same category." What they were really telling me was, "We are Tai, Ahoms are not, and it is better to leave it that way."

The monsoons turned out to be a great hindrance to my field research. The rains are constant in Assam, but the real problems started after the rains. Because most of the bridges to remote villages are made of temporary materials like bamboo and wood, they were washed away during the rainy season. Thus, communication thereafter ceased, sometimes for several months, and communities had to survive on air drops of goods by the military. In the end, however, it seems I was lucky, for not once during my research was I stranded, although there were several close calls.

Between September 1994 and February 1995 I concentrated on archival research. The Assam State Archive in Guwahati is a rich source for provincial papers. Although most of the collection for the preindependence period (prior to 1947) is not cataloged, the archive staff was immensely helpful in finding the material I needed. Two other important centers for archival research in Assam are the Directorate of Historical and Antiquarian Studies (DHAS) and the State Museum Library. Both of these centers have a rich collection of buranjis and artifacts of the Ahom kingdom, and I read several buranjis in the DHAS. Besides these state-sponsored archives, there were several private libraries and collections that I consulted, the most useful of which was the S. K. Bhuyan library.

Doing archival research in Assam is a fine art, and to access the material one has to go through several rites of passage. In my case, because I was "coming back home" to do research, the pressures and expectations to conform were even greater than if I had been a stranger. I had to prove that I was serious about my research, which required that I arrive at the archives before the gates even opened, and then be the last to leave. This proven, I had to learn how to "work" in the archives. Work meant accommodating several tea breaks (sometimes as many as six) with the staff and visitors in the canteen. Refusal to do so was not well received, nor would they understand that I had had too much tea. In addition, I was viewed as "too aloof, too Westernized." For this and other reasons, at times my work moved at a slow pace. Occasionally my father would drop in for a visit, and almost immediately the staff would attend to me with enthusiasm. However, not all was dull and tedious in the archives. There were exciting moments when new manuscripts were procured, and on two occasions I was consulted on new acquisitions. Also, I was always one of the first few to have access to the newly acquired documents. This was a great privilege and honor, for access to material determined my place in the "discourse community" in Assam and expanded the possibilities of my research project.

In late February 1995, I returned once again to do fieldwork in the villages. The village of Jahasuk, five miles outside of Dhemaji, was my base for the next month. Dhemaji is a small town bordering Assam and Arunachal Pradesh. The town has a mixed population, but very few "Assamese" people resided there. Most of the inhabitants are Tai-Ahom, Mishing, Miri, and a variety of other people who claim non-Assamese ancestry. Tensions between the two dominant groups—the Tai-Ahom and the Mishing—are on the rise, because the Mishing, who are the majority in the area called Cement Sapori, a few miles outside Dhemaji town, served notice to the non-Mishings to leave the area. Since then, the non-Mishing populations, in coalition with the Tai-Ahoms, have been trying to resist the Mishing, and this had given a new twist to the Tai-Ahom movement. In Dhemaji I was befriended by Puspha Gogoi, the general secretary of the Ban Ok, and by Umesh Chetia, a local journalist and political activist. Umesh Chetia took me around the "Tai-Ahom villages" and arranged meetings with several Tai-Ahom activists. In Dhemaji I did not live in the village, but rather took a room in the government resthouse.

Dhemaji is more political and therefore somewhat more volatile than Patsako. Tai-Ahom activism was very visible there, so much so that the first capital city of the Ahom swargadeos, Habung, was identified and claimed to be in Dhemaji. Several deodhai families were also promoting a Tai-Ahom religious revival under a banner called Phra Lung, which combined ancestor worship with certain elements of Buddhism and Tantric practices. Ahoms, according to the Phra Lung leaders, had to discard Hinduism to become Tai and thereby non-Assamese. Consequently, many in Dhemaji and the surrounding villages had converted to the new religion.

There was a certain undercurrent of political tension in Dhemaji. At times I was uncertain about being there. Because I stayed in the resthouse, I did not develop close friendships with people in the village. News about me had reached Dhemaji before I arrived. In Dhemaji I was viewed as the "researcher," and the people in general, particularly Tai-Ahom activists, were keen to cooperate with me. Their side of the bargain was that they thought I would represent the Tai-Ahom movement favorably. Somehow, they thought, my book would lead the state and national government to reconsider the demands of the Tai-Ahoms and reward them with the special Scheduled Tribe status that they desire.[17] While their view of me as the "researcher" gave me legitimacy and I earned the respect of people, I also knew that they were guarded during our conversations and that I was under the constant gaze of people who monitored all of my activities. I could not aimlessly walk around the village and stop by someone's home for a meal. Unlike Tai-Ahom villages in Sibsagar and Dibrugarh, where I conducted very few formal interviews but mostly engaged in conversation, in Dhemaji I had to arrange meetings in advance, and at times Umesh Chetia advised me to cancel my appointments. Despite these problems, Dhemaji made a special impression on me. Its natural beauty and rich, green undulating hills made the fieldwork aesthetically pleasing. Nights were deadly silent and every dawn was distinctly beautiful; indeed, fieldwork in Dhemaji was like a trip to an exclusive resort. At the end of March 1995, I returned to Guwahati and soon moved to Calcutta and from there to Delhi to do archival research.

The National Library in Calcutta and the Indian Archive in New Delhi both proved useful. The National Library has several out-of-print and rare books on Assam. Unfortunately, many of these materials are considered "too brittle for public use" and no one is allowed to read them. I suspect that this is one of the many reasons why the study of Assam has not developed in metropolitan centers like Calcutta. The Indian Archive in Delhi has a rich collection of colonial papers and documents, but unfortunately many of my requests to see them were turned down. Most of the documents on Assam are labeled "sensitive material" (even some of those dating back to 1910) and are available only by permission from the Ministry of External Affairs. As my experience proved, permission was hardly ever granted. Nonetheless, taken as a whole, my time spent in India was an enriching experience. I learned the Tai-Ahom language, which enabled me to read the *Ahom Buranji*. I also read a large number of Assamese buranjis, colonial documents, and government reports; I met and talked with several Tai-Ahom activists; I observed and participated in Tai-Ahom religious, social, and political events; and I made several friends.

Following my time in India, in July 1995 I traveled to Hamburg, Germany, to meet Berand Jan Terwiel, an anthropologist specializing in Tai-Ahom rituals and religion. Terwiel shared with me his field experiences during his trip to Assam in 1979, when the Tai-Ahom movement had just started. It was very useful to compare his notes with my own because I was thus able to follow the course of the movement from the time it began. In September I went to London. In the British Museum Library and the Oriental and India Office Library I was able to read all the materials—colonial papers and rare out-of-print books written in English and Assamese—that I could not access in India. In January 1996 I once again traveled to Assam in order to fill in gaps in my research and observe the ongoing Tai-Ahom events. During this time I was able to visit Thailand, where I had several conversations with Thai scholars who were doing research on different aspects of Tai-Ahom history, culture, and community.[18] These conversations made me aware of the ongoing intellectual and political exchanges between the Thai and the Tai-Ahom scholars, and they helped me to understand the transnational dimension of the identity movement. My research efforts to this point were formed into a dissertation, and I received a Ph.D. degree in 1999, but it was not until 2001 that a narrative of the community that calls itself Tai-Ahom began to take shape for me. I could now venture to write the story of Tai-Ahom history and negotiate my own voice alongside the stories and voices of the people claiming to be Tai-Ahom. Like my multisited research, the manuscript traveled with me wherever I went. The locations of writing were multiple—Guwahati (Assam), Dhaka (Bangladesh), London (United Kingdom), and Chapel Hill (United States)—and each site in some way influenced story telling about the Tai-Ahom.

### SELF AND COMMUNITY: MAKING SENSE
### OF ASSAM'S HISTORY

I undertook the study of Tai-Ahom history and the identity movement for several reasons. As a student of history in India I did not have the opportunity to study Assam's history, and as such I could not understand where the Assamese fit into the Indian historical imagination. Even today, in textbooks of Indian history Assam is absent. The story of its erasure goes back to the British colonial period, when the enterprise of finding, knowing, and writing the history of "natives" of India was undertaken. Colonization provided the motivation to construct a history that depicted differences between ruler and ruled and to create power for the masters. However, by the mid-nineteenth century, India was no longer seen as the distinct other after the Aryans were "discovered" and made the founders of Indian civilization. British historians quickly connected this group of Indians to Europe. Thus an Indo-European race was born in colonial discourse, and Indian history was connected through the travesty of racial theory to Western civilization and peoples.[19] Indian history, thus, entered the Western academy through the portal of dependency on Western culture and civilization.

The British entry into the province of Assam followed after most of India was colonized and the first history of India was written. In Assam, colonial agents confronted a mix of plains and hills peoples who were not Aryans. The abstract idea of racial/cultural affinity between the British and Indians on the basis of an Aryan connection was put to a severe test. Instead, in Assam, colonial agents listened to overlapping folktales inhabited by generic, nameless characters of unknown origin, and events that floated outside a fixed time line of Aryan history. Colonial confusion found its solution by making the non-Aryan(ized) peoples and cultures of Assam into absent subjects; a place and people where history was made "unthinkable."[20] For a brief period, in the late nineteenth century, the unthinkable history of Assam was made somewhat thinkable as powerful men were identified and duly acknowledged as the ruling community. These rulers the British called Ahom, but they dismissed them as a "dead" community of rulers when they failed to identify a specific community. Ultimately, in colonial narratives the people of Assam as a whole were transformed into anarchic frontiersmen without history—unknown and unknowable. Their sole use was as sentries safeguarding the ordered, known, stable colonial domain of British India.

The tenets of colonial thinking concerning Assam survived. Indeed, as the history of India became more and more known through research and writing, the silence concerning Assam became established.[21] In undertaking my research on the history of Tai-Ahom I immersed myself in a local history project to highlight a silenced episode in the national narrative. The story of Tai-Ahom is not simply a reminder of an absence in the national narrative; it is much more than that. Its absence serves as an instance to locate the "moments" and actors in the plays of power that have created a discourse today put in the service of the nation-state to use and abuse for further self-glorification and control of the past. The erasure of Assam from the history of India illuminates the process and power of standardizing narratives. People in Assam for the longest time believed they had a history that did not deserve mention. Hence they never asked that it be announced and made thinkable within the paradigm of Indian history.

This book is not an attempt to insert Assam into Indian national history. Rather, the issue I want to highlight is epistemological and methodological: Have the modern histories of India that claim to be counter/alternative histories broken the bond of philosophical and intellectual dependency on the colonial narrative?[22] Indian history is bound both mentally and physically. Organized by certain themes and places, it draws its narrative limit where initially colonialism and now the nation-state has fixed its cultural borders. Within this narrow confine it is further delimited by a very modern assumption that history radiates from the center. Only those segments of the periphery historically connected to the center in some subordinate position can be part of the paradigmatic narrative. Indian history inherited this model from the colonial style of narrative, and it upholds it even today.

The central position in Indian historical narrative is given to the Gangetic plain (although today attempts are being made to include the history of the areas south of the Ganges, too).[23] The Gangetic plain is traditionally seen as the land of Aryans and the birthplace of Hinduism. Even the postcolonial narrative has a fixed gaze on the Gangetic plain, in the nation's capital at Delhi. But what about the histories and cultures that do not connect to the central radial? "Border crossing" is not encouraged in Indian scholarship and historians are not yet ready to tell a different narrative based on human interactions located in a different center, such as the crossroads of Assam where Delhi meets Rangoon. This book is the first attempt to tell a story from the central position of Assam and the Tai-Ahom.[24] Such an endeavor is ultimately iconoclastic because it is conceived as an effort to dismantle the bounded official histories that politicize and demarcate the past into spatial, temporal, cultural, and religious units that are constructed and artificial.[25]

As a professional historian I understand the subject of history to be the act of bearing witness. Historians normally bear witness to things and events that happened in the past. The past is elastic and can stretch to several hundred, even thousands, of years before our time. But history is not a project of the past only. History is alive and constantly happening.

To bear witness to history as it is taking shape is risky and problematic, for we do not have the luxury of time to distance ourselves from events and actors in order to comment on it "objectively." The problem of "objectivity" notwithstanding, doing contemporary history provides new meaning both as a commentator and participant in the process. The recognition and investigation of this process—the double-edged power of history, history as a narrative and history as action—became for me the compelling reason to undertake the Tai-Ahom project. On the one hand, it allowed me the privilege of an old-fashioned historical adventure, to follow the trail of manuscripts (buranjis/puthis) and within them to try to locate a Tai-Ahom past. On the other hand, it threw me into the throes of a contemporary identity movement in process, making me both a commentator and an agent of the process of making a new history. The plot of history has finally turned for me: there is no defined subject or fixed narrative; history has become perpetual.

This book is concerned with the specific problem of a community seeking identity in the present. The Tai-Ahom community is marginal, confined to a remote corner in India. Their story is no more than a "fragment" within the larger discourse of the histories of modern communities.[26] But the study of a fragment is important because the alarming tendency of the newly produced national history of India is to repress and silence the diverse histories and memories of the groups and communities that constitute the Indian union. A careful investigation and recognition of fragmentary histories—the small voices in the margins such as the Tai-Ahom—is essential, for as Prasenjit Duara (1995) reminds us, history must be rescued from the nation.

>>>>>>>>>>>>>>>>>>>>>>>>>>>>

# PART ONE

<<<<<<<<<<<<<<<<<<<<<<<<<<<<<

*Historical and Comparative*

>>>>>>>>>>>>>>>>>>>>>>>>>>>>

*Perspectives on Identity:*

<<<<<<<<<<<<<<<<<<<<<<<<<<<<<

*Indian, Assamese, and Tai-Ahom*

>>>>>>>>>>>>>>>>>>>>>>>>>>>>

# CHAPTER 1

# Identification in India

At midnight August 15, 1947, the nation-state of India was born. The inaugural moment of India was marked by extreme violence, the memories of which are indelibly etched in the psyche of the people who lived through the horrific experiences of independence and partition.[1] The new nation-state of India, officially declared as a sovereign, socialist, secular, democratic republic consisted of sixteen states and nine union territories (at present it consists of twenty-eight states and seven union territories). "Secular nationalism and centralism," in the words of Sugata Bose and Ayesha Jalal, were the underlining principles of independent India (1999, 202). Centralism, however, was immediately challenged by regional states, and the relationship between region and center became strained in the subsequent decades. Problems between Delhi and Assam, the principal state of the northeast, emerged quickly. The contestation between center and state was an anticipated problem. Congress stalwart Sardar Ballabhai Patel warned Prime Minister Jawaharlal Nehru about the northeast in particular when he stated that "the undefined state of the frontier and the existence on our side of a population with affinities to Tibetans or Chinese has all the elements of potential trouble between China and ourselves. . . . The contact of these areas of north-east with us is by no means close and intimate. The people . . . have no established loyalty and devotion to India . . . European missionaries and other visitors had been in touch with them, but their influence was, in no way, friendly to India or Indians" (cited in Kaul 1967, 220–22).

In the newly created political union of India, the northeast was not the only region that did not seem to fit. Glaring differences between the various communities that constituted the Indian populace were more visible than the similarities, and there was no glue to bind them together. In fact, challenges to the national state emerged immediately after independence. In the northeast many groups of Nagas revolted against their inclusion in India, and in the north the Kashmiris asserted their right to autonomy. In south India, in the early 1960s, the Tamil movement emerged and challenged the cultural and political hegemony of north India. The demand for Khalistan in Punjab in the 1980s marked the rising tide of secessionist movements. Many more regional and local nationalist movements emerged in different pockets of India and challenged the hegemony of Delhi. In 1979 in Assam the All Assam Students Union launched an identity movement demanding the deportation of all immigrants from Assam to safeguard Assamese identity. The Assamese identity movement led the way for the emergence of new and parochial movements in the region. These include the Bodoland movement, which emerged in 1987 to demand a separate autonomous state within Assam; the movement launched in 1989 by the United Liberation Front of Assam to secede Assam from India; and the Tai-Ahom movement for the separation of identity of the Assamese and the Indians. Recently, groups of Dimasa and Karbi in Assam have also launched their own identity movements.

Scholars of Indian history and politics categorize under the generic label "subnational" these movements as well as many more that are ongoing in India (Mitra and Lewis 1996; S. Baruah 1999). The concept of subnationalism is highly problematic when applied to the constructed nation-state of India;[2] the term "local" may more accurately describe these regional movements. By describing them as local, however, I do not mean that they are discourses that are isolated and bounded to a limited territory. Rather, I use the term local to distinguish the identity movements from the national movement to homogenize Indian identity. The national movement, as is generally understood, is linked to capital, the West, and, at present, to the discourse of globalization. Local movements, on the other hand, attempt to override the power of the national. They seek to create a "different" sense of collectivity based on specific constructs that are emotional, sentimental discourses that give meaning to locality and enable the construction of a "homeland" as a different space from the homeland of "others."

In his 1882 lecture "What Is a Nation?" Ernest Renan argued that a nation is founded on the site of suffering, for "to have suffered together . . . unites more strongly than common rejoicing" (1999 [1882], 153). Suffering creates cohesiveness and brings disparate groups together. In other words, the memories of loss can provide a site for people to convene as a nation. The local nationalist movements in India claim that the communities they represent are sufferers within the nation-state. They have been marginalized economically and politically, peripheralized socially and culturally, and their narratives are erased from the annals of national history. They are thus reduced to the subjects of the powerful, moneyed interest groups that control the nation, and the state has failed to protect their rights. They are the victims of the national enterprise. The leaders believe local movements will enable them to overcome erasure from national history and empower their communities politically and culturally to transform memories into action. Hence, although the local nationalist movements ongoing in India have different agendas, strategies, and goals, their common project is to undermine the national center. In turn, they are creating new labels to identify with and they are demanding benefits that are presently denied. Ultimately, what these movements seek to accomplish is to democratize the national site of power and politics and to be able to practice citizenship based on rights and choice. The issues of local nationalist quests in India are multiple. Because I am mainly concerned with the issues and movements in Assam, in this chapter I will focus on the politics of identity in postcolonial Assam in order to understand the contemporary manifestations of a Tai-Ahom history in process.

Identity politics in Assam are framed within larger questions of Indian national identity and politics. Questions such as what is Indian identity and whose history constitutes national history in India are crucial to understanding the struggles ongoing in Assam. In this chapter I first investigate the historical processes and actors that constructed the concepts of India/n to show that national political actors forged a unity among the disparate groups and communities by invoking categories and symbols acquired mainly from the colonial period.[3] I undertake an investigative approach for analysis to show that in postindependent India the constructed label of Indian was made accessible to a select group of north Indian citizens who became the primary members of the nation-state while others were reduced to different levels of secondary citizenship. Built into the system of privileges and denial were the politics of religion and location that were deployed to include and exclude certain groups of people.

Later in this chapter I document the political processes that have taken place in twentieth-century Assam in order to highlight the strategies and goals of the Assamese and the Tai-Ahom identity movements. First, I outline the Assamese identity movement, which used language politics to contest Indian identity. I then outline the Tai-Ahom movement, which has challenged the concepts of both Assamese and Indian in Upper Assam by using a memory of connections to regions outside India, particularly Upper Burma and Thailand. I present the Assamese and the Tai-Ahom identity movements as strategies used for bargaining and demanding citizenship rights that continue to be denied to most people in Assam. In this sense, both of the movements are politics of opposition to the homogenization of identity that the label of Indian seeks to establish. By beginning the historical narrative of identity in the twentieth century, I highlight how groups of people create their collective identities and emphasize the role of modern memories and historical constructions in the project of identity politics. The labels Indian, Assamese, and Tai-Ahom, as well as several others under construction in Assam, are predicated on creating collective memories and a sense of belonging that are mobilized and crystallized in a specific moment of history and thus lead to different outcomes.

### NARRATIVIZING NATION:
### THE CONSTRUCTION OF INDIA/N

The term India/n was first created by the Persians in the fifth century B.C. Following the Persians the Greeks and the Arabs used the label for the multiplex, polyglot communities of the subcontinent with whom they entered into practical and commercial interactions. They called these peoples Hindu/Indica after the Sindhu/Indus river. According to Andre Wink, the Arabs first demarcated and defined the area "as a civilization, set it apart and drew its boundaries. . . . In a political-geographical sense, 'India' or Al-Hind . . . was an Arab or Muslim conception" (1990, 5). Toward the end of the thirteenth century, the Arab term "Hind" was Persianized into Hindustan, meaning Hindu Land. It is essential to remember here that the name Hindu at this time did not identify a religious community but referred mainly to geography. The influence and adaptation of Persian language and culture is intimately connected with the spread of Muslim political power into the subcontinent.

In the eighth century a group of Arab Muslims established a commercial and political kingdom in Sind in the northwest frontier. Over time, commercial interaction culminated in conquest, and in the thirteenth century the Delhi sultanate was established. In north India the Muslims, like their Hindu counterparts, were various. In the Indian texts we come across several names for Muslims. Sometimes they are referred to by the ethnic term Turuska (Turks) because several groups of the conquerors hailed from different Turkic backgrounds. Local people also referred to them as Yavanas, a geographic appellation that was also used for Greeks. In many Sanskrit texts they are referred to by the cultural epithet *mleccha*. Notwithstanding these markers of identification, everyone within the overarching sultanate was referred to as Hindustani, meaning inhabitants of Hindustan. Babur, the founder of the Mughal dynasty in 1526, noted in his memoir that the culture of sixteenth century "India" was not exclusively Hindu or Muslim, it was Hindustani (Babur 1996 [1483–1530]). The bond of connection between the diverse Hindustanis was a spoken language also referred to by the name Hindustani. This language emerged from the hybrid Urdu language, a language that scholars believe to have developed in the area of Delhi in military camps and in the Sufi establishments of Nizamuddin and Hindawi. This language had its roots in the local indigenous dialects of the Ganges plains.[4]

In the second half of the nineteenth century, the British colonial administration claimed the scepter and became India's rulers. The colonial administration's obsession with fixing the boundaries of people and territory led to the creation of new labels. The decennial census, started in 1871, organized the diverse people into a hierarchy of castes and tribes. Hindustanis were transformed into many different demarcated societies and were labeled Indian by the British. Further in the tenure of Lord Ripon (1880–1884), as Metcalf and Metcalf (2002, 117) have shown, the community called Indian was divided into "majority" and "minority" groups based on their religion, where Hindus became the majority group of Indians and Muslims the minority. However, administrative codification failed to give texture to the label Indian. An enterprise of history writing was undertaken by the colonial British administration to investigate and formulate a narrative and to make Indians a historical subject. Native elites from both the Hindu and Muslim communities were interlocutors in the colonial enterprise.[5]

In 1826, the colonial administrator James Mill published the first modern narrative of Indian history, *History of British India*. Later works, including Mounstuart Elphinstone's *The History of India: The Hindu and Mohammedan Periods* (1872) and Vincent Arthur Smith's *The Early History of India from 600 B.C. to the Mohammedan Conquest* (1878), created a linear, periodized narrative. Colonial historians told a story of India in a chain of episodes in which one event led to another and culminated in the entry of the British.

The periodized history made different groups owners of fragmented segments of the past. In the colonial depiction of history, which was based on ontological, ethical, political, cultural, and geographical schema, "ancient" India was made into Hindu history and deemed more "Indian" than that of others. The period following the ancient era was called "Medieval India" and was converted into a period of Muslim occupation. Between these two extreme classifications of "Hindu" and "Muslim" Indians, colonial scholars located a variety of people they saw as Indianized/Indianizable. These peoples were identified as the "indigenous," "tribal" people spread throughout the subcontinent with high concentrations at the frontiers, and with local systems of administration and communities. Nineteenth-century colonial practices and administrators created for the land and people of India a metahistory of identity, and over time the concept of "India" underwent more radical changes.

By the mid-nineteenth century, the political fervor against colonialism and a newfound consciousness of Indian identity motivated the several newly identified and hierarchical caste communities to organize themselves. They formed *sabhas* (organizations) and *samitis* (associations). Initially these sabhas served as sites for religious and social discourses. The Brahmo Samaj founded by Ram Mohan Roy; the Poona Sarvajnik Sabha founded by Mahdev Ranade; the Servants of India Society founded by Gokhale; the Arya Samaj founded by Dayanand Saraswati; the Ramkrishna Mission led by Vivekananda, and others became centers of Hindu reform and revival. Among the Muslims, the Deoband movement emphasized the role of religion and reform in defining community and identity in nineteenth-century India. Supported by the Western-educated Indians, some of these sabhas became centers for political mobilization against British colonialism and thus created a space for presenting new visions of Indian identity.

The politics of late-nineteenth-century India were determinedly anticolonial. The anticolonialist leaders rejected the British representation of India as a divided land and people and, in turn, forged an imagination of a national unity. Hindu and Muslim were now represented as a composite community that bore little resemblance to the layer cake of British historians. The nationalists emphasized the "blended past" of Indians; but to construct Indian they had to invoke colonial paradigms. One such paradigm that persisted was the categories of Hindu and Muslim communities. Religion became an important tool for group identity and for imagining community in late-nineteenth-century India. Also, an appeal to Hinduness was expedient for the nationalists to bring various caste groups together and thus create some semblance of unity, which they thought could not be achieved otherwise. Hence, while rejecting the colonial construction of "Hindu" and "Muslim" history, the nationalists had to lean on the cultural commonality forged by "popular Hinduism" and generate a vocabulary of resistance to arouse the masses against the colonial regime (Khilnani 1998; Guha 1997). Some of the anticolonialist Hindu leaders such as Bankim Chandra in Bengal, Bal Gangadhar Tilak in Maharastra, Lala Rajpat Rai in the Punjab, and even Gandhi, the undisputed leader of the Indian National Congress (INC), embraced a Hindu religious vocabulary as a weapon of resistance against colonialism.[6]

These leaders had different imaginings of what constituted Hindu. Although disagreement was the order of the day, by suggesting and acknowledging different formulations of the Hindu, they also created a fundamental ambiguity of who is an Indian and created a gap between the diverse Hindu groups and "others" that could not be bridged. While the nationalists of the INC rejected the colonial image of the Indian as a generic Hindu, by emphasizing numbers they made Hindus, at three-fourths of the population, the "majority" community. But nationalist leaders argued that the Hindus were by no means the only community of Indians. Muslims, Christians, Sikhs, and the other religious groups that made up the remaining one-fourth of the population of the subcontinent were Indians, too. They were, however, "minority" communities. Thus, in producing the idea of a single India, nationalist narratives disrupted colonial categories but re-created distinct positions for different groups. The majority Hindus became primary in Indian identity construction, while everyone else followed behind them.

In 1918, when Gandhi took over as leader of the INC, a rudimentary concept of India was developing that was supported by the masses. The disappointments of World War I made the people of India "ready to storm the gates of the British Raj" (Bose and Jalal 1999, 137). People were willing to die for an idea—Hindus, Muslims, and Sikhs. But as the anticolonial movement grew, the factions that had come together in the struggle became increasingly suspicious of the intent and activities of each other. The Muslim minority group, in particular, organized themselves as a separate political party and revived the Muslim League (founded in 1906) to represent their cause. Mohammed Ali Jinnah, an erstwhile congressman, became the leader of the Muslim minority group. Alongside the development of separatist politics, by the beginning of World War II India was facing a severe economic crisis and the majority of India's poor were hit hard. In August 1940 the radicalized masses responded to Gandhi's call to join the "Quit India" movement and demanded that the British leave India. This probably was the last successful attempt of the INC to create and present a combined unified front of Indians against colonialism, but it was not enough to overcome the divisions of religious politics. The tenuous concept of India/n as a composite land and people unraveled soon thereafter.

After the general elections held in 1937, the division between the INC and the Muslim League (ML) became more apparent and thus divided the nationalist enterprise. In 1940 the ML, under the leadership of Jinnah, in its Lahore meeting passed a resolution demanding independent Muslim states in the northwest and the northeast of India on the grounds that the Muslims of India were a distinct nation. Ayesha Jalal argues in her book *Sole Spokesman* (1985) that at this stage neither Jinnah nor the Muslim League envisaged Pakistan as a separate entity from India, but rather used the concept of nationality as a strategy to gain power for the Muslim political voice. Nonetheless, the divisions grew between the anticolonialist groups—the INC (dominated by Hindu leaders) and the ML (led by Muslims)—which led to the creation of two distinct imaginations of the past, Hindu and Muslim. Supporters of both communities through violence and mayhem enacted these in reality. The rampant communal violence allowed the British government to suggest a plan for the partition of India on religious grounds. This plan was unveiled on June 2, 1947, and the final transfer of power was conducted hastily in August 1947 rather than June 1948, as was previously agreed on. The haphazard partition and dismemberment culminated in large-scale communal violence on both sides of the divide, in both India and Pakistan.

Independence solved one problem in that it brought an end to British colonialism. However, it also created several new problems. Although a large number of Muslims migrated to Pakistan in 1947, the bulk of the Muslim population stayed in their homelands in India. Hence, at the end of colonialism and at the creation of India, along with inheriting an antiquated history of the past, the modern state had to deal with the unresolved problem of qualifying the concept of "Indian." The populace continued to be diverse—Hindus, Muslims, and many other religious groups made up the communities of India. The gap between an abstract idea of a single shared history and the lived reality of diversity continued to grow; it was left to the apparatus of the modern nation-state to formulate a narrative that might bring together the many and different groups of the new Indian citizenry.

## MAPPING THE INDIAN "GEO-BODY"

We know from scholarship on nationalism that nation building is a continuous process (Gellner 1983; Hobsbawm 1983; Smith 1986; Anderson 1991). In India, as in almost all other nation-states, the nation's construction has a long history. The process of imagining India as a single unit emerged in the late nineteenth century. The imaginings in the arenas of anticolonial politics, such as the elite site of the INC, Hindu, and Muslim political and cultural organizations, were various, as they were in the sites of revolt of subordinates groups across British India. As Bose and Jalal have argued, "it was during this period that the idioms, and even the irascible idiosyncrasies of communitarian identities and national ideologies, were sought to be given a semblance of coherence and structure . . . to the emerging discourse on the Indian nation" (1999, 107–8).

Of the plethora of local narratives devised by Indians, the nationalist narrative of Jawaharlal Nehru enunciated in *The Discovery of India* (1946) was the most forceful. This narrative lucidly connects thousands of years of history—beginning from the Indus Valley civilization (3500 B.C.) to the period of the nineteenth-century anticolonial struggle—as a continuous story of the "Indian" people.[7] Nehru's creative narrative fashioned a cultural and political space whereby everyone living in India could claim an Indian identity based on shared national, political, and cultural aspirations. Simultaneously, contradictory religious narratives also emerged and divided India among religious communities. B. G. Tilak (1938), V. Savarkar (1923), and S. Gowalkar (1939) presented Hindu culture as the bedrock of Indian history and identity. Before them, Sir Sayyid Ahmed Khan had emphasized that Muslims were a separate *qaum* (nation, so to speak), although he did not oppose the idea of an Indian nation (Bose and Jalal 1999, 124). By and large in the late nineteenth and early twentieth century, the myths about the past and present of India, although variously imagined, transformed the space and mentality of the people and generated a politics for national struggle. Political persuasion and anticolonial movements in the early twentieth century created the rhetoric of "nation," and in narrative the nation was born. As Sudipta Kaviraj has argued, "India, . . . is not an object of discovery but of invention. . . . The idea of nationalism stitches together, in ways that are not seriously and minutely analyzed, social groups and communities of people . . . who would not have considered themselves as one single people, having a single political identity" (1992, 3). The assumption of a common India was quickly challenged after independence, and many groups started to ask whose history was represented by the national narrative.

Grappling with the rising discontent over representation in the national narrative, the government, headed by the Congress party under the leadership of Jawaharlal Nehru (1947–1962), immediately promoted a version of India/n, under the catch phrase "unity in diversity." In Nehru's tenure the reorganization of India based on linguistic division (1956) was meant to overcome the dominance of religious divisions. Central to Nehru's India was a concept of planned economy: he presented economic development as a way out of age-old vices and discriminations. Alongside the schemes of economic and social planning, the Nehruvian administration encouraged a new writing of Indian history. D. D. Kosambi's (1956) seminal narrative of Indian history presented a new focus on economic and social transformations and continuities in the precolonial period. Rather than focusing on the divisions created by the religions of the different ruling dynasties, his story of India emphasized the material, economic, and social concerns that were shared by the vast numbers of Indians. Kosambi's narrative suggested a pragmatic approach to dealing with the diversities within the body politic, but this strategic exposition never became popular except among a limited academic community. It was soon superseded by a very different version of cultural history produced under the aegis of the Bharatiya Vidyabhavan series. This postcolonial narrative of the Indian past was mired in the vocabulary of religious culture and presented a limited understanding of demarcated communities.

The construction of a single nationhood was not confined to the site of historical narratives of India. Nation had to be identified, and the map was deemed a handy tool to use to do so. The map of independent India was created in 1954 and was based on the imperial map of India created in 1899.[8] The colonial and postcolonial maps encapsulated the "geo-body" and made it into both a political entity and a sociocultural space. The concept of India as a nation-state was brought alive and a cultural-historical vocabulary that included Aryavarta, Bharatvarsa, and Hindustan mediated an imagination of a timeless entity called India. The classical concept of Aryavarta as the dominion of *Aryavamsi* (Aryan land) was reinserted by the Bharatiya Vidyabhavan scholars, and using the emphasis laid on the religious mapping by Gowalkar and Savarkar, Aryavarta was also designated to be Punyabhumi, "the land of virtue" and the realm of Rama Rajya.[9] The other term, Bharatvarsa, likewise was embedded in a cultural-religious space and was designated as Deva Bhumi, the land of gods.[10] Although in the postcolonial narratives terms such as Bharatvarsa, Aryavarta, and so forth were meant as markers of the cultural space of India to create pride in the past, the vocabulary (because it was steeped in the Brahmanic Hinduism of north India) skewed the imagination of modern India. The realm of Aryavarta remained narrowly restricted to the Gangetic delta of the north. The people in the regions immediately outside were reduced to the realm of mythical beasts and demons and were variously called *asuras, danavas, dasyus,* and *mleechas* (demons, monsters, subterranean, casteless, and polluted peoples). The favored position of north India within the geo-body, as nationalist historians rightly argued, would not be acceptable to the country at large.[11]

To correct the problem the English name "India" was popularized, and the three terms—Hindustan, Bharat, and India—were used interchangeably to mean the same territory and cultural space. All of these terms were also made more elastic than Aryavarta. Along with reinventing the geographic scope of the terms, a revival of cultures outside the Gangetic region was also supported. The revival of south Indian languages and cultures was accompanied by a newfound interest in the study of the classical "sangam literature" of Tamilnadu, and this was uplifted to the level of the Sanskrit texts of the Aryans. Tamil was promoted as a sacred language of the gods and Shiva was deemed its architect (Hellman-Rayanayagam 1995). Further, to generate southern pride and confer to it a glorious position in the long history of Hindustan/Bharat, the powerful Tamil empires of the Cholas and Pandyas were discovered and entered as subjects of research. In a sense the expanded Hindustan became a Hindu land. Nonetheless, the history was promoted as the history of India/ns, and although it addressed the people living within it as one community, it continued to use a vocabulary that privileged certain groups only. Hindu was the one category that remained unhyphenated within this narrative. All others developed in interaction with the term "Indian" and became hyphenated categories. Thus, there were now Indian-Muslims, Indian-Christians, and so forth. The lexical position of the communities determined their status within the modern nation-state. The postcolonial narrative was conceived as an enterprise to correct the problem and make Indians of everyone in India. But it managed, once again, to exacerbate the differences, and "Indian" continued to be a contested site of identification.

In the late 1980s and early 1990s, the contestation and claim over history, nation, and identity in India reached a feverish pitch. To settle the uncertainties and create a final definition of Indian history, on December 6, 1992, a group of Hindu nationalists under the leadership of L. K. Advani of the Bharatiya Janata Party (BJP) marched to the site of Ayodhya. The Hindu fundamentalists claimed Ayodhya as the birthplace of lord Rama, and razed to the ground a sixteenth-century Muslim mosque built by the first Mughal king, Babur, which allegedly was built on Rama's birth site. This political performance by the BJP and the activities of religious politics that have developed since then are meant to create a center for India, a Rama Rajya from which "Indianization"—or more aptly "the Hinduization of India"—can radiate to create one people, one nation, and one culture or *Hindutva*.[12]

### A NOTE ON *HINDUTVA*: THE WEAPON OF CONTEMPORARY POLITICS

Vinayak Damodar Savarkar was the architect of the word Hindutva.[13] In his seminal book, *Hindutva: Who Is a Hindu?*, Savarkar writes: "*Hindutva* is not a word but a history . . . Not only a spiritual or religious history of our people as at times it is mistaken to be, . . . but history in full. Hinduism is only a derivative, a fraction, a part of *Hindutva*. . . . Hindutva embraces all the departments of thought and activity of the whole Being of our Hindu race" (1923, 110–11). He goes on to say: "The first and most important qualification of a Hindu is that to him the land that extends from Sindhu to Sindhu is the Fatherland (Pitribhu) the Motherland (Matribhu) the land of his patriarchs and forefathers. . . . This land to him is not only a Pitribhu but a Punyabhu, not only a fatherland but a holyland. . . . That is why the Mohammedan and Christians . . . are not and cannot be recognized . . . for though Hindustan to them is Fatherland . . . yet it is not to them a Holyland too. Consequently their . . . outlook smack of a foreign origin" (113). Savarkar's Hindu ideology of India made Indian identity and the country into an ethnoreligious community. This definition of community was further emphasized by Gowalkar in *We and Our Nationhood Defined*, where he writes: "The non-Hindu peoples in Hindustan must adopt the Hindu culture and language, must learn to respect and hold in reverence Hindu religion, must entertain no idea but glorification of the Hindu race and culture . . . In a word: they must cease to be foreigners, or must stay in this country wholly subordinated to the Hindu nation, claiming nothing, deserving no privilege, far less any preferential treatment, not even citizen rights" (1939, 55–56).

In Savarkar's and Gowalkar's expositions, "Hindu" and "India" share an organic connection.[14] Being Hindu qualifies one to a race, culture, tradition, religion, and community that is exclusive. They are the unhyphenated Indians, the true citizens. The rest of the populace are categorized within schema of conquest, occupation, conversion, and the like and thus deemed unauthentic. They are forever relegated to a secondary position. Further, they were suspect as citizens for their interests supposedly lie outside India, according to Hindutva's claim. The Hindutva ideology transformed the meaning of "Indian" and made Hindus the primary Indians, which is more than a legal, official identity. The aim was to guarantee certain groups of citizens of the modern Indian nation-state privileged rights while denying the same to others. To be able to do so, the ideology of Hindutva emphasized that the progeny of the Muslim invaders must be vindicated, which would enable Hindu Indians to become wholesome and realize their original glory.

This assertion was notably vocalized on May 27, 1996, on the occasion of the inauguration ceremony after the BJP came to power under the leadership of Atal Bihari Vajpayee. Vajpayee declared: "India is not a few decades, nor fifty years old. India is five thousand years old. And I am proud to claim the history of the five thousand years as my history."[15] The statement by the nation's leader reveals the current concept of what is India and who is an Indian. The BJP's ideological foundation in Hindutva can survive and prosper by erasing the history of Muslims in India. Muslims, being deemed as a conquering group, have their history reduced to a story of occupation, and the BJP government wants the populace to forget and force this history out of collective memory. The only past worthy of remembering in the space of Indian history is thus the "Hindu past."[16] In this new partnership of religion and identity, the victims are not simply the minority Muslim communities but the vast majority of the Indian populace. The pernicious linkage between identity and religion has created deep divisions, and in the caste-ridden Hindu society only small fractions of the upper caste, which are a minority group within the nation, are the beneficiaries.

Nearly ten years after the destruction of the Baburi mosque, Ayodhya continues to be a wrecked and contested site; it has already claimed the lives of several people, even as far away as Godhra, Gujarat. At the same time, as the identity of India/n is forcibly imagined and every attempt is made to homogenize and create a monolithic religious group of Hindus, in many segments outside the site of national discourse, local movements championing local identities are proliferating. Many of these movements are challenging the concept of what is Hindu, as well as what is India, as the central government continues to manipulate, under the banner of Hinduism, a politics and identity that fail to provide unity.

To sum up, it is quite obvious that "India," "Indian," and "Indianness" are vague terms. We have seen that the initial British colonialists in India, perplexed by the diversity at hand and the need to classify their subjects in order to rule them, transformed the diverse people of the subcontinent into fixed categories demarcated by caste, tribe, and religion. These categories were not based on empirical evidence but on an ontology in which natives were far inferior to the British. These categories have come to stay. Today, those who can be located within these labels can find a place and a name with which to identify. They are people "included" within the categories of "majority" or "minority" groups. But what about those who do not figure within these categories? In postindependent India, an appeal to make the so-called "excluded" people nominally Indian was taken up in the Nehruvian period, and it succeeded on paper (in the constitution) but failed in reality. Even today class, religion, region, language, and culture continue to divide the "excluded" people from the caste-based north and south Indian Hindus and the minority communities of Muslims. Are these groups "Indian"? This question has been raised time and again by colonial, anticolonial, and now postcolonial politicians and administrators.

## THE UNTHINKABLE INDIAN:
## WHERE DO THE "EXCLUDED" FIT?

The category of excluded communities was created by the British in the Constitution Act of 1935 to describe the communities not directly administered by the provincial legislatures. In the official British circles, another representation of the excluded groups was also created: they were "tribal" people without a "real" history, akin to savages. In 1857, Sergeant Carter (posted in Assam) observed, "though being used lately to see such large tracts of country without dwellings or inhabitants one almost feels disposed to fraternize with the first savage that turns up; and so far as looks go, such of the natives as I saw today, are perfect savages indeed" (n.d., 3). The colonial version of the savage frontiersmen was reinforced by previous fanciful descriptions of medieval travelers. Assumptions were also authenticated by the texts of Brahmanic Hindus that referred to these people as the *asuras* and *mleechas*—the demons and outcaste groups—because they lived in regions that were outside Aryavarta. Such a placement outside the lineage of Aryavamsi and the dismissal from the category of human, because according to Hindu concept they had no *jati* (a birth-based community), destined the "excluded" communities to be peoples without histories and thus without identities. Colonial historians justified this position (Mitchell 1883, 30).

The colonial goal was to create a population in the frontiers loyal to the interests of the British Empire. But in so doing, they distanced these people further from the rest of India. Most of these communities were separate among themselves; and because they were distanced from the rest of India by the British policy of "inner" and "outer" line administration for the region, they were practically unknown. In the postcolonial period the people in the frontiers became even more isolated because they had little or no contact with the central administrative system, and increasingly their activities were viewed with suspicion. In short, the colonial policies of India to have a separate system of administration and control of the excluded areas secured for the people a position at the bottom of the scale of Indians where they were forever doomed to be only dubiously Indian. In 1950, the framers of the Constitution tried to remedy this hopeless situation. Under the Sixth Schedule of the Constitution, in addition to the category called Scheduled Tribes, the government devised a new classification called "scheduled castes," so that some communities that were tangentially connected to the Hindu belief system, but outside the four principal caste groups, could be located in this classificatory scale. Many groups in Assam, as well as the rest of India, found themselves classified in this category. Those groups who were outside the Hindu schemes of people and identities were transformed into Scheduled Tribes. Although given a place within the label "Indian," they were deemed to be different from "real" Indians.

The government of India considers the scheduled castes and tribes of the northeast to be the most distant "other." Although they are not restricted from interacting with Indians, the government keeps them in their place, so to speak. A period of political tutelage is needed to make them Indian, according to the government, and making the northeast a restricted area, as I discussed in the introduction, has enacted this. New Delhi's cultural and political outlook toward these communities has, in turn, generated among them a strong resentment toward the national state. A historical example illustrates this point. In January 1948, when Robert Reid, exgovernor of the northeast provinces, was on a tour of Nagaland, he received news of the assassination of Mahatma Gandhi. Feeling "a shock of pain," Reid wanted to share his grief with his host, Changrai, the chief of the Konyak Nagas. But Changrai did not know who Gandhi was. Reid writes, " 'I said, he is responsible for the British leaving India. It is he who got India its independence.' 'I see,' said Changrai, 'it is he who has caused all this trouble for the Nagas.' " Even more significant was the reaction to the assassination. Reid told the Nagas: "A Hindu youth had put three bullets into [Gandhi], one in the chest and two in the belly. They listened to the details with delighted amusement and . . . they all laughed aloud."[17] Nagas believe that a great man must be scalped, because that is the only way to acquire the life substance of heroes and chiefs. Gandhi was not scalped by his enemies but shot, a method of execution that illustrated to the Nagas that he was not a great man. On the other hand, people outside Nagaland cannot comprehend the Naga practice of scalping and dismiss it as a barbaric custom. The problem of untranslatable cultural norms has widened the gap, but the Indian government thinks this chasm must be overcome, even by force if need be, in order to civilize and Indianize the Nagas. Thus, huge numbers of army personnel are deployed to Nagaland to violently force Indianness on them. Today, in postcolonial India, Nagas feel there is no honorable place for people like them, yet they are compelled to concede to an imposed Indian identity, which they feel can neither accommodate their peculiarities nor let them be different.

The residents of Assam have also experienced a gap between their own self definitions and the imposition of "Indianness" by the state. In the period of the independence struggle many Assamese, although they joined in the anticolonial agitations and struggles of the INC, were not wholly convinced that the rhetoric of "Indianness" included them. In the late nineteenth century, a concept of *asamiya jatiyatabadi* (self-awareness) took root and an ideology of Swadhin Asom (Independent Assam) surfaced. I would argue that the nineteenth-century Swadhin Asom movement, although it purported in its choice of vocabulary to be a nationalistic struggle, was not like the anticolonial struggle of the INC; that is, it was not a freedom movement directed against the British. The Swadhin Asom movement was anchored on the foundation of a quest for identity through self-awareness. The effort was to investigate, understand, and manifest an Assamese identity that would be recognizable to those within and outside. According to the politically conscientious Assamese intellectuals and middle class—men like Lakhinath Bezbaruah, Ambikagiri Raychoudhury, Kamala Kanta Bhattacharjee, and many others—self-recognition was primary for community participation. Assamese language and poetry became the tools to express this consciousness and sentiment. Ambika Giri, in his poem "Mine Is Not the Song of Laughter," eloquently expressed this sentiment. He writes:

My song is an endless heat
Coming out of a hundred burning losses, insults, humiliations;
It is the fiery vapour
Oozing out from the imprisoned energy of the soul
. . . . . . . . . . . . . . . . . . . . . . . . . . . . . . . . . . . . . . . .
It is the self-denying sentiment
That blows away meanness, cowardice, helplessness;
It is the common seal
That impresses with one form, one colour, one expression
. . . . . . . . . . . . . . . . . . . . . . . . . . . . . . . . . . . . . . . .
It is the voice of humanity withered
Under a mountain load of insults;
It is the voice of pride incarnate
That condemns the vanity of oppressors.[18]

This and other poems written in the early twentieth century depict the Assamese yearning to be both part of a larger whole and to affirm a specifically Assamese identity. Finding this identity was both the quest and the project of the Swadhin Asom movement. Over time, particularly after independence, the self-awareness struggle in Assam took many different forms. The most easily articulated sentiment was an aversion to the "imposed" Indian character, which was deemed Indian "colonization."[19] Different interpretations of the meaning of Swadhin Asom emerged and took shape in the last few decades of the twentieth century, and various groups have claimed to be the architects of Assamese identity.

## POETICS OF SELF-AWARENESS, POLITICS
## OF THE ASSAMESE

The historical literature on Assam suggests that the concepts of Assam and Assamese were created toward the end of the seventeenth century after repeated violent encounters with the armies of Delhi, who had led their soldiers to Assam in the hope of gaining access to a new territory and the trans-Himalayan trade.[20] The definitive attack took place in 1661–1662 under the command of the Mughal general, Mir Jumla, when the reigning king, Jayadhvaj Sinha, was forced out of his capital city of Garhgaon. To regain his throne he had to make a treaty with the Mughals, which he then immediately spurned when the Mughals retreated from Assam. The Mughal literature on Assam that emerged followed the trajectory of the violent attacks and became obsessed with the recalcitrant "savages" at the frontiers who could not be subdued. The so-called savages, who refused to acknowledge Mughal overlordship, were described as a group of Acahmers/Achams, which in the Mughal literature were depicted as witches and magicians. Thus Mughal historians explained defeat at their hands.

The "Baharistan-i-Ghaybi" of Alauddin Isfahani, alias Mirza Nathan, a Mughal general in the reign of Jahangir (1605–1636) is by far the earliest known eyewitness account of the Acham people. Isfahani describes the people as savages and magicians. To make his point he provides an extensive description of the practices followed by Achamers in warfare and worship. He writes: "It is the custom of the Acham that whenever they engage in a war, they perform some sorceries . . . According to the custom they build one raft of plantain trees . . . and performed puja, i.e., worship of the devils, on it, in the following manner. They sacrificed a black man, a dog, a cat, a pig, an ass, a monkey, a male goat, and a pigeon, all black. Their heads were collected together and placed on the raft along with many bananas, betel leaves and nuts, various scents, mustard seeds and oil, rice paste, cotton seeds, vermillion, and then the raft was pushed adrift."[21]

Likewise, the "Fathivah-i-Ibriyah" of Shahabuddin Talish, a late-seventeenth-century chronicle that commemorates the Mughal invasion of Assam of 1661–1662, describes the kingdom as a "country alarming of aspect, depressing to live in and unpleasant to the sight . . . a region apart from the land of men."[22] Talish describes the "subjects of the proud Acham Raja called Giga Singh Swarga"[23] as constituting two groups: "the Achamers" and "the men of the mountain who have not submitted to the king of Assam, but do not dare to rise against him." About the swargadeo (Giga Singh), Talish writes: "He regarded himself an incarnation of the Creator . . . The king did not force adherence to any particular faith or sect on any men of his kingdom, as long as they admitted his claim." The "Achamers" are deemed "sorcerers," and are "regarded by Hindoos to have descended from a race different from that of Adam . . . They ate whatever they found, and ate every kind of flesh, except human flesh." He goes on to describe the people of Acham as "decisive, energetic, ready to undergo great fatigues and to bring to a successful end the most arduous undertakings. . . . Dying, killing, fighting hand-to-hand are the things at which they excel. They are more cruel, pitiless, knavish, astute, hypocritical, inhuman, and bloodthirsty than any people of earth. This is what their appearance is like. . . . Men shaved their beards, moustache, eyebrows, and hair. If any one set aside this custom, he is accused of following the custom of Bengal, and he is put to death at once . . . Some Achamers call themselves Muslims, but they are Achamers in their habits, and Mussalman but in name."

In addition to Talish's account and his description of the Achamers, a Dutch mercenary named Glanius, who accompanied Mir Jumla to Assam, left a chronicle of his observations. In this, the first European impression of Assam, Glanius refers to the "people of Assam" and distinguishes them from the "Antropophages or Man-eaters" that were "the enemies of the king of Assam." From him we learn that "the inhabitants of the country of Assam are a superstitious people, who worship a Cow, and consequently never kill any of that kind. Their temples are full of the images of these creatures, the greatest part made of gold and silver" (1682 [1673], 169–70).[24] He adds that a distinguishing mark of the "Assam people" is the royal burial custom: "As for riches we wanted them not, having found good store in graves. It being the peoples' custom to inter with their dead, their best apparel, money and the greatest part of their servants; whom they bury alive, to bear their masters company" (175).

Thus in the medieval chronicles the concept of "Achamers" developed within narratives of Mughal power. The story was framed in a way to make it acceptable within the Delhi circles. The Mughals, who could not defeat the Achamers, had to make sense of them to explain why they could not be subdued. A perverse picture of the savage culture of Achamers emerged, backed by descriptions of their activities as sorcerers and witches. Almost all of the medieval chroniclers agreed that Achamers were invincible and, hence, could not be brought under Mughal rule and civilized. While the negative descriptions of Achamers of the Mughal literature can be debated and refuted, one thing that clearly set apart the Achamers from their neighbors is the figure of the swargadeo, who brought together various communities into a body politic. In the Mughal literature it is almost certain that "the Achamers" refers to the group living in the domain of the swargadeo. Nearly four hundred years later, it is not possible to ascertain if the local people ever referred to themselves as Achamers. The Mughal description of the people of Assam is telling, but it is definitely not a unique description of the people of Acham.

When the British entered Assam in 1792, according to colonial records they confronted "a country entirely unexplored by Europeans . . . a kingdom of great extent surrounded on all sides by natives with whose very names [the British] have been hitherto entirely unacquainted."[25] The initial penetration into the unexplored frontier tracts brought the British face-to-face with a diversity of communities. So amazed were they by the landscape and the variety of people there that early colonial reporters found it extremely difficult to classify them. In mapping the territory, only a small portion was considered "inhabited land"; the rest was deemed "uninhabited jungles," "unexplored hilly country," "uninhabited tracts," and "the most impassable in the world" (Burrard 1914, 4). The representations of the people matched such attitudes toward the place: colonial administrators shamelessly admitted that "there is no doubt a feeling that Assam [is] more or less a land of rakshas [demons], hobgoblins and various terrors."[26]

From 1820 to 1870, a vast number of photographs of the people of Assam were produced in their "natural settings"—surrounded by forests, hills, and animals—to provide concrete evidence that they were indeed subhuman.[27] The colonial photographers' perceptions of the people coincided with and strengthened the deeply held beliefs of the administrators. For the initial period (1820s and 1830s) there are no visual images of Assamese, although there are a variety of images of "tribal" groups. Among the labels and descriptions are "Dooaneeah," "a mixed race,"; "Muttuck," "hill tribe"; "Naga," "marauding hill tribe"; "Kookie," "robber tribe"; "Singpho," "warlike frontier tribe"; "Jaiantia and Kachari," "freebooters and plunderers"; "Mishimi," "lazy and barbaric hill tribe"; "Abor," "uncouth-mannered hill tribe"; "Simong," "hostile tribe"; "Miri," "dirty and exceedingly poor tribe"; and "Aka," "dirty tribe."[28] Although classified under several different categories such as "animist," "Hindus," and "unknown," there is not a single instance in which the British photographers acknowledge the tribes and communities as respectable people. Rather, they are represented in various colonial publications and journals as an undesirable mix of dubious, deceptive, and unpleasant subjects.

Over time, however, the colonial administration realized that different kinds of subjects had to be demarcated to run an administration. The "tribal" communities living in the hills, they found, were not easy to

"The Assamese." (Courtesy of the British Library)

subdue. Indeed, the colonial government decided it was judicious and cost effective to leave these people to manage their autonomous administrative units while protecting the frontier of British India (Elwin 1969). The tribal areas were demarcated by the "inner line," and direct colonial administration was established in the "outer line" area. Several legislative acts accompanied these demarcations; and by enacting categories such as Excluded Areas, Partially Excluded Areas, and Tracts, the interaction between hills and plains was restricted and then finally stopped. This allowed the British administration to take direct control of the valley areas or "plains" territory. Assam Valley was thus immediately transformed into a revenue-generating province, and the subject community was demarcated as a plains people, or a group of taxable, revenue-paying peasants. They were called "Assamese." There are few documents and even fewer visual materials on the Assamese in the colonial archives. Moreover, in the three extant pictures in the India Office Library in London, the Assamese are represented as a poor agricultural community, but there are no descriptions accompanying the photographs. Ahom is totally absent in these records and pictures.

Over time, as colonial rule expanded and new areas and people were brought under the provincial administration of Assam, in several quarters questions were raised if the label Assam and Assamese needed to be changed to suit the different local names of the people. Strong reservations were expressed about changing the name, however, with the most vehement criticism from the tea industry that was well established in Assam.[29] The government accepted that "the important commercial interests represented by the tea industry would complain if the name of Assam, now so widely known in the markets of the world as the chief source of Indian teas, were to disappear from the list of the Indian provinces."[30] That colonial economic interests won the day was hardly unexpected: colonial interest in Assam definitely did not center on its people; but rather on exploration, dominance, and exploitation. The term "Assamese"—created, established, and widely circulated in colonial publications and administrative circles—produced a community on paper; but the people who were called Assamese could not come to terms with the colonial representation of them as a single subject community.

Alongside the British codification of Assamese, internal formulations were also under construction, but local representations were remarkably different from the colonial versions. In 1836 a petition by Moniram Dewan, the appointed agent of the rulers of Assam to the colonial administration in Calcutta, outlined a definition of the Assamese. Moniram Dewan defined the Assamese "jati" as comprising various peoples: Brahmans, Khetree, Bor Koleeta, Soroo Koleeta, Keot, Koch, Koomar Koleeta, Matee Koleeta, Hindu Chutia, Ahom, Boorook, Kacharee, Moran, Chandal, Toorok, Gorea, Dom, Hari, and Maria.[31] As is evident from this statement, Moniram tried to represent the Assamese as a composite, multiplex, fluid society that included the ruling class of Ahom, as well as Brahmanic Hindus, various groups of "untouchables," and Muslims (Gorea), to name a few. Although there is some controversy about Moniram's intentions for consciously generating an Assamese identity, his initial definition of the Assamese, which is not different from the composite society created by the swargadeos and described in the buranjis, became a rallying point.[32] The blending of the various people into the Assamese produced a term with no clearly defined community or history. The local people who were included within this "us" of Assamese society did not find the construction confusing because historically they had learned to live within a "blended" community of sorts. As such, the term gained immediate currency, and a population called Assamese in the northeast frontier slowly emerged as different from the people living in the hills.

Until 1967, the multiplicity of Assamese constituents survived. But, an Assamese identity was generated and upheld at the cost of many other local identities—identities that demanded recognition. The Nehruvian attempt to recognize the uniqueness of various tribes and communities led to a remapping of the region, and in 1967 new names for ethnic and tribal groups entered the vocabulary of postcolonial India. At the end of the reorganization a community called the Assamese was isolated from other groups in the northeast. The Brahmaputra Valley was christened Assam proper and deemed to be an Assamese space. The mentality of the postcolonial government toward Assam did not change, however, but continued to marginalize both the people and the region. In time, this led to a new and metamorphosed struggle among the Assamese to define themselves. Today, when people refer to themselves as Assamese, they articulate a historical position and a cultural and political sentiment that is underscored by a feeling articulated as "we are different from Indians." Although it is not quite clear what counts as Assamese even today, it is worth investigating the story of how Assamese identity has come to be defined in terms of its difference from Indian identity. Through what strategies and channels of articulation has this sense of difference emerged?

Assamese history is complex because although it belongs to everyone who lives in Assam, it is not the story of a specific community in the general terms of "ethnic" and "religious" communities. Many kinds of people make up the Assamese today. As I explain in the introduction, the Assamese language provides some sort of definition for identity construction for those within Assam. But with the expansion of colonialism and the emergence of new communities of non-Assamese speakers within Assam, complications of who is Assamese also surfaced. Language has been at the crux of the issue: the shared Assamese language became the key signifier of those who are "Assamese" and, as a result, those speaking other languages became recognized as "others." Bengali speakers in particular were seen as a threat to the preservation of Assamese identity.

The struggle to establish Assamese as the principal language of Assam has a long history. The language problem emerged as soon as the British established their rule. The Bengali clerks who were the backbone of the colonial administration in Assam deemed the Assamese language to be a corruption of Bengali. Influenced by this view, in 1836 the colonial government dropped Assamese from public documents, education, and administrative and judicial use.[33] The Assamese people widely denounced the arrogance of this act, and in 1838 Ananda Ram Dhekial Phukan, author of the first Assamese grammar book, petitioned the British government to reintroduce the vernacular language rather than to continue to impose Bengali, which he argued "is a foreign language . . . which is but imperfectly understood by the teachers themselves, not to speak of the pupils."[34] The American Baptist Mission played a crucial role in supporting the Assamese language movement. With their help, Phukan started a literary publication called *Orunodoi* (The new dawn, 1846–1883), which became the mouthpiece of Assamese nationalism. Language politics became the channel for new demands: even after Assamese was reintroduced in the schools in 1873, agitation for Assamese identity recognition continued. The grievances were mostly economic, and language became the tool to articulate the emotion and experiences of marginality and peripheralization. The ideology of Swadhin Asom brought together different groups.

Like most nationalist movements, the project of making an Assamese identity was an urban intellectual phenomenon. The intellectuals of Assam who were centered in Calcutta played the most important role. This period of activism paralleled some important changes in India, such as the partition of Bengal (1905–1911), that directly affected Assam. The Assamese resented being lumped with East Bengal, and they were much relieved when the partition was revoked in 1912 and Assam was once again made into a chief commissioner's province. The politicization of the masses during the partition agitation was a resource to harness, and a variety of social-political organizations emerged as a consequence. Their concerns remained economic, and the revitalized Assamese language served as a tool to articulate their grievances and invoke memories of the glorious past of the swargadeos' rule. Jnananath Bora's writings provide an entry point into the mind-set of Assamese intellectuals and the course of the Swadhin Asom of the period. In one of his articles called "Asom Desh Bharatbarkhar Bhitarat Thakibo Kiya?" (Why should Assam stay within India?), he argues that the regeneration of Assam is possible only if it is separated from the rest of India. He claims that "the Assamese have always lived in a distinct country with its own distinctive administration . . . The course of our history is totally different from that of India's. India's history is not our history. . . . Like Burma, Afghanistan, or Thailand, Assam has always been a neighboring country of India" (1938, 264). The agitational mode expressed in the writings and speeches of men like Bora continued throughout the period of the anticolonial struggle and afterward. In fact, the ideology of separation—cultural, political, and social—that was articulated in this period resurfaced many times in post-colonial Assam alongside the definite and concerted effort of the national state to claim Assam as a Hindu majority state. Vigorous memories of the separation of Assam from the rest of India made a comeback in the 1960s Assamese language movement; in the agitation for Assamese identity led to the AASU in the late 1970s and early 1980s; and again in the discourse of the ULFA that survives even today. The later movements were able to gather strength when the rural masses joined in the hope of achieving an equitable redistribution of the state's resources.[35]

In the postcolonial era, the Assamese identity movement became a multiclass ethnic struggle. It started as a cultural movement: in addition to the Assamese language, cultural artifacts became tools for negotiating identity in the public sphere. Dress played an important role. Assamese women abandoned the sari and donned the locally woven *mekhala sador*. Many men, although they continued to wear Western attire, also wore a *gamusa*, an Assamese scarf, to establish their newly found sense of themselves as Assamese. The gamusa symbolically became the *koboj kapur*, the cloth that soldiers of the Ahom kingdom wore when they fought the enemy. New stress was placed on the Assamese language, and several schools were established proclaiming an Assamese medium of education as opposed to the English medium instruction of the missionary-run schools. Even the urban elite took pride in sending their children to Assamese medium schools. Assamese songs, which were always quite popular, now became vehicles of political as well as emotional expression. The songs of Bhupen Hazarika in particular impassioned the people to reclaim "golden Assam" from foreign hands.[36] The celebration of Rongali Bihu (Assamese New Year) became a public affair. Huge celebrations were organized for public consumption, and food became a celebratory aspect of being Assamese. *Kharodi* (mustard paste) instead of north Indian pickle, *pitha* (steamed rice cakes) instead of roti, *tenga* (sour soup) instead of curry, *akhoy* (puffed rice) instead of bread, and a host of other common local foods were popularized. But the movement was not simply confined to articulating and promoting self-awareness among the Assamese. The Assamese also became belligerent toward the Bengalis, both Hindus and Muslims, who were settled in Assam. Hence, alongside the development and engineering of cultural identity, social discriminations against groups of "outsiders" became rampant. Although no precise definition of "Assamese" was determined by the mass uprising, it became clear to people that being Assamese was a shared, intimate, personal "thing" that belonged to the people of Assam and differentiated them from their neighbors, the Bengalis, and by extension from Indians. Being Assamese remained a question and a quest for everyone in 1970s Assam.

Research into the economic condition of Assam proved crucial in this phase. It soon became evident that the main problems were the growing poverty of the state and the local people and the influx of foreigners who were putting pressure on the land. The literature that was generated during this period is immense, and it is not possible to address all of it in detail. However, a rough guide to the rhetoric and issues offers a general outline of the direction that Assamese politics took in the 1970s and early 1980s. The capital growth of Assam in the 1970–1980 decade was very limited, 0.4 percent compared to 1.4 percent for the rest of India. In the same period, the rate of unemployment among educated youth was 43 percent. The growth of jobs in the public sector was, in turn, stagnant. Of the 4,500 people employed in the northeast railway office in Guwahati (one of the main establishments for employment in the city) over 59 percent were non-Assamese. In the industrial sector similar discrepancies are evident. While Assam produced the largest amount of tea for India (55 percent), its share from sales tax was merely $22 million, half of what West Bengal received ($42 million) for auctioning Assam's tea. According to calculations of market price and profit estimates on the tea trade, India received $5,250 million for the period of 1962 to 1976 (Misra 2000, 123–25). The balance of trade has never favored Assam, as is evident in all other industrial sectors, such as plywood, coal, natural gas, and petroleum. Indeed, the situation is almost unbelievable in the case of the returns for oil and gas. On the eve of the AASU movement (1979), Assam received for its crude oil less than $2 (Rs. 42 based on the rate of exchange in the 1970s) for every ton (production was about 3.5 million tons annually). The royalty rate was revised somewhat in the early 1980s, and Assam received initially $10 (Rs. 325) and later $17 (Rs. 578) per ton. In the matter of sales tax on crude, Assam received a little over $2 (Rs. 54) per ton, while Delhi received $24 (Rs. 991) per ton. Similar statistics can be quoted for all other profitable raw materials and commercial production in Assam, clearly illustrating that private business in Assam was the monopoly of "foreign" or non-Assamese merchants and traders.

The combination of economic marginalization and lack of representation for bargaining with the state was aggravated by the influx of immigrants, both Indian and Bangladeshi, into Assam. There is a great deal of debate on the impact and changes in culture and economy effected by the settlement of "outsiders" (Guha 1977; Hussain 1993; Weiner 1988). The AASU student leaders in the early 1980s on the one hand used the sentiment of economic marginalization to rouse the masses to struggle against India, and on the other created awareness of the problem of unrestricted immigration of Bangladeshis that pitted Assamese against Bengalis. Needless to say, the cleavages deepened between Assam and India and the Assamese and the non-Assamese.

Initially, the multiclass alliance of Assamese led by the AASU seemed somewhat successful. By emphasizing economic discrimination and cultural marginalization, the AASU leaders were able to shift focus from differences between the groups of Assamese—Hindus and Muslims; Upper (eastern) and Lower (western) Assam—to give their struggle some unity. The AASU-led movement also created outlets for the public display of identity that became political tools. The catch phrase of the AASU leaders was "Come, come. Come out and be Assamese! Drive out the foreigners from your midst." The emphasis was to publicly declare a single, monolithic identity. Added to this sentiment of a single undivided community of Assamese was the handy tool of the economic deprivation of the populace. Slogans like "We will give blood, but not our oil" and "Save Assam today, to save India tomorrow" became fuel for the fire of Assamese nationalism and spread the movement to the distant corners of the northeast. The Nagas and other tribal organizations showed solidarity and publicly participated in the agitational programs organized by the student leaders of the AASU. For a brief moment in the early 1980s the Assam movement became the symbolic struggle of the northeast—for "plains" and "tribal' people too. Poets and activists together cried out, "Victory, mother Assam." Some of the most angry outpourings were directed against the Indian army, one of which admonished the army in these words: "Indian army, we donated blood, knitted woolen garments for you in 1962, 1965, 1971. In return you have rewarded us with raping our mothers, sisters in 1980, Shame! Shame!" Indeed, the Assamese became a violent, angry community. Curiously, the anger was formulated against the Indian state but the violence was directed against another enemy—the so-called Bangladeshi immigrants in Assam.

How was the Bengali created as the "other" in Assam? To answer this question we have to return to colonial politics. Colonial exploration into Assam had established several profitable business and industrial establishments for which labor was imported from outside, mainly from Bengal and Bihar. The colonial authorities also encouraged the settlement of people from East Bengal throughout the late nineteenth century. Particularly after the partition of Bengal (1905), Assam was linked with East Bengal and migration was officially endorsed. That colonial authorities officially encouraged the migration of East Bengalis into Assam was made clear by Governor Reid in his confidential reports. He writes: "In recent years, however, i.e., since the year 1905 or thereabouts, Muslim immigrants, mainly from the Bengal district of Mymensingh, have tended to flock to this valley in ever increasing numbers. Mr. Mullan in his Census Report of 1931 describes the invasion as the most important event in the last twenty-five years . . . [an invasion] destined to destroy more surely than did the Burmese invaders of 1820 the whole structure of Assamese culture and civilization, [one which] foretells that in another thirty years Sibsagar district will be the only part of Assam in which an Assamese will find himself at home."[37]

What is interesting about Reid's comment is that it shifted blame away from the colonial administration and its policies (which were designed to make serious demographic changes in Assam) to a group identified as Muslims. These Muslims were then blamed for the problems between the local and the newly settled communities. In these and other colonial documents, the term Bengali was replaced by the term Muslim, and Muslims and the Assamese were pitted against each other. Clearly, the divide and rule policy of the British found a home base in Assam, as it had already done elsewhere in India. The rhetoric of a threatening Muslim/Bengali community that was likely to become a majority group in Assam whipped up sentiment and directed political action throughout the 1950s and 1960s. In the 1970s and early 1980s, the problem of Bengali Muslim settlement in Assam became crucial to the Assamese identity movement. The AASU leaders hoped that by identifying the "foreigners/Bangladeshis" they would be able to formulate an Assamese identity. But much before any constitutional process could be outlined for shaping AASU rhetoric, violence against so-called Bangladeshi Muslims became rampant. The spark of anti-Bangladeshi violence was lit in a small village called Nellie, not far from Nowgong, in 1983.

Nellie became testimony that the student-led movement had lost its nonviolent, economic moorings and had become influenced by the religious politics that were driving a wedge into the Assamese community. Muslims of Assam became frightened that the Assamese identity movement was veering into a religious communal struggle. To placate Assamese sentiments, the student leaders of the AASU denied their hand in the massacre. To prove it they made sure that organized terror against one village or community was not repeated after the Nellie incident, and no villages in Upper Assam have been exposed to communal violence since that time.

The Assamese identity movement took many different forms after the Nellie incident, and increasingly it became more convoluted. The AASU was one group of leaders, but they did not control the political development in Upper Assam. A new group called Juva Chatra Parishad emerged in Upper Assam and, over time, the more radical group ULFA took over the leadership. Curiously, after 1983 and the forced elections conducted by Delhi in Assam, the enemies of the Assamese also multiplied. The ULFA and their supporters in Upper Assam declared that the main enemy was the Indian state, while the AASU leaders continued to harp on the rampant settlements of the Bangladeshis in Assam and demanded their deportation. Besides dealing with the Bangladeshi question, the AASU leaders had to deal with many new groups demanding recognition of their separate identities within Assam. The Bodos, in particular, became the most vocal anti-Assamese group in this period.

The anti-Bangladeshi rhetoric in Assam has limped along, but now its focus has shifted from Assam because the BJP has transformed the concern into an all-India issue. Recently, Deputy Prime Minister L. K. Advani made public statements that twenty million Bangladeshis are living in India, many of them in the northeast, and that they should be expelled. There is no evidence that such huge numbers of Bangladeshis are living in Assam, but rhetoric can easily create reality in India. Does this mean that the Assamese and BJP agendas have become one and the same? Is the Bangladeshi/Muslim their common enemy? The Assamese, as far I know, would be devastated if the Assamese identity struggle and the BJP's Hindutva enterprise were to be assessed as similar and directed against a common enemy. As Parag Das, a prominent Assamese public intellectual once told me, "The majority in Assam may be Hindu, but we are not Hindus like the Indians. Our struggles can never be the same."[38] This is not the view of intellectuals alone. The imagined panoramic view of a future single Assamese-Indian identity does not address the variety of identities that local people in Assam are attached to. As such, the BJP agenda has not succeeded in Assam despite their active political work in the region for over a decade. For the time being, however, the anti-Bangladeshi rhetoric is allowing some groups in Assam to devise grand theories of encroachment of land and resources, population pressure, and possible Muslimization of Assam, and so on. Grand theories may create an awareness of important issues, but they do not provide answers. In the years since Nellie the so-called Bangladeshis continue to be part and parcel of Assam and her problems.

Before we continue the story of the Assamese identity movement, a short note on the impact of Nellie on the Assamese-Muslim psyche is necessary. It appears that the massacre at Nellie outraged the minorities. Many responses emerged from within the Assamese-Muslim communities. Since then many Muslims became active in the AASU movement to establish their Assamese loyalties; others became active in the All Assam Muslim Student Union and religious-based political parties, particularly in the Barak Valley and in Dhubri, Barpeta, and Rangiya in Lower Assam, and demanded explanation of minority rights. In Upper Assam, it appears that many Muslim communities withdrew from the public sphere, while others tried to reassert their loyalty to the national Congress party and hoped for a political solution for Muslims in the formation of a new Congress ministry. My own family's reaction to Nellie and what followed thereafter is mixed. My father tried to make sense of the massacre by blaming "outsiders." As an academic and a supporter of regional identity he could not accept that (Assamese) students committed the violence at Nellie. Perhaps he was right because as long as AASU and then ULFA have held sway Nellie's communal/religious violence has not been repeated in villages in Upper and Lower Assam. But other forms of ethnic violence have become more common since then. In Western Assam, particularly in

Kokrajhar, Bongaigaon, Rangiya, and Barpeta, clashes between settler communities and Bodos are often reported.

My mother responded to the Nellie incident differently from my father. She was less concerned with questions of origin and motivation and more concerned about the effects of the violence on everyday people. She was among the first few to organize relief work for displaced and destitute women and children. Because at the time I was not in Assam but away in college, the Nellie incident did not raise questions for me about my Assamese identity. I think many Assamese-Muslim families, like mine, reacted variously to the Nellie incident. Clearly, the incident did not create a consensus but rather generated a debate concerning the place of Muslims in Assam. Twenty years later the spirit of the debate is less prominent, and Assamese-Muslims have settled back to their "Assamese lives." The memory of Nellie lingers but does not draw new images of fear and anxiety among Muslims and thus does not translate into a concerted political movement. Nonetheless, Assamese-Muslims, like Muslims all over India, are now more aware that the BJP supporters are ready to call them "outsiders" and that they could be potentially vulnerable to violence directed against them. Muslims in Assam are far more fearful today than they were during the Assamese identity movement led by the AASU.

After Nellie, the code of Assamese changed somewhat. To give coherence to the agenda of Assamese, some of the AASU leaders formed themselves into a political party called the Assam Gana Parishad (Assam People's Association) or AGP. This group has benefited the most from the Assamese movement. They capitalized on the prevailing situation of Assamese sentimentality and politicization and floated themselves as a political party in the 1985 elections. They made the subject of being "Assamese" their central discourse and then told people how to behave, look, and speak, in order to claim an "Assamese" identity. The local media, the television channels, and the movies made by the supporters of AGP became tools for the propaganda that was used to make "good" Assamese. However, voices of opposition grew, and increasingly many began to complain that the AGP government-sponsored image of the Assamese was not very different from the Indian national propaganda of a composite Indian identity.

Many believed that the concept of Assamese was suppressing other forms of local identities, particularly those of people who were not within the orbit of the Guwahati-led Assamese AGP party. In retaliation against the Assamese identity movement, resistance movements under different banners emerged, such as Bodo, Tai-Ahom, Dimasa, and Karbi. All of these movements worked on the margins of the Assamese Hindu community and its politics. What these new labels signified was difficult to understand immediately, and there may be many different explanations for the variety. The boundaries of self and other within these groups shifted with such ease and frequency in this period that it was hard to keep pace with them.[39] The Bodoland movement within Assam has been most effective. They have successfully claimed they are not Assamese and have created an autonomous Bodoland with the help of Delhi (Baruah 1999). Alongside the Bodoland movement another "ethnic" movement emerged in Upper Assam: the Tai-Ahom movement.

The Tai-Ahom movement is both a sociocultural and religious-political movement that claims the difference of the Tai-Ahom from the Assamese. The movement views the Assamese as a religious group, as representatives of the majority Hindu community, and as a territorially bounded society that represents the people and issues of Lower, not Upper, Assam. Moreover, the Tai-Ahom leaders deem the AGP government and their AASU supporters as appendages of the Indian state. On the other hand, Tai-Ahoms see themselves as the primary community that represents the heartland of Upper Assam, the districts of Sibsagar and their surrounding areas, where the authentic Assamese self prevails. Additionally, as the progeny of the swargadeos, they believe Ahoms uphold the autonomous history of Assam before its occupation by the British and then the Indians. Ethnically, they claim they are Tai, which situates them as Buddhist and not Hindu. The suffix Tai invokes for Ahoms a mythic connection with Southeast Asia. Another area of cleavage between Assamese and Tai-Ahom is class. The people who identify as Assamese are mostly from middle- and upper-income groups—professionals, bureaucrats, and business people. Conversely, the majority of people who claim Tai-Ahom identity are lower-income peasants and working-class people. Ahom propagandists believe that if the power of the middle-class Assamese is reduced within Assam, it will solve the problems of the marginalized and disempowered groups. They think it is the Assamese community, created by the AASU and AGP stalwarts, that has refused to sever their cultural and political linkages with India despite their rhetoric of Swadhin Asom, and that this issue has been the greatest bane to the local people and culture of Ujani Aham.

What is Ahom? How did the term Ahom gain currency in the narrative of postcolonial Assam? While the attempt today is to present Ahom as a single ethnic community, the history of its construction is far more complex because it has involved multiple agents and different representations. An investigation into the question of Ahom requires a stage-by-stage approach. Ahom politics became prominent in the early twentieth century through social engineering and discourses between power groups in Assam. The modern historical itinerary of Ahom is intimately connected to the political history of language groups and the sentimentality of difference between Upper and Lower Assam, as well as the caste and religious differences, discussed above, that have constructed the Assamese. In the climate of burgeoning identities in the twentieth century, Ahom leaders generated a reading of Assam's past that enabled the construction of a new label and politics of Ahom. But it is very important to remember that the twentieth-century politics that have constructed both the Assamese and the Ahom have their legacies in the colonial period. These, in turn, borrowed from previous narratives of community in Assam.

Toward the end of the nineteenth century several organizations were formed to voice the sentiments of the Assamese people. One such organization was the Asamiya Bhasa Unnati-Sadhani Sabha (Assamese Language Improvement Society—ABUSS / ALIS) formed in 1889. Constituted in Calcutta by Lakhinath Bezbaruah and Chandrakumar Agarwala (a Rajasthani who settled in Assam), the aim of the organization was, in the words of Moheshwar Neog, "to bring together all the literature available in the Assamese language; . . . to render into Assamese . . . important works in Sanskrit and other languages; . . . to increase [the] interest of the people in reading newspapers; and to establish one literary language for the whole of Assam" (1979, 3). This was an initial attempt to make one single community of Assamese-speaking people in Assam, a group that could learn to represent themselves through their language and to demand for themselves certain political and social rights in keeping with the spirit of the anticolonial struggle led by the INC. Within Assam, around the same time, Gangagovinda Phukan established the Assam Desh-Itihasi Sabha (Assam Historical Society). The rise of Assamese associations were seen in some quarters as a move of upper-caste Hindus to join the Assamese struggle with the INC, and in reaction an Ahom sentiment developed. One of the first instances of this development was in the site of British colonial documents. Henry Hopkinson, the colonial representative in Assam to the governor of Calcutta, writing in 1873, asserted the need to recognize Ahom as the pristine name and identity of the people of Assam. Hopkinson writes: "It would be better to substitute Ahom, Ahomeea or Ahomese as the name of the language to be used in Judicial and Revenue Proceedings in the valley districts of Assam instead of Assamese, for Ahom is the vernacular word, and Assamese borrowed from the Bengali for Ahom. So that in employing the word Assamese we are discrediting and contradicting ourselves at the outset, by using a Bengali word to explain we will not use Bengali (in Assam)."[40]

Internally, too, this was an important moment for constructing Ahom. In 1893, a group in Upper Assam formed the Ahom Sabha (AS). The AS started its career under the leadership of a local historian and politician named Pandmanath Gohain Borooah. In 1910, the AS changed its name to Ahom Association (AA), and in 1915 all local units were amalgamated under the banner of the All Assam Ahom Association (AAAA). The AAAA appealed to the people of Upper Assam not to give into Congress politics in the region, but instead to work for the "improvement of the lot of their Ahom people by working with the British." It further emphasized the "separate and communal identity" of the Upper Assam people, apart from the other peoples of India. As a mark of this separateness, the AAAA asked them "to shed their incredible attachment to Hinduism."[41] By using the rhetoric of something called the "Ahom people," the leaders appealed to people to invoke a historical memory of difference, rather than to concede to the political rhetoric of the INC, which was seeking to make Assam part and parcel of India. But it was not easy to make people suddenly think of themselves as Ahom, because they did not know what Ahom meant. Indeed, many of them later stated that they had never before seen an Ahom.[42] For most of them Ahom meant a royal person. Neither their fathers nor their grandfathers had ever interacted with royalty or the kind of royalty that the politicians were claiming to be "Ahom."

"Ahom" entered the domain of political history in twentieth-century Assam as an unknown and undefinable term. In the official publications of the time, the Ahom were not represented as a community separate from the larger group of Assamese. Even AAAA leader Padmanath Gohain Borooah, in *Assamar Buranji; or The History of Assam* (1906) and *Buranjibodh; or Lessons on the History of Assam* (1922), presented the Ahom as the principal group in Assam, but he did not define the Ahom or explain the difference between them and other Assamese groups. But from these words a crucial symbol of Ahom identity was developed and given form in the figure of the swargadeo. Swargadeos were represented as the founders of Ahom, beginning with the messianic hero called Sukapha. The aim of this kind of history was first to create a narrative to enable children to remember "salient names and dates . . . [and] map Assam in the context of the heroes" (Borooah 1906, 1–3).

To formulate a central narrative, a variety of stories, myths, and legends of kings and dynasties of Assam (some real and some unreal) were made up. Borooah developed a historical narrative in which one dynasty followed another in easy succession without break or disruption. This trend of history writing was not unique to Assam but was copied from the colonial model that had already narrativized a linear story for India in the early nineteenth century. The assumption that Assam was one unified space, culture, and society allowed for the interchangeable use of terms such as Pragjyotishpur, Kamarupa, Kamata, and Assam to refer to a single kingdom, a kingdom that was prominent under these various names at different periods of time. What is curious about this narrative is that the *danavas* and *asuras* (demons and monsters), who were treated as "rejects" in the narratives of Brahmanic Hinduism, found a place of pride and were honored alongside Krishna, an important deity of Hinduism, as the founders of the polity of Assam. What was the reason for doing so? Was it a deliberate attempt to mark a separation from the Aryan cultures and people? An investigation of the preface of Borooah's *Buranjibodh* will help us to understand this question.

> From Sadiya to the river Karatoya it is claimed to be Assam division . . . This whole region in ancient times was known as Kamarupa . . . The Hindu and Buddhist peoples lived here. The Muslims and Christians came later. There were many tribal peoples . . . In ancient times this land was ruled by danavas and asuras. Mahiranga Danab was probably the original king here. Among his successors, Narakasur [also a demon] became a very powerful king. He was a Janak king, and came to Assam from Bihar. In his time, this land became Pragjyotishpura. Krishna attacked and fought against Narakasur and made his son Bhaggadatta the new ruler. Sadiya was ruled by Vidharbha raja, whose daughter Rukmini was wedded to Krishna. The Baan king of Swarnapith [whose subjects were monkeys] married his daughter to Anirudha, Krishna's grandson. . . . The Tai people came from Burma. . . . They were

Buddhist people. . . . But to conquer land they moved south-west, intermixed with the hill tribes, and adopted their religion . . . Sukapha, a prince of Mungrimungram, the original kingdom of the Tai people, came to Saumar [Assam] in 1229. . . . The Ahom kings ruled for six hundred years. (1992, 1–13)

The swargadeos of Ahom were particularly valorized for mitigating all the differences among the various groups in Assam to facilitate the creation of a unified Assamese jati. In Borooah's words, "In combination (with all the people, the swargadeos) formed a new and separate jati . . . known as Asam. From the word Asam, the word Aham, and again from Aham, the word Assam originated" (1906, 46).

In this and other narrative constructions Borooah singlehandedly created a metanarrative of Assam. The origins story was made believable by rendering the Ahom, a group of settlers, a very special place as royal heroes who transformed into community architects and sought and achieved unity among the various groups. Also, by starting the narrative of the community outside Assam, in a mythical land called Mungrimungram (vaguely identified as somewhere in Burma), Borooah created a connection with regions outside of India, and thus shifted the core of Assam's political identity beyond the reach of Aryan cultures and communities. This shift was crucial for rejecting the politics of the INC, which was seen to represent the upper-caste Hindus of India. This narrative should have been very appealing to the Swadhim Asom movement promoted by the Assamese intelligentsia. But it was not to be.

The differences between the two, the Assamese and the Ahom, were noticeably generated from within Assamese society. The upper-caste Hindu Assamese had long desired and worked hard to be included among the Aryan communities of north India. To accept the narrative of the Ahoms would mean sharing a past with people who were considered outside the fold of Brahmanic Hinduism—people without jati and purity. Hence, to assert the difference, in 1915 Tirtha Nath Goswami, a priest of the neo-Vaishnavite sect in Assam, published a book titled *Mular Pora Haral Bhongoni Ripunjay Smriti Ba Prayachitta Bebhasthabidhan* in which he claimed that the Ahoms, like many other peoples of Assam, were *antarjya* or outcaste groups, and thus depraved, lowly, unredeemable, and polluted people. They, the upper-caste Hindus of Assam, according to this version, were not part of such a community but were related to other groups of Hindu Indians. The AAAA leaders reacted by demanding that the book should be recalled. Failing to achieve their purpose, they declared that the book was a reminder of the "ungratefulness of the Hindus and Brahmins who took numerous benefits from the Ahom kings, but never appreciated it."[43] Needless to say, the relationship between the so-called Ahoms and the Assamese Hindus worsened.

In 1917 the Assam Sahitya Sabha (ASS), a literary body convened as the successor of the ABUSS, subverted the AAAA meetings by assembling in the same venue in Sibsagar. The ASS was dominated by neo-Vaishnavite Hindu priests (*gossains, satradhikars*)[44] who refused to allow members of the AAAA to meet along with them because they were considered members of polluted castes. (It was not until 1974 that the ASS opened its doors to the various "tribal," non-Vaishnavite peoples of Assam.) In 1927, another association, the Assam Sanrakhyan Sabha (Assam Protection Society, or APS) was "constituted for safeguarding the essence of Asamiya culture."[45] The various Assamese associations, dominated by caste Hindu office bearers and members and using the rhetoric of safeguarding the "Assamese language," tried to erase the languages and cultures of tribal and outcaste Hindu groups. Not surprisingly, the relationship between the Hindus and others broke down, which forced the APS, in a meeting on May 23, 1926, to proclaim, "We are not Hindus, Muslims, Dafla, Miri . . . ; we are Assamese."[46]

Constructions of the Assamese as a composite society were formulated to arrest the breakup of the groups. But, the narratives continued to privilege the caste Hindu community within it. A common Hindu religion, Hindu myths and stories, and the dominance of Aryan culture persisted even in this new twentieth-century narrative, although the discourse shifted a little. In one account, titled *Asamar Athutajatir Uttpattir Bibaran* (The origin of the eight clans of the Assamese), the Ahoms were "discovered" to be the mukh jati (principle community) (Barua 1923, 61–72). Assumptions were validated by quoting from obscure Sanskrit materials written in Assamese that helped to imagine the Ahoms as an Indic (Aryan) people (Barua 1923, 61–72). The story reported that a group, originally comprising the army of Lord Krishna, migrated from Assam to Burma, where they were called "Shans," a name derived from Syam, another name for Krishna. In the course of time, some Shans returned to Assam and founded the Assam kingdom. The Shan/Syam, according to this version, is the original name of the Ahoms.[47]

The move to make Ahom part of Assamese Hindu society did not, however, convince the Ahom leaders. Even as late as 1928, the ASS made no attempt to recall the much-hated book *Ripunjay Smriti*. This led to massive agitation among the so-called Ahom supporters in Upper Assam. The next session of the AAAA, held in 1935, attracted a huge crowd, including women. It appeared that the division between the Assamese and the Ahom had become more than a political stance—it became an identitarian issue. Ahom leaders declared that the politics of the Ujani Aham were separate from the path followed by Congress supporters, and they demanded a distinct place for the Ahom within Assam, which they now called "Ahomstan." This demand was backed by many groups, including the Muslims of Upper Assam, who saw the Ahom movement as a formulation of a local politics. The Ahom then claimed Ujani Aham (rather than the colonial demarcated region of Upper Assam) as a foreground marker to conceive a people, history, and identity. The movement focused its concerns on the allegedly outside/external agents of Congress and their reshaping of the course of the Assam peoples and cultures. They chose to withstand this intrusion with select memories of the past, conveniently revitalized to contrast local and national developments. Hence, although the groups that came together to formulate the Ahom were multiple and had different resources and memories to construct their origin myths, they then were joined in a shared cause of common interests. The break between the Assamese and the Ahom was situated in this discourse. Those who claimed Assamese identity wanted to be part of India on their terms, while those who professed Ahom claimed Ahomstan in Ujani Aham as a separate entity from India. The tensions between these two memories and their differing associated political identities were elaborated in rituals, performances, and collective actions (which I will discuss in detail in chapter 4).

The notion that one must belong to the Ujani Aham and the Ahom in order to express one's identity was mobilized to direct political action throughout the 1930s and 1940s. The attachment to the label became so intense among certain groups that when a rumor had it that the term "Ahom" would be deleted from the forthcoming census report (1941), the Ahom movement leaders organized the "Mongolia" groups—the Kacharis, Muttocks, and Deuris—to devise a racial politics that claimed Ahom identity. They vehemently opposed the scheme of tabulating "Ahom" as "Hindu" and demanded a separate electoral constituency.[48] They failed to gain this, however, and thereafter submitted a memorandum to the British administration requesting that Ahoms should be made into a "racial minority community."[49] They also demanded that they should be demarcated as a scheduled tribe community. Although they were of the Assam Valley, Ahom leaders, by invoking a common agenda of racial politics, constructed themselves as leaders of a group who represented a specific unresolved problem in the northeast—that is, the relationship between the plain and hill peoples. Hence, they purposefully collected every fragment of evidence that could be used to disconnect themselves from the Assamese Hindus.

Following the "Quit India" movement (1942) and the success of the Congress in the Assam elections (1945), the AAAA impressed on the British government the need to include the Upper Assam districts in the proposed northeast frontier province. They hoped that the demarcation would entitle the people to certain privileges accorded to hill districts and make them separate from the caste Hindu Assamese. They proposed the creation of a new religion, called Nam Dharma, to counter the influence of orthodox Hinduism. The AAAA and Ahom Student Association of Jorhat continued to lead the political struggle. They recommended contacting the Shan states beyond the Patkai hills in Burma to connect Ahoms with groups outside the region. On August 15, 1947, when India became independent and Assam was constituted as one of the states of India, in utter frustration the AAAA boycotted the independence day celebration.[50]

Demarcating the state of Assam as the place for the Assamese did not solve the problem for Ahoms. They continued to hold on to a belief that they were a separate community from the Hindu Assamese. Ujani Aham, the original settlement of the Ahom swargadeos, was invoked and historicized as a place that had produced a distinct Ahom community. Political discontent over the mapping of this place within India was expressed in a discourse that claimed that the Ahom people had interacted with the land of Assam in a unique way that had produced an agrarian culture imported from Southeast Asia through their migration and settlement. To enumerate this connection between people and place and show its linkage with peoples and cultures outside India, in 1968 Padmeshwar Gogoi, a professor at Guwahati University and a self-proclaimed Ahom, wrote a book titled *The Tai and the Tai-Ahom Kingdom of the Brahmaputra Valley*. The book achieved two aims: it established the Ahom as a Tai community in the academic arena, and it presented the Ahoms as a distinct group that could subvert Assamese and Indian identities at the frontiers. Gogoi's position as a professor of history lent credence to the term Tai-Ahom and facilitated the circulation of Ahom history.

Since the 1960s, Ahom political identity construction has become highly malleable and exclusively instrumental in achieving specific outcomes to benefit particular groups of people as they locate themselves within a certain discourse, territory, and memory. Today the political makeup of Assam has become highly charged because it has been drawn into the workings of the nation-state's homogenizing discourse of Hindu nationhood (although as a lesser member). This discourse simply does not tolerate localized, fragmented, and subversive forms of being such as the Ahom, which claims transnational interests and a non-Indic past. Whether these tensions will fuel a creative process or mire the people of Assam in an endless battle (within as well as externally with Delhi) remains to be seen.

In sum, we have seen that the labels Assamese and Ahom emerged in conversation with and in resistance to the political activities and identities constructed by the INC during the anticolonial movement. In the early twentieth century, leaders and communities in Assam also tried to create principal and secondary communities and identities. The Aryan Hindu or "high" identity of the Assamese and the "low" Ahom identity of the outcastes mirrored one another and testified to the liminal understanding of self and other in Assam in the beginning of the twentieth century. Over time, as Assam became more drawn into the orbit of INC and caste Hindu politics, the Ahom identity became representative of a precolonial, prenational (Indian) past of Assam, a gateway to imagination, autonomy, and independence. While the meanings ascribed to being Assamese and Ahom are contestable and lacking "evidence," they rely on memories that were created for them. The collective codification of Ahom and Assamese was a British colonial enterprise embarked on for political and economic purposes. What they came to represent in the twentieth century is fuzzy and messy, but the process of the construction of both of the categories is known and can be documented. The next chapter addresses the colonial processes that constructed the Ahom and the Assamese concepts, processes that became the font for postcolonial politics.

**CHAPTER 2**

*Colonial Origins of Ahom*

A short distance from Sibsagar town is Garhgaon, the Ahom capital of yesteryear. In Garhgaon is the well-known edifice called Kareng-ghar, a multistoried masonry structure on a large acreage of land. It is a singular building—curious because it stands by itself without any other structure to accompany it. It is, moreover, of impressive proportions. Local histories and most people in Assam will tell you that the Kareng-ghar was the Ahom royal palace and was built by the swargadeos a long time ago.[1] To the Ahom people the specific history of the monument is not important; rather, its importance is in the assertion and belief that it was an expression of Ahom power and artistic style. It is easy to make this connection because there are no other buildings in Assam that compare to the Kareng-ghar. But, questions arise when considering the purpose and use of the building: Was it built as an ornamental rather than a utilitarian building?[2]

During my stay in Assam I visited the Kareng-ghar several times looking for insights into the Ahom dynasty. Could the building tell me something about the people who lived in it and used it? But the monument did not tell me a thing. It stood there mute, forlorn, and indifferent. A rusty signboard with its white paint peeling and the letters barely discernible described the structure as "Kareng-ghar: Ahom Royal Palace built by Swargadeo Rajeshwar Singha (1751–1769) of the Tai dynasty," adding that "the architect was Ghansyam, a Muslim from Bengal converted to Hinduism."[3] The signboard was put up by the Archeological Survey of India to protect the monument under the Ancient Monuments and Archeological Sites Act of 1958. However, after putting up the signboard, it appears, the government forgot all about the place. There was no other visible input by the government to maintain the premise. The large grassy acreage surrounding the building was overgrown. Cows and goats were grazing there, and village children ran around, playing hide and seek. Although few people seem to visit Kareng-ghar, once during a weekend visit I saw several Maruti cars parked outside the gates, and inside the compound under the spreading branches of the old trees a few families had spread out their picnic lunches and were enjoying an afternoon meal.

I was curious to know what brought them there. Kareng-ghar is too remote and also too publicized in tourist brochures. A visit there requires a trip to Garhgaon either by riding on an uncomfortable local bus or by driving there in an expensive private car (something few can afford). Once one is there Kareng-ghar is the only site to see. The nearest village is several miles away. Thus I approached the visitors with my question: What brings you to the Kareng-ghar? Without exception, they all said, "It is a good place for a day out with the family. Also, because it is part of our history." This was followed by a recitation of the other Ahom structures of Upper Assam that the swargadeos had built and that they insisted I must see. Some even offered to show me around the Kareng-ghar complex. Although there was not much to see because the engravings on the outer walls are in very poor condition, I was curious how my guides would read these depictions. Of what remains on one wall, one can make out the shape of a mounted warrior on horseback; on another wall elephants and deer are in a garden. Elsewhere, there is a boar and a bull engaged in a fight, a meditating ascetic, and several garden scenes depicting exotic flowers. My guides tried hard to offer some explanations of this medley of images by repeatedly reminding me that the Ahom swargadeos were great builders. But when I asked why they considered the Kareng-ghar an Ahom building, and why the engravings would be considered "Ahom," they could not provide an answer.

How did the Kareng-ghar develop the reputation of being an Ahom palace? Who were the first people who saw it, and what did they think of this building and the people who used it? The Mughal commander, Mir Jumla, was the first outsider who entered Garhgaon, which he even occupied for a few months in 1662 to 1663. Sahabuddin Talish records in detail the Mughal campaign to Assam in the *Fathiayah-i-Ibriyah*, but nowhere in the chronicle do we find mention of the Kareng-ghar. Obviously, the building that stands today and boasts to be an Ahom palace did not exist before the Mughal invasion. The Assamese buranjis state that after the Mughal invasion, Rudra Singha (1696–1716) employed several "Bengali" masons to construct brick buildings (Saikia 1997, 99–100). The Kareng-ghar was built by these masons who created a structure that reflected their architectural knowledge in both form and style. Robert Jenkins, the first British political agent of Upper Assam, affirms that masonry construction was introduced in Assam by Mughal artisans. In his journal on Assam, he states that "the royal buildings were made by Hindustani architects, for the hunts depicted on the walls . . . depict sawery camels, animals totally unknown to the Assamese and bullock cart carriages, which are also foreign to the province. The Palace of Garhgaon," he concludes, "is a Hindustani structure."[4] While local records and British colonial accounts agree that "outsiders" introduced masonry buildings to Assam and that the Kareng-ghar is a product of that interaction, colonial accounts tell us something new about the patrons of this and other buildings of Assam. They tell us that the buildings at Garhgaon were built by Ahom swargadeos. Jenkins writes: "A temple was . . . there, and the religious ceremonies performed are said to have been those of the ancient Ahom dynasty."[5] Who are the Ahom, and how did a story about this dynasty emerge in colonial literature?

In this chapter I will investigate the processes and representations of the Ahom in the British colonial accounts. I explore how memories and histories of the Ahom were constructed, invented, and presented in different colonial accounts; the official, academic, and popular narratives that, over time, local people used to construct their own set of memories of Ahom. I argue that the processes of construction and representation in the colonial period, beginning from the late eighteenth century until the end of colonial rule in 1947, reflected activities and ideas that were current in England. These processes spanned sociological, cultural, and economic issues. In the first phase of colonial construction, interests in antiquarian and civilizational issues that were fashionable in England dominated the study of tribes and groups in Assam. Orientalist assumptions led to finding a group of rulers who were called Ahoms. It appears that with the increase of knowledge of the "Assam frontier," which coincided with the intellectual drive in racial studies (following the development of the theory of social Darwinism), British colonials changed the story of Ahom to fit current racial terms. The colonials in the late nineteenth century literature designated the Ahoms as a race of people who migrated from Southeast Asia and were "Hinduized" though a process of settlement in the plains of Assam. Still, they were presented as "uncivilized" due to their practices of blood rituals. The backwardness and "barbarity" of the Ahom rulers justified the imperial ideology of conquest and the establishment of "good government" in Assam around the mid-nineteenth century.

Following the conquest the political economy of colonialism directed the annihilation of Ahom once it became evident that there were financial gains to be made by occupying the Assam frontier. As a consequence, the Ahoms were declared "dead" in the colonial records and a transformed community of Assamese subjects replaced the Ahoms. They were identified as the future tax-paying labor force for capitalist development in Assam. Thus an Assamese community was born in colonial economic ventures and revenue records. I would argue that the externally defined criterion of the "apathetic Assamese" and the development of capitalist agriculture in the nineteenth century resulted in a strange convolution of local history, denying people the right to claim a past and create belonging in a homeland. Assam Valley thus became a venue for colonial capital growth where old history was erased and new histories and communities were made up to serve colonial goals.

### INVENTING A PAST: INSERTING AHOM INTO
### COLLECTIVE MEMORY

In 1792, a contingent under Captain Welsh came to Assam in search of the *burkendazes* (mercenaries) who had fled there and were suspected of creating turmoil in the border region. According to Dr. Wade, who accompanied Captain Welsh as assistant surgeon of the mission, this was the first opportunity to gather information about Assam and Assamese who were practically unknown."[6] At the end of Wade's eighteen-month stay, he compiled an account of Assam "from authentic documents . . . and partly derived from the information of intelligent natives as well as from [his] observations."[7] This he presented to Colonel Kirpatrick to acquaint the Bengal administration with the geography and political situation of the eastern frontiers. In his account, Wade identified the rulers of Assam as Ahom. He starts the history of Ahom by recounting two "origin myths," which he implied were not "factual" knowledge but were based on the legends and beliefs of Ahom deodhais.

The first "myth" that Wade recounts is both curious and unique. It is not narrated in the buranjis of Assam, and Wade does not specifically tell us where he collected it. In the preface of his account, he informs us that he recorded the story from some deodhais, who are not named. Hence, neither the author nor the authenticity of the tale can be verified from this and other accounts. Wade's recounting of the story of Ahom origin begins in these words:

Droopudee, Aoturra, and Hoobhuddra, wives of the Pandow, were involved in hostilities with Doormerikh and the other wives of the Kowrow . . . In the midst of their lamentations [the Kowrow's took] a resolution . . . to address their supplication to Sreekrishna. "Thou art our Lord," they cried "for we have lost our spouses. . . . The Pandows have destroyed our Lords and have used their dominions. Do thou grant us thy protection and restore us to our property, with thy assistance we shall prove victorious." Bhagwan appeared before the supplicants. He promised to take the same care of them as of his own person, and to accomplish all their wishes. Exulting in the favor of the God, the heroines prepared their arms and mounting their horses and chariots advanced to attack the Pandow in the dead of night . . . Judishter was confounded at the appearance of female combatants. But the Panchoo Pandow without consulting Sreekrishna advanced to the attack on foot. "Ye feeble women," exclaimed the Pandow, "what can tempt ye to oppose the vigorous arms of man? Your destruction is inevitable." "We come," replied the princesses, "to revenge the death of our murdered Lords," and a shower of arrows succeeded the reply. The Pandows in vain discharged their arrows; the princesses were invulnerable while every arrow from their hands inflicted painful wounds on their adversaries . . . At length Judishter fled from the field and left his four brothers engaged with the princesses.

Judishter threw himself at the God's [Krishna's] feet, uttered his complaint and entreated his protection. Sreekrishna . . . directed him to send immediately to Dewaraka and convey his [Krishna's] eight wives from there to the scene of action; where in conjunction with the wives of the Pandow he promised they should obtain a complete victory . . . Roqminee, the principal wife of Sreekrishna, was chosen by Droopudee for her charioteer by command of the God. . . . Droopudee with innumerable arrows . . . drove the destructive instrument with such force, as swept Doormerikh with her hundred chariots, charioteers and combatants in a whirlwind through the air, and precipitated the whole army on the mountains of Odoigeer.[8]

The Kowrow who had fainted now recovered their senses and addressed their supplications to Sreekrishna. The God appeared and gave them assurances that wherever their destiny might place them, they should enjoy prosperity. Sreekrishna immediately repaired to Indreh and addressed in the following manner, "Hasten, O spirit, to the arms of Doormerikh, and a son shall arise from your embraces whose power shall extend to the west as far as the Domunni rock, and his provinces shall become populous, rich and happy. . . . Indreh in compliance with the Mandate of the God, delayed not his visit to Doormerikh. . . . In the course of time a son was born. . . . Indreh and his attendant spirits . . . rendered the earth clear and level; constructed a fortress which far surpassed the works of former times, and raised habitations which gave the name Ghurgown [Garhgaon] to that city . . . Indreh appointed the divine youth Raja of this city; and the sons of the other princesses who had experienced the embraces of various celestial spirits became Patro-muntree [ministers]. The Rajah . . . obtained the title of Swurgee Dhiu [swargadeo] from Indreh before the return of the latter to his heavenly mansion.[9]

This story of the origin of Ahom represented by Wade can easily be recognized as reminiscent of the Mahabharata tradition, but it is also unique in many ways. Without doubt, the origin myth departs on many levels from "normal" Mahabharata discourse, thereby providing numerous vantage points from which to examine the processes of production and the interplay of themes and traditions of the varied origins in Assam. The traditional story of the Mahabharata, which is a narration of struggle between the clans of the Kaurava and Pandava, told through the battle of Kurukshetra, is significantly altered in this account. In the Assamese version, the protagonists are not men but rather women. Pandava (Pandow) men are represented as weak figures hovering on the sideline, while Kaurava (Kowrow) women are depicted as brave warriors blessed by the supreme deity, Sri Krishna, in their enterprises. The layering effect that is prominent in the story indicates that such a story was produced at a time when society in Assam was undergoing some radical transformation. The impact of a new religion—Hinduism—is evident in this myth of origin, but it is also clear that its influence as yet was not dominant because the externally borrowed characters from Hindu myth were manipulated to fit internally accepted social context. As far as I know this is the only version of the Mahabharata in which women are represented as protagonists who founded a kingdom. This version never gained wide acceptance, perhaps due to its peculiarity, and outside the pages of Wade's account we do not hear again this myth of origin of the Ahom kingdom in a female line of warriors. It is important to note that although Wade presents this myth as a story of the Ahom origin, nowhere in this origin myth do we encounter the term Ahom. Wade, however, accepted it as an Ahom story because it records the founding of the city of Garhgaon, the capital of the Assam kingdom, and thus forced a meaning about a community that was absent in the original version that he recorded.

The second story presented in Wade's account differs from the first. This second myth is a more popular version and it is repeated in many Assamese buranjis. The second myth reads as follows:

> Rishi Bashistha lived by the Dikhow and wanted to make a place of worship similar to the Bararusee [Varanasi?] of the west and to give that river his own name. . . . In this spot he buried one thousand salgram [symbolizing the worship of Shiva], in the middle of which he placed one of the stones called Luckkeenarain. He also planted vegetables . . . and performed daily the mode of worship called Poorachurrum. Indra Deo was apprehensive that the devotees who frequented this temple would all be received into heaven; and gave orders to the kains over which he presided to inundate the country and destroy the pious edifice with the sacred plants and everything belonging to the temple. A deluge in obedience to his commands involved the whole in ruin. . . . The rishi cursed, "thou evil spirit, mayest thou transmigrate and be regenerated in peasants of the vilest caste" and addressing his curses to the river which had overflowed the temple, he prayed . . .
>
> The rishi forgave Inder. But he commanded him to associate with a female of a vile caste. Shama (the celestial wife of Inder) in this birth . . . was a Nara princess.[10] Her mother's name was Koonghdemalka, her father's name Samdam . . . Shama was impregnated by the celestial Inder. She had inquired of Inder if he intended to come to her, on which the god replied, "Ahim/Assim" (I will come, I will come) and thus the word Ahim/Assim which characterizes these people and the country . . .
>
> The child was born in 4041 kaljoog. He was named Swarga Narain. He was followed by his son, Pameepungh, who had two sons Suoka-rulphah Bhur Burra and Sookaphah Cueta [Sukapha; this is the spelling used later on]. When Pameepungh died he was succeeded by his eldest son, who was expelled by the younger brother. Sookaphah addressed himself to his brother with a declaration that he disclaimed to live under his government. He accordingly absconded and returned with . . . 12 commanders and 350 fighting men, 2 elephants, 2 conductors, 30

horses and horsemen . . . Sukapha and his men migrated westward . . . [and] captured many villages and a large amount of booty . . . Sukapha left for heaven after ruling for forty-five years in Assam.[11]

The story goes on to record that the king of the Naras tried to bring back the recalcitrant chiefs of Assam to their fold. Instead, the chiefs declared independence and thus, according to Wade, the dynasty of Ahom rulers was established in Assam.

Wade's "Account of Assam" was not published, but the Ahom origin myths therein found fertile ground for new imaginings in the minds of the colonial agents. Ahoms were now easily explained as a "foreign" warrior class who migrated to Assam and married local women to start their line of rulers.[12] This mythic-history of Ahoms served two purposes.[13] First, the British were able to "understand" and interpret the Ahom rulers' backgrounds and, second, they were made into liminal actors on the borderland between British India and Southeast Asia. Identity was constructed for the Ahoms, but it was made fuzzy and it has remained so since then.

Walter Hamilton, a colonial agent who introduced the term Ahom in his *East Indian Gazetteer*, suggested that the "Ahoms or the governing class of Assam . . . descended from the companion of Khuntai." To explain his theory of who Khuntai was, he constructed a fantastic story: "Many ages ago two brothers, named Khunlai and Khuntai of the Shan[14] race, came to a hill named Khorai Khorong, which is situated south of Garhgaon. Khuntai stayed in the vicinity of the hill and kept in his possession the god, Chung. The country is ruled by his successors. They eat pork, beef, and all other food that shock the piety of Brahmanical Hindoos and drink wine without restraint or remorse of conscience. . . . The Deodhaings were then their spiritual guides, performing worship to the god Chung with great mystery and secrecy, and possessing some books called Bulongi, written in a character which appears on the old coin, and which seems to have a strong affinity to that of Ava" (Hamilton 1928, 74–75). He also asserted in another account that "the names of the kings strongly resemble the Chinese."[15]

However, the colonial agents did not exclusively formulate the Ahom past. Native intelligentsia adopted an "attitude of collaboration" (Chatterjee 1993, 26). In the mid-nineteenth century a corpus of Ahom myths of origin was gathered, and a local archive of the Ahom created the past. Both the homegrown accounts and the colonial interpretations presented the

Ahom as a group of warriors who came to Assam in the thirteenth century from Southeast Asia, possibly Upper Burma.[16] The local accounts, borrowing from the colonial, emplotted a historical memory of Ahom origin outside Assam, but almost immediately they domesticated their history by locating them as rulers of the Assam Valley. This domestication was made possible through a story of migration from Upper Burma to Assam, where the wanderers became known as the Ahom. Thus in local narratives the Ahom and the history of Assam were intimately tied together. Because these narratives were crafted and written by local individuals, almost immediately the colonial administration accepted them as the "true" history of the Ahom rulers. What is surprising, however, was that the enterprise of finding the Ahom past was not an Ahom activity, but was initiated by the British and backed by the local Brahmin elites of Assam, who, not unlike the British, were "outsiders."[17] The complex memorialization that developed from these efforts represented the assumptions of groups that assumed "natural superiority" over the community they were representing in their writings. In 1829, Anandaram Dhekial Phukan, a Brahmin gentleman and one of the first scholars of local history, wrote a history of Ahom. This was followed by the *Assam Buranji* by Kashinath Phukan in 1844, who was also a Brahmin.[18] In 1875, Gunabhiram Barua, another Assamese Brahmin, wrote his version of Ahom history. Anandaram Phukan and Kashinath Phukan wrote Assamese buranjis, while Barua dabbled at translating a so-called *Ahom Buranji* into English.[19] Printed versions of both Phukan's buranjis are available. K. Phukan narrates the origin myth of Ahom in these words:

> Tyao Aimakhamneng became the king of Maolung. He ruled for ten years. His son Sukhanpha succeeded him. In the kingdom of Mungmit-kup-king-nau (or, as the Assamese referred to it, Mungmit-kup-kling) Phutyaokhang ruled for seven years.... On his death, his youngest son, Sukapha, became king ...
>
> After eighteen years had elapsed (since Sukapha became king of Mungmit-kup-king-nau and Sukhanpha had ruled for eight years), Sukhanpha fought against the king of Junlung. Sukhanpha did not invite Sukapha to fight with him in this battle. For this reason there was a rift between the two kingdoms. Sukapha learnt that Sukhanpha was conspiring to capture him. So he fled to the kingdom of Mungkang.[20] There he befriended the king, Naisanpha, and procured the icon of Somdeo.[21] In lakli Taijepi, Ha Pak Kaw Sip, that is 590, or Ha Pak Kaw

Sip Leng, that is 591, in the first lakli, Kaptyao, or according to the Hindu calendar 1150 saka [A.D. 1228], on 15th Aghun, Sukapha moved southwards. From 16th Aughun, he became king of a section of Saumar.[22] Assam pandits were asked to reckon Sukapha's arrival in Saumar by going back to the time of Khunlung and Khunlai's descent to the earth. . . . From the time of Khunlung and Khunlai's descent from heaven, until Sukapha's migration to Saumar, Sip Et Tao or eleven singhas had elapsed.[23] From the first lakli of Sip Song Taosingha, Sukapha ruled over Saumar . . .

When Sukapha came to Saumar he brought with him 1080 people, one male elephant, one female elephant, 300 horses, Thaomung Kling Lunmang Rai Bura Gohain and Thaomungkangang Bar Gohain.[24] He brought all these along with Somdeo. . . . He defeated the nagas and occupied the region. . . . In 1163 saka, they established their capital city at Charaideo [a few miles outside Sibsagar]. In lakli Plekingti, 1164 saka, they contracted friendly alliances with the king of the Mataks, Badausa and the Barahis. . . . These Barahis began to talk . . . They said, "these men are heavenly creatures. Nobody equals them." Since then, they spread this information in the kingdom. The term Aham became established and from then on the kingdom and the people were called Aham. Since Aham peopled the settlement, the kingdom was called Ahamardesh.[25]

K. Phukan's story of Ahom origin gives us several dates, place names, and actors. The narrative of Ahom origin reads like an astrological chart prepared by a Brahmin to calculate time, the location of stars, their impact on particular events and people, and so on. This is not surprising because the art of calculating and predicting the future was a Brahmin trade in Assam, as elsewhere in India, which was used very effectively to gain power and endowments from royalties in perpetuity. Although we do not know the purpose of writing this buranji and the benefits acquired from it, we do know that Kashinath, like most Brahmins of his time, wrote his buranji in keeping with the Brahmanic tradition that emphasized dates and auspicious events. He informs us that his buranji is an authentic history of the Ahom dynasty, but can this material be used by historians today to reconstruct a plausible date and place of Ahom origin? My attempts to do so did not produce favorable results. No places recorded by Phukan (as well as other historians of Assam) can be identified in the historical and official maps of Burma. These place names do not exist. I suspect they are descriptive terms and not the real locations of places through which the early migrants passed. The journey of migration to Assam is hence not possible to document and map. Nevertheless, the mythic-history of Ahom origin constructed by K. Phukan became quite popular, and although it has been modified several times, it is one of the well-known versions that have appeared in later Assamese buranjis.[26]

The origin story in Barua's *Ahom Buranji* reads as follows: "In the beginning there were no gods and men . . . All things were in a condition empty and chaotic. . . . In the sky were the golden eggs. . . . The eggs hatched and became kings . . . the vapor of the eggs became clouds . . . the blood of the eggs became water . . . they of the celestial eggs came forth in splendor" (1985, 1–4).[27] Khun Lung and Khun Lai were deemed by the chronicler as the splendid creation of the gods and were established as the ancestors of Sukapha. The Ahom rulers of Assam, according to this narrative, descended from these celestial beings through Sukapha (Barua 1985, 10–25).

The person called Sukapha, who appears in all the narratives about Assam and is considered by historians of Assam (both colonial and local scholars) as the founder of the Ahom dynasty, is a very intriguing figure. Based on a cursory examination of some of the tales prevalent among various Shan groups of Upper Burma, I have found that Sukapha is a shared hero who appears, with minor orthographical changes, in all of their ancestral trees. For instance, in the Hsenwi chronicle, Hsö Hkan Hpa (A.D. 1152–1205) is described as the most notable king of Mong Mao. The story retells the fabulous adventures of an unusually brave male hero who attacked and defeated the Chinese, invaded the Lao states, Chiang Saen, and the Yonok country, and became the overlord of Manipur, Arakan, and Assam. The Hsenwi chronicle mentions the conquest of Assam in these words: "When they entered Weh-sa-li[28] some cowherds reported the arrival of Kaw-sam-pi, from the country of white blossoms and large leaves (Mao kingdom). The ministers submitted without resistance, and promised to make an annual payment . . . Hkun-sam-long, the brother of the king, arranged the tribute and withdrew his army from Assam" (Milne 1910, 22–23).

The Mao Shans of Moguang in Upper Burma also claim the same personage of Sukapha (Choa Kam Pha) as their ancestor. They described Chao Kam Pha as the greatest of their rulers who ascended to the throne in A.D. 1220. It is said that in the early half of the thirteenth century, Choa Kam Pha's brother, Sam-Lung-Pha, the ruler of Moguang, undertook a variety of military campaigns, including a campaign into the Upper Assam Valley "where he conquered the greater portion of the territory then under the sway of the Chutya or Sutya kings" (Elias 1876, 17–18). These two myths from different sources are definitely not exhaustive. A careful investigation of myths from Upper Burma and the regions of southern China, I suspect, will produce several other similar tales. The origin myths of the three traditions stated above enable us to see some sort of historical connection between the region of Upper Assam, the so-called Ahom kingdom, and certain regions and peoples within present-day Southeast Asia. But these myths also create some serious confusion about the place of Sukapha as the founder of Ahom rule in Assam. He is shared by too many communities, and he is claimed as the founder of each kingdom almost around the same time. One cannot help but ask if Sukapha is really a historical figure or simply a story, a convention so to speak, to start the narrative of a community in many shared traditions. Retrospective significance, I suspect, was probably given to Sukapha by these communities in order to start the story of their origin as a political entity. It is not really clear from the evidence collected so far whether or not the events that are claimed in the Assamese buranjis as the work of Sukapha were really his feats.

Nonetheless, these stories of origin can be fascinating. They are a gateway to understanding the collective consciousness and ritual of community formation. Repetition is the key in these narratives, and by telling them many times a memory of the past is generated, embedded, and made believable, although very little evidence is presented about the details. How did this myth of Sukapha and Ahom develop locally in Assam? All historical narratives draw on previous understandings. In Assam the historical influence of cultures and memories from Southeast Asia, particularly Upper Burma, are noticeable, and their progress can be traced over time. The process of borrowing this memory of Sukapha from Upper Burma is recorded in the buranjis. Wade was informed that the tradition of buranji writing, beginning with Sukapha, developed in the reign of Siva Singha (1714–1744). According to his informant, a deodhai, "Sree Sree Surgadeo, king of kings, lord of the lightening and of the royal canopy capped with gold, Sootunphah [Swargadeo Siva Singha] . . . condescended to order that the following history should be written by Khoon Kiowlong Raj Muntree, who is the head of the Bailoong and the Ahum tribe, named Munmoohun. . . . Swargadeo inspired that the histories of his predecessors should be compiled, the succession of Ahum monarch mentioned in detail, and the books called *Roopoot*. That the history should only contain the names and transactions of the swargadeos."[29]

From the Assamese buranjis we learn that the reign of Rajeshwar Singha (1751–1769) was the period when a genealogy of the swargadeos, beginning from Sukapha, was fixed. This tradition of buranji writing was emphasized by his successor, swargadeo Gaurinath Singha (1780–1795), who sent Assam pandits to Upper Burma to collate the history of his predecessors from the records of the Buddhist temples. This group from Assam, the buranji tells us, was particularly motivated to find the history of Sukapha and to copy any buranjis that included him in their narratives (K. Phukan 1906, 8). It is not surprising, therefore, that the buranjis all reiterate the same tales of the swargadeos originating from Indra who is connected to the hero called Sukapha, because they were all copied from the same source. It is not possible now to know if there were many chronicles with stories of Sukapha, or if there was one chronicle in which all the stories were compiled. The Assam scribes evidently copied their story from the same source, and hence we have very little discrepancy for the early period of "Ahom" rule. Sukapha was found, adopted, and a "fixed" narrative of the past was created. This past was invoked whenever the origin of Ahom was discussed, beginning with the local people's initial encounter with the British agents and continuing on with any interested listener, including me. What Trouillot calls the "storage model" of memory-history was put in place and invoked whenever necessary (1995, 14). With the passage of time, the memory-history of the "foreign" royals was indigenized, co-opted, and transferred to the collective in the Assam Valley. It became their history and memory.

In the early nineteenth century, the potent combination of British curiosity and the readiness of local scholars to share the story of the "Ahom past" created a narrative of Ahom rulers. Along with this narrative, a euhemeristic tradition developed, and men like Sukapha became deified as gods. The historical personage called Sukapha became shrouded in mystery by his assigned position among the gods. The subsequent limitation closed the possibility of analyzing him as an actor in history, made him unreachable, and, ultimately, unknowable. The "unknowableness" of the origin of Ahom created several problems and enhanced the opportunities for the British to create their own history of Assam. But, most important, it created a negative mindset. Ahom was seen as a people without a clear history because they had no real founder, only tales of an ephemeral figure founding a community. Thus, while stories of the Ahom became objects of antiquarian interest, as a group they were considered "unknowable" and thus a people without a history. The colonials created history for the Ahoms; the same architects also denied history to them. It is this confusion that plagues the story of the Ahom even today. One must negotiate with the problem of presence and absence, a legacy of colonial historiography, to understand what was and is Tai-Ahom.

Despite the assumption of the colonials that the Ahom was "unknowable," in the mid-nineteenth century several versions of the story of Sukapha and the Ahom community were constructed and put into circulation. The colonial motivation to create an Ahom past was not questioned by the local people: they were not in a position to challenge the colonials dabbling with their past. Rather, through repetition of the myths (even by local scholars) the divine origin of the Ahoms and the concepts of creation, rulership, and history were linked together and made into memory "objects." Today, many Tai-Ahoms unquestioningly believe as a fact that from the gods to Khun Lung, Khun Lai, and Sukapha a linkage has been created for them. Whether these stories are true or fabricated is not the point; the power is in the narrative that makes the community believe in an alternative past, which they need to keep their community alive. The British agents were able to tap into local versions of mythic-history and use it—first to "understand" the groups they were dealing with and, second, to outline a history of rulers beginning with Sukapha and continuing to the moment when they (the British) found and positioned themselves as the new rulers of Assam. To become the rulers of Assam, the British had first to deal with the swargadeos. It is at this stage, once again, that we encounter another level of complication in the narrative on Ahom in the colonial period. What is amazing is that the ruling class of Assam, who were supposed to be the true "Ahom" in the story, did not recall that they were Ahoms when the colonials asked them about their identity.

### WE/THEY ARE NOT AHOMS:
### NEW IDENTITIES IN THE MAKING

Swargadeo Purandar Singha, the last Ahom ruler (as it appears from his correspondence with the British agents) did not conceive of his past in terms of being Ahom. Neither did his rivals to the throne nor the nobles of his court claim that their ancestors were the foundational "Ahom."

Such a claim would on the one hand have reduced the gods from swarga-deo or heavenly beings to human beings, and, on the other hand, would categorize Purandar Singha as the ruler of a specific ethnic group, which he resisted because his subjects constituted a multiglot and multiethnic polity. Instead, for the royalty the past remained distinctly ambivalent. When political settlements had to be made with the colonials, the royalty represented themselves as the "household" of rulers and avoided making a connection to an ethnic identity. An investigation of their writings demonstrates that attachment to any group, if there were any attachment, was murky.

In 1820, one of the few instances when the king of Assam, Purandar Singha, wrote directly to the British government in Bengal, he asserted his rightful claim to the throne in these words, "both myself and my forefathers are the descendants of Rajah Indur [Indra], and we never have been nor am I now paying tribute of my lands to any one."[30] Another contender to the throne, Bisonath Singha, the *jaub raja* (crown prince), appealed to the colonial agent, Robert Jenkins, to support his candidacy because his father was the Tipameah Raja of the Tipameah household. Likewise, the letters from the chief ministers of the kingdom, first the Bura Gohain, and then the Bor Gohain, who supported different candidates to the throne, never attached the label Ahom to their candidates. The Bura Gohain dismissed the rights of Kamleshwar Singha and Chandra Kanta Singha to claim the "Charung race," although they are "understood to have a distant connection with the Surgadeb/Rajah."[31] According to the minister, only the Tungkhungia family, to which Purandar Singha belonged, had the right to be swargadeo. The Bor Gohain, on the other hand, supported Chandra Kanta Singh because he "belonged to the Charung tribe, i.e., the Maharaja Singha Deb Gouree Nath Singha's descent."[32]

The passages cited above can be somewhat misleading if one is not aware that these names refer to places and not ethnic groups. The name Tipameah is derived from the place called Tipam; likewise Charung comes from Charing, Tungkhungia from Tingkhang, and Dihingiya from Dihing. Suhungmung or Dihingia Raja (1497–1539) started the practice of deputing princes to administer these places. He designated his four sons as the chiefs of the four provinces of his realm: Charing, Dihing, Tipam, and Tingkhang. Later on, the area of Namrup and Simaluguri were also made into princely provinces. Six clans, or *faids*, sprung up from this arrangement. Over time the title of Charing Raja became a customary appellation for the heir apparent. Gadadhar Singha (1681–1696) was Charing Raja, although he belonged to the Tingkhang household. Puran-dar Singha requested that the British confer this title to this son, Kam-leshwar Singha, who was also from the Tingkhang household.[33] It appears that a prince could move between these households—that is, a Tingkhang prince could become a member of the Charing household, and thus be-come the Charing Raja. Likewise, princes from other households could move to the same position of Charing Raja if the swargadeo or, in the colonial period, the British agent, so desired. The fluidity that marked royal identity in Assam as late as the nineteenth century is very important to bear in mind.

Royal memory, like identity, in this moment of encounter with British colonialism, did not produce a fixed genealogical map. The passages quoted above show that the royalty of Assam failed to define its identity and claim its heritage from a fixed line of historical personages—that is, Ahom ancestors. As a result, the royalty could not make use of a narrative of Ahom that had gained considerable political cachet among the colo-nials and make a bid for an independent princely state. Instead, the Assam king invoked a mythical character, Indra (Indur), as his historical ancestor who, he claimed, endowed on him and his ancestors the right of rulership. The British were not at all convinced of the story of Indra as the founder of the line of Assam kings. They were already aware that it was a narrative trope in India that had no historical value. Since the swargadeo could not prove his legitimacy as a "true Ahom" and thus of the ruling class, the British deemed he had no right to continue to rule.

On the other hand, communication from the Raja of Burma to the king of Assam claiming him as his "brother from olden times . . . since the days of Chowphah Chukapha Rajah" fanned British suspicions about the swargadeo's relationship with their enemy, the Burmese.[34] It is necessary to note here that even the Burmese king did not use the term Ahom, but rather invoked a long memory of connection with the Assam kingdom through Sukapha, who, as noted earlier, was a quasi-historical figure shared by many groups. The British used the correspondence from the Burmese court to their advantage, and thus, despite the swargadeo's re-sistance, the British represented the rulers of Assam as having a strong affinity with the Burmese. Walter Robinson categorically asserted that the "Shyans became Ahoms or Asoms in Assam . . . [when] they conquered the south-western extremity of the valley, and their conquests, together with the settlements of the colonists of this race, led to the permanent distinction of Kamrup from Assam, or Lower from Upper Assam" (1841, 2, 4). John Butler reinforced Robinson's hypothesis concerning the Burmese background of the Ahom. Butler concluded that "Assam was invaded in 1224 A.D. by a band of Ahoom or Shan adventurers" (1847, 127). The early colonial agents emphasized this story despite the lack of any historical evidence of a "dynasty . . . and of an ancient hereditary aristocracy" of Assam emerging from Burma, and it led them to suspect that "Assam . . . differ[ed] from most other countries that have been acquired in India . . . render[ing] it doubtful whether [they] shall obtain the quiet submission . . . of the present generation."[35] The letter and the myth of Ahom that the colonial agents had at their disposal helped to connect the rulers of Assam and Burma, and apprehensions about Burmese influence and interference in the administration of Assam were cast to justify British annexation of the region.

To accomplish the annexation, alongside political and strategic developments every effort was made to undermine the power of the swargadeo who was a symbolic center for local imagination and could fuel passion against the British and for autonomy. Hamilton, one of the earliest architects of the Ahom concept, also became an active proponent of debunking the power of the swargadeo. He began to cast doubts about the existence of "real" Ahoms, and to justify his supposition he developed another story of their early settlement in the Assam Valley. His observation that "Ahoms on their arrival had no women, but espoused those of the country" allowed him to conclude that there were no pure Ahoms, but "illegitimate issues of these families . . . many of them probably descended from the soldiers and servants who accompanied the princes."[36] This justified to him that the ruling king was not a purebred Ahom, and hence did not have the divine mandate to rule.[37] Buchannan's assumption of the "impure" blood of Ahom royalty was reinforced by W. W. Hunter, who compiled the first census reports on Assam. In explaining who the Ahoms were, Hunter wrote: "Ahams, the descendants of the ancient rulers . . . have freely intermixed with the people of the land . . . and have now sunk to the level of poor cultivators. They are converted Hindus . . . numbering about 94,304" (1879, 235–39). In 1891, the ethnographers E. T. Dalton (1872) and H. H. Risely (1891) both concluded that the Ahoms, descendants of a proud race of Shans, had degenerated into superstitious, backward, apathetic Assamese. Almost immediately, the colonial census makers, taking stock of the new outlook, deemed the Ahom as a "Semi-Hinduized Aboriginal group of Assamese" (Hunter, 1879, 236).

Once the fear of a Burmese annexation of Assam was reduced and the psychological and political feat of reducing the swargadeo into a nonentity was accomplished, the colonial government pensioned off the various contenders to the throne. Gradually colonial interest in the Ahoms also disappeared. In 1838, Jenkins wrote to Bishonath Singha, "formerly Jaub Raja of Assam," that "the British government did not . . . admit the right of [Bishonath Singha] or any other of the *Rajah race* to be Rajah of Assam" since they had "conquered Assam from the Burmese government." Affirming the end of Ahom rule, Jenkins informed Bishonath that "the British government conceiving that it would be gratifying to the nobles and the people of Assam had set up an *Assamese prince* Poorundur Singh as Rajah over half of the country."[38] In this and other letters to follow, the label Ahom was dropped and the swargadeos were reduced to nothing. "Ahom" was made unthinkable, and a new category called Assamese was discursively introduced into public documents. The colonial agents, who only a few decades ago had set up an intense search for the Ahoms, now became engaged in undoing the history of the "ruling class." The category called Assamese, who were imagined as low, debased, and servile, became handy for this purpose.

### THE ENTERPRISE OF COLONIALISM: MAKING THE ASSAMESE, CREATING GOVERNABILITY

The end of Ahom rule fulfilled multiple purposes. It established British rule firmly in Assam, and a fresh canvas was drawn up to sketch a picture of a new history of Assam and of a community called the Assamese. This moment was historic: Assam was mapped within British India and permanently delinked from Burma and the rest of Southeast Asia, areas with which Assam had shared historic and cultural connections for centuries.[39] The inauguration of the process of the "Indianization" of the Assam Valley happened subsequently. The target community through which this new development was forged was a new decontextualized and ahistorical community called the Assamese. The memory of the Assamese was connected to the Indian and Hindu communities, and local identities in Assam were transformed. The movement from one label to another was a process that affected the community immediately and continues to plague society even now, as I demonstrated in chapter 1. In a sense the moment of colonial intervention was a moment of creation of history; it was marked by an abrupt end of one kind of history and the emergence of another kind. The change involved more than a change of label. Society and culture were radically transformed and fashioned to suit colonial needs.

Major John Butler constructed a simple yet devastating story to explain how the Ahom degenerated into the Assamese. According to Butler, "the downfall of the Ahom kings of Assam may be attributed to their becoming proselytes to the Hindoo religion in the reign of Jeydhoj Singh (1654) . . . Initially, all the offices were confined to Ahoms, but after the reign of Rudra Singha when more of them became converts to Hinduism, they were admitted to a share in the public employ" (1855, 223). Butler identified the Assamese as a quasi-Hindu quasi-Ahom community whose "character . . . cannot be better illustrated, than by noticing some of their customs . . . The general mode of fighting is abuse with gross foul language, pulling the hair, and striking with the elbow, not the clenched fist" (228). He identified them further as a "licentious, degraded race, degenerating rapidly" (246), who could be redeemed "by the introduction of a more active and industrious people, who might stimulate the natives to increased exertions" (229). Remarking on the character of the people, Butler writes: "An inveterate indulgence in the use of opium . . . and their spare diet have [their] influence . . . and consequently [they are] slender, effeminate and indolent . . . their morals are extremely depraved and their manners servile and contemptible. Nor are the women one whit superior to the men; and although they are far from possessing attractive persons, they are utter slaves to the worst licentiousness" (134–35). William Robinson, a pioneering tea enthusiast who spent several years in Assam, supported and reinforced Butler's impression of the "insipid, dull Assamese," and added to the fast-growing negative body of literature concerning the group (1841, 5). The mid-nineteenth-century colonial literature, although perverse and racist, provides an excellent scope to probe into the characterization of the Assamese; one can say that from the colonial point of view the Assamese were a "stupid" people.[40]

How strange, then, that the British should take an interest in the group called the Assamese and the place called Assam, which many had publicly bemoaned was a land where "there [was] nothing visible . . . but mud and jungle."[41] Official ambition was however, markedly different from rhetoric. Simultaneous with the representation of the people as "barbaric and jealous" (Hamilton 1828, 74–75) colonial surveyors emphasized "the conspicuous position the place [held] as the scene of great commercial advantage to British India" (Robinson 1841). "Assam is not a country for diamonds, but it is for gold-dust, and what is much better, for industry in

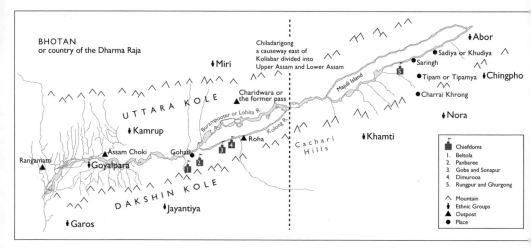

Colonial map of Assam. (Courtesy of the British Library)

trade," Wade wrote to Fowkes, a colonial trader in Bengal. Wade and his successors knew they could "do well in it."[42] But how was such a goal to be fulfilled in a country with a stagnating economy where the people were suspected of suffering from a "death-like inertia?"[43] The early colonial agents argued against the establishment of direct administration in Assam, fearing that the "character of the peasantry, their ignorance, the difficulty of pushing an investigation through the medium of individuals who . . . [had] little knowledge . . . of the European character . . . and dependence on the superiors as their all in all" would burden them without financial rewards.[44] Upholding this logic for twelve years, from 1826 until 1838, colonial agents in Assam engaged in a game of hide-and-seek with the political future of the province without assuming direct administrative responsibilities. Instead, they left the administration of the province to the exking Purandar Singha on his promise to pay fifty thousand rupees in cash as an annual tribute.

Granted, this was not a huge sum of money for economies with a developed cash system. But in Assam, "under the ancient government, the revenue was principally raised by a capitation and hearth tax; and by the ryuts giving a certain portion of their labour for the benefit of the state" (Scott 1832, 21). Peddling trade, toll tax, and plunder were the means through which the swargadeo built a capital reserve. The demand for cash by the British stressed the limits of the royal household.[45] The question that arose in Assam was what would be the source for paying tribute to the British? The representative agent of the British administration in Assam, David Scott, recommended a survey of the land to develop a new taxation system. Also, he encouraged the production of silk for the market, which previously was a cottage industry intended for local use. The effort of David Scott was aimed at improving the economy on the basis of local resources and skills, which he argued would enable the colonial administration to collect the required revenue and improve the lot of the people. The labors of the colonial administrator were strengthened by the missionaries, "with the view of raising these rude people in the scale of society."[46] Hence, along with introducing new cash crops, the Bible was translated and distributed among the people. But it soon became apparent that "it did not operate so well as might be expected; and the [tax system] was apparently an institution far advanced for the existing state of civilization in Assam."[47] The preliminary revenue system and the colonial economic schemes of Scott were immediately undone with a new policy of private landholding introduced by his successor, Robert Jenkins.

The process of new colonization started with a thorough exploration and systematic survey of land completed by Lieutenants Wilcox and Burlton. The survey report proved that Assam was rich in timber and other natural resources and had a potential for tea cultivation (Phillimore 1945). Colonial logic then deemed it necessary to occupy the province and establish direct rule. But they had to overcome another problem: the mosaic of communities identified as the subjects of the exswargadeo did not make a good first impression on colonial agents. They saw the people as "warlike," "marauding," "lazy and barbaric," "dirty and exceedingly poor," "treacherous"—in short, a motley group of unpleasant subject communities. To establish colonial rule and direct administration, colonial agents realized they had to create a governable society of subjects. It was in that context that the group called the Assamese was created by differentiating and demarcating them from those thought of as savage hill people, and from the "dead" Ahoms (Hodson 1987 [1937], 39). The Assamese were thereupon introduced in colonial documents as the potentially revenue-paying peasant class.[48] In 1838, the British established direct rule in Assam, and the Assamese community paid the cost of the administration. The defunct royalty pleaded and bargained, but their days had passed. Colonial rhetoric promised a "good and efficient government" to the Assamese people, something they insisted was absent in the previous administration.

Almost immediately on assuming the reins of government, the colonial administration immersed itself in developing agriculture and commercial enterprise for profit. Toward this end the traditional system of labor for land ownership was abolished. The idea was to attract a European planter class to invest in the land to grow commercial crops such as indigo, sugarcane, and tea, while displacing the local peasants from their lands through discriminatory land revenue policies. Jenkins rationalized that the Assamese who held on to their land had to pay "sufficient tax" so as not to inhibit the development of commercial cash production for the same land by European planters. Hence, in 1839–1840 a new land tax system was introduced. The entire region of Upper Assam was divided into *mouza* or territorial fiscal jurisdictions and land was categorized as *bustee* or homestead, *roopeet* or low paddy land, and *furinghutee* or high paddy land. The homestead tax was fixed at two rupees per head, one rupee per poorah (approximately three-fourths acre) of roopeet land, and eight anna for each poorah of furinghutee as well as for each poorah of grazing and noncultivatable land. In 1844–1845 the tax for roopeet holding was increased to one rupee and four anna. The taxes were then increased in the following decades without undertaking a survey of production and settlement work. For people who were not used to paying in cash or who did not raise crops for the market to sell for revenue, the new system was oppressive. The colonial administration, however, went ahead and divided the entire country—which was nearly four hundred miles in length with a population of 1,590,573 people—into 130 mouzas. A new proprietary land system was introduced, complete with title deeds and lease terms (Mills 1854, 1–2; Guha 1991). Needless to say, the colonial economy was totally new to the populace of Assam. As Jenkins himself observed: "In Assam no ryot [tenant farmer] had to pay tax for grazing, cutting of timber and he is free to plant anything . . . Every ryot is equal and independent of every other ryot of whatever caste, and there never were village servants . . . The Assamese . . . lived principally upon rice, and wear clothes in their own silks and cotton and none of them have ever been traders, nor are they now . . . The trade of the province was consequently confined to the sale of such articles as would procure for them the salt of Bengal, and few luxuries and necessaries they wanted . . . not obtainable in their own country."[49] A similar observation was made by Hunter: "The Assamese of Sibsagar are not a trading people, and nearly everyone raises enough on his own holdings to provide for the wants of his own family. Salt is almost the only article for which he has to go to the market" (1879, 251).

The locals could not comprehend the cash economy launched by the colonial government. They had neither the means nor the knowledge to make the shift from their self-sufficient homestead economy to raising crops for sale in order to pay taxes. Consequently, according to Mills, the peasants fell "into the hands of Kyaiis and Bengalees . . . [who] made them advance at an almost incredible interest for impossible returns, and then ruined the defaulters in the civil courts" (1854, iv). Moniram Dewan, the representative of the exswargadeos, made a petition to the British to draw their attention to the problems that the Assamese were facing under the new administration. He lamented: "A number of Assamese are out of employ, while the inhabitants of Marwar and Bengalees from Sylhet have been appointed to Mouzadarships; and for us respectable Assamese to have become ryots of such foreigners is a source of deep mortification."[50] In many cases tenant farmers unable to meet the revenue demands had to give up their furinghutee land. For the most part, in these and other newly reclaimed areas and in wasteland, European planters started cash crop production for which they did not have to pay tax.

The idea of introducing foreign enterprise and capital into Assam, taken up by Robert Jenkins, was much acclaimed by the colonial government. The growing prospect of tea cultivation in Assam became the guiding principle in the new land-settlement policy for enterprising European planters. Wasteland Rules were drawn up in 1838 and 1854 providing lease to applicants who could show they could invest three rupees per acre of land of over a hundred acres or more. This new policy of capitalist agriculture immediately ruled out local peasants and farmers from taking advantage of the situation. The money crisis that they faced dispossessed them from their own land.

To the developing shortage of local capital and the growing poverty of the Assamese (due to the new land revenue system), the British added another problem by introducing opium as a commodity for trade. Poppy grew abundantly in Assam, but "the natives . . . were unacquainted with the manufacture of merchantable opium" (Hamilton 1828, 243). Early on, the colonial agents made a note of the availability and home use of poppy in Assam, and on becoming rulers of the province they pursued a vigorous policy to introduce commercial poppy cultivation. The colonial dictum for introducing opium as a cash crop was, according to Mills, based on the argument that "three-fourths of the population of Assam are opium eaters, and men, women, and children alike use the drug. At the same time . . . very little of the terrible effects of eating it is witnessed in the appearance of the people. The use of opium . . . [has] almost become necessary . . . and in a damp country like Assam it is perhaps beneficial if taken in moderation [,] but experience has shown that to allow every man to grow the plant . . . is most injurious to the morals of the people. *Opium they should have*, but to get it they should have to work for it" (1854, 6; emphasis mine). In 1847–1848, in an effort to pursue this policy, 772 poorah of land was brought under poppy cultivation; in 1849–1850 it was increased to 1,107 poorah, and by 1852–1853, five years after poppy was introduced as a cash crop, the acreage of land under cultivation had nearly doubled to 1,311 poorah.

Along with expanding the cultivation of the crop, manufactured opium was introduced in the markets. From 1835 onward, the British had entered the trade in opium selling at five rupees per seer (a colonial-era measurement equal to 250 grams). By 1860, the opium trade was a government monopoly. Further, it was deemed a criminal offense for nonlicensed growers to cultivate poppy, even for personal use.[51] This was in utter disregard to the age-old convention that entitled each household to produce amounts sufficient for personal use. Between 1873 and 1874, there were as many as 5,137 opium shops in the 6,776 villages counted in 1881.[52] Indeed, there were almost as many opium shops as there were villages in Assam. Licenses were sold to the highest bidder so that more revenue could be collected. Between 1875 and 1879 the total opium revenue was Rs. 1,225,141 for 1,874 maunds (1 maund is approximately 34 kg); in 1905–06 it was Rs. 1,955,706 for 1,415 maunds; and by 1920–1921 it was Rs. 4,412,308 for 1,614 maunds. In defense of its opium policy, the British government reasoned that the "people required it in order to protect themselves from the diseases that are prevalent in a very damp and malarial climate like Assam . . . and to deprive the people in remote villages of their unrestricted use of opium would be to subject them to great hardship even to danger of fatal illness."[53] The colonial administration encouraged the cultivation of poppy, and the growth of the economy based on currency encouraged farmers to convert from paddy to poppy cultivation. This conversion, along with the increasing consumption of opium, resulted in the general ruin of the Assamese society in the 1850s, as is evident from the number of representations made to the government to "forgive tax" at this time. The acreage of paddy decreased considerably over time as more land was brought under poppy cultivation, and both new and settled lands were given up for commercial crop production to European settlers.

I have chosen here to introduce the dual story of the emergence of the "Assamese" and the end of the "Ahom" in the mid-nineteenth century through the medium of colonial land revenue and opium policies because they are intimately interlinked. Such economic ventures empowered the colonial government financially and politically, ultimately enabling them to control Assam's communities, even their production of history. In the British administration of Assam, Edward Gait is most noteworthy in combining the roles of administrator of the Assamese and of historical narrator of the Ahom. His book *The History of Assam* (1921) neatly covered the gaps between the two labels and packaged it as one history. Like his predecessors, Gait represented the Ahoms as Shan invaders who followed a leader named Sukapha and settled in the upper Brahmaputra Valley in A.D. 1228. Sukapha's progeny became swargadeos and ruled Assam continuously for six hundred years with a large group of ministers, administrators, and subjects, according to Gait. He states that the early settlers married locally in order to establish administration and increase the number of Ahoms, and in the course of time they became Assamese. What is notable about this narrative production is that nowhere is the state of the economy mentioned, nor is reference made to the development of the Assamese community through the colonial administrative and revenue policy. Instead, Gait seamlessly wove the Ahom and the Assamese together and presented his story in the past tense. The Assamese farmer of colonial Assam did not merit further investigation. Gait's narrative became very popular, however, because it was written for public consumption and not simply for administrative knowledge. Following the production of Gait's history, a new approach to the history of Assam emerged.

Local scholars of Assam, like S. K. Bhuyan, devoted themselves to the task of expanding Gait's history. Through the repetition of the same story line, local memory was restructured, and the study of all things Assamese became an academic exercise for local intellectuals. The Directorate of Historical and Antiquarian Studies (DHAS) was established in 1904 with this purpose in mind. Public space and memory in Assam from that time on would belong only to the Assamese but not the peasant society—only the Assamese that the British had constructed. The historical Assamese presented by the local literati was clearly an imagined group within Assam, for they could neither explain nor locate themselves in a specific community. One might say that the educated middle class thought of themselves as Assamese and claimed this fuzzy identity. The linguist G. E. Grierson (1904) facilitated this process when he declared Ahom a dead language, and the Assamese language became the only local medium of exchange in Assam. The final erasure of the Ahom occurred in 1931, when the label

Ahom was dropped from official records because it described a mixed (unidentifiable) community and an obscure, forgotten religious tradition. From then on in Assam there were clearly only two groups—the British administrators and the Assamese subjects.

Colonial administrators determined the presence and absence of communities in the historical accounts they constructed. The abrogation of Ahom rule and the emergence of the "Assamese" as a revenue category must be evaluated within this system that first created inequalities and then imagined new beginnings and made them "facts" of the past. The people who once were considered Ahom ceased to be considered royal and/or noble; rather, they were transformed and subsumed within a category called Assamese. Ultimately, the Ahom and the Assamese were presented as one and the same community. The arrangement finally put into practice was rather simple: the Ahom became a topic of history, a dead story of mild interest to antiquarians, while the Assamese emerged as an economic category that could make British rule in Assam successful.

Having created the Assamese, the colonial administration lost interest in them, except as an economic category. They were reduced to *kaniya*—lazy, apathetic, indolent, degraded people.[54] The perception of the Assamese being lazy led to the importation of laborers from Bengal and Orissa to build railway tracks and to work in the tea plantations, collieries, and petroleum fields, new ventures of colonialism in Assam. Indeed, at the heart of the British labor policy was a concerted plan to create fragmented and dependent subaltern groups bound to the work sites, who were unlikely to form communities of opposition in the frontier, which the British knew would be a dangerous and difficult situation to control. The representation was widely circulated that there is nothing that an Assamese can or will do. Henry Hopkins, the agent to the governor general in Assam, wrote extensively on the subject of why local Assamese should not be hired by the new British administration. He explained: "However carefully their selection is made they cannot on the whole be expected to be much above the levels of the general capacity of their countrymen and I would rate the capacity of the Assamese . . . as much below that of other races in India . . . They are acute and subtle but nature has over bountifully supplied them with the means of gratifying their material wants . . . and *their addiction to the vice of eating opium has caused them to be apathetic, enervate, and self-indulgent* . . . The official class though I believe they had been bettered by our teaching, are yet not so far advanced as to have entirely parted with their national character and they cannot be trusted."[55]

In Assam, the local Assamese became the disinherited masses, gradually falling into an abyss of poverty and social vice. Rising revenue demands, importation of labor, and the denial of employment to local people combined to make the people of Upper Assam, the erstwhile subjects of the swargadeos, the most abject population within the province. Adding to these woes, rampant land acquisition for cash crop production by European settlers forced many small peasants out of their fields. They were driven out of their land to forage in nearby forests, where they settled new village communities.[56] These marginal communities today form the backbone of the Tai-Ahom revivalism movement.

### THE ECONOMICS OF BEING ASSAMESE

Alongside the propagation of opium cultivation and use, other commercial ventures were started in Assam. But the local people—the Assamese—were largely kept outside of the operations and did not share in the benefits that followed. In fact, most communities of Upper Assam were utterly neglected while their land was confiscated for tea plantations. Fearing that "some [British] gentlemen [were] preparing to cultivate tea . . . over the maidams [tombs of dead ancestors]," the deposed swargadeo, Purandar Singha, made a final appeal to the colonial administration to stop the rampant land grabbing. He explained that "these tombs are in a manner holy with us and the cultivating of tea or any thing on them . . . has caused me great distress and I have addressed you entrusting that they will be ordered to leave these remains and repair those they have destroyed."[57]

*Maidam* was the royal burial site used by aristocracy and royalty. The system of "giving maidam" involved burying the deceased king with all his belongings, material goods, wives, slaves, and the lukurakhun or pallbearers. According to *Satsari Buranji* the practice of giving maidam involving the sacrifice and burial of people with the king started in the reign of Suhungmung in the fifteenth century, and continued until the reign of Pramatta Singha in the mid-eighteenth century. The burial custom of the Ahom royalty seems unique, but as a practice of worship to the god-kings, it is not peculiar. Human sacrifices to gods and goddesses were common in the region of Assam, and among the hill tribes these rituals were related to fertility cults. The custom of scalping that was practiced among various hill groups of Nagas was said to capture the "life substance" of the victim so that it could be offered on behalf of a dead chief to enable a better life for him in the next world. The Lakhers, a small "tribal" community in the

Lushai hills of Mizoram, buried along with their chief several slaves to enable him to make his journey to the next world.[58]

In the Assam kingdom, because swargadeos were worshipped as gods the burial ground or maidam was consecrated as a sacred mausoleum. The first royal cemetery of the swargadeos was established in the first capital city, Charaideo, on the hilltop. There swargadeos, queens, and princesses were buried along with the Mughal generals who had been captured and beheaded (Gogoi 1976, 90, 92). Over time, new maidams were established and they stretched from Jorhat to Dibrugarh in Upper Assam. Until the end of "Ahom" rule, maidams continued to be sacred grounds where only royalty and aristocracy were buried. As a result, for the last swargadeo what stood above the earth (the mounds) and what was underneath the ground (the bones of his ancestors) were very important. These sites housed the memory of the past and its glories. The mounds symbolized height and achievement and were the central points establishing the might of the royal family among their relatives, villages, title holders, and even strangers. Literally, the ancestors on the hill of Charaideo created identity for the royalty and served as the binding force for the multiglot and multiethnic subject population. Thus when the relics were desecrated and tea was grown over them, Purandar Singha, the last swargadeo, made his feelings known to colonial agents. Maybe this appeal came too late, for the governor general did not stop the process that was underway in Assam. The requisition of the elevated maidam lands, considered good for tea cultivation (because tea plants require good drainage), did not stop despite the swargadeo's request for the colonials to do so. Today the main tea belt in Assam spreads from Charaideo to Tinsukia, and it is literally built on top of the bones and remains of the royalty and aristocracy of the erstwhile Ahom kingdom.

In 1834 the governor general set up a committee to explore the possibility of commercial tea growing in Assam. The systematic cultivation of tea began in 1837, and the first batch (350 pounds) was auctioned on January 10, 1839, in London. Tea became the new commercial venture in Assam, and several business houses in London set up offices and plantation companies to tap directly into the tea business. In 1839, Robert Bruce and his cohorts founded the Assam Company, which was followed twenty years later in 1859 by the Jorehaut Tea Company. The power and influence of the tea companies in the administration of Assam increased tremendously as their revenue kept growing. In fact, it would not be an exaggeration to say that Assam was created sometime in the mid-nineteenth century as a result of the global trade in tea. For an average British person, as Reid recalls, "Assam was merely a place connected with tea and perhaps big game."[59] Later, the tea industry lobbied hard to keep the name Assam, the brand name of the tea that sold in Britain, when questions were raised about renaming the area the Northeast Provinces.

Alongside the tea plantations communication and production networks developed, so that the tea grown in Assam could be transported immediately to Calcutta and from there to London for the world markets. Steamers provided the linkage between Assam and Calcutta, and the British-owned India General Steam Navigation Company carried out most of the transactions. Because internal river transport proved unprofitable, the development of roadways within Assam was initiated. As early as 1845, the Assam Company claimed that it had opened and repaired over eight hundred miles of public roads. The effort was to connect local tea gardens with the outside world, particularly for business and commerce. Weekly markets were started where established traders and peddlers participated. It was in this context that a class of enterprising money lenders and businessmen, commonly called Marwaris, emerged. The Marwaris migrated from north India and Calcutta and settled in Assam, and they became the contacting agents for the planter class with Calcutta and enabled the easy transfer of money in the form of bills of exchange, or *hundis*, to and from the tea houses in Assam and elsewhere. The entrepreneurial class of Marwaris and European planters became the main beneficiaries of the growing capitalist economy in Assam.

Kenneth Warren of Warren Tea Industries, who worked in Assam from 1906 to 1923, recounts in an oral interview that when his father "arrived in Assam in 1859, there were only two roads—the Rangagora and Jaipur roads, both military roads. The country between Sadiya and Dibrugarh was virgin jungle." In 1906, when he arrived at the Hansuwa Tea Estate at Dibrugarh, a totally different scene welcomed Warren. He states:

> I was disappointed at finding that Dumduma and the district of Dibrugarh, the distance was so civilized. I had expected judging from the things my father had told me about the olden days to land in a bungalow surrounded by lots of forests with lots of elephants, tiger, deer, game and all that on my doorstep. Rather, I found myself in a civilized district. We had six gardens of our company nearly touching each other. There were several other gardens and companies too. There was a club for us in Doomdooma. We played tennis and polo three times a week.

The club was the meeting place. . . . There was a [horse] race meet in all the principal towns—Dibrugarh, Tezpur, and Jorhat.[60]

While life for the English planter class had improved tremendously through capitalist enterprise in tea, the growth was not on the same level for the local people. In fact, their lives correspondingly had deteriorated, and the income generated by the tea industry was not returned to local businesses. The statistics for the year 1844 prove the point. The Assam Company's cost for tea production for that year was Rs. 127,000. The salary of the twenty-five European officers, according to H. A. Antrobus's *A History of the Assam Company* (1957) was no less than Rs. 30,000, or about a quarter of the production cost. Presumably, most of this amount was saved by the officers or spent outside, as spending in the "jungles of Assam" was not even a consideration. Initially, even the rice for the coolie laborers was not bought in Assam but rather imported from Bengal. Similarly, other essentials like mustard oil, sugar, and the like were procured from outside the state. The Marwari agents were important in this long-distance trade: even packing boxes were bought from Calcutta and Chittagong and, until 1847, from Britain. Nothing reveals the lack of investment in Assam better than a note in the company's handbook: "It was the Company's normal policy to purchase the bulk of the gardens' requirement of stores in the United Kingdom and ship them to India. This heading of stores covered not only cultivation tools, factory maintenance materials, such as belting, paint, oil, grease, etc; but tea chests, steel works for building, machinery spares, and tea-making machinery itself" (cited in Antrobus 1957, 240).

Seventy or so Chinese men were employed by the Assam Company. They received Rs. 20,000 annually until 1843, which was four or five times more than what the local Assamese laborers as a whole were being paid. A reliable source is not available for the wage earned by local people from the tea industry, because their employment was seasonal and hence temporary. It was reported however, that there was a chronic shortage of labor in the tea plantations, which suggests that local people were not sufficiently employed because they were somehow considered unfit for labor. Added to the problem of investment in Assam the colonial economy, due to its overenthusiasm for tea cultivation, led to the stagnation of rice cultivation. As a result, the price of rice and other essential commodities increased steeply. Instead of sharing the burden and encouraging food production by making the tax somewhat equal (in fact, tea planters were allowed to cultivate as much land as they could, tax free), the average rice farmer was forced to pay four or five times more in tax. The policy was thus aimed to force the peasant off his land and make him a laborer on the tea plantation. This would have led to a greater reduction in food production, as was the case; although not many Assamese joined the employ of the tea plantations. Increasingly, the plantations became more dependent on outside commodities, thereby leading to further distance between the local economy and capitalist development under colonialism.

By the end of the nineteenth century, Assam became deficient in food grains. By 1901 over one fourth of the total settled land of Assam Valley, or 642,000 acres, was under exclusive proprietary rights. Of this acreage, over 85 percent was held under privileged terms, which meant little or no tax was charged. Only 15 percent of the tea planters paid a comparable rate to that placed on the peasant holdings. But not all of the land that was given up for tea cultivation was really used for that purpose. Why did the government allow the European planters to hold land in excess and not make it available for the local population to offset the food shortage? It appears that this policy, along with the increase in land revenue demand on peasant holdings and the increasing monopoly price on opium, were meant to force the local Assamese farmers from rice cultivation to tea plantation laborers. This policy move had partial results. In 1868–1869, there were 18,783 local laborers compared to the 21,667 imported laborers working on the plantations (Guha 1991, 191). But this pattern was not sustained even after the revenue demand was increased between 1867–1868, 1872–1873, and again in 1893.

The dependence on foreign labor from famine-strickened "tribal" areas from the rest of India grew correspondingly. Large-scale labor recruitment started in the 1870s: from 1870 to 1900 the nonindigenous population increased from 100,000 to 600,000 in Assam. During the same period the local population decreased. In the 1870s the total population of Assam was around 1.5 million, which grew to 2 million in 1891. In 1901 the local population of Assam was still 2 million, and owing to a black fever epidemic the local population decreased by 6 percent. The demographic changes of 1871–1891 were economically very important. The rapid increase in the number of immigrants from other parts of India, combined with the stagnant local population growth, created an imbalance in the distribution of the resources and benefits derived from the modern sector (tea, petroleum, and coal). The Assamese peasants continued to be limited to growing food for subsistence and thus they were not competitors in the market economy.

On the other hand, the remittances out of state increased. Not only was the rich planter class sending their high dividends and savings from their high salaries overseas, but the poor wage laborers imported from outside Assam were also remitting their hard-earned money to geographic areas outside Assam. The net remittances increased from Rs. 90,000 in 1880–1881 to Rs. 500,000 in 1897–1898, and thereafter to nearly Rs. 5,000,000 by 1904–1905. Even the money that remained within Assam for development and capital growth did not reach the local people. Employment as clerks and service personnel was confined to non-Assamese, mainly Bengalis. Marwari traders, on the other hand, held a monopoly on the entire internal trade, including the export of lac, rubber, cotton, pepper, and silk and the import of various manufactured consumer goods and essential items like wheat flour, edible oil, ghee, refined sugar, and piece goods (Guha 1991, 188, 196). The exports and imports from Assam increased rapidly during the last decades of the nineteenth century, but imports always remained around 50 percent of exports (mainly tea). In 1883–1884 the total export surplus from the Assam Valley was Rs. 11,000,000, which increased to an annual average of Rs. 18,000,000 from 1892–1896. The return flow, however, was no more than Rs. 2,000,000 per year (Guha 1991, 197). Thus, at the end of the nineteenth century, Assam was a classic example of an economy gone awry. The divide between the traditional subsistence sector and the capital-intensive, highly monetized sector was gaping. Added to the existing scarcity of rice and food grains as well as the general poverty of the people was the visitation of another disaster: in 1896 a major earthquake rocked Assam. Most of the people in Upper Assam lost whatever little they had, and their situation worsened.

The poverty of the Assamese in the late nineteenth century was contrasted by the wealth of the planter class, which could now invest in technological developments to facilitate tea production and distribution. In 1828 coal was mined in Safrai, near Moran—not far from Sibsagar. Coal mining in Makum started in 1865 and in Ledo in 1882. The establishment of coal mining was of great importance to the tea industry, which until then had depended on wood fuel for running the factories. In 1867 petroleum was accidentally discovered in Nahor Pung, near Jeypore, close to Namrup (now a thriving center of the Tai-Ahom movement). More oil fields were found in Makum and Digboi. Immediately in 1889, by a proclamation of Queen Victoria and Lord Salisbury, secretary of state for India, a blanket concession for ninety-nine years was given to the British Burmah Oil Company for the exploration and exploitation of the petroleum fields in Assam and other areas under British rule.[61] The local entrepreneurs could not safeguard their interests in the crude petroleum of Assam, and by 1926 the oil fields in Digboi were producing 660,317 barrels of crude.[62] Until 1947, Digboi remained the only oil field locally important to the empire and, later, the Indian nation. In 1885 the first railway in the Assam Valley was constructed between Dibrugarh and Sadiya by the Assam Railways and Trading Company, thus connecting the distant tea plantations with the Brahmaputra River.[63] For the time being this railway became the major means of communication with the outside world. Further, the construction of railways, collieries, and oil-drilling operations created a substantial demand for bricks, and in 1890 brickworks were established at Ledo, in Margherita, not far from Digboi.

Forty-one European men managed the oil, coal, and railway enterprises for the empire in Assam.[64] Likewise, all the tea planters were British, mostly from Scotland.[65] The Digboi oil fields were developed for the production of crude oil only; no investment was made for a refinery in Assam. In fact, in 1963, when the government of India in a joint venture with Burmah Oil completed the longest pipeline in South Asia (from Naharkotiya in Upper Assam to Barauni in Bihar), Assamese crude oil was transported at an exorbitant price to a refinery in Bihar, thereby generating little employment or revenue in Assam. The tea industry similarly generated little or no income for the local people. The lack of employment of local Assamese in the colonial establishments, monopolized by the Bengali babus, meant the Assamese could not access and influence colonial policy making for Assam.

The attitude of the Raj toward the people of Upper Assam added to the existing problems. Colonial agents decided that "to an ignorant, stupid and bigotted people like the Assamese, abstract studies are often difficult and unattractive even when communicated in the most common language" (Mills 1854, xxx). Hence the policy was to leave them uneducated and thus open to further exploitation. An English tea planter's wife summed up colonial logic for the lack of an education policy in Assam. She wrote: "There is a little school [in Sibsagar] but in that environment education was not very necessary and anyway, the people are not very intelligent."[66] The sad irony in this story is that while from the beginning the colonial government recognized "the many points of interest in Assam," that interest was confined primarily to the documentation of "descents, customs and languages of its numerous . . . tribes and cultures" (Robinson 1841, 2). Colonial agents and explorers compiled information without taking any interest in indigenous perceptions, knowledge, and communities. K. N. Panikar has argued, in Assam, as in the rest of colonized India, "intellectual curiosity apart, the sheer compulsions of rule dictated the need to contend with the past. The colonial concern with the past, however, was not merely an exercise in 'knowing,' it was an effort in constructing it anew as well" (1995, 108). Once the project of collecting the histories of the various groups of Assam was completed, the census records and categories created, a revenue system established and running, and a system of colonial development put into place, the colonial authorities lost interest in the people and their future.

In the face of an oppressive present evident in an impoverished economy and the marginalization of local culture and community, within certain circles a nostalgic memory and emotion concerning the past began to surface. Almost immediately, after Assam was demarcated as a separate province from Bengal (1874) and again during the partition of Bengal (1905–1911), local awareness of Assamese identity and the Ahom past emerged under the leadership of many organizations (discussed in chapter 1). These groups and organizations had little power to interfere in colonial economic matters. Instead, they concentrated their collective energies on regaining and recovering the history of Assam to create pride in the past. Men like Moniram Dewan, Haliram Dhekial-Phukan, Anandaram Dhekial-Phukan, and Gunabhiram Baruah, all of whom were Brahmins and middle-class gentry, tried to speak for all of the Assamese people. No doubt, these efforts created their own problems. The past propagated by these intellectuals and their organizations verged on the unreal. Following in the line of colonial narratives, they constructed their own Assamese past. The attempt was to create a proud, independent people. Along with the rising tide of Assamese middle-class consciousness, Ahom organizations also emerged. Both Assamese and Ahom organizations invoked the swargadeos as their ancestors, and they were depicted as noble rulers. The Ahom group in particular emphasized the story of migration from Upper Burma. But the swargadeos were also presented as the founders of a settled community in Assam, a valley dwelling; civilized people who differed from hill peoples or uncivilized "tribal" others. It is indeed strange that the colonized subject in Assam, in order to regain some level of dignity and pride in the past, resorted to the colonial framework and conceived themselves superior by typifying other groups in the northeast as low and uncivilized.

The mind was truly colonized in Assam; was there a way out? To probe into this question, I lived in several villages and spent time in "important places" to meet and talk to local people about their memories of the past. The Kareng-ghar was one of those places. But whenever I raised questions about Ahom history, memory, and identity, I encountered the same stories recorded in colonial history books. There was no local or separate memory of the people of Assam. Such encounters made me very uneasy. Was there a time when there was an alternative way of remembering and recounting the past? To find answers to this question I turned to the local literature of Assam, the buranjis.

# CHAPTER 3

# The Memory of the Local:

# The Stories the Buranjis Tell

Buranjis record the history of Assam. I grew up with this assertion, but it was not until 1992 that I saw a buranji. The buranji that Domboru De-odhai showed me was allegedly a thirteenth-century chronicle (later I learned it was a late-eighteenth-century copy). It was written on *sachipat* (bark of aloe wood) and the narrative was in Assamese, or so it appeared to me. Although I did not get an opportunity to read this buranji in the course of my stay in Assam, I was able to read several buranjis at the Directorate of Historical and Antiquarian Studies in Guwahati (DHAS) and the Tai-Ahom Jadughar in Sibsagar. Buranjis tell various tales of the swargadeos and their activities, wars and alliance making, nobles and court politics, exchanges with rival courts and their representatives, natural calamities and auspicious sightings, and religious rituals and worship. In short, the images are multiple but there is one center: the swargadeo.

History in Assam, as determined by the buranjis, is a narrative of kings, where the stories were updated in the reign of each successive king. Buranjis of later periods had new and more detailed information than did the buranjis of earlier periods. As such, each new buranji invoked tales told previously and added new ones current at that time of writing, thus providing continuity and reminding readers of the deeds of previous swargadeos. Recycling is the ethos of buranjis, and hence authorship is not important. Most buranjis are anonymous, and they are rarely dated. For the compilers, the structuring of the material was crucial to producing a narrative, but within that structured narrative divergent tales about swargadeos and their rule were told. Buranji writing was not an exercise in creating ethnic pride or claiming an ethnic identity. The predominance of the swargadeo culture undermined the possibility of any new consciousness, and thus buranjis, in the end, served the purpose of maintaining the institution of kingship in Assam—for, above all, these chronicles were written for royalty. History and epic were one and the same in precolonial Assam, and the remembering society ordered and constructed its memories through the memory of kings and not their own past, even if there was one to go back to. Swargadeos and legendary heroes belonged to Assam and that made the people and the region unique, or at least those who wrote these stories said so. Identity emanated and resided in that understanding. What was this identity?

The precolonial memory of identity in Assam was heterogeneous. Identity was neither particularistic nor unknown but ambivalent, multiple, and fluid, as it is today. Ahom was not a specific group identity, but a position connected to a place—that is, Ahom was only in the domain of swargadeos. One could say that the Ahom were the king's men. This is what I understood after reading several buranjis. The story of the Ahom, as told in the buranjis, can be retold in many ways. The postcolonial leaders and colonial agents told their versions; these I have presented in the previous chapters. In this chapter, I will tell the story of Ahom that the buranjis recount. It is a precolonial tale, nuanced and entwined in the discourse of ambivalence. Within it is an elusive and intriguing shape of something called Ahom. I am not assuming that I can tell the story of the Ahom as the contemporaries who wrote the buranjis told them. My location as a twenty-first-century historian reading precolonial accounts belies such a possibility.

### REMEMBERING ORIGINS: THE TALE OF HEROES

The *Satsari Buranji* inaugurates the establishment of an Ahom polity in Assam by the legendary Sukapha. Part of this story is offered as follows:

> In ancient times, even after three yugas[1] had elapsed, Brahma [god of creation] could not create man. Hence, he planted a gourd tree. Inside it were humans, they sprung out from the fruit. They knew nothing and were like beasts. In order to civilize these creatures, Lord Indra sent Nangkun.[2] They became his subjects. Satya Yuga ended in peace. . . . In Treta yuga there was discord. The strong began to oppress the weak. Indra prayed for peace. He also sent his two grandsons. . . . They came down on a golden ladder.[3] In this way, Indra sent his two grandsons, Khun Lung and Khun Lai, to earth. They descended in Mung-ri-mung-ram.[4] But there was an argument. Khun Lung went back to heaven. Khun Lai stayed on earth. . . . Khun Lung's progeny ruled the king-

dom. . . . Four thousand two hundred years of Kali Yuga had transpired. The Nora king's sister, Nangnaam, was his wife.[5] She was expecting a child. He sent her back to her father's house. Sukhrangpha was born in his grandfather's home. Another sister had a son named Sukapha. He said, "two tigers cannot live in one den. Two elephants cannot stay in one stable. Two kings should not stay in the same kingdom. Hence I would like to go to the southern region. You continue to be the king here." To this Sukhrangpha replied, "very well, you may go. But send me tribute every year." He gave Sukapha 9,000 men, a lot of jewelry, bows and arrows, spears, one male and a female elephant, a trainer for the elephants, and thirty horses with blinders. . . . Somdeo was the god of wealth, prosperity, and knowledge . . . in that year, Somdeo had to be worshiped. They found that the icon was missing. They realized that Sukapha had taken it with him. The king sent his men to bring back the icon. They fought with Sukapha's men. But they were defeated and had to return. The migrating group (under Sukapha) captured many villages along the way, and got a lot of booty. Those who resisted were killed and their brethren were forced to eat human flesh. . . . He crossed the Namkiu lake and arrived at Khamjang.[6] . . . Along the way, a number of people were captured. They were either Chutias, Morans, [or] Barahis . . . given names according to the task they performed.[7] . . . Women were introduced in their band. . . . From Tipam they crossed Dihing, Dikhou, and came to the banks of the Dilimukh.[8] . . . In the south there were the Kacharis,[9] in the north were Barahi-Morans. After an extended discussion the Barahis agreed to supply firewood. They said, "these people are not simply anybody. They are heavenly creatures. Their physical attributes say so." . . . Thus the king and his men, from now on, were referred to as Ahom. Four Barahi-Moran princesses were taken in marriage by the king. . . . In the temples of the Morans and Barahis, Sukapha offered sacrifices. The spirits were appeased. Thus Sukapha took over the place and the political system. He had two sons and one daughter. He ruled for thirty years. (Bhuyan 1960, 1: 1–20; translation mine)

Carefully plotted, the *Satsari Buranji* strings together a series of fragmentary episodes focusing on themes such as evolution, exploitation, and competition, as well as dismemberments and reorganizations in which both gods and men are presented as equal partners undertaking a shared journey spanning several epochs. The narrative, as we know, begins with the story of gods descending to the earth on a golden ladder and establishing their "home" somewhere in Upper Burma. There they found a polity and became known as Nora. In the Assamese language, Nora signifies a male person. In a way, one can say that gods became human (men) in Upper Burma, or so they are assessed in the buranjis. The Nora kingdom slowly expanded to bring in new peoples and territories. Eventually, though, the divine progenies were motivated to look for new areas and people to rule over and, as a consequence, a group under the command of Sukapha decided to migrate westward. They encountered many new people on their way. While many of these people joined them voluntarily, others fought and were killed in the struggle for control.

For me the key issue here is not the myth itself but rather the motivation that created the myth and the outcome it produced. While the buranji pays a lot of attention to the dual phenomena of dismemberment and reorganization, its main purpose is to direct the reader's attention to the process that inaugurated a glorious history of the itinerant community in the Upper Assam Valley. Social, political, and mystical developments, it seems, transformed them into rulers and enabled them to become the Ahom there. Leaving no space for ambiguity, the narrative establishes Sukapha as the foundational character of the story in Assam. In Assam, Sukapha became the fountainhead of an "unequal, peerless" group of Ahom, the buranji tells us. It is necessary to recall that the narrator does not give any more details about this newly constituted Ahom community. We do not know what made them Ahom, except that they were the followers of Sukapha. Aside from his presence in their midst no common ethnicity, language, or religion bound the group together. We do not even know who they were and what motivated them to join Sukapha in his mission of conquest. It seems the narrative functioned as an epic whose main purpose was to commemorate the deeds of Sukapha, the hero. His followers are posed in the story to glorify the activities and accomplishments of the hero. The narrative is not a story of Ahoms but of Sukapha, who is the main character. Like the bulk of Sukapha stories that have circulated in Assam, this one was not dated or signed by an author.

A question that immediately arises is what was the purpose of such a telling? Also, what was the connection between the signifiers of Sukapha and Ahom? Sukapha, as I argue in chapter 2, cannot convincingly be proven to be a historical personage, nor can we conclude that he was an invented character. The power of the story of Sukapha lies in the fact that it served as an aid to order a narrative and structure a political memory that undid the messy and multiple memories of the diverse groups that made up the populace of precolonial Assam. By prioritizing Sukapha as a hero par excellence with a divine mandate to rule the Assam Valley, it became possible to project a noble and heroic identity for those associated with him. It appears that contemporaries understood this metaphor of Sukapha and used it to generate a story of a polity. Within the polity, it appears, were some men who were designated as Ahoms. For the scribes of the buranjis it mattered little to define the Ahom in black-and-white terms. Several centuries later, it has become very difficult to understand the buranjis' meaning of "Ahom." This problem is of concern to me because I cannot determine definitively what "Ahom" meant in precolonial Assam. Yet any attempt to analyze the history of this label results in a direct encounter with a full-blown identity movement that has been launched under the same banner. Is there a way to make the precolonial Ahom comprehensible on its own terms? Does the Ahom of the buranjis share an affinity with the current meanings of Ahom as an identity? To enter into a dialogue with these various time frames and understandings of label and identity we have to engage with the stories that the buranjis tell (like the one referred to above), for we have nothing but the memory stored in the buranjis to go back to in order to find the Ahoms. While the story of Sukapha stands uncontested, there is some debate concerning what should be the name by which we should refer to these chronicles. Some prefer to call them *puthis*, meaning "religious" books; others call them buranjis, meaning "history" books. The naming is crucial, for therein lies the enigma: is it mundane history or sacred philosophy that the narratives memorialize?

### THE MAKING OF BURANJIS

The etymology of the term "buranji" is a matter of debate. In 1794, Wade first came across some chronicles that he called *buloonji*: "roopoot" histories or "documents of knowledge" of the swargadeos, which he compared to the Japanese "boronjis" or "sacred letters."[10] Beyond making this flimsy linguistic correlation, Wade did not investigate the history and tradition of buranji writing, although he met some of the last scribes of these texts. G. E. Grierson, who compiled the *Linguistic Survey of India* (1904), proclaimed that the word buranji is an Ahom word, made by combining three separate words: "bu"—"ignorant," "ran"—"teach," and "ji"—"storehouse." Put together, the words meant "storehouse to teach the ignorant"

(67). Although Grierson did not know the Ahom language, his interpretation became the standard explanation for the term. Thus it is no surprise that local scholars of Assam, namely Numal Gogoi and J. N. Phukan, both of whom claim to be Tai-Ahom, have questioned the colonial usage in these accounts. Gogoi suggests that the documents should be called *pulanchi* because they were "the papers of grandfather to grandchildren" (1987, 162). Phukan compares them to the "Che Chi" accounts, which he says is the Chinese history for historians, a tradition of writing that, he posits, migrant groups brought with them to Assam from Yunnan—their original homeland. He argues that initially this genre did not have a name, but "as Ahoms were exposed to the Sanskritic tradition a term was developed from the local Pali and Sanskrit languages, and it probably stands for Puran Panji" (1994, public lecture). While academics are anxious to fix a label, the chronicles themselves do not engage in name calling. In fact, the chronicles hardly ever refer to themselves as buranjis. One of the first chronicles in which this appellation appears is the *Tungkhungia Buranji*, written in 1804. Following it, in 1835, we see Kashinath Tamuli-Phukan use the term for his narrative, which he titled the *Assam Buranji*.

Even more confusing are the questions of how and why the tradition of buranji writing developed in Assam. Were these accounts written in the language of the Noras, the ancestors of Sukapha, or in the language of another group that brought with them an advanced writing system and introduced it into Sukapha's band? How did the collective that was in its formative stages decide what of their diverse memories to include and exclude? In other words, whose stories are recorded and what was the purpose? Were they written for a general audience of listeners and readers, or were they specifically meant for royalty? Many more questions can be asked, but the fact remains that buranjis do not give us too many hints about how we should approach them. Buranjis communicate messages that are difficult to grapple with and analyze from our current standpoint. At best, we can evaluate them as texts or documents rather than read them as "sources" from which we can mine a specific history of a defined group called the Tai-Ahom.

Consider the question of the origin of buranjis that were recorded in a late-seventeenth-century manuscript. The story of the origin of buranjis is recounted in these words: "He, Sukapha, crossed the river Namkiu and arrived at Khamjang. There he counted his people—sixty people had died, seven were lost. Rajadeo Sukapha said, 'whoever dies, whoever we capture, any conversation that takes place on the way, must be recorded.' "[12] This particular reference is retrospectively considered to be the genesis of buranji writing. If it is true, this was a major transition: a motley group of migrants were not only able to identify a need to record their activities, but were able to produce a technique and format that guided the transformation of oral accounts and memories into a written record. Further, they were able to use writing as a tool for embedding recent community memory, so that in the process of migration and settlement in a new territory, information concerning the followers of Sukapha, those who constituted the "original" community, was not lost. The way the story is told in this buranji is that every activity was to be recorded as a tool to conserve facts, a process that aided in the internalization and conceptualization of a new kind of social memory. Thus, the actors of history also become narrators of historical developments and commentators on their experiences, and consciously collated and connected them to tell a story of themselves. While this is not impossible (throughout human history people have told stories of themselves and others), it is somewhat difficult to accept that a conscious writing system developed within the uncertain conditions of migration in the thirteenth century. Also, this account does not convincingly tell us how this recorded memory was put to use. Writing can develop in "simple" subsistence economies with less pronounced social hierarchies, but like Jack Goody (1986), I believe the potential of utilizing complex narratives as an artifact is only possible in complex productive and exploitative economies. In precolonial India this developed in stratified palace and temple economies. The drive to create and legitimize narratives was intimately tied to the drive of certain groups to acquire and keep power.

From the buranji literature that has survived through time, we learn that the seventeenth century was a period of intense activity focused on community organization and on the consolidation of state power in the swargadeo's domain. Cynthia Talbot (2001) has argued that in the Deccan, around the seventeenth century, court chronicles began to be written in response to several political and social changes that were taking place. Norman Zeigler, in his study of Rajasthani chronicles (1976), emphasizes the intense political activities in the region during the late sixteenth and early seventeenth centuries and suggests that chronicle writing developed as an "adaptive response" to Muslim conquest and the threat it posed to local power positions. I agree with both of them that rapid changes in internal and external conditions in seventeenth-century India prompted different communities to create some sense of order of the past and present and record what they thought relevant. But I would hesitate to say that the tradition of buranji writing in Assam emerged suddenly in the seventeenth century, as much as I am critical of the local Ahom historians' claim that buranji writing developed in the thirteenth century. Tale telling in the swargadeo's domain undoubtedly developed as a process, and the recording of old and new tales was meant to take account of the processes of change, adaptation, and integration that happened throughout the rule of the swargadeos. This is evident in the narrative style, the stories that buranjis tell, the orthography that borrows from different sources and tells of interactions and exchanges through time, the composition of buranjis that mix a variety of legends current in different time periods, and the like. On the whole, buranjis enumerate a historical process; they are not artifacts of single momentary experiences.

From the buranjis we learn that in the seventeenth century several Brahmin families were invited to take high positions in the swargadeo's administration. They were employed as representatives of the swargadeo in foreign courts—such as those in neighboring Koch, Tripura, and Manipur, and those as far away as Bengal in the west and Burma in the east.[13] The activities between the courts and the need to create political supremacy and legitimacy for the Ahom swargadeo, one may suppose, intensified the tradition of buranji writing. This writing on the one hand established a "pioneering story" of the polity, simulating a "common memory" of the past for the various people; and on the other hand, it glorified the swargadeo in foreign courts by creating linkages between him and the gods and the well-known heroes of shared cultures and regimes. We can see these themes in several buranjis that were written to record the visits and exchanges between Assam and foreign courts.[14] One can assume that to the listening audience within the domain of the swargadeo, the meaning and uses of the texts in external circles were not very important concerns. Still, they must have been drawn to the praise and rhetorical dramatizing of their rulers and probably accepted the stories they heard about the swargadeos. Facilitated by the repetitive mention of gods and heroes, who had been carefully inserted into the narrative at key points, the audience remembered the basic outline and accepted the structured vocabulary of community genealogy. The pioneering story of the swargadeos as the fountainhead of the community in Assam was established.

Internally, an "oikotype" ("home type"; Fentress and Wickham 1992, 74) memory was thus founded, and a narrative of community followed.

A close reading of the chronicles to evaluate their prose style, orthography and language, narrative structure, and stories indicates that buranji writing developed and took off in the late seventeenth century. This tradition continued until the first half of the twentieth century. Some popular buranjis, like *Assam Buranji Puthi* (1906) and *Ahom Buranji* (1923), were commissioned by colonial officers. These are not wholly new texts but were compiled from several older buranjis that contained scattered information. The new colonial buranjis were printed and produced as if they were history books, which in very dramatic ways transformed the nature and context of buranjis in Assam.

Almost all buranjis, whether of the seventeenth century or later, claim to be narratives of the genealogy of the swargadeos. The *Tungkhungia Buranji* opens with the lines "Homage to Sri Krishna. Homage to Ganesh . . . This buranji is . . . Sri Sri Tungkhungia Vamsavali [genealogy]." The *Assam Buranji* describes itself as an account of the genealogies of the "lunar line" of the kings of Assam. Titles such as *Raja Vamsa Katha* ("Narrative of the royal family"), *Raja Vamsavali Katha* ("Narrative of the genealogy of kings"), *Janma Katha* ("Narratives of origin"), *Purushar Vamsa Katha* ("Narrative of the genealogy of ancestors"), *Ahom Swargadeo Utpatti* ("The origin of the Ahom kings"), and *Rajanam Charita* ("Narrative of royalty") or simply *Vamsavali* ("Genealogy") are commonly used to describe the contents of buranjis. Although tracing the roots of the swargadeos and placing them in the right order on a genealogical chart was the main focus of the buranjis, the emphasis within the narrative became the praise of the king. This was used to remind the audience of the glory of the ruler, and they were invited to partake in the aura of sacred kingship.

Like Brahmanical astrological texts, buranjis, particularly the ones that cover the early periods, provide a lot of details regarding the date, especially the months, and *saka* (year), of events relating to the swargadeos.[15] Natural occurrences and calamities were also of great concern to the scribes. This detailed record keeping allowed for calculations, predictions, enumerations of auspicious and inauspicious times, and so on. A temporal sequence was strictly maintained; keeping the narratives simple allowed for several repetitions. Despite the temporal emphasis, the chronology of the buranjis is not dependable for historical reconstruction, and several violations in recording the events and actors are noticeable. These violations lead me to conclude that buranjis functioned as a rhetorical device to forge a sense of coherence for community and memory in Assam, and a structured genealogy facilitated the process, but it was not used or seen to be like modern history books of our time.

Perhaps it would be easier to understand the nature of buranjis if we put them in the context of the place wherefrom they emerged. One can say that buranjis are, and are about, the varieties of interactions and exchanges that were taking place in Assam. In this sense, the text, the society, and the place served as and became a crossroads for meeting, assimilating, and restructuring various influences and communities. Memories overlaid memories, and the narratives became vehicles and documents of the crossroads. The process was continuous as new sets of images were added to include the expanding audiences in extended settlements.

The natural tendency in the buranjis is to suppress what is not meaningful to the fluid communities at the crossroads of culture and history, and to substitute with what seems appropriate to the audience. Thus, in the buranjis of Assam we find a variety of images but no definite descriptions of groups. Fluidity and elasticity are the two themes that are emphasized. An illustration to this effect can be gleaned from the *Satsari Buranji*, which records events in the reign of Swargadeo Pratap Singha (1603–1641). In this tale, the emphasis is put on maintaining elasticity so as to avoid the demarcation of communities within the swargadeo's polity. The logic for this is expressed in the voice of a minister who reminds the king: "In the past, your ancestors attacked and killed the enemy and thus expelled them from the land, but they did not erect walls. If ramparts are now built, they will become unalterable boundaries between the Kacharis and us" (Bhuyan 1960, 163: 76, translation mine). In this and similar tales, the buranji upholds the fluid identity of a crossroads society that discouraged separation between communities.

Exclusive, demarcated identities were perceived as counterpolitic. Arguably, identity was not unknown to the people, but fixity was not the ethos. Thus, the boundaries between the "us" and the "them" remained flexible. There is nothing in the *Satsari Buranji* to tell us specifically who is "us" or what constitutes "us," but we are made aware that "us" is not different from "them"—the Kacharis. This relationship is emphasized again in another buranji. When Swargadeo Jayadhvaj Singha's (1648–1663) army attacked the small kingdom of Gobha the Kachari men ran away, leaving behind the old, the invalid, and the women. At nightfall, the women came out of hiding and found to their surprise that the swargadeo's soldiers looked and behaved no differently from their [Kachari] men. They befriended the soldiers, saying, "You are no different from us. We are alike" (Bhuyan 1990, 132: 228). In a context of fluctuation and change, the consciousness of "us" and "them" was never firm, and the stories of similarity linked people together and made the polity an interactive place for several different groups and communities. The buranjis adhere to these themes and create stories that serve as vehicles to join rather than separate the people. The narrative of the buranjis maintains the multiplex experiences of the various peoples. The institution of the swargadeo served to realize a polity and gave some coherence to its fluid culture. Yet, the emphasis on the "swargadeo culture" was not intended as a single, fixed center. Buranjis served as documents of power, stabilizing while maintaining fluidity.

One may wonder if the tradition of writing buranjis was a specialty of the polity founded by Sukapha. A careful examination of neighboring communities and cultures in the eastern region shows that it is a shared tradition. The Kochs, Kacharis, and Jaiantias also maintained the tradition of writing.[16] Small chieftains like the Bara Bhuyans, Chutias, and even the Dimarua had their chronicles (Gait 1963, viii). The *Rajamala*—a narrative of the kings of Tripura—was well known to the Assam scribes.[17] In this context it is plausible to suggest that buranji writing was part of a common tradition of the region. One can also see several parallels between the buranji tradition and the Puranic writings of ancient India. Like the Puranas, buranjis are records of the past and memorize embedded and externalized history. However, there are also several differences between the buranjis of Assam and the writing traditions of the neighboring courts. Buranjis were never written in Sanskrit but rather in Assamese, and occasionally in a Tai language that is sometimes referred to as Ahom, although this language was unknown to most of the populace of Assam.[18] For certain, Brahmin priests who would have been illiterate in their language did not write Ahom buranjis. Hence, Ahom buranjis do not uphold or claim to be the written tradition of a Brahmanic (priestly) or a Kshatriya (warrior) culture.[19] They are manuals of local shamans, deodhais, and bailungs who wrote about kings and their activities for rituals of divination and oracle telling. Often in these documents the writing is accompanied by symbolic and intricate drawings that were designed to predict political and religious activities and their outcomes for the royalty and their supporters (Terwiel and Wichasin 1992). Many of these documents were written or drawn on cloth, as well as on strips of cane, bamboo, and wood, and were used for esoteric rituals and worship activities that were kept extremely secret.[20] It appears that this style of buranji writing lost its prominence in the latter periods as the importance of Brahmins increased in the court.

The discovery of some of these Tai-language buranjis by colonial agents led to a gross oversimplification that fueled the idea that a "foreign" group had migrated from the hills of Burma into Assam, established an Ahom kingdom, and used the buranji literature to record their history and culture. By one stroke of the colonial pen, buranjis were made into the history books of the Ahom. They also were fixed as a single genre together with the Assamese buranjis. But for scribes and audiences then, and now for readers like me, this supposition disrupts another logic, the logic of plurality that guided, shaped, and created buranjis. Buranjis followed different styles of writings, their contents are various, and they served a variety of audiences. There were specific buranjis written for *chaklang* marriage ceremonies, which were read aloud (Bhuyan 1990, 260: 146–47). There were buranjis that were written to defame a rival noble (Tamuli-Phukan 1906, 55; Bhuyan 1931, 256–63), and some written to glorify kings or to construct genealogies of the royalty and nobility, as previously described. A seventeenth-century buranji sometimes told different stories compared to the eighteenth- and nineteenth-century buranjis. Likewise, the orthography, language, structure, and so on differed among buranjis. The intermingling influences and processes that produced buranjis as a voice of and about the crossroads were lost when colonial historians strung together all of them as one body of literature. Context was replaced by assumptions in the colonial period and the power of colonial assumptions facilitated a narrativization of these texts as the history books of a defined Ahom group.

The peculiar political considerations that shaped the British "finding" of the Ahom and their books (buranjis) has not been questioned by local scholars. Rather, they have accepted the colonial reading of these texts without evaluating the chronicles and the plots they convey. Buranjis and Ahoms—terms unfamiliar to most local people during the swargadeos' rule—today define a specific group and their history. As a result the multiple moorings and processes of construction that characterized the writing of the buranjis have been lost, along with the shared traditions and crossroads culture that they invoked.

Why should we be bothered with the colonial transformation of buranjis? Quite simply, because this transformation has silenced all other possible readings of the chronicles and has imposed on them a presence (that is not there). The singular reading of buranjis as the history of Ahoms happened in the interaction of two unequal institutions: on the one hand was colonialism, backed by the apparatus of a state that was determined to discover a history of the natives; and on the other hand were the local people who were diverse, powerless, and had multiple and messy memories about their past. The messiness was reordered by the colonialist who made history in Assam an ethnic artifact of the Ahom. Both history and the contents of the buranjis were thus fixed. The neatly packaged story of an Ahom community served colonial purposes, as we saw in the last chapter. But should the colonial representation be our determining lens now? Given that conditions have changed, we can reexamine the buranjis and the stories they tell on their own terms as well as consider their use in the present Tai-Ahom movement. Will that allow us to extract an "authentic" history of the Ahom past? I seriously doubt it. Nonetheless, engaging the chronicles and their stories generates a dialogue that can acknowledge the multiplicity of possible readings. In my opinion it is in such a dialogue, and in the acknowledgment of varied perspectives, that we can find some authenticity.

### THE "US" AND THE AHOM

The hundred or so buranjis at the DHAS in Guwahati and at the Tai-Ahom Jadughar in Sibsagar tell manifold stories of the "Ahom kingdom."[21] I have not read all of these buranjis, which was neither possible nor necessary because most of them are copies of copies. As mentioned earlier, all contain a standard story. Generally buranjis invoke a format that begins with the story of Sukapha. This format is characteristic of the nature of their production and is meant to uphold the swargadeo culture. On the one hand, in these chronicles stories of common people and their communities of origin are not recorded at any great length. To acknowledge them would have meant recognizing the specific communities and different groups, and doing so would have gone against the swargadeo cult as the one and only legitimate center of identification for the polity. On the other hand, because the groups that came together under the swargadeo's administration were diverse, they had to be represented, if at all, as a composite community living within the swargadeo's domain. Thus, along with the discourse of the cult of the swargadeo, the buranjis developed a narrative of the "us" group that was to serve as an identity for the people.

The "us" in the swargadeo's domain, the Assam Valley, was a fluid, inclusive, and amorphous community.

The creation of the "us" group was a continuous process. The intermingling of several groups, some situated close to the powerful center and many others far removed from the center of the swargadeos' administration (and only connected through the network of several intermediary officers), did not solidify into an easily identifiable "us." Nonetheless, the metaphorical "us" kept alive the ethos of fluidity; the crossroads did not become a site for a fixed identity. Within that lucid space of "us" an administrative pyramid was also put into place as a strategy to maintain the balance of power and relegate duties.

At the top of the pyramid was the swargadeo. The office of swargadeo was limited to six princely families: the *mels*, or estates, of the Saringia, Dihingia, Tipamia, Tungkhungia, Namrupia, and Samuguria. These names were all derived from their places of residence. For example, the *Deodhai Assam Buranji* informs us that after "Sukapha descended to the plains, his three sons came and settled in the area which is now called Tingkhang. The one who settled there is called Tinghkhangia or Tungkhungia. The other one settled in Dihing and is known as Dihingia, and the one in Upor Saring is called Saringia" (Bhuyan 1990, 223: 129; translation mine). In the course of time, three more mels were created; and thus the number was raised to six royal houses from which the swargadeo selected princes. Additionally, the offices of three *gohains*, or nobles the Borgohain, the Bura Gohain and the Bar Patra Gohain—were created.[22] These men controlled most of the populace of the kingdom, which was divided into several *faids* or service groups. The direct control of the service groups, which meant a control of the labor force, made these nobles very powerful, often more powerful than the princes. In precolonial Assam, where tax was not in cash but in kind, control of labor was crucial. In order to restrict the expanding power of the three principal nobles, the swargadeo created several new offices and increased the number of nobles in the kingdom. Along with the three gohains, the offices of the Bar Barua and Bar Phukan also became very powerful. In 1826, when the British first occupied Assam, the nobility was a sizable group. This probably led the colonials to think that there were two defined ethnic groups in the Assam kingdom—one made up of Ahoms, from which the sovereign and nobility were selected, and the other made up of the diverse ethnic groups that formed the commoners (Hamilton 1828, 1: 171–75). The faids that were controlled by the nobles were conglomerations of *khels* or labor units. The entire male populace of the kingdom was divided among the khels; some were skilled, others were unskilled *paiks* (laborers).[23] A paik or individual laborer was the smallest unit in the khel. As an individual the paik had neither identity nor a place in society. He was located and categorized within a *got*, which was formed by a combination of four paiks. Several gots made up a khel. To inhibit khel solidarity, paiks were constantly moved from place to place and between khels. Any form of resistance by a paik was severely punished. The creation of the khels and faids allowed for the construction of the "us" community as an administrative device; its shape, numerical strength, and composition were subject to continuous change and reformulation. A single definite identity for the populace was still unthinkable in precolonial Assam.

What was the political appeal to creating the unbounded "us" rather than devising and maintaining group identities based on ethnicity? First, the logic of the time was state building. The efforts and activities of the administration concentrated on the acquisition of territory and new groups of people. By so doing, the swargadeo's administration enhanced its resource base and enabled further expansion. In a nonmonetized economy such as Assam, wealth was calculated in terms of the labor that one controlled. The acquisition of new people made new settlements and expansion possible and, in turn, glorified the swargadeo even more. We have several examples in the buranjis that elucidate this crucial political strategy. For instance, in the reign of Pratap Singha (1604–1648) a census of the population was undertaken to determine the numerical strength of the kingdom, identify gaps in the service groups, and create new faids to facilitate the swargadeo's mission to become most powerful king of the region.[24] As stated in the *Satsari Buranji*,

> *Those who were in the kingdom, as well as those outside the regular settlements, were now put together.* Three men formed a got, twenty of them were a *boratu*, one hundred were *saikiatu*, and a thousand were a *hazarika*. In this way the entire population of the kingdom was counted and categorized. The subjects asked the eldest daughter of the king to represent their grievances against this compulsory division and settlement. The king did not pay any attention to this complaint. The king summoned the three gohains and directed that they should distribute the people according to the position of the commander. . . . Archers were given eight pura of land and ordinary paiks were given seven. . . . In this way the gohains divided the land according to the regulation and placed the

men according to the recent arrangement. (Bhuyan 1960, 3: 164; translation and italics mine)

Second, the political process of state building was combined with economic motivation. As shown above, by bringing together—sometimes with the use of force—a varied and expanded populace within the swargadeo's administration, a vast community of workers was created. Originally many belonged to "enemy groups" who were defeated and incorporated within "our territory and constituted into one big community and kingdom" (Bhuyan 1960, 3: 161–62; translation mine). The creation of this "us" group facilitated the construction and narrativization of a new history. The buranjis delivered the story line and embedded a new memory. Differences between the varieties mattered little—it was the laboring potential of the men that mattered to the swargadeo and that was extracted through complex rules and regulations. The warrior-agricultural ethos of society deleted all ethnic markers of the subject groups. Rather, the domain of the swargadeo became an eclectic space in which the rituals, customs, traditions, and so on of Bantun, Akhaampha, and Tungkhul Naga tribes, along with those of Morans, Barahis, Sungis, Chutias, Kacharis, Jaiantias, Brahmins, and "Bangali" (Muslims) meshed together and created a haphazard syncretic "us" community. It is to this unmistakably loose, undefined subject community of "us" in the service of the swargadeos that the buranjis often refer to. The system of the creation and the domination of the "us" community was both a political and economic exigency (A. Guha 1991).

The buranjis rarely mix the terms "us" and "Ahom." The Tai buranji does not refer to Ahom; rather the people of the swargadeo's realm are described as *kun-how/roa*, which translates as the generic "us." In the Assamese buranjis, occasionally, we find reference to the Mungkungia Ahamia people,[25] but the commonly used term for describing the populace is *ami*, which, once again, translates as "us." The appeal of strategically creating the "us" community began in the seventeenth century, as discussed earlier, but the process of making the "us" group continued over time. In buranjis that record the events of the late eighteenth and early nineteenth centuries, we find several references that reinforce the ethos and continuity of the "us" community. For instance, in the reign of Rajeshwar Singha (1751–1769), several groups of runaway soldiers from Manipur—along with their king and members of the royal family—came to the swargadeo's domain and sought his protection. Rajeshwar Singha

settled them near Disao and gave them a *khat* (estate) for their maintenance. Even after the return of the Manipur king to his domain, this group
continued to live in the swargadeo's kingdom. They became known as
Mugul and their settlement became Mugulukhat (Tamuli-Phukan 1906,
55; translation mine). In the eyewitness records of Captain Welsh and
Jenkins of 1794, we come across references to the integrated Manipuri
community in the swargadeo's army. This, along with the presence of a
variety of people that together constituted the populace, led Captain
Jenkins to the conclusion that "the population of Assam is of very mixed
origin."[26]

If new people were constantly incorporated into the "us" community
that kept growing, how did they discern their place within it? In other
words, was there some identifiable element that made the system comprehensible and accessible to the people? The "us" in the buranji literature,
we have seen, stood for a fluid, generic society. It was a changing body, and
consistency was created by the khel system within which a paik found his
place. Khels, as we have noted, were either part of a mel or faid. These
institutions had two common features: first, they were administered by
one of the six princes or a high noble; and second, they had a spatial
location, which became their label of identification. Built into his system
of association of people with place was the tendency to underplay ethnic
identification and uphold the association with the swargadeo and his
domain as the only conceivable and necessary location of identity. Hence,
when we encounter a specific group in the buranjis, it is really the place
name that is emphasized as the context and location of identity in the
swargadeo's domain.

The swargadeo's domain was a cluster of places, but it was not a continuous territorial unit that could be mapped like a modern country. Rather,
it was made up of many places, some of which were contiguous while
others were dispersed. It was emplacement within the domain that gave a
place its meaning and rendered identity to its inhabitants. A place was
recognized as important only if had a sizable population. Ultimately, people were more important than land, because population in Assam was a
scarce resource. The swargadeos were so invested in keeping the people
they had acquired that they created strict laws to maintain khels and
forbade khel members from traveling outside.[27]

Although the swargadeo's domain was not a defined territorial unit,
it had some distinguishing symbols—such as rivers, forests, and hills—
that served as tools to conceptually demarcate "our" space from that of

"others." Within this range of natural features, the Luit River (also known as Brahmaputra) was upheld as the principal marker. Its tributary, the Namdang, delineated the eastern boundary, and the Manas River flanked the western confines of the swargadeo's domain. Within this space, the scattered, multiple communities constituted "us" and assumed the place names as their identity. Beyond this were "others." Like the "us" community, "they" were an undifferentiated category. The groups constituting "they" were recognized only after alliances were made; then they became *datiyali*, or "neighboring" people, such as the Bhuts (Bhootan), Naga, Mikir, Gobha, and the like.[28] Besides these groups, the Assamese buranjis often mention the "Bangalis," who are referred to in the Tai buranji as "pay-fang-kaw" ("foreigners who crossed the boundary over and over again") to designate the armies that came from the west, from Bengal and beyond, as far as Delhi. This memory of violence associated with the label "Bangali" fuels contemporary anti-Bengali and, ultimately, anti-Indian, campaigns in Assam.

Then, as now, terminology demarcated the world and created a new episteme of identity in the domain of the swargadeo. The buranjis tell us that besides the preponderate "us" group there was another class of people, so to speak, who were called Ahoms. Mention of the Ahom is rare, but it occurs in different settings and conveys a variety of meanings. Evidently, Ahom was a complex institutional naming scheme, which opens up new questions about how to define and understand the Ahom in precolonial Assam. Today, many have made the Ahom past a simple explanation by claiming that the terms refer to an ethnic group. Padmeshwar Gogoi almost singlehandedly determined this trajectory when he wrote his much-acclaimed book, *The Tai and the Tai-Ahom Kingdom of the Brahmaputra Valley* (1968). This categorization foreclosed the possibility of reading the story of Ahom in any other form or shape. Today, the identity seekers of the erstwhile domain of the swargadeo claim they are the Ahom, and by that token they package their history as a single story, removing all traces of the multiple possibilities of their varied backgrounds. I, however, venture to read the story of the Ahom that is told in the buranjis somewhat differently.

The "Ahom" were made by swargadeos to serve their administrations. It was an honored clique to which few men were elevated. But it was neither an ethnic community nor a family inheritance, but rather an identity marker, something to which many aspired but was achieved only by those whom the reigning swargadeo favored to induct into the clique. It was gender determined, for the rewardees who became Ahoms, it is evident from the buranjis, were all men. Depending as it did on the desire and discretion of the swargadeo, becoming an Ahom did not mean that one remained in that position for a lifetime. Indeed, the identity was not permanent but a variable condition easily undone whenever the swargadeo desired. I will discuss the loss of Ahom identity, but first we need to understand how the Ahom was constructed in the reign of different swargadeos.

It is in the buranjis that we encounter Ahoms. Hence, we have to go back to them and engage them to understand the meanings of being Ahom that they convey. In these narratives, the Ahom is not treated as one single entity. The process of making and becoming an Ahom, it seems, evolved through the rule of different swargadeos. The earliest mention of Ahoms comes from Sukapha's period. Sukapha and his two principal nobles are not designated "Ahom" in the buranjis, but his grasscutter and pigkeeper and some of his "warriors" are called Ahoms. Allegedly, twenty-three houses of Ahoms accompanied Sukapha. Along with this group of "regular" Ahoms were another three households of "irregular" Ahoms, although the buranjis do not explain the differences between the two.[29] All of these men, in the course of migration, espoused Barahi women, and a new group called Kadami Ahoms emerged from these unions. No mention of this group is made in the later periods; most probably they were absorbed and distributed between the regular and irregular Ahom groups. The Moran, Barahis, and many other groups were designated as *aniyamar*, or irregular Ahoms.[30] Thus, the "foundational moment" of the Ahom is also represented as a moment of confusion in the buranjis, but I believe this was a political and ideological necessity, because it was one way to leave the context of the Ahom ambivalent and undefined, open and inclusive. The only characteristic that the buranjis claim was shared by the ever-expanding body of Ahoms was that they accompanied Sukapha in his migration to the Assam Valley. In the early phase of settlement in the valley, nothing restricted the easy mixing and intermingling of the migrants with local groups. Within the space of a short time, it appears that Sukapha had a sizable following—an indication of bigger things to follow.

The seven chronicles that were included in the *Satsari Buranji* were compiled in the late seventeenth century. These chronicles tell us that in the sixteenth century, after the defeat of an important local group called Chutia, the power of the migrant warrior-agriculturalist group increased manifold, and their leader was elevated to the status of a swargadeo. The first king to use the appellation of swargadeo was Suklenmung (1539–1552). His predecessor, Suhungmung (1497–1539), was the founder of the office of the swargadeo. Immediately on creating this office, barriers were set up between the high nobles and the commoners and the easy mixing of cultures and people that took place at the level of daily life was discouraged by royal mandate. One can read this as the beginning of class consciousness in the swargadeo's domain. Those who were considered to be or who became Ahoms were demarcated from others. The separation between the two classes—the Ahom and the non-Ahom—was implemented in various ways. Here, for instance, is a comment from Suhung-mung's reign: "The king ordered that all the sons and grandsons of the former chiefs should be brought to his presence. Each of them was given a unit to command. . . . Those that were born out of wedlock were designated as Handique. They could not become princes. They could socialize with Ahoms. The Ahoms could eat from their plates. . . . The grandchildren of the Barahis, who had joined Sukapha—Thamithuma, Thakunath, Thakunkhun—were appointed as the governors of the swargadeo. These men were named Chutia. The commoners were called Chetia. . . . Because of centuries of intermarriage and social interaction with the local people many Ahoms had lost their heritage. The Ahoms who could be identified were accounted for and their status quo was recognized and maintained" (Bhuyan 1960 1: 12–14; translation mine).

Further, in the reign of Surumpha Bhaga Raja (1641–1644) rules were created whereby commoners were forbidden from "building homes on stilt and beams . . . or wearing gold beads, rings, and thuriya.[31] Even Ahoms were to live according to their standard. If they tried to exceed their position they would be put to death" (Bhuyan 1960 1: 28; translation mine). The disorderly past in this way was somewhat ordered, and a class of nobles associated with the swargadeo was created and the maintenance of status was strictly regulated. For those who lived within the domain of the swargadeo the differentiation in rank was emphasized by the use of certain objects as markers of identity, although even at this stage official regulations were not sufficient to fix the boundaries between the commoners and Ahom nobles.

Regarding the institution of marriage one would expect that to establish and maintain kingship and the clan identity of Ahom nobles rules about who could marry whom were also put into place, so that Ahom men had to marry Ahom women. Clearly, however, this was not the case.

The buranjis repeatedly remind us that only men accompanied Sukapha on his initial journey, and in the process of migration he as well as his companions espoused local women. According to the buranjis, Sukapha married four Moran and Barahi women. Likewise, his principal officer, the Bura Gohain, married a Moran woman. The son who was born of this union became the Bura Gohain on the death of his father, and the office continued to be a monopoly of the family for a very long time. The practice of endogamy was discouraged for it was not politically useful. The inclusion of different groups through marriage augmented the strength of the new group of settlers and the ambition to become rulers of the valley motivated the continuation of this practice. Toward this end, swargadeos contracted multiple marriages to make political alliances. Moreover, the king married any women who caught his fancy. Pratap Singha (1603–1641) married a Kachari slave woman, and he gave her son the name Lukmai and raised him as his own.[32] Siva Singha (1716–1744) on becoming swargadeo took his wet nurse, who was the daughter of Lahtokia Koch, as his mistress. He also married Phulmati, a temple dancer, and made her his chief queen. On her death, the king married her sister, who was previously married to Miri Handique Halal Bar Gohain, and bestowed on her the rank of chief queen. Also, he took in marriage another man's wife, Aakori Gabhoru (Bhuyan 1931, 37; Bhuyan 1960, 3:253). Examples like these abound in the buranjis: they recall that the swargadeos and the principal nobles engaged in very suggestive and promiscuous relationships with women of different social and class standings and ethnic backgrounds. Slave women were the most exploited category in precolonial Assam, and they represented different groups—Kachari, Jaiantia, Naga, and others. What is interesting, however, is that some of these women, as noted above, were able to reach the highest available position of chief queen, and their children were recognized and awarded high offices based on their ability and became part of the nobility, the so-called Ahom group.

Almost all of the high officers in the swargadeo's administration came from ethnically mixed and different class backgrounds. For example, in the case of the Ahom noble Lai Handique, "Bandukiyal Bargohain's daughter was given to Lepati Gohain of the Buragohain faid. She brought with her a Kachari slave woman and her son, whose parentage was unknown. Lepat Gohain used to cohabit with the Kachari slave. He used to call her son his Lai Pu [first born] . . . One day he took the boy to the capital . . . [because] the swargadeo requested to have the boy . . . Hence forth, the slave boy and his family were recognized as Lai Handique and given a high office."[33]

The buranjis record that Bhatiyapariya Naubaisa Phukan's family (a high noble) belonged to "the illegitimate children of a Kachari slave woman." Likewise was "the family of Narakonwar Phukan and Nara Bailung. They were part of the dowry and had come as slaves." In a similar vein the buranjis tell us that "Saiyania Handique had brought a pregnant woman to his house. She gave birth to a boy . . . Later he became Naubaisa Phukan." This flexibility of position was not limited only to people who located themselves within the "us" community: "In the reign of Dihingiya Raja [1497–1539] a Goriya [Muslim, possibly a prisoner of war] was commissioned to build a daul [temple]. He made a very beautiful building. The king was very pleased and gave the Goriya rewards and the name Daul Chetia."[34] By this act a Muslim was made into an Ahom noble. This is not the only case; many similar stories are available in the buranjis.

The background information on the origin of the Ahom nobles often suggests mixed and quite dubious family histories. The class of Ahom nobles did not have an affinity to their ethnic backgrounds, nor were they a class of hereditary aristocrats. Ahoms were a much more dynamic group than that, as they were made up at the behest and desire of the swargadeo. Class and family background mattered nothing at all in the selection of nobles.

From the very beginning until the end of the swargadeo's rule in the nineteenth century, Ahoms were created from the different groups constituting the "us" community. My own family history fits into this narrative. It appears that a Muslim ancestor named Sheikh Azimuddin came to Assam in A.D. 1596. We do not know much about him, but his grandson, Sheikh Kailam, who was married to a local woman named Labanya (believed to be a daughter of an important functionary of the swargadeo), was awarded the title of Namati Saikia—that is, Saikia of the newly settled estate in Nazira, near Sibsagar. The title was accompanied by a large land grant and several items of nobility, namely the *hengdan* (sword of honor), two *botas* (copper trays for presenting betel nut, a cultural tradition for all formal exchanges), and gold jewelry such as thuriyas. The reward of the title was recorded in a copper-plate inscription (still owned by the family).[35]

Interestingly, when I returned to Assam to undertake research on Tai-Ahom history and identity, I visited Namati, Nazira. There I met my extended family in the village, some of whom are presumably "Ahom"

Hindu, and some "Ahom" Muslim. Both sides of the family welcomed me and expected that, like them, I could make sense of our hybrid, murky past. Although the narrative is not seamless, they were able to understand it and live without too much confusion. They also assumed that I was undertaking research on Ahoms to find "our" identity. That I made a separation between my personal and intellectual pursuits was not important to them, and they told me time and again that "you are like an Ahom in your speech and actions." Although the meaning of this notion was not explained to me, it is clear that the creation of likeness, of "being like them," was an attempt at inclusion. The erasure of difference between them and me and everything in-between was evocative and reminiscent. They were thinking back to a time when "us" in Upper Assam was Ahom, the ethos that made the swargadeo's domain powerful and unique. However, when I asked them what made them Ahom they explained that it was their history and their past, which we know now was a royal recognition and favor. Their concern, like many others in Assam, to fix and claim an identity as Ahoms is an aspiration that has its roots in the present. Their predecessors, I suspect, the so-called Ahom nobles, who actually lived within the domain during the rulership of the swargadeos, paid scant attention or interest to identity issues. This is not to say that becoming an Ahom was a small thing. It was a very privileged position, and the awardees understood the power that they enjoyed in the form of the land and labor that accompanied the position. Precisely for this reason, becoming an Ahom could not be reduced into a simple label of identity. It was vested with many facets of power and responsibility, and the awardees understood these to come with their temporary honorary status. Therein lies the difference in the approach to and perception of the importance of the Ahom, then and now.

The swargadeos, by and large, are never referred to as being Ahom in the buranjis, however. One can say that they were above any sort of categorization, being deemed gods on earth, but a more mundane explanation can be found in the family background of some of these men. For example, when he ascended to the throne the famous swargadeo Pratap Singha (1603–1641) had to declare, "I am the son of a mere Gohain's daughter,"[36] thereby taking into account his mother's nonroyal background. Gobar (1675), first in a long line of Tungkhungia kings, was born of an incestuous union between Rangdoi and her nephew, Chaopam Gohain (Bhuyan 1931, xviii). His successor, Sudaupha (Parbatiya Konwar [1675–1679]), used to refer to himself as a peasant. The lack of association between the term Ahom and the swargadeos continued until the end of their rule, in 1826, as discussed in chapter 2. The swargadeos never claimed to be Ahoms or to become Ahom; however, they designated who could and could not be Ahom.

Overall in precolonial Assam, like the "us" group, the Ahoms were intertwined with the swargadeo culture. Becoming an Ahom was thoroughly dependent on the whims and desires of the swargadeo and his two principal nobles, the Bar Gohain and Bura Gohain. Birth did not play a role in conferring or guaranteeing the place of an Ahom to an individual. However, on becoming an Ahom, a person acquired an identity different from his natal family, khel, or associates. For instance the *Ahom Buranji* records that "Rupchand Barbarua of the Bakatial Ahom ghar was originally a son of a rope maker of the Baruk Chutia family and worked for a Mussalman before he was made a Barbarua" (Barua 1930, 31; translation mine). According to this evidence the progeny of an unknown Chutia rope maker in the employ of a lowly foreigner became one of the five most important nobles of the kingdom. On his appointment as Barbarua, Rupchand discarded his Chutia family. This was not an isolated case.

A similar story involves Tingkhamiya Hatisarat. Legend has it that "when Sukapha came to Tipam, he met a Moran family. The Moran was named Khingkhing. His son was called Khimrat. In the reign of Sukhampha Khura Raja [1552–1603], Khimrat's grandson became Sitpatar. His family joined the Buragohain's faid and they were designated as Tingkhamiya Hatisarat. They became Aaham."[37] Another example is Papung Ahom's story. In the reign of Suhung (1675), in Sapungbaruk Bargohain's ghar, a slave woman gave birth to a boy. This boy claimed that he was from the family of the Bargohain. The Bargohain was enraged and wanted to kill him, so he fled and sought refuge with Khampeng Buragohain. The Buragohain gave him the name Papung and appointed him as an Ahom.[38]

This great fluidity of movement is dramatically exemplified in the story of Kam Ligira, who was an indentured servant. According to the story, "He was appointed as Tipamiya Phukan. His mother was a ligiri [female indentured servant]. His father joined the khel of Miri Handique" (Bhuyan 1932, 74; translation mine). Another example from the reign of Suhung is of the story of the Naga Bar Phukan, who was one of the five principal officers in the central administration. It is said that "in the Bar Patra Phukan's khel there was a Barahi named Lahar . . . He was childless and so he adopted a Banpha Naga boy. When Lahar Barahi died, his son was appointed as Liksawan Bora [in charge of slaves] . . . Swargadeo was pleased with his performance and the Naga boy was made the new Bar Phukan."[39] These few examples, as well as many others available in the buranjis, make it apparent that being Ahom was an acquired status. It was not a birth condition but a situation, a placement within the higher echelons of society that was acquired through services and favors. No doubt, once this status was achieved, many of the new awardees constructed glorious genealogies and became very attached to them. In what follows I will provide some examples from the buranjis.

Kirti Chandra Barbarua, one of the high nobles, found out that people were gossiping about his background in a menial family. The enraged noble convinced swargadeo Rajeshwar Singha (1751–1769) to confiscate all the buranjis in the kingdom and burn those that were not favorable to him because he wanted to put an end to the story of his humble past. In Assam even today people talk about a buranji called *Chakarepheti Buranji* (The hooded cobra), which documents the history of all the nobles and swargadeos who came from low and dubious backgrounds. I believe this buranji was available until a few years ago, but now it has "disappeared." Evidently, at some point during the rule of the swargadeos, the enterprise of making lofty family genealogies for Ahom nobles had become a serious matter. At least it was for those who were upgraded to this position. Once they became Ahoms, they wanted to project it as an inheritance, if possible, to legitimize their position. By the late eighteenth century, in the buranjis we find there were two classes of people in the swargadeo's domain: the undeciphered "us" group and the gentrified Ahom officers who originally rose from the ranks of "us." But once they "arrived" at that elevated position they downplayed the memory of their past. Lingering traces of their unattractive past were removed by such drastic measures as burning buranjis. As a result, buranjis were decontextualized and transformed from narratives of heroes into artifacts of identity construction. In the recent Tai-Ahom identity movement, the use of these chronicles for this purpose has intensified.

In short, buranjis narrated the story of nobility and divine rulership, which, in turn, made them part and parcel of the expanding power of the swargadeos and the class of administrators called Ahoms. The intimacy between the two, the Ahom and the buranjis, deepened over time even as tensions between them were also exacerbated.

Becoming an Ahom did not mean one had the privilege of being in that position forever. Consider the story of Lailang Baruk, a commoner, of the Saupungbaruk Buragohain faid: "He was taken to the forest in Dihing . . .

and abandoned there. He adopted a son of a Dihingia Ahom. His children were known as the family of the Buragohain. In the reign of Bura Raja [Pratap Singha] . . . the family of the adopted son of Lailang from Dihing was stripped of their title as Gohain . . . They ceased to be Gohain, and assumed the title of Saianiya Handique [an Ahom title]."[40] An ordinary person, it appears from this evidence, could rise up in the hierarchy and become a noble, but he could also lose this status quickly. This story and many more in the buranjis document the process of losing Ahom status. That such a loss was possible is extremely interesting and revealing.

Identity, as I have argued, was not unknown in the swargadeo's domain. Besides the "us" there were Ahoms, and both were very self-conscious positions. Hence the argument does not rest on a specific sense or lack of identity in precolonial Assam. Rather, texts show that identity was not a fixed, permanent thing that once acquired remained changeless over time and place. Identity, whether it was being a part of the "us" group or being a more elevated Ahom, was elastic and temporary. No person within the swargadeo's domain had a fixed and stable location. It was the possibility of movement between these different labels of identity that kept the people, culture, politics, and society in motion. No doubt at times it produced tension, but transience was the principle understood and appreciated by those who joined the collective "us" or were made Ahoms.

This reading no doubt will be disagreeable to many who see the label of Ahom as an entry point to becoming a defined group and who read their past as a seamless narrative of ethnicity or ethnic identity in the making. Many also want the Ahom today to be different from the Assamese Hindus, and to assert such a difference they become adherents of the Phra Lung religion (which I will discuss in chapter 5). The struggle to become a known, recognizable group with defined boundaries of identity is something I can understand. Like everyone else from Assam, I am part of a marginalized, subjected community. But to make oneself included, known, and accepted does not require creating a myth of a past and propagating it as the history of the people. Such an effort, I fear, will create a new language of power that will include some and deny others a place and, as such, will undoubtedly perpetuate an unevenness in representation. In other words, I am arguing that the present reading of the Ahom as a historic ethnic group does not solve problems but creates new ones.

The possibility of changing labels, and along with them a family's status, were privileges available in the swargadeo's domain not only to free men (paiks), but also to indentured servants (*ligiras*) and slaves (*bondi*). It is said that "a family of the slaves of the Rebati Goan, Tangali Uruwa, changed their status from slaves and intermixed with the Rebati Gaon Ahoms."[41] The Rebati Gaon Ahoms are known as *aniyamar* (irregular) Ahoms. Swargadeo Pratap Singha's mother belonged to this group. The story of origin of the Ahom noble Bhatiyapariya Naubaisa Phukan is similar. According to the records: "Originally, his family derived from the illegitimate offspring of the Barakiyal Bargohain's slave, the daughter of Tiperah Kachari. Some of them moved to Saring and took the name Chengrai. To this day, some of the sons and brothers of the Tiperah Kachari are slaves in the faid of the Borgohain."[42]

Thus in the swargadeo's domain nothing was permanent, bounded, and demarcated. The Ahom, as we have seen, emerged as a class of high officers in the buranjis, but it had different shapes at different times. In the buranjis, on the one hand, we hear of the "peerless" Ahoms of Sukapha's polity who conquered, subjugated, and founded the kingdom in the valley. These men are remembered in these narratives for their glorious feats, not for their ethnic background. On the other hand, the buranjis also tell us about the licentious and dubious activities of Ahom nobles as well as those of the swargadeos. The discourse about Ahoms, both in implicit and explicit terms, establishes that it was an identity that called for a "blend-ing" of various sorts. Everyone within the polity had the potential to fit within this category. Ethnicity was not the factor that made an Ahom but rather the favor of the swargadeo. Hence, in the reign of different swargadeos the composition of the Ahom nobility varied. There was no template to follow but a recurring pattern of the Ahom as a variety makes one suppose that "mixing and matching" was the ethos that constituted the blended Ahom.

If we are to chart the "blended" group over time, the picture we get from the buranjis reads like this:

In the reign of Rudra Singha [1796–1714], the Ahom officials were: Thaomung Tima . . . of Barahi origin . . . ; Thaomung Kataki was the son of a female slave of the king . . . Chao Thumlung Bargohain was a Kachari; Chaophrang Buragohain was Matak; Chao Senglung Bar Patra Gohain was a Matak of Jakhalanburiwa Matak family. Thaomung Pan-lung was of Kachari origin. Lashaikhampeng Chaophrang Buragohain was the son of a female slave; Lashai alias Maupia was of Naga origin; . . . Kalangshu Phukan was the son of a female slave; . . . Momai Tamuli[43] was of Lukurakhun family. (Barua 1930, 31–32; translation mine)

The list of "Ahom officials" in the reign of Lakshmi Singha (1769–1780) is similarly eclectic:

> The swargadeo appointed new Ahom officials. The son of Bakatiyal Rajneog, Bhadrasen, was made Barbarua. The son of Dalbandha Buragohain, Bailung, was made Bargohain. A member of the Kaboighariya Buragohain, Gohain Hazarika, was made Buragohain. From the Maran patar faid, a Bar Patra was appointed. From the family of Lai Handique, Bahmuwa was appointed Naubaisa Phukan. From the family of Lahan, a Dekaphukan . . . from the Dafla Duaria family, Mohan, was made Ghora Barua . . . The son-in-law of the wet nurse was appointed as Chetia Phukan. He is a Kachari by origin . . . Deka Phukan was appointed from the family of Miri-Handique. In this way, in keeping with the age-old traditions the deserving from each ghar/household were given royal offices. (Bhuyan 1932, 68–73; translation mine)

In the reign of Kamleshwar Singha (1795–1811) the Ahom officials were:

> Dihingiya Phukan was a Miri-Handique, Nibukiyal Rajkhowa was from the Kukurasuwa ghar, Lanmakhuru was Khargoriya Phukan, Tipamiya Phukan was of the Chetia Patar khel . . . Saudang Barua was from the Saudang jat, the barua of the Saudang is Fhisi by jat, Raidongiya Barua is Sanuwal Kachari, his brother Majau Melaiya is Bhandari Barua, Tamuli Phukan is from the Brahman Kakoti ghar . . . The grandson of Daulay is Bhandari Barua and is a brahman . . . Gajpuriya Rajkhowa is of the Pakhimuriya jat, Dikhoumukhiya Rajkhowa is Tangsu by jat, Na-Meliya Barua is Gayan by jat, Khanikar Barua is Barahi by jat, Sangrung Phukan is Ukanimari Chetia by jat, Majumdar Barua is Ganok, Guwahati Dekaphukan is Lukurakhun. (Bhuyan 1932, 183; translation mine)[44]

The lists of officials that can be taken from two different buranjis that spread over a period of two hundred years confirm that the Ahom refers to a conglomerate of heterogeneous people who were carefully selected and brought together by royal mandate to assist in ruling the kingdom. Creating this group conferred power and legitimacy on the swargadeos in the eyes of their rivals—the Kacharis, Tripuris, Bengalis, and many others. The creation of this loyal class of Ahoms was politically a very clever move that enabled the swargadeos to exercise immense power that perpetuated the obedience of the "us" community. For the services they rendered, the Ahoms were guaranteed certain privileges, but the benefits were not permanent. By emphasizing the fluidity of this identity, the swargadeos controlled and directed the continuous movement within and beyond this group which, in turn, never allowed for developing any sense of loyalty to or cohesiveness of the group. Ahom was not an identity to die for in precolonial Assam; in fact, nobody could even claim ownership of this label because it was left to the discretion of the swargadeo to award or demote a person to and from this status. Although this curtailed the development of group solidarity, in a peculiar way it provided various options to individuals. One could change one's affiliation to another khel or faid, as described above, and thus build a new identity and a new history for oneself as well as one's family. In one lifetime, a person could change his identity several times. Thus we see in the swargadeo's domain that the narration of identity is the story of fluid exchanges, marked by temporariness and by fluctuations determined by royal activities and policies.

In precolonial Assam labels carried little weight—the focus was on the person. This does not mean that personhood was acknowledged in the structure; indeed, the opposite was true. A person was a subject of a system in which the swargadeo ruled supreme, and one could be moved at will and given new identities by the swargadeo. In this way identities like Ahom were constantly created and dismantled. Over time, the concept, number, and role of the Ahom also changed. Continuous expansion of the population and the domain of the swargadeo resulted in many changes and made the label even more desirable, but also more slippery and untamed. All of those who participated in this order had to adjust to the vagaries that were a part of it. To contemporaries the ideology and phenomenon were understandable and manageable, but to us as modern citizens with fixed national identities it appears arbitrary and perplexing. The problem of identity or understanding the Ahom of the buranjis is really a modern dilemma. The lack of acknowledgment of our limitation has, in turn, made Ahom thinkable only in the ways the colonial agents had taught us to think—that is, that Ahom is a "dead" community, an "unthinkable" historical group in the present.

The "unthinkable" Ahom has a long history. Heretofore I have engaged stories of the Ahom and the Assamese told by different narrators. These stories are diverse and even contradict one another, yet a common theme runs through them: they are all "myths." Even the play-by-play account of the different time periods, actors, activities, and descriptions does not outline a clear image of Ahoms, but rather gives interpretations of what possibly made up the Ahom without fixing a historical analysis.

The slipperiness of these myths aside, what is more important is an investigation of the process of myth making, which was never even. A definite hierarchy exists among these myths. The operative myth in India today labors hard to fit the group called the Assamese within a national narrative. The Assamese in the national imagination are a tamed, Hinduized, plains people, who are upgrading themselves to become "civilized" through the state's economic and cultural development interventions. One has only to see television narratives of the new Indian, such as the song and dance routine of "Hum Sab Bharatiya Hai," to understand this enterprise of the modern state's attempt to make Indians of the Assamese. There is no place within this project for historic images of the Ahom, and for ambivalent and hazy non-Indic memories of a past. An investigation of the national process at work in Assam and of the silencing of local narratives makes it quite obvious that the new national myth is premised on colonial myths concerning the land and its people.

The categories of the past—swargadeo, Ahom, "us"—were transformed as soon as the colonials entered Assam. In colonial documents and minds, the term Ahom no longer referred to a fluid, official position but was made into a group identity, passed on from one generation to the next. Ahom was transformed into an ethnicity; discourse entwined the ideological assumptions of the colonial state with the need of subject communities to find a place for themselves in a drastically changed world. The locals, confounded by the dismal loss of power of the man they thought was a god, found the swargadeo replaced by a foreign colonial state and could offer no resistance. The colonial construct of the ethnicity of Ahom gave the outgoing nobility something to cling to. Many thought in these changed circumstances that if they could claim a past as Ahoms, they could benefit in the new administration. They could claim it as an inheritance and make some gains as nobles of yesteryears. They were bringing their old, outmoded sensibilities to a radically altered context that did not do them any good. Even so, in the 1881 census, 179,314 people in Assam claimed to be Ahom; in 1891, the claim was made by 153,528; and in 1909 the number of claimants increased to 178,049 in the census tabulations. In the meantime, as I discussed in chapter 2, in the site of colonial administration the category called Ahom became less and less important. Ahoms were reduced to the level of picturesque savages, and finally they were eliminated for they did not fit the new ethos of the colonial economic enterprise in Assam. In 1931, they were told they did not exist anymore. Instead, the populace of the Assam Valley was given a new label, Assamese, and organized as a subject community of obedient tax-paying peasants.

The elimination of Ahoms by the colonials is bothersome, but it was preceded by another even more blatant lie, that of the "discovery" of the Ahom. This lie was created to facilitate the construction of a group of hereditary rulers and nobles from whom the colonials might inherit power and legitimize their administration in Assam. The colonials claimed that they got their information about this ruling community of Ahoms from the buranjis. It is true that the buranjis provide several images of the Ahom, but for certain they do not present it as a definite community/ group. The Ahom in the buranjis was both an idea and a system designed to strengthen a pluralistic crossroads society and culture. The end of the fluid, multicultural past in the colonial period was the beginning of a problem that continues to ail Assam even today.

The colonials killed the history of Assam. All that is left is myth— uneven, unequal, and created.[45] The creation of the myths of Assam and its people were accomplished by "outsiders," first the colonials and then the Indian nation-state. Backed by power, their myths were transformed into believable "facts." The power of these myths for a long time closed the possibility of investigating the story of Assam and the Ahom beyond what had been imposed. Government rules forbade "foreign" scholars from undertaking research in the region. The people of Assam, living with limited opportunities in a backward state with poor education facilities, and cut off by geographical isolation and bad communication, remained quietly dormant for a long time. Recently, though, under the banner of several different groups, they have constructed new identity movements. The Tai-Ahom identity movement that emerged in 1981 is one of them. What is the goal of its members? Immediately, it appears that they want to become known as a group called the Ahom. What Ahom will mean is still under construction. But a long-range view of this and other movements ongoing in Assam is to create a collective that can rise up and resist the intrusion of others into their home ground. The politics, society, and economy of Assam, they claim, must be made autonomous. In short, their attempt is to undo the history of silences and disempowerment and launch a new beginning. Before one gets too carried away by these move- ments, however, it is useful to remember that like all other myth-making enterprises that came before it, the contemporary Tai-Ahom movement is a construct. For the leaders of this movement, it is easy to make up the Ahom however they desire, for there is no fixed narrative to overburden new imaginings. The only new thing about this myth-making process is that now it is possible to bear witness to the phenomenon and construct our own narrative. Contemporary Tai-Ahom history is an experience for many in Assam, direct and accessible, but it has not become less complicated, as we will see in part 2.

>>>>>>>>>>>>>>>>>>>>>>>>>>>

## PART 2

<<<<<<<<<<<<<<<<<<<<<<<<<<

*Tai-Ahom: A Language*

>>>>>>>>>>>>>>>>>>>>>>>>>>>

*and Culture of Emotion*

<<<<<<<<<<<<<<<<<<<<<<<<<<

# CHAPTER 4

# Rationalizing a History

Bhupen Hazarika, the most acclaimed poet/songwriter in postcolonial Assam, has created a rich imagery connecting the people of Ujani Aham with the Luit River. Repeatedly in many songs he reminds his "young friends of Luitpaar (river valley) [that] no one compares with [them]," because in them he sees the spirit of struggle to survive, for which they have "entered the battlefield with the promise to fight until death." The "foaming Luit" mirrors their "determination and mental prowess [and] in acknowledgement" he sings, "bows its beautiful head to you." In another song (written by Jyotiprashad Agarwala), Bhupen Hazarika celebrates the "new generation of men and women of Luitpaar" as "the eternal sentinels, . . . the brave ones who have overcome the fear of death to carve with their own hands a new society . . . weave new dreams . . . make a revolution without fear."[1]

I have heard these and many other of Bhupen Hazarika's songs since my childhood. For my generation, his songs were our only narrative source for imagining Assam's historical past; our school textbook history rarely mentioned Assam. The narrative of Assam created by Bhupen Hazarika is a marker of postcolonial history, but it evokes memories of a time and place that no longer exist. The river, Luit, which Hazarika celebrates as the life blood of Assam, is a compelling image, but a historical investigation of both the Luit and Hazarika's sources of information about the river and its people is impossible because there is no Luit anymore. Sometimes, I wonder if there ever was such a thing.

In many probing conversations with Assamese people, including those living both inside and outside of Assam, I have searched for the meaning of the Luit. Often I have been told that "Luit is a site of nostalgia. It is not for real." Or I have heard people make statements such as, "I have heard about Luit from my grandparents. But I am not certain what they were talking about." When I asked my father (who was supposedly from Luit-paar, as a native of Sibsagar in the heartland of the Luit Valley) about Luit, he told me that "in the old days they called the Brahmaputra River, Luit. When we were young, once in a while, we also referred to it as Luit. It is no longer the case. Now we come across the term Luit only in poems and literature. Neither Luit nor the culture of Luitpaar is there anymore. It survives in our imagination, at best, in our language, our speech, but the place is not like it was before. The area of Luitpaar today is Upper Assam. But Luitpaar is not simply the bounded territory of Upper Assam. It is more than that, much more than an administrative unit."[2]

What is Luitpaar and who are the "Luitporia" that Bhupen Hazarika sings to and my father so fondly remembered?[3] How did the place change, and why is it only in the site of creative writing and fiction that Luit is mentioned? Even if the place and culture are dead, I thought, as I traveled in Ujani Aham, I should be able to locate something and be able to talk about the place and culture of Luitpaar, however imprecisely.

In this chapter, which is based on my fieldwork in various villages, I introduce several strands of emotions, politics, culture, and society that reflect the construction of Luitpaar that is taking place in Ujani Aham and in the discourse of a Tai-Ahom identity. The images and stories seem to blend with the rhythm of the agricultural cycles. Among the multiple stories, tales about the "golden days of the swargadeos" and the "peer-less" Ahoms were very popular and frequently told, at least in the 1990s. Traveling along the river valley through the villages, I also heard the murmurs of a political movement called the United Liberation Front of Assam (ULFA). It seemed to be connected to the Tai-Ahom movement, but nobody wanted to discuss it with me. Instead, we talked about Tai-Ahom history and their lost identity in Luitpaar. People readily shared with me information about the Tai-Ahom movement and their claims. Loss of land, social and cultural exclusion, and economic and political marginalization, it seems, have brought together disparate, fragmented, and marginal groups in a shared cause to recover an identity called Tai-Ahom along the Luit.

In the first part of this chapter, I explore the linkages between people and place—traditions, culture, and economy—to show the development of a "psychological ecology" (Gallagher 1993) in Ujani Aham that shapes and nurtures the discourse of the Tai-Ahom identity along the Luitpaar. In the second part of the chapter, I investigate the historical processes of the Tai-Ahom movement to show how it has constructed a rich imagery of Luitpaar in the postcolonial period. My argument is that the current construction of Luitpaar and Tai-Ahom consists of loose collections of stories and traditions—constellations of particular environmental, emotional, and cultural variables that are dialogic in context. Tai-Ahom is not a fixed ethnic community (even now) but is constructed through negotiations between many groups and leaders who, in turn, are transformed by the images of Tai-Ahom. As a result, both the people and their discourses are undergoing many changes in Ujani Aham.

If Ujani Aham is the imaginary space of Luitpaar and the homeland of Ahoms, what is it that facilitates the connection between them? Is it a memory that links people and place? How does this memory serve the current Tai-Ahom movement? Before we can engage these questions, it is necessary to remind ourselves that Ahom in the historical records was never the identity of a defined, singular community. Rather, it was an administrative category devised and maintained for the consolidation and enhancement of the swargadeo's power. Despite the absence of a historical, ethnic Ahom community, many people today do not hesitate to claim they are Ahom. Likewise, they claim a particular place as the Ahom homeland. It is in Ujani Aham that they aim to regain their lost glories and recreate the "golden days of Ahom rule." Driven by need and a psychology of neglect and economic marginality, the place has become a repository of dreams and aspirations for the future. New doctrines of being Ahom incorporate the past of colonial accounts and buranjis and make new versions out of these. They claim that the past belongs to the people of Ujani Aham, and that they are the progeny of the "peerless" Ahom who were noble, glorious, and powerful. A direct connection is made between history and ethnicity, or at least, the discourse of ethnicity. Skewed though this may be, this new version of the Ahom motivates the people to envision a hopeful future. Their hope is to reclaim land and resources in Ujani Aham, get fixed electoral constituencies for Tai-Ahom candidates, and become a Scheduled Tribe group, which would ensure that they benefit from many privileges.

The current Tai-Ahom political movement, not unlike the fluid label Ahom, is unclear, variously imagined, and there are many different articulations and discourses. Also, the movement has multiple locations. Of these, three sites—local, national, and transnational—are most important and most easily identifiable. In the next chapter I will discuss these sites and the performances of identity in them by various agents. In this chapter, I am concerned with the emotional and cultural mapping of Ahom in a place—that is, with the structuring of "being Ahom" in Ujani Aham and the discursive use of memory and myth to create a limited identity politics.

### THE POWER OF PLACE

Ujani Aham is not a territory identified in official maps. It is a matrix of spatiality that has been constituted by processes of migration as new waves of people and culture entered and left their imprint on the banks of the Luit. In the buranjis, the term "swargadeos' domain" encapsulated the nature of this area and its culture of hybridity manifested in the crossroads kun-how ("us") community. The kun-how community, as we have noted, was constituted by a variety of peoples combined and consolidated into a polity. In the swargadeo's domain, identification of those within the kun-how community was never firm. The composite kun-how community shaped the culture of Ujani Aham as a distinct "blended" space and, in turn, the ecology of riverine Ujani Aham transformed the multiple communities into agrarian societies. One informed the other, and the process of construction and reconstruction of both place and people were simultaneous and continuous. Ujani Aham, like Raymond Williams's Welsh village, is a "place that was being received and made and unmade" (Harvey 1996, 29). Despite continuous changes and tensions between the settling communities, a relationship between people and place developed and became embedded. In short, Ujani Aham became a history of a place in motion that represented a culture belonging to and shaped by the people of that place.

In administrative terms, the districts and communities of Golaghat, Jorhat, Sibsagar, and Dibrugarh to Sadiya, and Lakhimpur all the way to Dhemaji, are loosely considered the area of Ujani Aham. This broadly coincides with the cartographical space of colonial "Upper Assam." It is a large and heterogeneous territory, inhabited by a variety of people, including tribal and plains people, Hindus, Muslims, Christians, and "others." Many of the communities to be found in the region have little in common in terms of culture and religion. Yet a majority of them share a condition of poverty, as well as a deep consciousness of neglect—which in Indian circles is referred to as "backwardness"—that fosters a feeling of displacement.

The term "displacement" generally evokes a sense of loss of place through migration, forced eviction, and movement—in short, physical dislocation. The people of Ujani Aham are not physically dislocated in that sense. They have not recently moved to or from another place. Although anchored in their own "homes" they nonetheless share a mentality of "displacement," fostered by a sense of cultural and economic marginality within the modern Indian nation-state. Many people feel threatened and alienated.[4] To this sense of psychological alienation is also added real economic neglect, which is evident in the lack of capital investment in small or heavy industries, and the lack of skill training, educational opportunities, job possibilities, and so on. These are the bottom-line issues that create, nurture, and sustain the feeling of dispossession and thus dislocation in Ujani Aham that many described to me during my conversations with them.[5] To this is added a daily encounter with what is referred to by local people as "Indian colonialism." This rhetoric has gained ground as the commercial enterprises in the region—transport, tea plantations, food distribution, tourism, print and media journalism, and other businesses— became the monopoly of non-Assamese people, which started in the colonial period. Further, the control of the state bureaucracy and the management of the public-sector industries of oil and gas refining are in the hands of non-Ujani Assamese people. To top it all, the Indian army has several battalions of soldiers posted in the villages to monitor local people and their activities because they are considered ULFA supporters and are suspected of having linkages to the rebel organization. The people of Ujani Aham have come to view themselves in this situation as a "minority," living without power, resources, or a voice in the administration, economy, or politics. In the face of this depressed present, the past has acquired a new meaning, and some people have started to look for an alternative in the present in order to find a sense of community within the heterogeneous complexities of people and cultures and deprivations that surround them.

The memory of a "swargadeo culture" and the practice of agriculture, particularly rice cultivation, before colonialism introduced commercial cash crops like tea are important symbols for Ujani Aham people. They believe that the construction of the Assamese during colonial rule was the beginning of the end of their local identity. One can argue about the degree of authenticity of this claim, for we know that before the people of Ujani Aham were transformed into Assamese not all of them were Ahoms. Although local people responded to my alternative reading in different ways, depending on their level of education and association with the current Tai-Ahom movement, one thing they all seemed to share was fear and a mentality of being under siege by "outsiders" in their "own home." It is this sense of threat that has made them conscious that they must forge a unity. The memory of the "swargadeos' rule" and their shared pecuniary condition encourage people in Ujani Aham to think of themselves as different from other groups in Assam and India. Nowadays, this awareness and persuasion has taken shape as Tai-Ahom.

The idea of being Tai-Ahom in Ujani Aham is facilitated through some enduring social forms such as food, festivals, myths, and legends. It is a social understanding, not merely a philosophical and a political one. Social forms and practices have become tropes for "spatial telling" (Carter 1987, 346) and the site of community construction. There is a strong tendency among proponents of Ahom to idealize these practices and make claims that they are ancient and traditional. When one compares them, however, to social and cultural behavior elsewhere in Assam (and in some other parts of each India), it is hard to avoid concluding that these traditions are widely shared. They are not, in short, original or specific to Ujani Aham, and neither do they have any specific meaning. Yet, the people who claim to be Tai-Ahom today try to locate and find themselves in these practices and insist that they and their practices are unique to Ujani Aham. The sharedness of these practices in Ujani Aham has given the residents a lobby, a prerequisite to stage their grievances in the public sphere. It is necessary to remember that the symbol of the rural life of Ujani Aham is not a permanent thing, and it may soon give way to other forms of identification, other kinds of discourses, and other markers. For the time being, the image of a rural Ujani Aham facilitates the construction and continuity of a Ujani Aham community. The community, as we know, is not homogeneous. The unity of the diverse groups brought about by the Tai-Ahom movement is fostered by a connection of the people with the river, Luit, which flows through the place. By the banks of the Luit, an Ujani Aham community has been produced and reproduced. I intend to focus on the constructions of the social in Ujani Aham, but before doing so I must explain the connection between these people and the Luit River.

## A RIVER RUNS THROUGH IT

The imagination of Ujani Aham as separate from the rest of Assam, and of Tai-Ahom as the emblem of Ujani Aham identity, are concepts that flow in the rhythm of the Luit.[6] The Luit is not a well-known river. It is a little, curved outflow that annually drenches the plains of Ujani Aham, and by flooding the area it creates fresh silt beds for the rice cultivation that sustains the populace living along its banks. Unlike the Brahmaputra River, which is commemorated in history books, the Luit is not the subject of historical celebration.[7] The only known mention of Luit in precolonial accounts is in Kautilya's *Arthashastra* (1984, 190). He identified the region and communities as Para-Lohitya. A clear reference to the river was also made in the early colonial maps, which delineated a section of the Brahmaputra in Upper Assam as Lohit (Luit).[8] However, over time, the name Luit/Lohit was dropped from the maps, and the entire river was renamed Brahmaputra, with the region itself called the Brahmaputra, or Assam, Valley. While others forgot or relinquished Luit, the people who lived along its banks continued their allegiance to the river. The mentality of attachment and claim over Luit does not, however, translate into fixing a distinct location on the ground as the space of the Luit. For outside observers this lack of geographic specificity highlights the fact that the collective memory of the Luit is an internal, emotionally driven entity, and those who claim it as their own have created this memory in a manner that is accessible only to them.

Outside Ujani Aham today no one thinks of the Luit as a separate river. The Luit is swept into the turbulent Brahmaputra in Assam, linked to the Tsangpo in Tibet, and emptied into the Padma in Bangladesh. For the people of Ujani Aham—the Luitporia people, to borrow Bhupen Hazarika's term—the memory of Luit evidently matters a great deal. It is not a singular memory but a string of very powerful and poignant emotions that facilitates the narrativization of a story of Tai-Ahom today along its banks. Luitporia people, despite the differences among them (which are many), are able to devise a plan, shape a direction, and transform the mythical lore of the Ahom past into agendas and plan for action in the future. The stories of the river, as a result, become very important to them, because the river belongs to them and the stories are about them.

Today, the symbolism of Luit as *our* river and the Luitpaar (banks) as *our land* and *our home* has been established as the site for expressing a passion for belonging and recognition. In the Assamese language "home" is denoted by the plural term *amar ghor* (our home). Ghor is both the abode of a family and the place of one's roots. In a wider context, the family home and the community's home, Assam, is not demarcated. Ultimately, those who claim their origin in Assam see themselves as one family. For this family of Assamese, Assam is "homeland" as well as the hearth of their ancestors.[9] Thus, they establish an exclusive connection to the place. With the settlement in Assam of many different groups of people from different regions of India, Nepal, and Bangladesh, however, new developments and associations with the place were generated. Now there are groups of people who live and work in Assam for whom Assam is not home and homeland. The local people distinguish them as videkhi, "foreigners," or Assambakhi, "residents of Assam."[10] With the emergence of these communities of videkhis and Assambakhis, an anxiety among the local people has surfaced. They seek to preserve the "ethnonational" (Connor 1994) integrity of their homeland by either driving out the "outsiders" or by claiming sections of Assam as their exclusive homeland. The Tai-Ahom claim to make Luitpaar their exclusive homeland is an attempt in this direction.

By this token other groups, including Assamese people who cannot claim their origin in Ujani Aham, will not have the same privileged position of association with the area. This is not merely an emotional claim. The leaders of the Tai-Ahom movement expect that through this claim and its recognition from the Indian government at Delhi, the Tai-Ahoms will become citizens of Luitpaar in the truest sense—that is, they will own the land and resources that they do not own now. Thus they will emerge as a community with power in their homeland in Ujani Aham. At the same time, they hope, the "old" history of the buranjis will enable them to find a shared emotional "home" with their Tai counterparts outside and beyond Assam, as well as in modern Thailand. The current demand to make Ujani Aham a Tai-Ahom homeland is very problematic, no doubt. Nonetheless, there is a "remembered connection" and an intimate association of the people with the place facilitated by images such as Luitpaar. The commemoration of the river valley as the home of Tai-Ahom has a long historical itinerary.

In the buranjis, the Luit was the channel along which the earliest myths and memories of the "us" community in the swargadeo's domain took shape and unfolded. Along the river's bank, the buranjis claim, the first immigrants under the leadership of Sukapha organized their initial settlements. Villages sprang up at Tipam, Dihing, Dikhou, and Dilihmukh; ultimately the settlers established the first capital city at Charaideo, a little hillock beneath which flowed the Charaideo rivulet (a tributary stream of the Dikhou connected to the Luit River).[11] Because rice cultivation was the mainstay, the early settlers at times occupied segments of the fertile banks to practice wet-rice cultivation. For this, they had to resort to different tactics, including war and bribery, to oust other groups such as the Kacharis who were also making claims to the banks at strategic points and controlling the water supply (Saikia 1997, 185). The ability to wrest control of the river valley and of river transport from the rival Kacharis made this migrant group the most powerful in the region. Over time, other local groups like the Barahis and the Morans who befriended the early settlers designated them as Ahoms—the unique, peerless group under the rule of a swargadeo. Ultimately, the control of the riverine plains and river allowed the swargadeo to become the supreme power in Ujani Aham, and rival groups were reduced to subordinate positions of vassalage.

The Luit continued throughout the period of the swargadeos' rule to bear witness to intense political moments. On ascending to the throne each successive swargadeo established a new capital city on its bank. Meteka, Rangpur, and Garhgaon are the best-known capitals other than Charaideo. These and other capital cities were all situated on the banks of the Luit's tributaries, in and around Sibsagar. In fact, the swargadeos drew their political boundaries where the Luit ended and merged with other rivers. The area around Sibsagar, the heartland of the Luit Valley, always remained the core domain of the swargadeos. Correspondingly, the importance of a place was measured in relation to its distance from the Luit. For example, the territories beyond Guwahati, in the west, were left to the "Bangalis." One can hypothesize that these areas were too far from the Luit and its tributaries and hence had little importance to the swargadeos. The same was also the case with the hills of Naga, Garo, Miri, and the Mikir settlements. For the wet-rice cultivators of the Luit Valley, the hills had little appeal because they had no potential for rice cultivation. This guaranteed the political independence of the hill tribes.

The relationship between the people of the swargadeo's domain and the river became passionate with the passage of time. The end of the rule of the swargadeos and the beginning of British rule intensified their connection. The mercantile colonial administration introduced brisk transport on the river, opening new ways to exploit manpower and natural resources. Laborers from Bengal and Orissa were ferried up the river to Ujani Aham to work in the tea plantations that developed not far from the river's banks. As a result, several new communities of "outsiders" were created in Ujani Aham, and the Luitporia people, diminished in number and strength, were pushed out of their homes and land to accommodate the colonial hunger for a cash crop economy and profit.

A few miles away from the Luit basin, colonial agents discovered coal, petroleum, and natural gas and exploited these resources to generate power for colonial factories and workshops. Much of the river and the riverbanks were used for the enterprises of the colonial economy, but few of the displaced Luitporia people could take advantage of the new benefits offered by the river and the fertile riverbanks that once formed their wet-rice fields. The longing to claim the Luit and Luitpaar today for those who identify with the Tai-Ahom movement has risen out of this dispossession. The river is more than simply a site for people to locate their memories of the past. It is also the place along which their social interactions and political encounters took place. It is a symbol of loss and history as well as real property to reacquire.[12] The relationship with the river is intimately political as well as cultural and economic.

A search for traces of what constitutes Tai-Ahom in Luitpaar or what is distinctly different between the Tai-Ahom people and the non–Tai-Ahom in the area did not produce concrete results for me. Initially, I found it very annoying that I could not pinpoint the differences and similarities between the two so-called communities. Over time, however, I realized that I had to take into account the world of human activities flowing along the river, (which let the people think they are "different"). Failing to do so, in my search of explicit constructions of what and who is Tai-Ahom, I was missing the richness of the variety of internal memories that motivate the construction of Tai-Ahom. The most poignant of these memories is the assumption that the Luit has existed since the beginning of time, for it is the one constant factor in the fast-changing landscape of Ujani Aham. One only has to listen to common villagers talk about the river to understand the sentiments associated with it. During my stay in several villages, I was privy to many heated discussions concerning the question of whether the river should be called Luit or Brahmaputra. The name Luit was the undisputed winner, for, as many said, "Luit and Brahmaputra may appear to be the same river, but they are not. Luit is the river that flows through Ujani Aham; Brahmaputra belongs to everyone—Assamese, Indians, and Hindus."

The appropriation of a place by people to produce a distinct identity is not unique to Ujani Aham.[13] In several African communities natural objects are viewed as guardians of the collective identity as a community. It could be a mountain or hill, and even animals and snakes can be seen as objects that inform and preserve the culture of a community.[14] As Keith Basso has pointed out, the connections between people and natural objects are both powerful and telling, "for whenever the members of a community speak about their landscape—whenever they name it, or classify it, or evaluate it, or are moved to tell stories about it—they . . .

represent it in ways that are compatible with shared understandings of how, in the fullest sense, they know themselves" (1992, 222).

However, the claims of the groups who call themselves Tai-Ahom today and identify their history with the Luit are not inconsequential. The imposition of the label Tai-Ahom on the landscape of the Luit has denied other forms of articulations of people who identify as Luitporia but not as Tai-Ahom. Luitpaar is their home too, but the right to claim the area as their homeland is silenced. For example, the Phakey, Aiton, Khamyang, Turung, Mishimi, Assamese, and others who live by the Luit are not allowed to suggest new interpretations, and thus the expectations of these communities have to be mediated to suit the Tai-Ahom movement. The silencing of other voices by one group in Luitpaar is open to criticism. Nevertheless, the brokering of an idea called Tai-Ahom by local politicians in postcolonial Assam has created a space for otherwise disassociated and disparate "excluded" groups to forge solidarity and use the platform of identity to devise political and social actions. In this newly created space, they have been able to imagine themselves as something other than the imposed label of Assamese. As a result, Tai-Ahom leaders have been able to successfully create an arena of social and political protest in Ujani Aham. The gaps between the present reading of the past and the stories that buranjis tell about the Ahom are underplayed, for what the identity seekers ultimately need is recognition, with or without a history to back the claim.

### CONSTRUCTING UJANI AHAM

Besides the Luit, there are other markers of identity for both the rich and the poor that make up the Ujani Aham lifestyle. Rice culture is a shared discourse and practice in the region. The old adage "tell me what you eat, and I will tell you what you are" (Braudel 1973, 66) is specifically relevant. Just as Ohnuki-Tierney found in Japan,[15] in Ujani Aham it is evident that rice mediates history to create a sense of sharedness, binding rich and poor alike in an "us" that distinguishes the group from "them." The metaphor of rice as a distinguishing boundary between the collective self of Ujani Aham and that of others extends to geography. The paddy fields of Ujani Aham are viewed as "our" land, "our" space, "our" markers of identity, something different that cannot be shared with the rest of the Assamese people. The Luitporia people's standard of respect for themselves and their neighbors is based on the quality of rice paddy they produce, not simply the quantity of rice, although the ownership of more and larger paddy fields makes a household more powerful in the village. During my stay in the villages, I heard and observed several family arguments over competing claims to rice fields. Everyone wanted a piece of land on which to cultivate rice and thus find a place to claim and belong. In others words, being a land-owning peasant in Luitpaar connoted an identity—Tai-Ahom as it is called today. This I experienced personally. Particularly around the villages in Sibsagar, where my land-owning ancestors are well known, I was received very warmly. Many even told me that they were "land-eaters" of my grandfather. A recognition of a shared past was thus established and the connection to a plot of land bound us together and made me part of a large extended family. The religious differences between me (a Muslim) and the tenant-farmers (Tai-Ahoms/Hindus) became irrelevant. Land is the god of peasants, as many of them explained to me. As partakers of the land settled by our ancestors, we were joined in a common faith. This creation of likeness had a tremendous effect on me. Although I did not understand how the cultivation of rice along Luitpaar marked their identity as Tai-Ahom, I realized that in an inexplicable way we were committed to establishing continuity. This is explained as Tai-Ahom today, but the real issue at stake is a claim to land and its resources, rice, and other crops that are part of Ujani Aham culture.

Given the importance of rice cultivation in the river valley, it is not surprising that among foods rice occupies a privileged place, and an impressive variety of rice products are made and used everyday. *Bhat* (steamed rice), *phita* (a variety of steamed rice cakes), *kumol sawul* (softened rice cooked and dried for use as breakfast cereal), *handa* (rice powder), *akhoy* (puffed, roasted rice), *cira* (flattened rice), and *bora sawul* (sticky rice) are the staples. Although rice is consumed all over Assam, as well as in eastern and southern India, people who say they are Tai-Ahom claim "[they] prepare rice differently from others. We steam rice in small pouches wrapped in a particular leaf that is found only in the forests of Ujani Aham."[16] In this and other instances food becomes a boundary for crafting differences and constructing identity. Aside from rice, in the villages of Ujani Aham most people have very little to live on and they eat what they can procure. I ate in several kitchens and was often served rice with a small serving of vegetables, mostly greens (picked from the backyard garden) accompanied by small portions of fish caught in the village pond. Sometimes even the fish was not available, and a meal could consist simply of rice, boiled potatoes, and some greens. On one occasion I was offered ants and ant-hill nests mixed with a fine paste of mustard seeds that was accompanied by a small glass of *lau-pani* (rice beer). This meal was considered a delicacy. In particular the rice beer was a treat, because it is served on very special occasions. On another occasion I was offered the meat of a sand lizard.[17]

The people in the different villages explained their dietary choices as a compulsion based on availability and as a result of their poverty. Every time I ate in their homes, people apologized for not providing me with "good" food. Initially, I did not understand what they considered to be "good food," and I assumed it was a customary gesture to apologize to guests because eating in company is a very formal activity in Assam. But as I continued to live in the villages, people felt comfortable enough to ask me questions about the food that I ate regularly. Often during these conversations they asked me, for example, if every day in America I ate "chicken, chocolates, and ice cream." These items they considered the markers of "good food," even if I tried to tell them otherwise. They moaned that as parents they could not provide these luxuries to their children, and stated that their children ate what was available, including wild plants and dead animals.[18] This was one reason, they claimed, that the caste Hindus looked down on their communities. Poverty plays a significant role in influencing dietary practices in the villages of Ujani Aham. Still, in an effort to craft their identity of difference, food items, such as the ones I have mentioned above, became important mediums for constructing Ahomness. In particular eating beef (which was served on rare occasions, such as festivals) and drinking lau-pani became associated with being Tai-Ahom. Thus food came to play a dynamic role in Ujani Aham, shaping the way people think about who they are and who their neighbors are, particularly the people of Lower Assam and the caste Hindu Assamese who do not share their food habits.[19]

Along with food, the practice of sericulture in Ujani Aham binds people in a shared culture. *Pat* and *muga* (silk yarn) derived from silkworms are used to weave a variety of clothes for both men and women. In nonindustrial Ujani Aham, every family weaves its own clothes. Although weaving is a woman's activity, its effects are felt in every aspect of village life. In a way it safeguards against and restricts the levels of penetration by outsiders into the clothing market.[20] Homemade clothes are rarely sold in the market. On one occasion a group of women told me that they refuse to sell their handicrafts because if they did so "everyone else would be wearing our clothes and we will lose our identity."[21] Because clothing matters, a conscious effort is made by people not to wear garments that can identify them with other groups. People of Ujani Aham who want to be recognized as different see their identity linked to, or expressed in, their dress. The shades of color, length, and kinds of stripes on men's lungis, the patterns woven on women's mekhala sador, and, above all, the fact that the clothes are homemade all assert difference. The adherence to local dress styles, patterns, and fabrics has had a positive impact in that it helps to bridge class and caste boundaries and temporarily knits the communities together.

Even more important than food and dress, the mark of Ujani Aham is its spoken language, a language its speakers consider to be pristine Assamese.[22] It is a symbol of a mix between the "Ahom" language (declared dead by Grierson [1904] and Gait [1963]) and a dialect of Assamese spoken in the Luit Valley. Although very few "Ahom" words have survived in the speech of Ujani Aham, the tone and inflection of Ujani Aham Assamese is influenced by local syntax and grammar, which privilege colloquial usage rather than the formal language of literary Assamese derived from Sanskrit, which is an external borrowing (Gogoi and Gogoi 1984, 282). The words or figures of speech of Ujani Aham are tied to tropes of interiority that reaffirm a distinct sense of "us."

These are some of the obvious markers of identity that most people in Ujani Aham provided for me when I asked what made them different from others in Assam. I found it hard to accept that these "things" made them Tai-Ahom, for there was nothing unique about them, nor were they peculiar to one community in Ujani Aham. They were shared experiences and attributes. In particular, lower-income families and lower-caste and non-Hindu people shared common food habits and dress styles. Once I accepted that these were common "things" and lived experiences for the majority in Ujani Aham, I also started seeing how these markers play a role in making Tai-Ahoms out of the disparate and marginal groups. Precisely because these "things" and experiences are shared, the leaders of the Tai-Ahom movement can use them in a strategic political language of disempowerment and marginalization, and rally the people to support their cause for a new identity. The ordinary everyday experiences are made extraordinary through conscious political and social efforts, and a discourse of Tai-Ahom is generated. This discourse has become popular. Food, dress, language, emotions, and social actions become "things" to express local views of what it means to be Tai-Ahom. The emotional discourse that describes the experience of being Tai-Ahom—words such as marginalization, disempowerment, and dispossession—constructs a place called Ujani Aham and, with it, a culture and politics of identity.[23] Reflection on the construction of specific symbols leads us to understand the performances of Tai-Ahom identity, much of which is a verbal claim about being different from "others." In the meantime, as the concepts of Ujani Aham and Tai-Ahom are developed and produced in Luitpaar, internal hierarchies of leaders and supporters, images and agendas, continue to contest and vie for the power to lead the identity movement.

The current Tai-Ahom movement is both visible and audible due to a number of reasons, which I will discuss in the next chapter. It would be a mistake, though, to assume that this is a brand-new movement. In Ujani Aham, throughout the twentieth century different leaders have assumed the mantle of Tai-Ahom politics and achieved limited success. Each attempt at constructing Tai-Ahom furthered the cause and delineated a shape that, over time, was transformed from a loose patchwork of symbols into a sharper image outlining an ethnic identity. The experiments with Tai-Ahom identity that are ongoing today are part of a series. To understand the current developments, the history of Tai-Ahom identity construction in the early twentieth century must first be investigated. In the rest of this chapter, I will explore the unfolding process of Tai-Ahom politics that led to the late twentieth century and the emergence of ULFA, the militant organization that radicalized the people of Ujani Aham. Although the Tai-Ahom cultural movement and ULFA were not really connected, the impact of ULFA on the movement was dramatic. As an organization, ULFA made groups like Tai-Ahom deeply aware of their subject position within India. Tai-Ahom, in this atmosphere of charged political awareness, became more than a label—it became a movement that galvanized all kinds of people to support an identity that promised dignity through recognition and justice and rights through the redistribution of resources and land.

### PEOPLE, PLACE, AND POLITICS: A TWENTIETH-CENTURY STORY OF UJANI AHAM

In the last decade of the nineteenth century and the first quarter of the twentieth, in a limited domain of Jorhat and Sibsagar, a small group of intellectuals began to revive the stories of swargadeos in order to construct a memory of an Ahom past. Men like Thanuram Gogoi, Surendranahth Gohain Barua, Radha Kanta Handique, Padmanath Gohain

Borooah, Sarbananda Rajkonwar, and Hiteswar Barbarua were the pioneers in this movement. They used this material to write history books about dead kings rather than to craft a new identity.[24] In their meetings they focused on discussions of genealogy, the origins of particular khels and the lineage of the khel members. Ahom was not yet a "public" object for mass consumption but a tool for elites to assert their privileged place.

Narrow definitions of the Ahoms as royals who belonged to the lineage of the swargadeos and constituted the elite class of Ujani Aham could not include in their narratives the vast masses of peasants who were the bulwark of local society. Hence, the Ahom-minded people of Ujani Aham felt that something more was needed to capture the imagination of the people and constitute a political organization. In the history of the Tai-Ahom movement this was the "moment of manoeuvre" (Chatterjee 1993, 81). Within and outside Assam important changes were taking place that forced a new discourse of the issue of Ahom and transformed elite expressions into a new kind of mass political sentiment that was brought together in the organization called Ahom Sabha (which I referred to in chapter 1). The story of the birth of Ahom Sabha in Ujani Aham is today told in very simple terms. Nabin Borgohain, a high priest in the present-day Tai-Ahom movement in Dhemaji, told me the story in these words:

> We were told by the Dadai purush gossain [Shankaria/Vaishnavite priest] that 300 maunds of rice were needed for the *rath yatra* [ritual celebration] during the governor general's visit to Assam [1890]. We collected rice from Tipam, Abhaypur, and Lakua. Under the supervision of Kaliabar Medhi and a magistrate, Sarubhaga Dihingia sent the provisions by boat to Sibsagar. The boat got stuck in the river and Hati Dihingia and Sarunath Dihingia, two Ahoms, went to help dig out the boat from the mud. Since the Ahom men touched the boat, the gossain decided it had become *suwa* [polluted]. They said Ahoms had polluted the sacred objects of the yatra by touching the boat! We—Ahoms—had donated our rice that we had grown, harvested, thrashed, cooked, and softened for the official guests. That was acceptable. But the moment we touched the boat it became polluted! The entire offering was thrown into the river. It became obvious to us that the Hindus will take our rice and our labor, but they cannot accept our presence. This was the reason for forming the Ahom Sabha.[25]

Following this incident, the Ahom movement started to expand, although Ahom politics continued to be a limited enterprise. A few deodhais and a small group of middle-class professionals in Sibsagar engaged in a discussion to make Ahom politics separate from the caste Hindu politics that had taken shape under the guidance of the Indian National Congress (INC). Toward this goal, in 1915 they took up the cause of promoting the Ahom language. With the help of a Buddhist *bikhu* (priest) from Burma, Ahom alphabets were designed and blocks were made in the Sreerampur Press of the American Baptist Mission in Calcutta. The support of the American Baptist group in Sibsagar was crucial. Additionally, the Ahom intellectuals of Jorhat, under the guidance of Radha Kanta Handique, also set up a Tai language school, but the results were not encouraging. The biggest problem was finding teachers who could teach the language courses. It was apparent that the so-called Tai-Ahom people were illiterate in the language of the early buranjis, and soon the project of language training was given up.

In the meantime, the INC party was becoming prominent in Assam. Ahom politicians saw the rise of the Congress in Assam as the ascendancy of Hindu power because they viewed the Congress organization as a mouthpiece of caste Hindus. Threatened by the INC's prominence, the intellectuals of the Ahom Sabha decided to form a political association called the Ahom Association (AA), and they invited all kinds of people to join the organization. The AA was meant as a platform to protest the rise of caste Hindu power in Ujani Aham (which I discussed in chapter 1). The 1935 convention of the AA in Dibrugarh was a massive affair, and the effects of the association's politics became evident when in the 1937 Assam Assembly election, four candidates of the Ahom Party won seats. In 1941 a new political group called "Sarbo Doll" or "All People's Party" was constituted by the various non-Congress political groups of Ujani Aham to contest elections against the Congress in Assam. The Ahom leaders of the All People's Party targeted the "Mongolia" groups—the Kacharis, Muttocks, and Deuris—to come together against caste Hindus. A major issue for them was how to create a separate electorate from the Congress in order to gain more political power in Assam. Toward creating the Ahom as a separate group within Assamese society, Handique wrote several "Ahom epics." His attempt was to "tell stories and events about our people and history . . . to create pride in our history" (1924, 2).[26] Surendranath Gohain, the leader of the People's Party, appealed to the British government that Ahoms be declared a "racial minority" in Assam, a demand that was not achieved.

After 1947, when India gained independence from the British, Gopinath Bordoloi, an Assamese Brahmin who formed a ministry as a Congressman, declared the Ahoms to be a "backward group," a categorization that had many long-term consequences. Although the term "backward" in this sense was meant as a political and administrative term, the label stigmatized the community as low, and in caste Hindu religious terms it indicated that they were a polluted group of people. Ahom thus became backward both politically and socially. The classification "backward" guaranteed few benefits for the Ahom: by being labeled as a "backward group" and not a Scheduled Tribe (ST), the Ahoms were left out of the Sixth Schedule of the newly drafted Indian Constitution that would have ensured them more privileges within the Indian union. The classification ST is not well explained in the Indian Constitution, but groups that are "geographically isolated, backward, and shy" are put in this category by the national government. The system of creating ST groups is continuous, as new groups are admitted into the classification. The ST classification works to give groups access to affirmative-action policies, and thus the lucrative benefits of economic and political gains drive many groups to claim ST status. The Tai-Ahom political leaders wanted to enlist their supporters as a ST group in order to guarantee some benefits to them. But they failed to achieve this goal in the initial period of the classification. Nonetheless, with each successive ministry in Assam, men who identified themselves as Ahoms gained limited political power and received ministerial offices. Purandar Chetia became a cabinet minister in the local Assam government, while Surendranath Gohain, the pioneering leader of the AA, became a cabinet minister in the national government. Soon after joining the coterie of parliamentarians, the Ahom leaders changed their political affiliation and joined the Congress party to ensure their continuance in office.

Arguably, the events of the early twentieth century and the politics of the AA generated an interest and a narrative that emphasized the swargadeo culture of Ujani Aham, thus setting the area and culture of Ujani Aham apart from the rest of Assam. The leaders of AA were using a memory of the swargadeos' rule as a tool to construct a political opposition that could defy the Congress's hegemony in Assam. The term Ahom from the buranjis served well for the purpose of bringing together certain groups of people with a common agenda, and through the efforts of the elite political group an alternative memory of Ahom power before the rise of the Assamese in colonial times was generated. Within the heartland of Ujani Aham, images of Ahom therefore quickly gained prominence and became a handy tool for bargaining with the national Congress party for more power in Assam. As a result, the plethora of images increased. It started with discussions about swargadeos and clan groups, as we have seen, but soon enough new tactics of racial politics were also devised and used for political purposes. Once these images became available in the public and political sphere, local people did not know what to do with their emotions about having become a backward/outcaste group within the Hindu religious fold. Nor were they sure what to make of the newly minted Ahom histories. The label Ahom that was put into circulation did not create an Ahom community for them. It only served the urban political elite who could now claim descent from rather remote and obscure warrior-administrators to carve out political careers for themselves. At this stage, a minor change of name, the construction of lofty genealogies, and membership in the AA was all that was needed to become an Ahom politician. Many in Ujani Aham saw the politics of Ahom as a way of challenging the caste-based Brahmin hegemony. While they called themselves Ahom, however, few changed their customary religious practices, which continued to be Hindu. The political discourse fostered by the elite and the common person's feelings of exploitation and marginalization that were embroiled with experiences of geographical and cultural difference in Ujani Aham came to a head in 1962.

### A PERIOD OF RECKONING: 1962

In November 1962 tensions between China and India reached a culmination in a full-fledged war in India's northeast frontier. The reasons for this conflict were many. In 1914 the British colonial government drew a line to demarcate the northern boundary between India and Tibet, which they called the McMohan line. The Chinese, however, never ratified or accepted this demarcation. When India became independent in 1947 it inherited the colonial map along with the people on the frontiers. The Chinese government protested this arrangement, but the Indian government showed no interest in engaging in a discussion about the issue. In 1954 the Indian government drew a new official map, but it reproduced the same boundaries that were on the British model. Needless to say, the Chinese refused to accept the Indian map. In turn, the Indian government, after claiming the northwest and northeast frontier areas, made few attempts to administer these territories. In the northeast the area between the "inner line" and the Assam plains was totally neglected.[27] The various tribal groups (the Monpas, Akas, Miris, Ankha, Dhaplas, Mishimis, etc) living in the area did not really know where they belonged—India or China. Meanwhile, the Chinese government, after annexing Tibet in 1959, tried to muster the support of their neighbors in East Asia by raising a general alarm against the foreign investments of the United States in South and Southeast Asia. China labeled India a pawn of the United States to justify its aggressive anti-India mood. In the end, the conflict between the large powers in the region—India and China—was a show of armed power based on serious miscalculations on both sides. The people living along the line of the border suffered the repercussions of such nation-state politics.

The Chinese army entered Assam on November 21, 1962. The army moved rapidly into the Assam plains and entered the town of Tezpur, which, according to B. N. Kaul, "was immediately deserted by the Indian officials and military. The civil authorities released convicts from jails. Banks were closed after they [Indian officials] had burnt their currency notes" (1967, 427). Residents of Lakhimpur, Dhemaji, Tezpur, and the like were forced to leave their homes in the wake of the Chinese occupation of the area. The people of Assam in general felt betrayed and deserted by the Indian authorities. Prime Minister Nehru's historic speech, aired on the national radio on November 22, drove the final wedge. He declared, "my heart goes out to the people of Assam, but I cannot do anything." The Assamese people were shocked and devastated. Buddheshwar Gogoi, a high school history teacher and the founding chairman of ULFA, described to me his impression of the 1962 debacle in these words:

> In 1962 the Chinese attacked us. We immediately heeded Nehru's call to give everything we had for the cause of saving our country [India]. We started a war fund and donated all our money, family jewelry; many people even donated their pensions; some even gave their land-holdings papers to the government. We were prepared to fight to save our country. But when the attack took place, the government officials backed off and abandoned us. . . . On the other hand, the Chinese soldiers, who were supposed to be our enemy, saved us that year. We had food because of them. You see, when people started fleeing at the wake of the Chinese invasion, the paddy in the field was not yet harvested. But we could do nothing. We were asked to evacuate. However, when we returned to our homes, we found that the Chinese soldiers

had harvested the grain, tied them in bundles, and stored them in the barns. We could not believe it. Our enemies had saved our paddy. We are farmers. Rice is our only wealth, and the Chinese gave it back to us.[28]

This candid narrative is full of implications. Paradoxically, while the people of Ujani Aham were preparing to "fight to save our country"—that is, India—the Indian government did nothing to safeguard them but left them exposed to the Chinese attack. In turn, their enemy—the Chinese—gave them back the thing they cared for most of all: rice, the fruit of their labor. This realization came as a shock to people. The initial reaction was disbelief, for until then Congress had pretended it cared.

The "Chinese Aggression," as the event is popularly known in India, revealed to the people the utter disregard with which the Indian state viewed them and the region of Assam. Almost overnight, everyone in Assam realized that their relationship with the Indian state had changed forever. The memory of being abandoned spurred reactions. After the attack on Tezpur and its abandonment by Indian officials, several residents of Guwahati met with some British officers who had flown a reconnaissance trip to provide assistance. A report in the *Daily Telegraph* on November 2, 1962, stated that the residents confided to the British, "at last, we know who are our real friends." In the traumatic aftermath of the Chinese aggression and the desertion by Indian civil and military authorities, people in Assam were asking one question: what happened? Failing to find an answer from the government in New Delhi, gradually people generated a self-imposed distance between themselves and the rest of India and hesitated to be identified as Indians.

In keeping with the mood of the times, the Assamese intellectual and political forces generated a consciousness of Assamese identity centered on the memories of "Ahom rule." A nostalgic reminder of the swargadeos and the historical autonomy of the place and people of Assam prior to colonialism became the key. Poems that were written in the period of the anticolonial struggle in the early twentieth century were recycled to create a new political spirit among the postcolonial generation in Assam. Nalini Bala Devi's poem *Janam Bhumi* (Land of my birth) became the sentiment of difference between Assam and India. Lakhinath Bezbarua's poem, "O, My Beloved Country—Assam," which was composed during the period of anticolonial struggle, was now sung as a regional anthem. This song is sung even today at public gatherings. Bhupen Hazarika's songs, such as "We Assamese People Will Never Be Impoverished by Any Calamity," helped energize local Assamese identity. By the early 1960s in this climate of local fervor, an Assamese identity movement emerged with a full-blown political agenda. The curious combination of the labels "Assamese" and "Ahom history" was not explained. The people of Ujani Aham, while they connected with the emotion of the Assamese movement and felt very distanced from Indians and Indian identity, were not convinced by the new direction of Assamese politics. In response, the members of the erstwhile AA convened their own forum.

The development of an Ahom movement alongside the Assamese movement happened in the wake of the government of India's decision to reorganize Assam in 1967. Assam was soon to be divided along linguistic and ethnic lines. In Garhgaon, Sibsagar, under the presidency of Padmeshwar Gogoi, an Ahom forum was convened. The *Assam Tribune* reported on June 8, 1967, that the leaders in the meeting urged that "a separate and autonomous Ahom unit [should] be formed with the contiguous Upper Assam districts . . . which met with sudden setback and continued to deteriorate under the hundred and twenty years of British rule, as well as under the present administration."

Immediately, more Ahom organizations emerged. Some of them, such as the "Ahom-Tai Rajya Parishad," The "Ahom Sabha," and "The Mongoloid National Front," gathered their forces together and became an amalgamated organization calling itself "Ahom Tai Mongolia Parishad." This new forum convened in October 1967 under general secretary Siva Buragohain of Jorhat. The organization demanded that a separate "Mongolian state of Ahoms" be formed in Ujani Aham, east of the famous Kaziranga game sanctuary. The *Assam Tribune* stated on June 3, 1967, that another Ahom leader, Khagen Saikia, who led the "Ahom-Tai-Rajya Parishad," demanded that there be a "creation of a separate centrally administered unit . . . in which Ahom-Tais and the various other tribes would enjoy social recognition and all political rights." The Ahom organizations that proliferated at this time expected that by making a lot of noise about Ahom and their "otherness" from the Assamese groups, the government at New Delhi would be impressed and give them some rights. Even students and intellectuals became involved in this effort to carve out a separate space for Ahoms within Assam. Professor Jogen Phukan presided over the newly organized "Guwahati University Tai Students Association," which, as reported by the *Assam Tribune* on October 5, 1967, passed a resolution that "Tai languages should be taught in schools and colleges in Tai majority areas; scholarships [should] be awarded to Tai students for pursuing higher studies in Thailand and Burma; proper care and preservation of historical documents should be taken up; and the publication of Tai historical manuscripts and development of [the] Tai Central Academy at Patsaku, Sibsagar were necessary."

Despite these intense efforts, the Ahom leaders failed to convince the Indian authorities that they should be classified as a tribal group and given the status of ST. After the reorganization of Assam, the Ahoms found that they were not classified as "tribal" but were made "part and parcel of Assamese society." In fact, this was done deliberately by the government so that all of Assam could be made into a large caste Hindu, but "backward," society. This development drove the wedge further between the Ahom and Assamese communities. Padmeshwar Gogoi's newly coined term "Tai-Ahom" inaugurated a significant change: Ahom became Tai-Ahom and Ujani Aham was deemed an Ahom space and connected to the history of the swargadeos. The appellation immediately narrowed the concept of what might count as Ahom. It implied a vague but important connection with the Tai people of Southeast Asia. Adding the prefix Tai to Ahom led to the construction and circulation of a new kind of memory in Ujani Aham. Tai-Ahom was now internally conceived of as not Indian, although those who called themselves by this label continued to live, as they had in the past, within the boundaries of the Indian nation-state. Their relationship with the Assamese also underwent some drastic changes. They agreed that they shared a common language, but beyond this neither their histories nor cultures were linked. The loose, fuzzy, indefinable Ahom of the buranjis was assertively transformed into an ethnic community through the political memorialization of Ujani Aham's past. The renaming made Ahoms into Tai—foreign, exotic, and different from everyone else in Assam. Even so, at this point, despite the active circulation of the label, it was not clear what Ahom meant to the people of Ujani Aham at large.

Thus, a new form of local politics was born in the 1960s, and it centered on making Tai-Ahom into an "ethnic" community. Suddenly Ahom was no longer a derogatory label for the low and sundry in Ujani Aham, as upper-caste Hindus believed, nor was it only a historical topic as the colonials had perceived. The rules of what and who could be Ahom were discursively altered by political developments in Ujani Aham. A unique aspect of the new Ahom enterprise was that it was not a sequential development. The process of experimentation with the label, the production of new meanings, and the consumption of Ahom were simultaneous:

discourse and practice went hand in hand. The label Ahom was put to use in political, literary, and cultural gatherings, including festivals and commemorative holidays in Ujani Aham. Alongside the intensified politics of Ahom, a value was also put on the term as a label, and it was exchanged for high-price government posts, important ministerial portfolios, and big gains. The direct gains that were made gave becoming an Ahom a greater allure among the masses. The heterogeneous components of Ujani Aham found in Ahom politics a reason to get together.

In contrast to the 1960s, in which Tai-Ahom politics became one of many local agendas, the 1970s was seemingly not an active period for Tai-Ahom politics in Assam. No doubt, in a limited domain of academia, Tai-Ahom became a subject of discourse, but its shape remained vague and unclear. To the populace of Assam, Tai-Ahom did not mean much. For children growing up in the 1970s, Tai-Ahom had no visibility. There were no special holidays identified as Tai-Ahom, no Tai-Ahom villages, no language called Tai-Ahom, no history lessons about Ahoms, not even Tai-Ahom festivals and food. In Ujani Aham, particularly in the district of Sibsagar, from which my family came, there were some vague reminders of an Ahom past in the art and architecture associated with the swargadeo culture. Most of these buildings, though, were in ruins: the Kareng-ghar, Rang-ghar, Talatol-ghar—as well as the *duals* (a type of temple) and several *maidams* (burial grounds), including Charaideo (the burial ground of swargadeos). They were all overgrown and the abode of wild animals. One heard stories of the "powers" of these places, but few actually ventured to visit them. Although Tai-Ahom was not really visible in the society and culture of the time, this situation would change. Throughout the 1970s, Tai-Ahom leaders focused on a cultural revival. The attempt was to construct a separate community outside of the rubric of the Hindu and the Assamese, so that they could continue their appeal to the government of India to make them a ST group.

The burgeoning politics of Tai-Ahom found several outlets. Political efforts to create an Assamese identity were already underway in the late 1970s, led by AASU. The Assamese movement, locally known as Ahamia Jatigathan (Community building), started in the early 1960s as a language movement directed against the Bengali-speaking people of Assam. By the 1970s, however, it became determinedly anti-Indian. In the 1980s, it changed course again and became anti-Bangladeshi Muslim. But as soon as the AASU took this turn, in Ujani Aham the Juva Chatra Parishad was formed to devise a local Ujani Aham forum and agenda. For people in

Ujani Aham, the menace of Bangladeshi settlers was not an immediate experience as was claimed by the AASU. In fact, the politics of Ujani Aham were more concerned with reviving a memory of the past, focusing on those aspects of Ujani Aham culture that would emphasize the non-Brahmanic elements of Assamese culture and society. The swargadeos of the erstwhile Assam kingdom became icons in the Chatra Parishad movement, and Ahoms became crucial participants in the new forum. Student leaders sought men like Domboru Deodhai to help them understand Ujani Aham's Ahom past. In the meantime, a group of Thai intellectuals launched a program to search for "ancestors" and during this search they found the Ahoms of Ujani Aham. I will discuss these groups and the alliances between them in greater detail in the next chapter, but here it is necessary to note that the gathering together of a variety of groups led to a further radicalization of politics in Ujani Aham and a more autonomous future was imagined. In the early 1980s, a new guerrilla movement—ULFA—emerged in Sibsagar.

Unlike the previous identity movements in Assam, ULFA suggested the use of violence against the Indian state as a main strategy of protest. They emphasized that the enemy was not the poor settlers from Bangladesh, because potentially they could be converted and made *natun Ahamia* (new Assamese) if they accepted Assam as their homeland and learned the Assamese language. The ULFA emphasized that the true enemy was the Indian state. The ULFA claimed that India had failed in every sense of the term to improve conditions of living in Assam and to provide opportunities for the growth of the people and the economy. They were now calling on their supporters in Ujani Aham to relinquish their attachment to India, despite the fact that the majority in Assam is Hindu, and declare war against the state on economic and political grounds. To quell the "militant terrorism" of ULFA, several military units were deployed to Assam.

As if state violence were not enough at this time, intracommunity clashes—Assamese Hindus against Bengali Muslims; and Assamese against non-Assamese—flared up. Violence became a sustained condition in Assam. In Upper Assam the Indian military ran amuck in the villages, and in Lower Assam violent clashes between plains' tribe groups such as the Bodos and settlers from Orissa and Bihar, as well as the so-called Bangladeshis, became the order of the day. The ferocious violence was all that newspapers could report on Assam, and the details of how many people were killed were publicized with perverse pleasure in the national press. Since then all that outsiders seem to know about Assam is the violence that was part of the saga of the land and people in the 1980s and 1990s. Understanding the relationship between the communities and violence becomes a major problem for those who do not know the histories of these communities and their interactions before the violence. For most people the identity issues in Assam are fitted within certain categories that totalize rather than emphasize nuance and variation. Some claim it is terrorism that is part of the psyche of the people of Assam; others reduce the struggle to a religious conflict of Assamese Hindus (potentially helped by the Indian state) against the Bangladeshi Muslim settlers; and still others claim that local people have no agency and it is the Christian missionaries and Pakistani Inter-Services Intelligence infiltrators who trigger and facilitate violence. These assumptions are simple and provide a recipe for grand theorizing. Indeed, this was one of the major complaints of the ULFA. They pointed out that although they represented the Assamese, the majority of whom are Hindu, their struggle cannot be subsumed and made part of the Hindu national struggle ongoing in the rest of India. ULFA claimed that the psychological, cultural, and economic distances between the Assamese and the Indians could never be overcome by pretentious claims of their common Hindu background. The rise of the ULFA, for the time being, shifted focus from the anti-Bangladeshi politics that had planted itself in Assam and made people aware of the larger and more problematic relationship with the state. But a people's movement against the state never developed because new political developments emerged in various pockets in Assam.

Throughout the 1980s the violence in Assam made people more restless, and the predictable outcome was the collapse of the concept of an Assamese community. A new movement called the Bodoland movement became one of the most vociferous and violent splinter groups, and its members dominated the politics of Lower Assam in the late 1980s. The Tai-Ahoms also gained ground in Upper Assam. They focused on constructing and publicizing a history of Ahoms by reviving obscure cultural practices and religious rituals. By invoking the swargadeos and Ahoms of the buranjis as their ancestors, they presented the "Tai-Ahom" label as an ethnic community. But unlike the "tribal" communities (of Nagas, Khasis, Mizos, etc.) that differed from Hindu Assamese in clear ways of religion, language, and culture, the so-called Tai-Ahoms could not really distinguish themselves from the Assamese. To a lesser or greater degree the groups that claimed to be Tai-Ahom resembled the Assamese Hindus, sharing with them the same spaces, language, food habits, dress, festivals, rituals, superstitions, and so on. Yet the newly constructed label Tai-Ahom appealed to many disempowered and marginal groups and gained ground in Ujani Aham. These groups found in Ahom a site to reject the label Assamese and carry on a protest movement against the institutions of Assamese power of Hinduism and urban elitism, which were connected with Delhi and the rest of India. "Ahomness" mattered to these groups, as well as to both the Indians and the Assamese, for claiming Ahomness was an affirmation of being different from these groups.

Within this space of protest, the voice of ULFA became more radical and prominent. The young men and women of the ULFA organization revived memories of 1962, the moment of departure from India. Buddheshwar Gogoi, the group's founding chairman, described to me the need for creating the radical organization:

> We forgot to remember 1962 for a long time. We forgot what the Indians had done to us . . . After India became independent, people in Assam continued to be poor. We tried to be good peasants and kept waiting for the government of India to deliver some real goods, which independence from British colonialism had promised us. People in Bengal and Bihar were enjoying the newly found freedom from colonial subjectivity and we expected the same. We, in Assam, had also fought for Indian independence against the British. . . .
>
> The Nagas, from the very beginning, understood the mentality of the Indians. We were the ones who thought, "we are Hindus, we are Indians." But now we have to remember 1962—the trauma of desertion, the betrayal of the Indians. . . . We had to take action against the Indian state and people.[29]

The young ULFA radicals initially pursued socialist political visions and dreamed of freeing Assam from Indian bondage and servitude. This rhetoric, initially rejected in the thriving metropolis of Guwahati and the satellite towns of Lower Assam that were connected by trade with the rest of India, received a hearty response in the villages of Ujani Aham. There, people saw ULFA as articulating their dreams and longings. Therefore, when the state deployed the armed forces to wipe out the ULFA cadres, the people of Ujani Aham sheltered the radicals in their homes and became their supporters. The resolve of the local people of Ujani Aham to support ULFA activities became stronger in the face of the army assaults. The military operations called Bajrang (1990) and Rhino (1991) created new waves of sympathy, and politics became more radical. The Indian military, after failing to break the ULFA organization through military operations, directed their attacks on the villages of Ujani Aham. In 1992, on New Year's Eve, the AASU called for a statewide *bandh* (closure of Assam) to protest the military atrocities that had been perpetrated against villagers, especially women (who in particular had been targeted). In this climate, a cultural identity like Tai-Ahom helped to unite the populace of Ujani Aham.

Emboldened by the ULFA leadership in Ujani Aham, the disgruntled and peripheral communities under the banner of Tai-Ahom made a demand for a homeland. This was projected as a new Tai-Ahom state, covering the areas from Sadiya to Kaziranga. Because ULFA was already talking about separation from India, the demand for a Tai-Ahom homeland did not surprise too many people in the region. By connecting Ujani Aham with the Tai-Ahom movement and the history of Luitpaar with Ahom history, the Tai-Ahom leaders and their adherents now defined and unified the concept of Ujani Aham, and their customs and practices were presented as part of a Tai-Ahom culture. The connections they made were no doubt fraught with problems, combining as they did emotions about past politics, longing for a new homeland, and feelings held by a variety of people otherwise not connected to each other. Moreover, by connecting Ujani Aham to Tai-Ahom, they left out several groups that could not claim the label Tai-Ahom and thus put them outside the space of the new politics.

The connections made by Tai-Ahom leaders between Ujani Aham, Luit, and an Ahom past must be critically evaluated. Otherwise, as David Lowenthal warns us, "history co-opted by heritage exaggerates . . . to assert a primacy, an ancestry, a continuity. It underwrites a founding myth meant to exclude others" (1994, 53). This is not, however, of immediate concern for Tai-Ahom leaders. They are more concerned with the people they have included within their new order then they are about those left outside.

What do the agents of the Tai-Ahom movement want to achieve? How is the construction of Tai-Ahom connected to radical politics of ULFA? Is it possible for the people of Ujani Aham to become Tai-Ahom and at the same time make a connection with Thailand? How do local politics interact and exchange with transnational interests? My travel to Assam in 1994 plunged me into thinking about these questions, and what I encountered was very convoluted and complex. In the following chapters I try to make sense of some of my encounters in the field. For both actors and witnesses alike, including myself, the Tai-Ahom movement involved a series of messy and troublesome events. In the next chapter I attempt to convey the more recent developments of Tai-Ahom as I have experienced them.

# CHAPTER 5

# Performance and Politics of Tai-Ahom

. On February 10, 1995, under the banner of the second Tai and Tribal studies international conference, leaders of the Ban Ok Publik Muang Tai and local tribal organizations along with Thai scholars and SULFA members (surrendered ULFA militants) gathered together in a remote village school in Sonapur.[1] The purpose of this gathering was to discuss strategies to increase the bargaining capacity of local organizations, vis-à-vis the state, in determining matters of economic and political importance.[2] Thus a barely known village and an obscure school on February 10 became the hub of intense discussions. There the participants agreed that the Tai-Ahom identity movement could serve as an agenda for gaining control of land, resources, and political power for groups that were dispossessed and marginalized by the Assamese caste Hindu communities. They were representing a variety of people, but this mattered little to the leaders. The coming together of the Ban Ok leaders, Thai scholars, and ex-ULFA activists was a historical moment, as I saw it. I was also struck by the political connections made by the leaders in their public speeches, using the images of swargadeos and precolonial Assam as their common denominator. The camaraderie between the groups was palpable, and I could not help thinking, like others around me, I suppose, that I was witness to a momentous gathering. Indeed, the convention was the site of a powerful statement combining a variety of agendas and groups that were otherwise disconnected.

The Tai studies conference was part of a long series of "articulations" (Laclau and Mouffe 1985) of the marginality and disempowerment of the people of Assam. This rhetoric had created several discourse communities throughout the twentieth century to project representative as well as parochial issues.[3] I have discussed in previous chapters the histories of the discourse communities of the Ahom and the Assamese that emerged in response to the articulations of the Indian National Congress in the early twentieth century. However, in the periods immediately following independence Assamese became the dominant discourse and Ahom was submerged within that articulation. In the late 1980s, a new discourse of the community of Tai-Ahom emerged again, and this time it addressed, on the behalf of several disparate and unrepresented groups, important historical grievances as well as current ones concerning the rights of citizenship as practiced in Assam.

### MAKING SENSE OF LOCAL NATIONALISM
### AND MULTIPLE DISCOURSES

The discourse generated by Tai-Ahom activists, with some support from the ULFA in the late 1980s, framed an ideology of "local nationalism." I see local nationalism as a movement creating a social and political imaginary in a specific, definable place (in this case Ujani Aham) to articulate wider political and social demands. Although rooted in a place, there is nothing particularistic or simple about local nationalism. It is a "moment" and a site that tends to overwhelm what is considered "national" to reconstitute new social and political conditions in a locality. The politics of local nationalism were aimed at gaining for Ujani Aham, in particular, autonomy in politics, culture, and identity. In this political assertion, the Tai-Ahom were supported in some measure by the ULFA, although the connections between the two were never really established or clearly articulated. Both organizations claimed that Assam's marginality had reduced its people from citizens to subjects.[4] This rhetoric reached out to a variety of groups at the same time. Regional and class boundaries in Ujani Aham were temporarily submerged and, by and large, the people endorsed the efforts of the Tai-Ahom and the ULFA leaders without making too much effort to investigate the politics and strategies of the leaders. The commonly experienced economic disempowerment and political marginalization, accompanied by the deeply felt antagonism toward the classes and groups of people identified as upper-caste Hindus (who were deemed to be representatives of the Indian state), allowed the people to come together in a common endeavor. In this context, leaders of different movements could generate images and narratives of the past in order to promise a political utopia in the future and a new identity for Ujani Aham as separate and different from Hindu India.[5]

The initial success of both organizations and the politics of local nationalism were determined by several factors. The leadership of ULFA in the early 1990s was in the hands of the Ujani Aham group led by Auro-bindo Rajkhowa, Anup Chetia, and Pradeep Gogoi, who were very sympathetic to the Tai-Ahom cause because many of their family members were involved in the identity movement.[6] As a result, Ujani Aham cultural, religious, and social performances enabled the construction of Tai-Ahom as an "ethnic" identity. And, with the help of ULFA, Tai-Ahom was transformed into a political movement demanding freedom in the frontiers. Curiously, the rhetoric of freedom did not focus on the emancipation of land and territory but on identity. Tai-Ahom was promoted as the original and autonomous identity of the Ujani Aham people. Leaders opined that Tai-Ahom was suppressed and submerged by other labels such as "Assamese" and "Indian." Only when their identity as Tai-Ahom was recognized, they claimed, would they truly become part of the Indian union. Then they would be free citizens who could claim an identity both intimate and personal.

A crucial factor in the efforts of both the Tai-Ahom and the ULFA organizations was the shared audience. This captive audience, along with a shared mystical past created and sustained by images of the swargadeos, made it possible to dream of a political utopia, a dream that temporarily bonded together the Tai-Ahom and ULFA movements. In the words of Pradeep Gogoi, the vice chairman of ULFA, "such a fire of freedom could only ignite and burn in the villages of Ujani Aham where hope had died."[7] The people living along the Luitpaar heard the call to engage in antagonistic politics. They became the agents who transformed the ideas of their leaders into action through cultural and social activities as well as through armed struggle. In the course of my stay in several villages I became acquainted with many young men and women involved in both organizations, all of whom fluidly moved between them, sharing their energies and resources. This fluidity was also well known to Hiteshwar Saikia, Assam's chief minister, who was rumored to have connections with the main leaders of both organizations.[8]

I am not suggesting here, however, that the two politically dispersed movements, the ULFA and the Tai-Ahom, can or should be evaluated as one large enterprise. Their agendas were not merged under a common banner. The Tai-Ahom leaders continued to represent an identity movement, while the ULFA made bold statements about seceding from India and making Assam independent (a new nation-state?). Their political strategies also differed. Tai-Ahom leaders emphasized the "production of culture" as the way to forge a new beginning, while those of the ULFA promoted armed struggle against the state. Hence, although Tai-Ahom leaders negotiated and received some help from ULFA, they were ultimately looking toward New Delhi to recognize them as a separate community from the Assamese and make them the beneficiaries of political and economic privileges, which were not available to them in their present condition. Also, when the founding leaders of the ULFA were forced to go underground after the military operations of Bajrang and Rhino, the ULFA shifted its headquarters to Lower Assam and their relationship with the Tai-Ahom movement ceased abruptly. Thus, analysis in this chapter of the combined articulations generated by the two groups is confined to the early 1990s.

Apart from the heightened local political consciousness generated by the leaders of the ULFA and the Tai-Ahom in Ujani Aham, a third and external factor also contributed to strengthening the platform of local nationalism. The Thais of Thailand had adopted the Ahoms as (one) of their ancestors after the first international Thai studies conference.[9] What had begun as a Thai academic exercise became fodder for both the leaders and supporters of the Tai-Ahom and ULFA organizations. A new representation of origins made it possible to imagine a history of Assam connected with Thailand that transcended the limits of the nation-state and Indian national identity. As a consequence, the Ujani Aham people felt more distant from Hindus and India. The ULFA did not have direct linkages with Thai scholars; at least no links are evident from the available materials. The Tai-Ahom organizations forged an alliance between ULFA and Thai scholars, and a Thai scholarly endorsement of the ULFA struggle for freedom was articulated at various conferences and in academic papers.[10] In addition to Thai academic support, ULFA also cultivated strong political and revolutionary ties with Kachin and Shan rebel groups in Burma. Such cross-territorial affiliations with Thai scholars and with Shan and Kachin rebels strengthened the movements in their home base in Assam but also made the discourse heterogeneous and brought to the fore divergent aspirations of local nationalism.

The Tai-Ahom discourse of local nationalism was controlled and directed by an organization called Ban Ok Publik Muang Tai. Composed of professionals, teachers, bureaucrats, and local village politicians, Ban Ok's main agenda was to produce a memory of the Ahom as an ethnic group based on a revised reading of the buranjis and the swargadeo culture and a constructed religion called Phra Lung, which claimed to differ from Hinduism. The efforts of the Ban Ok were endorsed and facilitated through overt and covert support by numerous agents. One of the most important local supporters of the Ban Ok was the chief minister of Assam, Hiteshwar Saikia.[11] While this may lead one to assume that Tai-Ahom was possibly a government-sponsored movement (due to the involvement of the chief minister), this was not the case. Tai-Ahom never became a statewide or state-sponsored movement. In fact the support it received from the Thai scholars and the ULFA made it decidedly an antiestablishment, antinational struggle as it looked at outside influences and agents to make its agenda broad based and transnational. Both leaders and followers of Ban Ok believed that with the help of Hiteshwar Saikia they would become a locally known community and that the ULFA would empower them economically, while the Thai scholars would make them a transnational community endowed with political power and cultural capital for exchange.

In this chapter, which is based on my fieldwork and oral histories, I document the articulations of Tai-Ahom leaders and organizations and show the convergence between the local agents, such as the Tai-Ahom, Hiteshwar Saikia, and the ULFA, and the transnational agents, such as Thai scholars and the Tai-Ahom identity movement. The alliances made by the organizations and leaders were not, however, permanent. The Tai-Ahom and the ULFA, it seems, quickly parted company, and very little is known of either their convergence or their parting. The connections between Tai-Ahom and Hiteshwar Saikia as well as the Thai scholars are better documented, and these relationships survived until 1997. In April 1996 Hiteshwar Saikia died, and in 1997 the Thai economy took a massive downward turn. As a consequence there were no more patrons to help sustain the Tai-Ahom movement. The period between 1985 and 1996 was thus the peak of the movement, and the production of Tai-Ahom at this time involved many leaders. Motivated by a desire to secure an identity, find a place, and "possess" a history that had been denied them within the national history and the national identity the movement had undertaken an intense search of the past during this period. The Tai-Ahom in this sense became an assertion and a demand to mitigate the marginality of Ujani Aham and its people. This ideology found many supporters and created a dynamic movement for a short time.

### TAI-AHOM ICONS: A TWENTIETH CENTURY PRODUCTION

George Coedés, in his book *The Indianized States of Southeast Asia* (translated into English in 1963), introduced the Ahoms as a Tai group to scholars of

South and Southeast Asian history and culture. But it was not until 1979 that Ahom history became a subject of discourse outside Assam. Political and academic interest in the subject of identity in Nehruvian India played an important role in prompting efforts to discover identities for marginal groups. In the decades following the reorganization of Assam (1967) and the division of the region into several small ethnic states, many more local identity movements emerged and bid for independent status. In 1979, the Assamese movement, led by the All Assam Students Union and Juva Chatra Parishad, made identity politics a lively platform for constructing an Assamese identity that boldly asserted its difference from the Indian national identity. That same year Berand Jan Terwiel, an anthropologist of Thailand who was undertaking research on the rituals of the Tai peoples of Southeast Asia, visited Assam and met with Ahom deodhais. The deodhais tried to convince Terwiel that they, too, were Tai. To prove it, Domboru Deodhai, along with several other deodhais of Bokota and Patsako villages in Sibsagar, put on displays of rituals. After a stay of eleven days, Terwiel found the *"informant's* statements and beliefs about their age-old tradition to be true," and he accepted the religion as a pre-Buddhist Tai religion (although Terwiel has since revised his opinion).[12] To the great advantage of the Tai-Ahom movement, Terwiel, in his voluminous study of Tai rituals (1983) mapped Ahoms as an ancient Tai community. Further, he identified Domboru Deodhai as the last of the original priests conversant in the ancient Tai rituals and the language of buranjis. This endorsement by a Western academic legitimized local claims and opened new possibilities for Tai-Ahom in general and Domboru Deodhai in particular. Both became distinct entities and soon Tai-Ahom was launched as a new identity movement.

Who was Domboru Deodhai? Why did Terwiel think he was the last "authentic" Tai-Ahom priest? These questions are hard to answer. Before 1981, Domboru Deodhai was unknown in Assam's public and political circles. In 1992, when I met him, he was very prominent within the Tai-Ahom movement and had a large following among the student members of the Juva Chatra Parishad and the Tai-Ahom activists in Ujani Aham. To an extent, his newly found prominence required an obliteration of his humble background. He was very reluctant to share any information about his childhood or religious training. Instead, he talked to me about his community and the Tai-Ahoms' loss of identity. He explained to me the need for Tai-Ahom identity in these words: "We were British servants. We had no identity. Our people retreated to the forests and remote villages when they drove out our swargadeos. Since then we have been practicing our religion and culture in our homes. Things are now changing. We have realized we have to find our identity. Hence I am teaching my grand-children all about it. Our religion and language are the bulwarks of our identity."[13]

Recently produced articles and political pamphlets concerning Tai-Ahom present Domboru Deodhai as someone who belonged to a re-spectable, although ordinary, peasant family (Gogoi and Gogoi 1994). Like his father, he combined agricultural duties with priestly activities. In Patsako, he was the deodhai of the village. His family commanded special respect in the village because they had in their possession several "very ancient texts of the Ahoms" that became part of Domboru Deodhai's inheritance. Terwiel had contacted him in order to see these manuscripts. After their meeting, two things happened that propelled Domboru De-odhai into prominence. First, the emergence of the Juva Chatra Parishad created a site for the development of a local Ujani Aham identity. The swargadeos, their culture, and the history of the Assam kingdom became the foci of revival. Men like Domboru Deodhai, who were the priests of an archaic non-Brahmanic religion, were presented as keepers of an alter-native non-Hindu/non-Indic past. Second, the Thai scholars' search for an original Tai culture led them to the historic Ahoms of the buranjis. In pursuit of ancestors they came across the Tai-Ahoms of Assam.

In 1981, when the first international Thai studies conference was held in New Delhi, Domboru Deodhai and several Tai-Ahom leaders were invited to participate in the gathering. Domboru Deodhai went to New Delhi with his manuscripts. At the gathering of international scholars he made a dramatic speech in which he called on academics and intellectuals to assist the Ahoms in finding their lost identity, an identity that he claimed was memorialized in manuscripts called buranjis.[14] Retrospec-tively, one can say this was the moment the movement was launched; Tai-Ahom was transformed from being a local to a national and international agenda.

The drama of his speech aside, Domboru Deodhai made a huge impact at this conference. Dressed in his unusual attire of a long, white silk shirt, a white sarong, and a large white turban, the wizened old man was a show stopper. No one could overlook him. Nor could anyone stop asking him questions about the bundle of manuscripts that he carried everywhere. Suddenly he became a celebrity; and scholarly curiosity about Tai-Ahoms and their buranjis was provoked.[15]

Invigorated by the exchanges at the conference, the Tai-Ahom delegates, soon after they returned to Assam, initiated a process to investigate the buranjis, for they assumed these texts would be their gateway to the culture, history, and identity that they had lost. Buranjis also were invoked as the repositories of a religion called Phra Lung, and swargadeos, in the present remembering of the past, were deemed gods. The mundane was transformed into the sacred. Domboru Deodhai was assigned the task of writing new prayers for the Phra Lung religion so that Tai-Ahoms could perform worship in a Tai and not Hindu manner. The 1981 version of Phra Lung was not the first attempt at creating a religion. In 1967, a similar attempt was made to distinguish the Phra Lung religion from Hinduism. But then, as now, the differences between the two were not clear. Phra Lung rituals, particularly their emphasis on ancestor worship, did, however, create a vague sense of difference between the Ahom and the Hindu Assamese. The prayers written by Domboru Deodhai also helped to formalize public and private religious and ceremonial Tai-Ahom gatherings during festivals. I attended some of these festivals during my stay in Assam.

Politics motivated the movements, but the leaders used religion to organize themselves through the Ban Ok. The society took up the cause of collecting and discussing, as well as "discovering," new buranjis in order to write a history of the Ahom as a living culture and community, a history that counters those written by colonial and postcolonial historians who had declared the Ahom to be a "dead" community. Nagen Hazarika, one of the active members, coined the catch phrase, "we revive, we survive." This summed up the agenda of Ban Ok.[16]

Both history and politics need a community to claim. Hence, the first task of the newly organized Ban Ok was to make a community. But, where were they to begin? There was no group called Tai-Ahom readily available. So the leaders of Ban Ok turned their attention to several Assamese groups in the heartland of Ujani Aham, as well as to small Tai communities, namely the Aiton, Phakey, Khamyang, Khamti, and Turung. The "Assamese Ahom" and various Tai-speaking groups were pooled together as Tai-Ahom.[17] Not unlike the swargadeos' efforts to create a body of subjects whose common thread was location within the realm, the new Tai-Ahom movement invoked the people who lived in Ujani Aham to claim Ahom identity. Curiously, in this enterprise, the Muslims who had a long history of connection with the swargadeos' administration did not join the Tai-Ahom movement. I do not know for certain if they were discouraged, or if the Muslim community of Ujani Aham did not feel it was their movement too. Why did they privilege religion over history? This is an important issue that can provide an entry point to the investigation of Muslim identity in Assam, but it is beyond the scope of my project here. Suffice it to say that due to this preselection, only the Hindu and Buddhist communities of rural Ujani Aham became the main participants in the Tai-Ahom movement.

The newly constituted community of Ujani Aham Ahom, however, needed to have some identifiers to distinguish itself. The revival of Ahom as a language was considered essential. Language has always been critical to identity in Assam. In the past, the battle was between Assamese and Bengali. Now Tai-Ahom challenged Assamese. The leaders of Tai-Ahom blamed Hindus for erasing the original Tai language of the buranjis and imposing Assamese on them. They suggested that the Tai-Ahoms should relinquish Assamese. The defunct Tai Language Academy at Patsako was revived toward this end. The chronic shortage of Tai language teachers was addressed by inviting Phakey Tai speakers to help in constructing a Tai-Ahom language. Marriages between Tai-Ahom and Phakey speakers gave a new boost to the language project.[18] Numal Gogoi, a founding member of the Ban Ok and a professor at Dibrugarh University undertook the compilation of an Assamese-English-Tai dictionary (1987) by collecting Tai words from old dictionaries along with current words from (Khamti, Phakey, Aiton, and Khamyang) Tai-speaking groups.

Despite the enthusiastic efforts of Ban Ok to find Ahom history and culture and introduce Tai language to the followers, the impact of the movement in its early phase remained very limited. The major problem was financial. Fortunately, in the mid-1980s Hiteshwar Saikia, Assam's chief minister, took over as Ban Ok's "patron" and donated one million rupees. Thereafter, Tai-Ahom and Assamese language books about swargadeos and Ahom history, journals and pamphlets about Tai-Ahom rituals and customs, and lexicons and dictionaries started to appear in bookshops all over Assam. Hiteshwar Saikia also gave money to celebrate events commemorating Tai-Ahom heroes and to institute public religious gatherings. The financial boost promoted the visibility of Ban Ok. Subsequently, the organization became the mainstay of the movement. When I left Assam in 1996, more than seventeen organizations were in the fray "fighting for the Tai-Ahom cause," but Ban Ok dominated the movement.

My encounter with the Tai-Ahom movement commenced in Namrup on February 22, 1994, on the occasion of the eleventh session of the annual Ban Ok convention.[19] I had traveled to Namrup with some trepidation. Known to be a base for ULFA activities in those days, frequent skirmishes with the Indian military took place there. The situation was made more delicate because there were rumors afloat that ULFA was going to call an Assam bandh to protest the killing of five of their activists by the Indian army. A bandh in this situation was bound to become violent with gunfire exchanges between activists and the army. But curiously the ULFA did not call a bandh immediately. Throughout the five-day period of the Ban Ok's convention (February 22–27), the ULFA maintained their calm. The day after the convention ended, the ULFA called a statewide bandh for fifty-six hours. I was struck by the mutual understanding between the two organizations, but few people took note of it. Discussions on the subject were not encouraged, and I did not push the issue. This situation, however, made me aware that the Tai-Ahom movement had the tacit support of the ULFA. To understand the Tai-Ahom claims and strategies, I realized one had also to take into account the activities of the ULFA in Ujani Aham, because both organizations shared the same space and audience.

When I arrived at Namrup on February 22, a festival and political celebration was underway. The site of the conference was a *mela,* as they are called in India—a secular festival of sorts on which Hiteshwar Saikia had spent a lot of state money. Tents of all shapes and sizes as well as pavilions were set up in a large open field. Some of these tents and pavilions were identified as places for "meetings" and "cultural activities," others were identified as "rest areas," "sleeping quarters," and so on. Outside this impressive "commemoration complex," huts and shops were set up. The whole place was transformed into a Tai-Ahom village, at least temporarily. Hundreds of delegates stayed for the five-day event, and thousands attended the daily open sessions.

I encountered a variety of events taking place simultaneously—festivals and worship, political discussions and arguments, and cultural performances and academic presentations on Tai-Ahom history and culture. Hundreds of thousands of people attended the sessions, and the spirit of celebration pervaded the atmosphere. Tai-Ahom revivalism was pageantry and politics, a "public enterprise" (LeGoff 1992) driven by the need to construct images of an identity in demand. Political speeches were the high-lights of the day, and cultural performances spiced the evenings. The Ban Ok's meeting was a political and economic venture as well as a spectacle.

The main issue promoted in this event was the revival of the Tai-Ahom language. The leaders of Ban Ok criticized those attending for abandoning their mother tongue in favor of the foreign, Sanskritized Assamese language. They asked the audience to reclaim the Tai-Ahom language and make it the language of their homes and hearts. At this point I was invoked as a "foreign scholar" who had come to Assam to learn the Tai-Ahom language. It was interesting that I was not introduced as an Assamese-Muslim woman, but as a person who had come from the West to learn Ahom. One may read this as an attempt to undermine and shadow my religious identity, which could not have been unimportant to the Ahom leaders of the Ban Ok who were making religion an issue to break away from the caste Hinduism. But by not talking about my religious identity and instead focusing on my intellectual quest, the leaders were impressing on their audience that Tai-Ahom deserved a place in history and was a historical project that could be reclaimed if they tried. I was thus trans-formed in that moment into a representative of that project and was presented as an example for others to follow.

Pushpa Gogoi, the chief spokesman and secretary of Ban Ok, asked people to open up communications with Thai people and to travel to Thailand, establish marriage relationships with Thais, and adopt Thai food habits, dress, mannerisms, and social culture. Acculturation with Thailand, he emphasized, would make Ahoms Tai, and only then would Delhi recognize Tai-Ahom identity. In that case, they would be historically connected to Thailand but also be citizens of India. In making this asser-tion of difference from the "Hindu Assamese," the leaders were speaking of an elsewhere, another identity, and of connections different from what they had at present.

The evening cultural performances carried the same message of mak-ing Ahoms Tai. Khamti, Aiton, and Phakey groups sang Tai songs. The so-called Ahoms sang in Assamese, eulogizing the migration of Sukapha and his men to Mung-dun-sun-kham (Assam). These songs were ironic because in this situation designed to make Ahoms more Tai, the transition had to be facilitated by a language and culture that the new Ahoms were rejecting. However, this was not a deterrent to the organizers, who had one task in mind: to advertise the label Tai-Ahom and persuade the masses to claim a Tai-Ahom identity.

What did this annual conference of Ban Ok mean to politicians, academics, activists, and the rural masses? Assumptions and purposes varied greatly. Politicians saw the event as an opportunity to garner support for their future elections. If becoming Ahom enhanced his or her possibilities for election, they were willing to assume the new label. Hiteshwar Saikia's ambition of becoming the sole spokesman for Assam was finding a receptive ground and was backed by Ban Ok. Therefore, he actively supported the movement. Academics saw the event as a site to publicly engage in a topic that they had long discussed among themselves. The notion of identity for the rural public, who made up the bulk of the crowd, was being shaped by this event, so it seemed. Those who were attending the convention, however, were somewhat confused. For them familiar customs, concepts, and identities were seemingly disappearing, as new ones were being formulated. Many things were happening, and too many leaders were making claims on their allegiance. Notwithstanding the messiness of the present, the audience, by and large, endorsed the demands. This was a repeated experience for me throughout my stay in Assam. I found from my conversations and interactions with people in Ujani Aham that many of them did not understand the current politics and public production of Tai-Ahom. But they participated in the movement. Many of them are still waiting for delivery on its promises. When will they become Tai-Ahom? If so, what will they achieve?

In the meantime, they were willing to tell me stories of the migration of their ancestors to Assam in the thirteenth century under the leadership of Sukapha. When asked how they knew this, they told me that they had "heard it in the meeting." While they regurgitated colonial and postcolonial versions of the past, beyond such narratives of history, there was no memory to draw on to tell another kind of story of Tai-Ahom. The majority expressed their lack of knowledge of Ahom in such statements as, "Ahoms were the ruler class, but we are simply village peasants." This was exactly what the colonial records had once said about Ahoms. It was evident in the meetings of Ban Ok that the same story of Ahom nobility was upheld. Only now, everyone who claimed to be Ahom was inducted into an ethnic group, some of whom could claim to be of royal and noble background, while others could be Ahom peasants.

Why were people willing to adopt the language of the new politics and claim an identity that they were not really a part of? What made the label relevant to them now? Many told me that being part of the grand meeting of leaders and politicians was an attractive break from the routine of village life. They could get a free bus ride and enjoy the colorful cultural performances. Moreover, it was also an occasion to meet and visit with relatives and friends. Such reasons seem simple, yet there was something more serious brewing in the conference and the rural masses were drawn into it.

The organizers articulated through imaginative, provocative speeches and performances why people needed to become Tai-Ahom. They made it evident that Tai-Ahom was aimed to create a space for the marginalized, dispersed peoples of underdeveloped villages to assert their rights. The label Tai-Ahom was a site to celebrate and use, despite differences among them. Ultimately, the movement's purpose, they claimed, was to serve as a language of opposition, a source for combating marginalization by caste Hindus. It was also a site from which to introduce a new set of leaders who could espouse the demands of the Ujani Aham people.

The Ban Ok's activities were not limited to annual conventions. Over the years, the Ban Ok was instrumental in establishing six *Sukapha bhavans* (centers) in various places, and they had planned several more. The bhavans were devised as outlets—spaces for performing and constructing Tai-Ahomness in the public sphere, as well as for mapping Tai-Ahom territory within the state of Assam. The song and dance routines enacted in Sukapha bhavans made up new traditions by reviving festivals and ceremonies recorded in the buranjis, while circulating and entrenching them through repetition. Over time, leaders of the Ban Ok expected these traditions and festivals to become embedded in community culture.

One of the first commemorative events taken up by Ban Ok was the celebration of Sukapha Divah (commemorating Sukapha). The first Sukapha Divah occurred in 1988. The event attracted a great deal of public attention, and through it Hiteshwar Saikia found another way to support the Tai-Ahom movement. Since the first successful celebration, the state government, under the directives of Saikia, declared December 2 as a regional holiday in memory of Sukapha.

In one such celebration of Sukapha Divah on December 2, 1992, the Golaghat chapter of Ban Ok, in a dazzling, colorful ceremony, presented Hiteshwar Saikia with a hengdan—an Ahom sword of honor—while proclaiming him to be a "twentieth-century Sukapha." He was also designated as the new swargadeo of the Tai-Ahoms. In his acceptance speech, Hiteshwar Saikia modestly asserted that he did not have the qualities of the mighty Sukapha, "who built greater Assam by uniting seven states." He lamented that "we are back where we were in 1228 A.D."[20] However, six months later, facing severe criticism from the press, which was mainly controlled by caste Hindu businessmen and intellectuals, Saikia called a press conference to relinquish the title of swargadeo. When I interviewed him on May 31, 1995, Hiteshwar Saikia noted, "I am not from the royal family. How can I be a king?" During my stay in Assam it became evident to me that although he had relinquished the title of swargadeo because it could prove politically harmful to his future career, he behaved like a patron, a swargadeo-like figure, for Tai-Ahoms. Hiteshwar Saikia brokered several deals for the group, some of which I will discuss below. As such, he managed to keep a tight control on the movement. The Tai-Ahom movement was a way to keep the ULFA activists reined in in Ujani Aham. At the same time it was not so powerful to dismantle caste Hindu hegemony in the valley. Hiteshwar Saikia found it convenient to support such a movement and keep many groups happy at the same time. He hoped to use them to his advantage in the next general elections.

On December 2, 1994, I attended the Sukapha Divah celebration at the Jayanagar Sukapha Bhavan in Guwahati at the invitation of Kiran Gogoi, an active member of the Ban Ok. The ceremony started with religious activities. Following the flag-hoisting ceremony, *tarpan* (homage to Sukapha) was offered. A hundred and one lamps were lit to establish that it was an Ahom worship ceremony. People made obeisance to a portrait of Sukapha. In this portrait, Pushpa Gogoi (the secretary of Ban Ok and the artist) depicted Sukapha as a proud (Mongol) warlord![21] The ceremony concluded after two hours of speech making. The theme of the speeches was along the lines of "remember Ahoms are not Hindu; the golden days of the swargadeos must be regained." This theme was presented in several different ways. When I was invited to share my research findings at this gathering, I decided to address the problem of the elusive beginning of Tai-Ahom history. My research so far had led me to tentatively conclude that the original story of migration under a leader called Sukapha was an oral tradition with no significant evidence to substantiate it. The "fact" of Sukapha was created in the seventeenth century when buranji writing became an established tradition in the Assam kingdom. I mentioned this and explained that although several communities in Upper Burma also claimed Sukapha in their ancestral tree, the narratives do not establish his ethnicity nor tell us precisely where he came from. I suggested that the migration story is a way of telling a history to begin the narrative of a community and that it need not be read as an actual journey. I also suggested that it might be possible to approach the stories of Sukapha as a metaphor of the shared cultures of Assam and Burma. No one contested my presentation that day. However, the next day the daily newspapers presented a totally different version of my talk. It read, "Yasmin Saikia, a Ph.D. scholar at the University of Wisconsin–Madison, USA, presently conducting research in Assam, presented her findings on the occasion of Sukapha Divah celebration. Ms. Saikia believes Sukapha is a Southeast Asian hero. Assam's position is unique because the mighty Sukapha founded the Ahom kingdom here."[22] It dawned on me then that my research findings could be harnessed to the cause of Tai-Ahom identity. I was not uncomfortable with this because I knew that like the multiplex versions of Tai-Ahom history floating around Assam, my version would form one of many transient explanations.

Another important public event annually celebrated by the Ban Ok is Me-dam-me-phi. This event focuses on the worship of royalty—swargadeos—who are claimed as ancestors of the present-day Tai-Ahoms. In 1991, the celebration of Me-dam-me-phi began as a mass celebration and, since then, January 31 has been identified as the day for annual celebration. Me-dam-me-phi became a site for political juggling and alliance making as Hiteshwar Saikia's men countered the previous government's supporters who were of the AGP party and represented the caste Hindu constituencies. Through this public celebration, Saikia sent out a clear message to his rivals that the new vision of Assam would be prepared by the Tai-Ahoms drawing on the concept of the swargadeo's domain. In the new Assam, Ahoms would rule.

In 1995, at the celebration of Me-dam-me-phi in Guwahati, three different sites of worship were set up. From my various conversations with different Tai-Ahom leaders, it appeared to me that Hiteshwar Saikia was the financial guarantor for all of them. Celebration in different locations helped to create awareness and reinforce the idea of a new Tai-Ahom religion. I attended the celebration held at Dispur, near the state capital. In a large open field, a makeshift temple called Seng Reng was set up. Three laymen were designated as priests for the occasion and conducted the religious function. The ceremony commenced with hoisting the Ahom flag. The newly made-up Ahom flag in white cloth had a dragon symbol across it. The dragon is not an Indian symbol, but is widely used in Tibet and China as well as in many parts of northeast Thailand. The dragon symbol of the Tai-Ahom flag was a way of asserting a non-Indic background and a connection with Asian cultures. After the flag went up, the three laymen officiating as priests read prayers to the swargadeos. In the

1980s, Domboru Deodhai Phukan had written these prayers. The entire ceremony was videotaped, presumably for mass relay later. The target audience in Guwahati was the emigré community from Ujani Aham who had relocated to the city over the years to access jobs and professional development. They came in huge numbers to the celebration and made it look like the Tai-Ahom movement was a significant phenomenon in Assam.

The Me-dam-me-phi celebration, unlike Sukapha Divah, was not an event that involved speech making and scholarly interpretations. It was fun fare that combined politics with cultural play. The religious aspects of the event were clear neither to the organizers nor to the audience. I observed that most of the attendees had no idea what to do when the worship began. Some bowed their heads, others folded their hands, and some continued to chat and chew betel nut. The priests made an effort to call on them to fold their hands and join in prayer. With a show of solemnity that controlled the crowd, the priests started their worship. They chanted the same prayer that they had read earlier in the morning, then more prayers were said in Assamese. Then they sprinkled on the audience holy water collected from the Brahmaputra River in Guwahati and distributed *prashad*—a concoction made of honey, milk, brown sugar, yogurt, and clarified butter. The worship was then announced to be officially over. The Me-dam-me-phi celebration did not seem very different from Hindu worship on the occasion of Saraswati or Lakshmi Puja.[23] The only addition was the distribution of *haj* (rice beer) among the men.

After the worship, people started milling around. Almost everyone was talking politics, with some venturing to project the result of the next general assembly election, which was to be held in 1996. The discussions favored Hiteshwar Saikia. In his political success, many saw a future for the Ahoms who would gain by becoming a Scheduled Tribe group. For the common man, though, it was not these long-term gains that mattered. What mattered more was the free lunch served after the ceremony. Meat is a very expensive commodity in Assam and few can afford it, but Saikia made it possible for them to eat meat to their hearts content and they were grateful. Me-dam-me-phi brought Saikia new prominence in the city, and his supporters were able to successfully uphold a public image for Tai-Ahomness.

When pressed as to whether or not participation in such events had altered their faiths, most people answered in the negative. They did recognize that by dislodging Brahmins and Vaishnava gossains from their positions of power, they were creating new possibilities for themselves.[24] In their religious celebrations Tai-Ahom laymen could now officiate as priests, a development that was evident at both the Sukapha Divah and Me-dam-me-phi functions. Because these were temporary priests, their impermanent position prevented any single individual or group of individuals from becoming keepers of religions and gaining power. Most welcomed this change.

For the adherents of Tai-Ahom, the emergent idea of Phra Lung religion was not yet neatly packaged. Hence, many followers, despite the rhetoric of relinquishing Hinduism, continued to cling to some practices and to Hindu icons in their private lives, as I found out during my visits to many Tai-Ahom villages. The ambiguity between belief and practice notwithstanding, under the direction of Ban Ok, at least at a public level, the new Phra Lung religion claimed to be different from Hinduism.

At a private level, too, rituals and celebrations were reshaped and took new forms under the tutelage of Ban Ok. Evidently, multiple practices were the order of the day and each household made up some customs that were convenient for the family. Phra Lung religion as performed in the private sphere varied from household to household. One private ritual of the new religion was called Dam Pata. The meaning of Dam Pata roughly translates as "commemoration of ancestral spirits." I observed two distinctly different renditions of this in people's homes, at Kiran Gogoi's house on June 13, 1994, and in Patsako on April 14, 1994. Clearly, the ceremony of Dam Pata was a new creation. There was no fixed text on which followers might rely then reproduce. Seekers of a Tai-Ahom identity were straddled between two locations—their Hindu past and Phra Lung present. Both traditions were enmeshed in their new worship system. In short, religion provided a connection to the past as much as it served as a gateway to something different; it involved a process of acceptance and resistance that was the ethos of the Ban Ok's cultural production.

In Kiran Gogoi's home in Guwahati, Dam Pata was a serious business with elaborate paraphernalia, and I suspected that the show was put on at least in part for my benefit, so that I, the research scholar, would get a "correct picture" of Tai-Ahom religion and culture. The worship was held in a room in Gogoi's home. Three trays of offerings were placed in the center of the room. The trays were made of woven banana leaves and straw. Each tray was designated for a deceased family member. On this occasion, Mr. Gogoi's father, grandfather, and patrilineal ancestors were the objects of worship.[25] On each tray were several offerings—eggs, rice, fruits, and rice beer. The trays were illuminated with earthen lamps. Friends of Kiran Gogoi officiated as temporary priests to conduct the ceremony. They started the chant, "Saw nuru, saw aw kai." Prayers were read in Assamese, invoking the gods and ancestors to bestow blessings on the Gogoi household.

Afterward, the offerings made to the ancestors were cooked and distributed among the visitors. Rice beer was the most important item in the array of sacred foods because Tai-Ahom ancestors, unlike Hindu ancestors, were believed to enjoy alcohol. Through the medium of food and drink, an exchange between ancestors and their progeny was believed to occur, and thus humans were privileged to partake in the food of the ancestors, who were now deemed gods. The Gogoi household was quite clear that in the pantheon of ancestral spirits there were no Hindu deities. In the 1930s, it appears that Kiran Gogoi's father had converted to Buddhism, and hence they identified themselves as Buddhist Phra Lung followers. They emphasized that they were not Hindu and that Dam Pata was not a Hindu ritual. This Buddhistic Phra Lung ceremony was considered very powerful as well as merit earning. After the feast, the worship of Dam Pata was over. On inquiring how often the Gogoi household performed this worship, they told me that this was the second time they had performed it in several years and they did not plan to perform it again for many more years. However, if misfortune were to befall them, they would invoke the ancestral spirits for safeguarding and assistance.

Contrary to what I had witnessed and was told at Gogoi's home, I found that Dam Pata did not have the overtones of a Buddhist ceremony in Patsako. Hindu deities were prominent in the Patsako celebration and cohabited the same space as new ancestors. In Patsako, Dam Pata celebrations coincided with Assamese Bihu—that is, between April 13 and 15. Assamese Bihu is a celebration of spring and marks the New Year for the community. The Tai-Ahoms in Patsako believed that originally the Assamese Bihu had been their festival, a "Tai thing" that had been subsequently transformed as Hindus took over and made it into their New Year's celebration. Hence, to break away from the Hindu Assamese Bihu celebrations, Dam Pata was devised as a community event in Patsako.

On the day of Bihu, I expected to observe authentic Dam Pata worship. Because nothing seemed to happen, I went to Nilima Barua, the local village teacher's home. Some members of the Barua family had earlier told me that they were "authentic" deodhais, although Nilima's father-in-law,

Jayeshwar Barua, who was over eighty years old and head of the family, on numerous occasions had tried to correct this misrepresentation for me. He told me that he had "forgotten everything about being Ahom" and he reminded me that he was "an Assamese Hindu." Because I was keen to see the performance of Dam Pata worship, he suggested that I go to his nephew Nandeshwar Barua's home. In Nandeshwar Barua's home, in a corner of the kitchen, four brass bowls, each containing a little rice beer, were set out in front of several pictures of Hindu gods and goddesses. The picture of the Hindu goddess Durga stood out. That was Dam Pata in the Barua family.

How does one read the two ceremonies that shared the common label "Dam Pata"? Evidently they differed. Differences of class and location influenced the performance of each ritual. Kiran Gogoi, a successful city-based lawyer and an active member of Ban Ok, organized an elaborate ceremony to represent the Tai-Ahom religion to me. It was a show as well as a venue for constructing a tradition for family members to imitate in the future. Nandeshwar Barua, a peasant who lived on the brink of poverty, could not put on the same show. Dam Pata was for his benefit, not a performance for others to consume. He had to make do with what he had—pictures of Hindu gods and rice beer. The latter, no doubt, was a prized commodity, for the rice he had available to feed his family was quite limited.

Beneath the layer of obvious differences, however, I also saw something in common. Dam Pata undisputedly was a very important event for both families. In their efforts to honor their ancestors, both Gogoi and Barua, along with many others seeking the label "Tai-Ahom," reordered the religious practices with which they were familiar. But they also were doing much more than that. By doing away with intermediaries like Brahmins, and by introducing alcohol (a substance most Hindus would consider to be polluted) as an offering to ancestors and gods, people who considered themselves to be Tai-Ahom Phra Lung worshippers were re-making their religion to suit their own terms. Through their practices they were also transforming Hindu gods. Sometimes this entailed renaming them. Thus, the Tai-Ahom goddess Hubasani combined the powers and qualities of the Hindu goddesses Durga and Kali and became one goddess in the Tai-Ahom religion, just as the god Phra combined Shiva and Buddha. The changes they made, they hoped, would define them as practitioners of another religion, one that was not Hinduism. Both symbolically and fundamentally, these people were trying to forge a separation and, through a process of appropriating and reformulating, gain acceptance as Tai-Ahom.

The efforts of Ban Ok inspired and mediated many cultural and political changes. One such development was the establishment of a center for Tai-Ahom studies. In 1992, Hiteshwar Saikia opened to the public the imposing structure of the Tai-Ahom Jadughar (Tai-Ahom House of Antiquity). Both Ban Ok and Hiteshwar Saikia hoped that the jadughar would become the future center for Tai studies in Assam. "Tai-Ahom things"—memorabilia of the royal period, buranjis, and other artifacts—were collected and put on display to showcase the glorious Ahom past. A research wing was also set up. But the jadughar, instead of becoming a center for intellectual exchanges concerning Ahom history, culture, and language, was transformed by the consuming public into a "sacred site." The reason for converting the museum into a temple, many explained, was because it was a house of their swargadeos, their gods.

The objects displayed in the jadughar were collected locally. People donated their heirlooms for a variety of reasons. Some were motivated by an altruistic desire to share their possessions with their community, a community that needed them to reconstruct its past. Many also gave to the jadughar in the hope that they would be rewarded for their contributions and that Hiteshwar Saikia would appoint their sons—Ahoms—to government jobs. The latter was the dominant reason. When the hoped-for appointments were not forthcoming, many donors reclaimed their artifacts. When I last visited the jadughar in March 1995, only a few buranjis were on display in the glass cabinets.

Although it was conceived as a study center, the jadughar never developed a library, although a Tai research aide, Tilu Hatibarua, was permanently appointed to facilitate the process of buranji collection and cataloging. Tilu Hatibarua is from Patsako. Her credentials derive from her father, a deodhai, who had assisted the colonial agent, Edward Gait, in compiling *The History of Assam*. Bidya Phukan, the late Domboru Deodhai's son, was appointed to be in charge of general administration. Mohan, a son of a deodhai from Patsako, held an administrative staff position in the jadughar. All the staff members were closely connected with the Tai-Ahom movement. Employment in the jadughar served several purposes for these young men and women. It provided a livelihood and, perhaps even more important, it gave them a new social position. As Mohan, one of the staff, said, "When I was a university student, my fellow students and others looked down on me as a pork and fowl eating deodhai. I was impure in their eyes. Since I have been associated with the Tai-Ahom jadughar, I have stopped thinking what the Hindus think of me. Rather, they are paying attention to us."[26]

The Ban Ok's most successful demand led to the creation of over two hundred jobs for Tai language teachers. Between 1992 and 1994, Hiteshwar Saikia approved these appointments in elementary and middle-level schools all over Assam. Conceived as a strategy to reward active members of Ban Ok, the government allowed anyone who could barely read and write Ahom to be appointed as a language teacher. The only criteria that these teachers had to fulfill was that they had to claim to be Tai-Ahom, and the school had to show an enrollment of five or more students willing to learn the Ahom language. From the very beginning there was a lot of skepticism among the Assamese, and it did not take long for different groups, including so-called Ahoms who did not support Ban Ok or Hiteshwar Saikia, to start questioning the reason for and usefulness of Ahom language training. Homen Borgohain, a noted "Tai-Ahom" journalist and a well-known political voice of the Assamese people, wrote a scathing editorial on March 25, 1994, in the leading Assamese weekly, *Asom Bani*, questioning the purpose of studying Tai-Ahom. He argued that because the Tai-Ahom language was "dead," it would not serve the goals of primary education even if the government revived it on paper. The editorial concluded that appointing Tai language teachers was a political ploy by Hiteshwar Saikia to ensure his victory in the 1996 general election. This did not fly well with Ban Ok. Homen Borgohain was viciously attacked in print and in person, and all Ahoms were asked to "socially boycott" him.

But the issue was not resolved by shunning Borgohain. The fact that Hiteshwar Saikia was using the strategy of "job donation" to garner political support without making a firm commitment to making these positions permanent caused much concern, even among supporters of Ban Ok. The Tai Education Council demanded that the appointments be made permanent. In April 1995 the organization put forward to the local Assam Assembly a list of grievances. They demanded that Tai language teachers be permanently appointed and officially recognized, and that the number of teachers be increased to a thousand. They also demanded that the Tai language be officially recognized in all levels of learning, teaching, and examination, and that a Tai Education Council and Tai Finance Cell be established in Guwahati to carry out the business of Tai education. So far, most of these demands have remained unfulfilled. By raising these issues, however, agencies such as Ban Ok and the Tai Education Council have been able to make Tai-Ahom identity a public issue and challenge the order created and maintained by elite Assamese groups.

While the Ban Ok has assumed the role of a chief agency in the cultural and social construction of Tai-Ahom, several other organizations have divided the turf on the political and economic fronts. When I left Assam in 1996, there were seventeen registered organizations and many subgroups. Numbers can be deceptive. The mushrooming of organizations did not correlate to a growing number of people identifying themselves as Tai-Ahom. Dispersed and distributed in several villages, the number of Ahoms, according to Ban Ok's estimate, was six hundred thousand. No doubt, this is a small number. But as I mentioned in the introduction, the Tai-Ahom movement (as a splinter group) has raised some serious concerns regarding the breakdown of the Assamese community. They have rightly raised the issue that the Assamese label today has come to be synonymous with caste Hinduism, and as such this label threatens to marginalize smaller groups and communities that are on the periphery of Hinduism or are not Hindus. Hence, Tai-Ahom has raised a very pertinent question about the drive to homogenize Hindu culture in Assam (as it is elsewhere in India) that goes against the grain of the multireligious and multicultural societies that together constitute the Assamese. Therefore, the important question is not how many Ahoms are part of the movement, but who heads the seventeen organizations that have created and maintained this protest against Hindus and the Indian state in general.

Predictably, a group of educated, urban men initially maintained a tight grip on the movement. But they soon had to accept leadership from many ancillary subgroups in the villages. In the rural areas, the Phra Lung Sangha (PLS) and the Ahom Land Demand Committee (ALDC) played very important roles. Women's organizations were visibly absent, with the exception of the Tai-Ahom Mahila Sangha.[27]

The PLS organization predates the Ban Ok. Founded in 1967 in Sibsagar by a group of Tai-Ahom professionals and deodhais of the local villages, the main effort was to revive religion through social and cultural changes. The Phra Lung religion was created at this stage, and included elements of Mahayana Buddhism, Tantric practices, and ancestor worship. Also, new dietary habits like eating beef and drinking lau pani were introduced. Although since 1982 the PLS has merged with Ban Ok, some differences among the members about accepting the dietary suggestions continue.

For instance, in the village of Barbarua in Dibrugarh district, the Tai-Ahom people were Shankari Vaishnavas. While critical of the Hindu caste system, they were equally reluctant to accept the dietary rules suggested by the PLS. They were aware that the mahant and gossains (Vaishnava priests), although financially dependent on them, did not treat them well. Many times when they visited their religious preceptors in the town for advice and suggestions they were not welcomed. When they would be allowed an audience, they had to squat on the bare floor, maintaining a respectable distance. The mahants never offered them food or water because they were considered polluted and vile—untouchables in caste Hindu society. The reminder of their "lowness," they told me, made them wary of institutional Hinduism, but they were reluctant to "give up [their] belief system." The new dietary laws of Phra Lung religion made it even harder. They explained that they could not discard the practices of their ancestors whose religion forbade them from consuming meat and liquor. Because ancestor worship was an integral part of Phra Lung religion, they reasoned that they too should be allowed to respect the beliefs and practices of their ancestors. Despite this, they claimed an Ahom identity and sought recognition as Hindu–Tai-Ahoms. In short, for many complex reasons some communities did not wholly integrate into, nor totally alienate themselves from, the identity movement.

The loose approach to religion continued, even as the deodhais of Patsako, with the support of Ban Ok, converted many to Phra Lung. The conversion ceremony was called Te-Te. Because the principles of Phra Lung were not determined, the ceremony entailed the convert pronouncing a simple verbal commitment to respect his ancestors. The conversion ceremony was conducted in Assamese. After the death of Domboru Deodhai, Nabin Borgohain of Jahasuk village in Dhemaji became the religion's high priest. According to him, he had converted over twenty-eight thousand people to the Phra Lung religion. I was really surprised when I visited him at his home and saw pictures of Hindu gods and goddesses adorning his living room. When I asked him the reason why he displayed them despite relinquishing Hinduism, he made the vague reply that "one day you too will have to deal with these gods and goddesses." Like Nabin Borgohain, the vast majority of Tai-Ahoms straddled two religious traditions—a form of Hinduism and a strong belief in ancestor worship. They could not tell for certain what was precisely their religion. As a general rule, the older generations in the villages were more inclined to Hindu practices, while the younger generations abandoned these in favor of Phra

Lung. In the event of mass conversion, a ceremony called Hu-pat (to kill a cow) was performed. Nagen Hazarika was instrumental in initiating this ceremony.[28] Although no one knows for certain the origins of this ritual of killing a cow to establish the finality of conversion, the ceremony of Hu-pat had become the fine line differentiating "real Tai-Ahoms" from "Hindus claiming to be Tai-Ahom."

Most of the supporters of PLS were not yet ready, however, to make a clean break from Hinduism. Thus Hindu and Phra Lung syncretic rituals were accommodated by PLS. During my stay in Dhemaji, on the northern banks of the Luit River, I heard several "accommodation stories" that explained the reasons for the rising popularity of the Phra Lung religion there. One story in particular enumerated for me both the process and context of the accommodation strategy. In Borjaha Sapori village, nineteen kilometers from Dhemaji, a woman was possessed by a god called Phura. Phura was described as a combination of the Hindu goddess Parvati and the Hindu god Shiva. One fine morning in February 1995, the possessed woman marched to the Seng Reng (Ahom temple) and, after devouring the blood of several live chickens, made divinations in the name of Phura. She warned the people that unless they and their neighbors immediately converted to Phra Lung, bad luck, loss of crops, epidemics, and disasters would befall the community. Subsequently, many in Borjaha Sapori converted. Following this, mass conversions in the adjoining villages created a sensation. The idea that Phura is the foundational deity of Phra Lung became widespread and to an extent enabled activists within the organization to establish a semblance of difference from caste Hinduism while accommodating the Hindu gods. Hindu and non-Hindu deities and spirits were allowed to cohabit.

Spirit possession is not unusual in Assam. What made the Borjaha Sapori story significant is the strategic connection between this village and the Tai-Ahom movement. Weeks before the dramatic episode, both Ban Ok and the ALDC had identified the village as the first historic Tai-Ahom capital city, Habung (as it is called in the buranjis). The press publicity that followed the woman's possession and divination lent credence to this speculation, and Tai-Ahom demands got a new boost. Although I was not "encouraged" to meet the woman, I watched the effects of this event from a distance. Drama notwithstanding, those actively circulating the message of "possession" were driven by another, more long-term, objective. They were using the event to fit the Tai-Ahom into the ST category in India.

Also, this demand for ST could be achieved within the constitutional framework of India. They identified obtaining ST status as a gateway for building their futures. But they were not admitted into the ranks of the STS in their earlier attempts in the 1960s. In 1981, Ban Ok made a new appeal to the Assam state government to recognize the Ahoms as an ST. This appeal, like previous ones, was turned down.

On August 9, 1995, the PLS once again took up the initiative and presented a memorandum to Narasimha Rao, then prime minister of India, demanding ST classification for the Tai-Ahoms.[29] This time, along with the memorandum, they suggested a redefinition of the term ST. They claimed that Tai-Ahoms, unlike other "tribal groups," were valley-dwelling people with a royal heritage. But like the "tribal groups" of the northeast, they were different from the caste Hindu Assamese. This difference, they demanded, should be recognized, and as an ST group they should be entitled to favored access regarding admission and employment in administrative, professional, and technical fields, several concessions for development and growth, and above all free aid money. Also, politically they demanded fixed electoral constituencies so that Tai-Ahoms could elect their own representatives and have a political voice. Apart from their religious difference from the caste Hindu Assamese, they asserted that they were Tai people living in India. They argued that their rights as a "minority" group would be protected only if they were granted ST status. This reading of the past, one that combined "tribalism" with "sedentarized royal culture," was a way to forge possibilities in the future. But, the requests were viewed with a great deal of suspicion, both in Dispur and Delhi.

To exert more pressure on the government to award them ST status, the ALDC was formed in Dhemaji. The ALDC emerged soon after Hiteshwar Saikia signed an agreement in 1992 with another group, called the Bodoland movement, which was also making claims that they were not Assamese and thus deserving of a portion of Assam for the Autonomous Bodoland Council. Concomitantly, Hiteshwar Saikia also promised the Tiwa, Lalung, and Mishings (inhabitants of areas north of Dhemaji, bordering the state of Arunachal Pradesh) their own autonoumous regions. On the basis of this pledge, the Mishing group started reclaiming land occupied by Assamese and others by serving notice to all non-Mishings, which included Tai-Ahoms in and around the Dhemaji region, to vacate their land. Dhemaji is made up of a conglomeration of sixty-five villages, of which fifty were identified by Ban Ok as Tai-Ahom. Most villagers did not have documents proving land ownership because these had never before been required. They were now threatened with landlessness.

In January 1994 in Cement Sapori in Junai, adjoining Dhemaji, the ALDC was formed under the leadership of Ratneshwar Borgohain to combat the Mishing threat and to demand a Tai-Ahom homeland. In August 1994 Ratneshwar Borgohain and Bikas Ranjan Buragohain, two prominent office holders in the ALDC, called a press conference at the Calcutta airport in which they threatened to wage a war against the Assam state government if it failed to provide for Tai-Ahoms a separate territory with autonomous administrative powers. A year later, on April 5, 1995, the ALDC organized a hunger strike to pressure the state government further. They demanded that the Assam kingdom that was annexed in 1826 by the British and incorporated into India in 1947 be returned to the Tai-Ahom, and that this area be declared the new Ahomland. The ALDC believed that if they could accomplish this goal, Tai-Ahoms would regain control of the resources and wealth of the region once ruled by their ancestors. Thus, they would vindicate the losses suffered for the last hundred and fifty years during British colonial and postcolonial Indian rule. The Ahomland envisaged by the ALDC was territorially mapped within the Indian union (as a temporary solution), but it was proposed as an autonomous unit. Within this area, according to the ALDC plan, a swargadeo would rule with a select governing body. The ALDC hoped that "in the future all the Mongoloid people of the sub-Himalayan region would congregate into one body politic and thus totally de-link from the Hindu state of India."[30]

By and large, most people in Ujani Aham viewed the ALDC's demand for a separate homeland as a romantic and utopian idea. However, they were willing to back the demand because they believed that the grievances of economic and political rights were real. Increasingly, people in the villages of Ujani Aham who felt dispossessed, marginalized, and oppressed identified with the ALDC. These people were already feeling hopeless about their integration into the mainstream Indian culture and economy. In this context, some degree of political separation from India seemed to be a good strategy. A demarcated space was viewed as a place where they would be Tai-Ahoms, not submerged under labels made by Assamese, Indians, and Hindus—groups that had exercised power over them. As the message spread throughout rural Assam, the rhetoric of "local nationalism" gained ground. The ULFA also spoke out for marginal groups and demanded political and economic rights for them. They had brought into the public domain questions and concerns about economic and social privileges. With the rising tide of political activities, the Ahom movement and the ULFA supporters in Ujani Aham became indistinguishable. Many activists hoped that through the efforts of both organizations, they would become real participatory citizens. No doubt, these decisions also led to much confusion, and rifts began to show in the Tai-Ahom movement. The Dhemaji faction led by the ALDC veered closer to the ULFA, and Ban Ok leaders took advantage of this by showing support for the ALDC. In other words, they gave tacit approval to the ULFA to carry on their armed struggle in Ujani Aham, a struggle that they hoped in the long run would enable the creation of an Ahom homeland separate from the Hindu Assam.

Throughout the 1990s the construction of Tai-Ahom identity was in process. The constant negotiations that defined the interactions between various agents kept the movement in motion. "Tai-Ahomness" could mean several different things to people within and outside the movement, as is evident through the activities (and goals) of the different organizations. One thing, however, was becoming clear. The Ban Ok's efforts to advance a Tai-Ahom identity opened the floodgates for many more new and vociferous demands claiming degrees of separation from established labels, institutions, histories, and icons. The ULFA, both politically and culturally, exceeded the demands of Ban Ok. The association of the three agencies—Ban Ok and its ancillary organizations like PLS and ALDC, ULFA, and Thai scholars—created new readings of Assam's past. As these took shape, they also produced new issues and problems. The stories of these agencies, even when combined together, do not make one narrative with a clear beginning, middle, and end. Instead, there were several stories of different beginnings, but there are no endings. Each episode was a fragment of dispersed and variegated movements. Toward the end of the 1990s, nothing was fixed, etched, or determined in Assam.

This messiness notwithstanding, the movement successfully brought most of the people in Assam to accept that "Tai-Ahom" was a historical category and even an ethnic community. The Tai-Ahom community (absent in the buranjis) became naturalized in the current narrative as the founders of Assam's history. There was no more space to question that assumption.[31] The stories about the Ahom past and the history of Assam were therefore decontextualized. To the new version the ULFA and Thai scholars added new lines and put them in circulation. People subjected these in turn to multiple interpretations. The stakes were raised higher and higher, and the label Tai-Ahom underwent several incarnations. How did the ULFA and these Tai scholars facilitate the Tai-Ahom movement? In the next section I will discuss this issue in some detail.

Buddheshwar Gogoi, first chairperson of ULFA, described to me his thoughts on the groups' struggle:

> In Bihar nobody is killed for speaking the local language, neither in Bengal. Why do they kill us in Assam? Why should we be afraid to say we want to speak our own language? . . . Over the river Ganges, in north India, there are no less than eighteen bridges. Did anyone lay down their lives to get these bridges built? Since 1960, in Assam we had only one bridge built over the Brahmaputra River, in Saraighat. When we wanted another bridge over the river, we had to call attention to this demand by laying down our lives. Have you seen or heard anything like this anywhere? The British colonialists have left India, but we have another set of masters who rule us from Delhi and Dispur. . . .
>
> Have you reflected on the terms such as "Operation Rhino," "Operation Bajrang" that were used for the military operations against the ULFA? Bajrang is the Hindu term for Hanuman's army of monkeys [in the Ramayana]. What is the message the government is giving us when they use these terms? They view us as animals, and we have to be controlled by the brute force of a superior human being. In Punjab, the military mission is called Operation Bluestar. But the people of Assam are made akin to animals. Don't our people see it—the humiliation? Some do, but men like Hiteshwar Saikia are shrewd, cunning, and wicked. They will do anything to dissuade the populace, make up new causes, and divert public attention. They will do anything to keep their *gadi* [political seat/power].[32]

Instead of opening new channels of communication with the state and national government, the ULFA's struggle created a mentality of being under siege in Assam, and the political regime at New Delhi handled the situation by unleashing a reign of terror. New Delhi deemed the ULFA's demands for economic justice and political rights as terrorism. The national government's paramilitary mentality became a major impediment to dialogue, according to Gogoi, but he also held the local government responsible. In particular, he saw Hiteshwar Saikia's conniving attitude as aggravating the problem. In fact, Gogoi went so far as to suggest that Hiteshwar Saikia was instrumental in floating parallel movements to divert public attention and support from the ULFA organization. He did not explain what these organizations were. Was it Tai-Ahom? Definitely, Gogoi and his cohorts were not against the Tai-Ahom movement. In fact, they were very sympathetic to it. What they resented, however, was that Saikia had assumed the leadership of Tai-Ahom people. The ULFA considered themselves the leaders of the communities in Upper Assam and Tai-Ahom was the emblematic cultural movement in the region. Throughout the 1980s and early 1990s both Saikia and the ULFA continued to vie for the exclusive leadership in Upper Assam.

The emergence of a militant organization such as the ULFA in Assam baffled many local politicians, scholars, and even radicals. People in Assam have suggested different theories and stories of the ULFA's origin, but nothing is conclusive. When I was undertaking research in some villages, often I encountered casual as well as serious discussions about the ULFA. From these discussions I gathered that there are multiple narratives of the ULFA's genealogy, which in turn makes it hard to construct one story. But one thing was certain, the ULFA originated to address the widely held perception that the Indian government was treating the Assamese people unequally and unjustly. We have seen in previous chapters that such grievances have a long history. Many believe that the emotions of suffering and hurts were first addressed by the Assamese identity movement led by the AASU. After the AASU movement lost its appeal when it became a parochial, urban upper-class movement driven by cultural and not economic issues, the ULFA emerged in the villages of Upper Assam. Unlike the AASU leaders, the ULFA leaders promised to lead a successful secessionist movement.[33]

According to this explanation, the rural middle class leads the ULFA. But an investigation of the ULFA's revolutionary documents, political agreements, and programs makes it evident that other networks and agencies, some internal and others external, have contributed to shaping the movement as well. Moreover, if we examine the leaders and their cultural and political orientations we find that the narratives of the past generated under the aegis of the Ban Ok and Tai organizations deeply influenced the ULFA's political language and programs. The ULFA's ideology eclectically combined information concerning the swargadeos' domain (found in the buranjis) with present populist demands for justice and economic rights in ways not very different from those demanded by the Tai-Ahom leaders.

However, ULFA maintained its differences with Tai-Ahom and did not merge with their organization. The differences between them had more to do with their strategies than with their ideologies. The ULFA planned an armed struggle with a view to secede from India, while Tai-Ahom groups focused on identity and public and official recognition of a different history. Still, they shared several connections. The main factor forging the connection between ULFA and Tai-Ahom was the social composition of their members. Almost all of the members of both of these groups initially came from the villages of Upper Assam. They came from both rural and urban areas and consisted of a variety of age groups. Very little about the actual composition of these groups' members was known outside their immediate circles. Because the locations of the strongholds of both organizations were obscure, the army often raided Tai-Ahom villages in search of ULFA activists. The villagers, no doubt, vehemently denied association with ULFA, and sometimes they managed to convince the authorities, but not always. The public silence about the connections between the two organizations notwithstanding, in private their leaders consulted each other on various occasions. During my stay in several Tai-Ahom villages that were claimed by outsiders to be "ULFA dens," I became aware of these exchanges. But an outline of the birth of the ULFA is necessary before we can analyze these connections.

When ULFA leaders narrate the story of the origin of their organization, they invoke a long line of separatist movements as their legacy. They begin their story in the 1960s, with the rise of the Tai-land movement, which was advocated by the All Assam Ahom Association.[34] In a published memorandum submitted to the Home Minister of India on May 28, 1967, the association stated: "This conference urges by a realistic appraisal of the historical antecedents and ethnic character of the tribes and races of Upper Assam, all of the Mongoloid stock, . . . that a separate Autonomous Unit be formed . . . for protection and free development . . . which met a serious set-back and continued to deteriorate under the hundred and twenty years of British rule as well as under the present administration for the last two decades of independence of India."[35] The memorandum, despite being very strongly worded and making a claim of racial difference from Indians, bore no visible results and the Ahom Association (AA) did not gain an inch of ground for a homeland. However, the rhetoric of political and economic injustice generated by the AA inspired a new politics in Ujani Aham. The potent combination of racial politics and the peoples' keen awareness of the neglect they had suffered during the colonial regime and that they continued to suffer under successive postcolonial regimes provided the strong sense of unity, motivation, and commitment that was necessary to sustain a fight for their cause.

Another organization that ULFA claims in its genealogy is the army of radicals called Lachit Sena. This unit was formed in 1968 to drive all non-Assamese away from Assam. The Sena defined the "Assamese" as a linguistic community; therefore only a small percentage of the people living in Assam qualified as such. This narrow definition of Assamese did not work, nor did the politics of intimidating the "non-Assamese" into leaving Assam. In 1977–1978, after a decade-long hiatus, a new Assamese politics emerged under the leadership of the AASU. Simultaneously, the ULFA claimed that a parallel organization called the Juva Chatra Parishad was formed in Upper Assam to reclaim the Jatiyatabadi (racial/ethnic awareness) struggle.[36] Several mediators worked to amalgamate the AASU and the Juva Chatra Parishad but without success. The leaders of Juva Chatra Parishad claimed that AASU differed socially, geographically, and politically from them.[37] Further, they viewed the amalgamation as a way to empower and legitimize the urban students of Guwahati, whose strategies of appeal to and compromise with the national government they could not endorse. The ardent members of the Juva Chatra Parishad wanted an armed struggle against the state.

Two prominent hubs of the Juva Chatra Parishad were in Namrup and in Sibsagar. These two units came together and pledged to form a new organization to regain the "golden Assam of the swargadeos." The inauguration ceremony was held in Tolatol Ghar in Sibsagar, presumably once a palace and capital complex of the swargadeos.[38] Gogoi recalled for me the actual moment of the birth of the ULFA, as follows: "At Tolatol Ghar we killed a raj hanh [goose] [and] arranged for haj [rice beer] and other ritual objects for the occasion. The ceremony was performed with full solemnity, keeping in mind the sacred space of the swargadeos, the Ahom kings, who were the only legitimate rulers of this country [Assam]. Gagen Handique slammed the bird against a tree, killed it and we took bloody *phuts* [smeared blood on the forehead]. We pledged to free Assam."[39]

In this choice of space as well as in the details of the ceremony, the ULFA activists forged symbolic connections with the kingdom of swargadeos that from then on would serve as the emblematic site of their struggle. The ceremony recalled by Gogoi was a modern re-creation of a deodhai ritual.[40] Also, the ULFA's central office was set up in the Talatol Ghar complex and named in Tai as *Dai Kao-Rang*. A "real" but "imagined" connection with the past and the culture of the swargadeos' rule was thus made. Many of the initial members, who called themselves Ahoms and Motoks, dreamed that after this ceremony they would once again create the golden days of the swargadeos.[41]

In the meantime, though, the AASU had laid the groundwork for an Assamese movement. To get the attention of the captive Assamese audience, the ULFA modified the orientation of their movement by expanding it beyond Ujani Aham and making claims to lead the Assamese Jatiyatabadi struggle. This was possible because the people of Assam had already identified the Indian state as one of its "enemies." This enabled the leaders to construct a monolithic community, the "oppressed people" of Assam. The ULFA envisaged that complete independence would only be possible if all Assamese—regardless of cultural, economic, social, and religious orientation—supported their cause. Thus, the ULFA increasingly, in public, tried to steer clear of "ethnic" identity movements such as Tai-Ahom and even the anti-Bangladeshi problem that the AASU wanted to discuss. Instead, leaders constructed their political discourse in popular-democratic terms, emphasizing common citizenship rights to all Assamese, old and new, in the future "golden Assam." But, in private, Tai-Ahom and the ULFA joined their efforts and resources the keep the leadership of the Upper Assam faction intact.

Whatever their public rhetoric, the idea of leading an all-Assam movement did not have deep roots in the practical programs and ideological orientation of ULFA leaders. Even as they made statements pledging a new future for Assam, they continued to link ULFA identity with a past memory of the swargadeos, icons of a history and culture that were specific to Ujani Aham. As such, the ULFA continued to be intertwined with the Tai-Ahom movement, at least for their supporters in Ujani Aham. The ULFA leadership also continued to be controlled by the Ujani Aham faction, which commanded all the key positions. The ideological orientation of this group expressed itself when they drafted a constitution for the organization.

Gogoi noted that "following the pledging ceremony at *Talatol Ghar*, a draft constitution of the ULFA organization was written in Namrup and a flag was designed in Sadiya, both drawing inspiration from buranjis."[42] Revolutionary changes were predicated on the establishment of a socialist economy, but as usual the ULFA leaders could not give up their royalist influences and assumed that the future state would be ruled by a swargadeo. The proposition made clear how little they had processed the principles and outcome of their struggle outside of the political and cultural imaginary of Ujani Aham. The dual-colored flag designed as an ULFA emblem was made of muga silk (Tai-Ahom activists claim that swarga-deos introduced the domestication of this kind of silkworm and, subsequently, muga silk production in Assam), which had a central symbol in green to epitomize Assam's meadows (Phukan 1994, 208–13). According to Gogoi, on April 7, 1980, the ULFA flag was hoisted for the first time at Charaideo, "to symbolically reconnect with the past—the first capital of the swargadeos—as well as to determine the new ULFA capital in Assam. A Dam Pata ritual was performed to appeal to the swargadeos for guidance to assist in the armed struggle to free Assam. Since then, the rituals of flag hoisting in Charaideo and [the] worship of swargadeos have become ULFA traditions."[43]

Today, ULFA members vehemently deny the Ujani Aham/Tai-Ahom makeup of the organization. Even the Assamese elite consider it unthinkable that a serious and massive endeavor for the freedom of Assam could be conceived and controlled by local politicians and intellectuals in Ujani Aham. Members of ULFA often reminded me that they represented the Assamese people at large, not a select community. Ironically, despite their stoic denial of parochialism, all of the important office bearers located themselves within "Ahom" royal genealogy. Also, all of the ULFA cadres apprehended by the police/military forces had historic Ahom titles—Phukan, Hazarika, Saikia, Gogoi, etc.—or had assumed Ahom pseudonyms.

In 1988 when the first round of arrests took place, it became apparent that the ULFA, despite its rhetoric of leading a popular-democratic struggle, was confined mainly to Upper Assam, and all of the important office bearers were from Sibsagar and surrounding areas. As a founding member of the ULFA told me: "It had to be so, because we were looking for support from the Shan and Kachin organizations and they had very little respect for Assamese Hindus. They had no faith that Assamese people could carry out a revolution. They dismissed them as a weak jati who cannot be fighters. In fact, they did a physical test on our boys. It is believed that a certain body part indicated Mongoloid traits in a person. They checked our boys to verify. Only when they were reassured, they were allowed into the training camp. Otherwise they were rejected and sent back home. The present ULFA boys do not know about this. They think the Mongoloid groups are very friendly with the Assamese people" (name and location of interview withheld).

Beyond this admission that the ULFA was organically linked to Ujani

Aham, the member refused to discuss with me any arrangements that had been made between the ULFA and the Kachin and Shan insurgent groups. Nor would he discuss with me the reasons why the ULFA publicly declared they represented the Assamese. When I reminded him that recently the ULFA stronghold had shifted to Lower Assam and was gaining popularity among the Assamese Hindu communities there, he simply remarked, "They are there now, but in the pan-Mongoloid cause they will not be of much use." He evaded my questions concerning the ULFA's constitution and its royalist aspirations, the reason why there was such a large pool of so-called Tai-Ahom young men in the organization, and why all of the top offices were confined to known "Ahom" members. Nor would he discuss any connections between the ULFA and Ban Ok's leadership. Such issues emerged instead during my village fieldwork.

In March 1994, when I went to Patsako village to discuss my project with the village elders, I found the young men to be quite hostile toward me. Later, I learned that two days prior to my arrival, a shootout between some ULFA supporters and the army had taken place at the edge of the village. Following it, the army raided the village in search of ULFA supporters. Thus when I showed up in the village, the young men expressed their doubts about my "real intention" and forbade the village elders and women to talk to me. It was a difficult situation, because in Sibsagar town, where I stayed for a while before I started my work in Patsako village, authorities had quizzed me about my real reasons for going to Patsako. A local Assamese politician told me, "So I hear you live in the ULFA den. Why? Are you sent from America to assist them?" He even cautioned me not to go there. I did not heed his advice, however, and I returned to Patsako to continue my research, this time with success. When my research led me to the political aspects of the Tai-Ahom identity movement, I was directed to "legitimate sources" outside the village. Often it turned out that prominent activists in the Tai-Ahom movement had affiliations with ULFA. In certain villages that I cannot name here (to maintain their anonymity), connections and interactions between Tai-Ahom activists and the ULFA became more obvious. Many Ban Ok members were ULFA supporters, and people talked quite openly about so-and-so's son being active in the ULFA movement. People even discussed how the top office bearers of Ban Ok shared close friendships with ULFA office bearers and how these friends had held discussions together in these villages.

But the connections between the two organizations were not obvious, and I did not deem it necessary to investigate them when I lived in the villages. I did not want to attract unnecessary attention and cause a police raid in villages inhabited by very poor people. But I knew that the language of emotions and revolt that circulated in villages was a combined rhetoric of Tai-Ahom and ULFA leaders. Both talked of political and economic justice as their goal, with the end of New Delhi's colonization of Assam. Hence, when Buddheshwar Gogoi told me stories of interactions between ULFA leaders and Tai-Ahom villagers that spanned a decade, I was not surprised.

The government at Dispur and conservative Assamese politicians, however, refused to link the two organizations and instead distinguished them in fine detail. Assamese politicians rejected the possibility that local people from Ujani Aham could lead a "militant" struggle. Hiteshwar Saikia's government saw the Tai-Ahom movement as his feudal legacy and refused to accept that Tai-Ahoms would participate in a freedom struggle. Both of these groups insisted that the ULFA was the brainchild of disruptive external forces. In doing so, they missed the point that these movements were making: that is, a demand to share in the rights and privileges of being Assam's citizens. Instead, the government and Assamese intellectuals dealt with Tai-Ahom and the ULFA in a piecemeal manner. But, they could not wipe out the movements. Throughout the active period of the ULFA and Tai-Ahom movements (1985–1994, after which many ULFA leaders went underground), regimes in both Dispur and Delhi refused to address the demands and grievances that both organizations were raising. The latter would have required a serious investigation of the role of the Indian state in the northeast, one that could potentially threaten India's interest in the frontiers by exposing its failures.

Information concerning the connections between the two organizations started trickling into the public domain once the state apparatus made a dent in the ULFA by "buying" some of its active members with huge sums of money. Sunil Nath, a SULFA (surrendered ULFA) and an Assamese Hindu, was the first to make this evident. During our meeting, he frankly admitted to me the connections shared between the Tai-Ahom and the ULFA. In his words: "The ULFA started as a pan-Mongol revival organization. The ULFA's ideology was not different from the Ahom activism that we see now. Rajiv Rajkhowa, alias Arbindo, was of the opinion that the golden days of the Ahoms should be regained. . . . Pradeep Gogoi endorsed this concept. . . . In the organization there was a tendency to show a great deal of respect to the Ahom officers. . . . The vice-chairman was said to be the descendant of Gomdhar Konwar [a scion of the Tungkhungiya royal clan, who raised a standard of rebellion against the British authorities in 1836], hence he commanded special respect. . . . Although we talked in terms of Assam, the idea was always concentrated around Ahom rule and the swargadeos."[44]

When I asked Pradeep Gogoi about ULFA–Tai-Ahom connections, he denied them. Yet he continued to talk about his dream of making a "golden Assam." His plan was to "build Assam with a few good men." "Arobindo Rajkhowa," he claimed, "is a good Ahom man, but Hiteshwar Saikia is of another kind. He is a magician. Between the two are men like Pushpa Gogoi, Nagen Hazarika, Romesh Borgohain, etc. They are trying to camouflage the situation by making people think all that Ahoms want is sociocultural recognition. They do not want people to judge Hiteshwar Saikia too harshly. . . . Ours is an armed struggle, to free Assam from Indian occupancy. . . . Such a revolution can arise only from the villages of Ujani Aham where people have no future, only a past to talk about. . . . Hence, the ULFA had to take the lead."[45]

Surprisingly, in spite of the vocal condemnation of Hiteshwar Saikia, in 1991 the ULFA leaders assisted his comeback. They called off violence during the election year, facilitating Saikia's successful campaign. When questioned about this, the ULFA leaders made no comment. Once again, like the connections between Ban Ok and the ULFA, the relationship between the ULFA and Saikia was shadowy but mutually beneficial. Ranoo Wichasin (1991), a Thai scholar who has visited Assam several times and is intimately involved with the Tai-Ahom movement, argues that the ULFA is a militant Tai-Ahom movement that would gain in power when the vast Tai-Ahom populace of Assam became more aware of their (non-Indic) heritage. She saw Saikia's role as one of facilitating the awareness campaign by donating state money to making the Tai-Ahom community visible.

Contrary to the expectations of some local and foreign factors, after the mid-1990s the ULFA rapidly lost power. It went through several internal changes that transformed its base of support. The Upper Assam group went underground and the movement lost its immediacy in the area, while linkages with rebel groups outside Assam became dominant. Then the governments in Delhi and Dispur declared the ULFA to be a terrorist group. The massive Indian military onslaughts under Operation Bajrang (1990) and Operation Rhino (1991) destroyed ULFA strongholds in Upper Assam. For a short time after these military operations the ULFA made a comeback, with the support of extraterritorial rebel groups, rumored to be of an eclectic variety of men from Burma, Nagaland,

and neighboring countries. The organization unleashed a reign of terror against prominent businessmen and politicians whom it deemed to be corrupt. Such rampant violence made many people uneasy. Many Marwari and non-Assamese businesses folded their operations in the region. Foreign businesses, particularly British ones, also quit their operations (including tea operations). In the meantime, the ULFA made huge monetary demands on the national tycoons, such as the Tatas who had a flourishing business empire in Assam, probably to buy arms that they needed to carry on their armed struggle.

The government at Delhi had to remedy the situation so that their big business supporters, who had heavily invested in tea and energy resource projects in Assam, could continue to function. Delhi deployed huge numbers of armed forces to suppress ULFA activities. The Indian Army was quite successful: ULFA leaders fled the area and went underground. In the vacuum that was created, activists from Lower Assam stepped in to take over the leadership of the ULFA. The ULFA became a fragmented organization; there was a weak wing in Upper Assam and a strong growing leadership in Lower Assam. Nalbari, in Lower Assam, became the hub of ULFA activities. Not long after, in 1997, Sanjoy Ghosh, a nationally recognized environmental activist, was assassinated, and the ULFA was blamed without proof. This came as a big blow. In the eyes of the local people of Assam, the ULFA activists were reduced to the level of common criminals. Thereafter, the Bharatiya Janata Party (BJP) government launched a double-edged policy to undermine ULFA organization. They started first by targeting the Hindu sentiment of the Assamese by organizing pujas, public rallies, and BJP yatras in Guwahati. At these events top BJP politicians, such as L. K. Advani and Sushma Swaraj, made appearances. Second, the BJP launched a campaign to "buy" the loyalty of the Assamese. "Economic packages" for the so-called development of Assam were handed out in the form of central educational institutions and industries. These institutions were to be controlled by New Delhi. The national government's message was "India cares about Assam." To receive the attention of Delhi, local communities had to accept the BJP's mandate of linking Assam with the rest of Hindu India. Alongside the economic packages, the BJP government deployed huge military forces to villages in Assam to impress and frighten the gullible and weak. Once again, the anti-Bangladeshi card was trumped up and the state made its alliance with the Assamese leaders to divert attention. Most people in Assam today have relinquished the ULFA agenda out of fear of army reprisal and greed. In the end the ULFA did not gain much for people in Assam in general or in Ujani Aham in particular. It had promised autonomy of identity, economy, and politics. Relative to the past Assam today has been more drawn into national politics, but not as an equal player. It has become the site for political games of national parties, and the people are pitted against each other in the name of religion, culture, and class. Ujani Aham continues to be poor, neglected, and isolated.

In summing up the relationship between the Tai-Ahom movement and the ULFA, it is necessary to remember that publicly the ULFA never talked about reviving Tai-Ahom identity. Instead, it made claims of leading a secessionist movement that would enable Assam to break away from India. Toward this end its leaders embraced a number of agendas to draw different groups into the movement. Initially some of these agendas were very attractive to people. As membership grew, ULFA leaders carved out a space to promote an Ujani Aham ideology. In this space the stories of swargadeos were retold, and the ULFA made the autonomous precolonial swargadeo's kingdom of Assam the political quest of the Assamese. The swargadeo's domain, the ULFA promised, would be regained and Assam made independent. While the ULFA claimed everyone living in Assam within this future, the Tai-Ahoms were forefronted as the main beneficiaries because they represented a direct linkage with the swargadeos. Thus, without openly endorsing the Tai-Ahom identity movement ongoing in Ujani Aham, the ULFA made explicit connections between the past and future by claiming that only a return to the swargadeos' rule would make Assam truly free from India economically, socially, culturally, and emotionally.

The Tai-Ahom movement, not unlike the ULFA, pursued the same goal of returning to the swargadeos' rule and culture. However, some of the methods for achieving these goals were different. The Ban Ok's strategies were particularly different from those of the ULFA. But leaders of both organizations maintained a cordial relationship, as I found out time and again during my research in Assam. The obvious connection between the two organizations bypassed almost everyone's attention. The ULFA leaders represented themselves symbolically as the inspired progeny of the swargadeos—the proud, valiant, independent-minded citizens of Assam. While they continued to base themselves in Upper Assam, they also created linkages with new networks, including those of politicians and public figures outside the region. Parag Das, who was rumored to be "one of the brains behind the ULFA," once confided to me, "do not be surprised if you see Arobinda Rajkhowa or Anup Chetia in Hiteshwar Saikia's house. The

ULFA can carry on their activities because there are many important politicians, businessmen, and scholars who are covertly supporting them."[46] For certain, the ULFA managed to carry on their activities in Assam because they were protected, sheltered, assisted, and encouraged by local people. Most of this support came from people in Upper Assam. Even Hiteshwar Saikia, who opposed the ULFA because they challenged his claim to exclusive leadership, could not totally disconnect himself from them. Saikia, as well as the ULFA leader Arobindo Rajkhowa (and many more), locate their "home" in the same village in Nazira, near Sibsagar.

Ultimately, the ambiguity of the ULFA's ideologies, plans, strategies, cohorts, and confidants helped it to command a large group of supporters and to receive aid from many different quarters. For nearly a decade they controlled the politics of Upper Assam, where they destabilized the economy and government. Even today, when the ULFA has become more or less absent from active political life in Assam, the Indian army is still posted in all the villages, hunting for the last remnants of ULFA supporters. The Indian army has been there for twelve years so far, and it will probably spend many more decades in Assam. The Indian state appears to have conceded that the ULFA will never be fully driven out, because it coexists with the history and memory of Ujani Aham. In many ways this assumption is not misfounded. Although the leaders of the ULFA had to flee the area, people still talk about ongoing ULFA activities. Even today newspapers will report an "ULFA sighting." More important, the ULFA helped the people of Ujani Aham to harbor a dream that they had not dared to dream for a long time during and after the end of colonialism. For Tai-Ahom supporters, in particular, the ULFA's promise of bringing political autonomy and a revival of swargadeo rule to Ujani Aham continues to be a rallying point.

## THE EXCHANGE SPHERE:
## THAI INTEREST IN THE TAI-AHOMS

Conferences and seminars have provided a site for the Tai-Ahom movement to transform itself into a transnational issue. In turn, the Tai-Ahom movement was shaped by the political views of external agents who suggested new images for constructing, performing, and consuming identity in Assam. Did the Ahom leaders find Thai scholars to support their cause by plan or by coincidence? Either way, once they found each other at the first international Thai studies conference held in New Delhi in 1981, the attraction became mutual. The two groups sought out each other as friends and ancestors. The conference became the launching pad for a Tai-Ahom movement that exacerbated the differences between Assamese and Ahom, Ahom and Indian, by linking the histories of Assam and Thailand. This cncounter also transformed the Thai search for origins in Thailand and linked Thai history to Assam and Ahoms in India. This was a new addition to the Thai search for origin project that had already found and claimed linkages with groups in southern China, northern Vietnam, and even Laos. Who forged alliances with whom, and for what purposes, has become unclear over time.

Encounters between Tai-Ahom and Thai were frequent throughout the 1980s and peaked in the mid-1990s. When Hiteshwar Saikia passed away in April 1996, the Tai-Ahom movement lost its financial support in Assam. Also, in 1997 Thailand suffered a major economic recession. As financial pools within Assam and Thailand dried up, the Tai-Ahom movement was directly affected. Since then Tai-Ahom has become a dying chapter in modern Assam's political history. Although the Tai-Ahoms never managed to be recognized in Indian national history, for a decade and a half (1981–1997) they participated in exchanges with Thai activists that generated a new transnational discourse and new possibilities of identity that temporarily overshadowed Indian national identity at the margin of Assam. During this period Assam became a lively crossroads that facilitated historical and cultural linkages between South and Southeast Asia. Within Ujani Aham, the ULFA raised serious political questions about the rights and identity of people in Assam, which were addressed with the help of Thai scholars.

A group of Thai academics were the first to notice the cultural and political rift between Assam and the Indian state. Chatthip Nartsupha, a professor of economics at Chulalongkorn University, and Ranoo Wichasin, of Chiangmai Ratchabhat Institute, began in 1980 to take a keen interest in the Tai-Ahoms of Assam. Ultimately, they emerged as outspoken advocates for the Tai-Ahom movement in Thailand. Beginning in 1980, Nartsupha encouraged several young academics to study Tai-Ahom history, religion, and culture in Thailand, and Wichasin was one of his first converts.[47] Ranee Lertleumsai of Silapakorn University and Willauwan Kannittanan of Thammasat University also became actively involved in studying Tai-Ahom myths and religion. These scholars generated considerable interest in Tai-Ahoms in Thailand, and their work has resulted in an ongoing Tai-Ahom project at Thammasat University.

Chatthip Nartsupha's influence was not limited to the world of Thai academics. He was also influential in renewing the study of buranjis in Assam. In his public address at the second international seminar on Tai studies, held in February 1995, in Guwahati, Chatthip Nartsupha proudly recalled his role in the Tai-Ahom movement. Fourteen years ago, he said, he had encouraged Professor J. N. Phukan of Guwahati University to undertake the study of Tai-Ahom history. Chatthip Nartsupha had also influenced Professors Romesh Buragohain and Pushpa Gogoi to dedicate their academic and political energies to the Tai-Ahom movement.[48] The joint political and academic pursuits also led to close friendships between Nartsupha and Tai-Ahom leaders. Kiran Gogoi took great pride in describing his close relationship with Nartsupha and the friendship that had developed between their children. J. N. Phukan called Nartsupha "a friend and brother." Pushpa Gogoi and Romesh Buragohain considered Nartsupha a "fellow crusader in a shared battle." In the villages where I did my research, especially in Patsako, Chatthip Nartsupha was a household name.

Why was Chatthip interested in a local movement in Assam? To what use could he put the Tai-Ahom movement in Thailand? Interest in the Tai-Ahoms of Assam, like other adopted ancestral groups in East Asia, was mostly motivated by internal developments within Thailand. In the 1970s, as Western capital moved into Asia, Thailand became an important place for commercial investment. Chatthip Nartsupha, as a professor of economics and a Thai regional specialist, was distressed by the course of capitalist "development" in Thailand's society and economy. Some Thai academics feared that the "foreign-aid" agencies that were dumping money and experts into Thailand would erode village societies, impose western norms of economic development, and foist a value system that would go against Thailand's communal village system.[49] In response they developed a nativist political agenda emphasizing the "community culture" of villages. They hoped to empower villagers so that village communities could gain a foothold in national development projects and bargain on somewhat equal terms with the state in planning development. For this to happen, Thais needed an archaic, "original" Tai society that they could display as a model and inspire the "transformed" Thai villages to follow in its lead. Unfortunately, such a village society did not exist in Thailand, and what was absent had to be created. Textual materials on Tai culture and history were reread and new interpretations of the past were suggested. The forgotten and lost pristine village community was refound in the texts.

The groundwork for the construction of an "ancient Tai culture" had been prepared for a long time. In the 1960s, the story of Tai migration from a remote "homeland" somewhere in southern China gained currency and became part of textbook history in Thailand. Western scholars contributed by identifying Nanchao as the original homeland from where, they said, Tais migrated—some to the east and some west as far as Assam in India.[50] Such literature identified the Ahoms as the westernmost Tai group, and their buranjis were considered a depository of a Tai past. Scholars such as Terwiel (1983, 1994) even claimed that Ahom rituals, oracles, divinations, and ancestor worship represented the original Tai belief system before Tais converted to Buddhism. By and large, general Western scholarly assumptions concerning Ahoms fitted easily within the scheme of Thai academics searching for an antiquated Tai people and a life and culture before Buddhism and capitalism transformed Thai society. The "discovery" of Tai-Ahoms and their buranjis, deemed as the repositories of an isolated, archaic, genuine Tai community, was no coincidence because Chatthip believed that "ancient Tai identities are still preserved in these texts and words and reflect the continuity of these identities" (1996, 14–15).[51] Once claimed as an ancestral group, Ahoms became a subject of intense academic deliberation as well as a subject of more general interest in Thailand.

While Thai intellectuals such as Chatthip actively sought out an "authentic Tai village culture" to empower the local people of Thailand in the face of capital intrusion from the West and from the Thai government, Tai-Ahom leaders in Assam saw in the Thai endeavor an outlet for their political and economic ambitions. They seized this opportunity at the international Thai studies conference in New Delhi. Along with representatives from Thailand, Tai-Ahom delegates drafted a common agenda to explore their "shared" identity. The rather abstract and unknown category called "Ahom" in the buranjis was revitalized through discussions and became a platform for challenging Assamese and Indian identities. Its association with Thai history and culture made Ahom history exotic and different. Moreover, the newly found connection with Thailand provided an impetus for demanding ST status for Ahoms in Assam. The postcolonial state practices of economically neglecting and culturally marginalizing Assam within India were both challenged by obscure Ahoms with the help of Thai international support.

To facilitate exchange and mutual development, several levels of communication between Thais and Tai-Ahom agents were forged. Conferences accelerated the production of Tainess among Tai-Ahoms and provided occasions for frequent visits among the representatives. Since 1981 Thai scholars have visited Assam to participate in the annual conferences held by Ban Ok. Their presence at these mass gatherings made a big impression and led many in Assam to believe that Tai-Ahoms and Thais were related since time immemorial, although some also resented the attempt of Ahoms to become Tai by denouncing the Assamese. Among the youth in Ujani Aham there was a growing attraction to traveling to Thailand to connect with Tai brethren, whom they saw as models of economic success—a goal they too wanted to achieve. In villages I often heard stories about visits to Thailand. On these occasions, the entire male populace would gather to listen to the traveler's encounters in the "land of their forefathers." In these accounts, Thailand was presented as a place of pilgrimage where everyone was happy, kindly disposed, and successful. The narration would end with sighs of longing to "return to the place where we originally came from." Such repeated stories, at public and private gatherings, of travel to Thailand convinced Tai-Ahoms that they were more Thai than they had known. At the same time their distancing of themselves from Hindu Indians was becoming more apparent. Even Hindus in Upper Assam agreed without hesitation that "they [Tai-Ahom and Thais] were related in the past."

In addition to the Ban Ok's conventions, the conferences and seminars on Tai studies brought people together. Since 1981 two "international" conferences on Tai studies have been held in Assam. Hiteshwar Saikia funded both of these meetings and also provided financial assistance to enable Tai-Ahoms to travel from Assam to Thailand and even to London for conferences.

At the sixth international Thai studies conference, held in Chiangai, Thailand, in 1996, there were several sessions on Tai-Ahoms, and their history and identity was a hot topic of debate in the plenary session. Evidently, recognition of "marginal Tai groups living outside Thailand" was a serious academic concern.[52] My paper on the Tai-Ahom politics of identity did not go unnoticed. People were either very encouraging or highly critical of my approach. This was a surprise and a new experience for me because at South Asian studies conferences only a very few people had shown interest in the subject of Tai-Ahom. I found myself wondering whether Tai-Ahom was the subject of Southeast Asian history or of South Asian history? Of course, the real issue is the politics of production of academic knowledge that creates certain topics worthy of attention and silences others. Assam and Tai-Ahom, as I argue earlier, are unspoken subjects in Indian history. In the face of this ubiquitous silence, I see the effort of Tai-Ahoms to insert themselves in contemporary history as a challenge to the statist parameters of Indian history and politics. Hence, although they are a small movement at the margins of the nation-state, their efforts deserve scholarly attention and analysis.

Thai academic interest in and support for Tai-Ahom identity was only one aspect of a very complex relationship. It did not take long after the first meeting in 1981 for the label Tai-Ahom to become an item of transaction between the two interested parties. Notably, it resulted in a commodification of "Tai-Ahom objects." In several villages in Sibsagar, a large number of puthis were available that could be bought for an "attractive price." "Thai scholars," people told me, were "very kind and paid handsomely for puthis that they took back to Thailand for translation." Funding for the purchase and translation of buranjis into Thai came from the Toyota Foundation of Japan (Wichasin 1996, 14). In addition, on several occasions in my conversations from April 1994 to March 1995, different villagers also confided in me that when the Thai delegates would visit their village, they would stage rituals and worship for the Thais benefit.

The effects of the new commodity value of Ahom history and culture had an impact on my work. At times people asked me for payment in American dollars for the information they shared with me. Their logic was simple: "Thai scholars pay us, so you should too." On such occasions there would be heated discussions between those who located me as an "insider" entitled to receive information without payment, and those who located me as a "foreign returned" person. Those who wanted payment approached the business very pragmatically. While they considered me one of them, they also reasoned that I had to pay for information, because it would help me earn a degree and get a job. Their logic was simple: the Thai scholars are outsiders yet they support us, so why should not one of us support our cause? The Thai scholars were not the only ones determining the price of the Tai-Ahom past. Rebel groups from Burma and other countries had joined the fray and were helping the ULFA to reclaim the past to create a future in Ujani Aham. These groups had also raised the stakes of Tai-Ahom history, and now everything came with a price.

While Thai scholars generated income for Tai-Ahoms in Assam through travel, tourism, and the buying of "Tai antiquities," they also disseminated a wide array of "cultural goods" from Thailand to enable Tai-Ahoms to create Tai ambiance and lifestyle in order to distinguish themselves from the Assamese. Pictures of the Thai monarch and his wife adorned many Tai-Ahom homes and places of work and worship. Ironically, while Thai scholars sought a pre-Buddhist past in Tai-Ahom villages, people in Ujani Aham were rapidly converting to Buddhism, an enterprise facilitated by the direct involvement of the Thai monarchy's donation of Buddha images and other religious items to the newly converted communities in Assam. There was a competition among villages to acquire these important religious artifacts sent from Thailand. A market in Buddhist paraphernalia developed as a result, and demand exceeded supply. The most lucrative wares were *tankhas* (Buddhist art scrolls), handwritten manuscripts, and religious robes. From Thailand people sent such items to Assam to make merit. The Thai scholars, inadvertently, became conduits for these goods. They carried several of these as gifts to Assam between 1985 and 1995.

The Thai scholars definitely were not motivated to visit Assam for potential trade benefits. In fact, quite the opposite was true. For both Thai and Tai-Ahom proponents, the goal was, in Nartsupha's words, to "find" and "link cultures over state-borders . . . in order to look for the origin of Tai cultures" (1996, 21–22). Nartsupha insisted that buranjis were sources for the "study of the origin [of Tai culture], the starting point, and its formation process, since all it is at present is the result or the stream of the past that has been layered one over another" (23). The project of cultural awakening in Thai villages was to "bring history back to the village community where it belongs." This project constituted an "ideological war between the state and the village community" (22). Tai-Ahom served as fodder as scholars fought the battle in Thailand. The battle between groups with a vested interest in capitalist growth and those who resist it is ongoing.[53] For the time being, the "discovery of Tai-Ahoms and Tai-Ahom things" has created a venue for a political consciousness as well as a distinct commodity for consumption among Thais seeking a pre-Buddhist, precapitalist, exotic Thai history. In short, Tai-Ahom provides an imaginative space for a return to a pastoral village life that has been overrun by the new capitalism that is centered in Thailand's cities.

Perhaps the commodification of Tai-Ahom was more pronounced in Assam. Tai-Ahom leaders viewed their friendship with Thai scholars as an avenue for future economic growth. By the time I left Assam, the project had been quite successful and promised even more. Tai-Ahom leaders regularly traveled to Thailand (with funding from the Assam state government). While in Thailand, they stayed in Buddhist *viharas* (temples) and

Thai homes and universities to learn the different ways of making Tai-Ahoms fit into the mold of archaic Tai. They hoped that, in the future, Thais looking for a place to visit or in search of genealogical roots would privilege Assam over the other locations of ancestral groups and "find" pristine Tai culture in their villages.[54] In the meantime, the production and consumption of the label "Tai-Ahom" in Assam financially benefited several groups and individuals. It created new jobs, brought business to Tai-Ahom building engineers and contractors who built seng-rengs and Sukapha Bhavans, boosted the publication industry of Tai-Ahom books, and created new sites of political power. All of these activities also heightened an awareness of a separatist identity and motivated a local movement.

The political culture of the Tai-Ahom movement depicts what Amrita Basu calls creative tension (Basu 1992). The source of this creativity lies in the various axes of ambiguity and contradiction. The complex web of interpretations of Tai-Ahom by different agents with different agendas made it into many different things. But there have been too many images and expectations, too many different strategies and policies, and far too many leaders for Tai-Ahom to be a movement of a single defined group. Nonetheless, the Tai-Ahom identity movement has made impressive inroads into the psyche of the people in Ujani Aham. As a result it became a movement in its own right—different and separate from the Assamese. The Assamese have come to accept that those who say they are Tai-Ahom are different and are related both historically and ethnically to Thai people in Thailand. The efforts of the leaders have produced results. Membership in Tai-Ahom organizations grows daily. Why do people want a new identity as Tai-Ahom? What does the Tai-Ahom label provide them?

The main effort of the Tai-Ahom movement in Ujani Aham was to assert a political right to identity and to economic justice, things that the leaders of Ban Ok, the ALDC, and the ULFA claimed were missing within the present state structure. The combined efforts of these groups reflect a formative stage in local nationalism designed to counter the hegemonic power of Delhi and to demand a restructuring of policies and attitudes toward Assam, particularly Ujani Aham. Although Tai-Ahom initially appeared to be a "cultural" movement, the amalgamation of leaders and actors made the movement an agency for transformation in Ujani Aham. The label "Tai-Ahom" underwent significant transformations as a result, but it retained its central position as a focus for imagining a different past in order to etch a new path for the future—to regain the golden days of swargadeo rule, to affirm a Tai heritage, and to create potentials for economic development. The movements that used the label Ahom also created a distinct political and social imagery. The signifier "Ahom" became a means to register opposition to orders imposed by the Assamese and Indian states and mobilized Ahom history as a voice of protest (irrespective of how one read and interpreted its meaning). As we have seen, many movements in Ujani Aham used the language of Ahom history to forge new forms of consciousness and to advance their interests. The discourse of local nationalism was mediated and moderated by this central category and what it said to different groups. Their heterogeneous interpretations of Tai-Ahom allowed different groups to articulate the failure of the Indian national state in Assam, to register their grievances, and to demand a new political and economic reality—a reality that has remained elusive.

In this chapter I have investigated discourses produced by leaders who used Ahom for their various political and economic ends. In the next chapter I discuss the responses of everyday, ordinary people in villages and towns who shared with me their views and observations, longing and desires, and hopes and expectations about Tai-Ahom identity. These people wish someday to become known and recognized as a people with a history and an identity.

# CHAPTER 6

# There Was No Plot in the People's Struggle

In the first half of the 1990s the rhetoric of Tai-Ahom identity emerged as a dominant voice in Ujani Aham. With the help of Thai scholars, this rhetoric maintained a "domain of sovereignty" (Chatterjee 1993, 6) distinct from the political activities of the Assamese identity movement. Rituals and practices multiplied, and support from local rebel groups like the ULFA combined with the interest of transnational networks strengthened the discourse of Tai-Ahom. Oral accounts endorsed the presence of Tai-Ahom in all walks of life in Ujani Aham. During my stay in Assam, I encountered the images of Ahom everywhere. The people who upheld this identity varied widely, and although not all of them endorsed the various leaders and their strategies, they all had something to say about the identity movement and were associated with it at different levels of interaction and participation. Economic background, social status, place of abode, age, religious affiliation, and gender influenced people's thinking, and, subsequently, how much they associated with the movement.

Through political maneuverings, Hiteshwar Saikia shifted the focus of the movement from Ujani Aham and made it a political game that was played in Dispur. While the villagers of Ujani Aham were conscious that only a few men in Guwahati were controlling the activities of the Tai-Ahom movement, they also realized that the discourse about identity, if it would bear results, would ultimately benefit a large group that included them. Hence, these people were more than "listening subjects" (Foucault 1972, 52), they were participants in as well as agents of the movement. The village gathering places called *sabha* created space for discussion at the grassroots level. In these gatherings they discussed buranjis and Tai-Ahom religion and rituals, as well as politics. Discussions in the sabhas aided the creation of a standard version of Tai-Ahom history for active circulation and consumption. They also eliminated ambiguities: Sukapha was deemed a Tai-Ahom hero with divine qualities, the Luit Valley was accepted as the original place of the first Tai-Ahom settlement, and Ujani Aham was claimed as the "geo-body" of Tai-Ahom history and culture.

This version of Tai-Ahom history, as we know, has very little to do with factuality but rather is a charged emotional discourse. Whenever I asked for verification of what made people Ahom, the response was on the order of, "We don't have to verify anything. The buranjis tell us all about it. Unfortunately, nowadays, nobody reads them. Hence, you are asking this question." Clearly, these Ahoms were approaching the buranji texts as repositories of Tai-Ahom history. Although the majority of them could not read the buranjis, they ardently believed that the chronicles were records of *their* past. The people assumed that they did not have to clarify anything; it was my task to know the "truth"—something they already knew and were trying to establish. If, however, I insisted on knowing the name of a particular buranji that had in its record this information, usually the person would confide that they had not read it, but that they knew that Domboru Deodhai's family held a very old buranji with the history of Ahoms.[1] Or people would tell me that they discuss their history in the sabha, where they learn about their past, and history.[2]

What I want to emphasize here is that the people who now claim to be Tai-Ahom are not always clear about Tai-Ahom history, but they are emotionally attached to the label. This makes them believe that the Tai-Ahom identity movement is a valid one. They expect that the identity movement will enable them to return to a past forgotten for a long time, a past neglected and denied. However, a longing for return to the past does not mean a lack of interest in the future. In fact, the struggle for identity is an attempt to guarantee better opportunities, both in the present and in the future. In the meantime, the movement serves to express, in the words of Gabriel Marcel, a "passionate longing for the unknown" (quoted in Harper 1996, 36). Because the Tai-Ahom identity continues to be vague, even for those associated with it, the question that is often asked is what is the best method for continuing the struggle, and what will be the outcome? For most people and their leaders, there is no single strategy or fixed goal to work for. For many, any tactic and any level of success is acceptable.

As I demonstrated in chapter 5, under the guidance of the Ban Ok, the main thrust of the Tai-Ahom identity movement has become cultural revivalism and economic improvement. Political regimes have been expected to transform these demands into reality. Hence, to a large measure the Tai-Ahom movement could be easily co-opted by the state government, and it has become encumbered by the politics and politicians in Dispur. The revival of the Ahom language played an interesting though problematic role in the then new Tai-Ahom cultural revivalism. Moreover, attempts to have Tai-Ahom classified as a ST proved to be problematic. Still, many viewed obtaining this status as the quickest and most secure way of guaranteeing economic and political advancement. However, the Ban Ok's strategy of using cultural revivalism to make economic gains did not go unchallenged. Many Tai-Ahom leaders suggested violent means to gain Tai-Ahom rights and identity. The ULFA was one such organization. Although we cannot say that ULFA is the voice of the Tai-Ahom movement, its appeal to the so-called Tai-Ahoms of Ujani Aham was immense. Another organization, the ALDC, was also very attractive to the people, especially because it promised to make a new homeland for the Tai-Ahoms in Ujani Aham.

As chaotic a conglomerate as the Tai-Ahom movement is today, it is also undeniably a site that has brought people together in a common and deeply felt purpose. It is possible that the demand for recognition as Tai-Ahom will not be fulfilled for these people: their identity demands can be located in the circumstances created by political and economic factors, and these conditions may not remain constant enough to rally the group to continue their struggle. The course is not foregone. However, at this juncture, a more vital and interesting question that arises is why do people in Ujani Aham respond to the politics of Ban Ok, the ALDC, and the ULFA? One could attempt to reply by reducing this response to an outcome of elite-level politics, but such a reduction does not explain what drives people to relinquish Assamese identity. Definitely something more complex than the mere politics of elite power brokers is at work. Can we begin to understand why people are looking for belonging in Ahom? We have to recover the voices of the common people and situate their reasons by keeping in mind a historical framework that helps to explain why a new identity has appealed to the masses in Assam.

The reasons are neither orderly nor homogenous. Likewise, the processes and strategies for mobilizing to achieve these goals are fragmented and multiple. In this chapter, I will present a selection of these responses. My choices are based on the uniqueness or typicality of the responses. One common emotion that most people I spoke to expressed was a longing for a return to a place called "home." Home was described in many different ways. Some claimed it was Assam, others Thailand, and a few said they were from China. Home in their eyes was not a fixed place, but there was a time when they claim that they had had a home. In this sense, home was a temporal fixity rather than a fixed spatial location. The past was a time of home. In this there was consensus, although the past was a flexible notion. Some said that since the colonial period, the glorious days of the swargadeos had been lost and the people of Ujani Aham had been forgotten. Others said that after colonialism everything had changed. They were given different names and forced to relinquish their identities. Yet others blamed the present political regimes and the surge of Indian Hindu identity for excluding noncaste Hindu groups like Tai-Ahom.

Everywhere I went in Ujani Aham, people seemed preoccupied with images of the past, stories of lost glory, decay, demolition, and injustice. They were feeling very distant from everyone else, and a deep sense of alienation dominated village life. They hoped that if a "perfect" past existed, when their kings were gods on earth, they could establish a perfect future too. The two points of memory—the archaic past and the unknown future—dominated sentiment in the villages.[3] People lived in the memory of the past by telling stories of gods and kings, and in the memory of a prosperous future when they would become an ST group and receive the benefits and economic privileges of this status. The identity struggle in the present, in their estimation, was the bridge for connecting the two poles of memory. In this sense, the present nostalgia for the past was regenerative, and inspired diverse Ujani Aham communities to start new lives. Unfortunately, the leaders of the movements were so numerous, divided, and contentious that a variety of goals, strategies, and policies lacked grounding. Nonetheless, it was the variety of choices that were available to people that kept them engaged in the movement, and Tai-Ahom identity continued to be fluid, spontaneous, and under construction.

## IN THEIR OWN VOICE

I gathered most of the information given in the following sections from conversations, almost all in Assamese, with a wide variety of people in several different villages and towns. My family connection to the places and peoples of Ujani Aham helped me immensely in establishing ongoing conversations. Being a Saikia from Sibsagar was an asset, and to this was added my late grandfather's prestige as a schoolteacher of the town high school at Sibsagar. I was immensely privileged to have access to the information, people, and ideas that allowed me to see the Tai-Ahom movement from within—as it was happening in the villages of Ujani Aham and in the political core of Guwahati.

I have divided the information that I gathered from the different groups not by class or caste but by social roles. I have identified three different social groups: educated urban professionals, religious leaders, and youth. No doubt, the dominant voice in these conversations is male, for men usually assumed the role of spokesperson during our discussions. Occasionally women also spoke out, although this happened mostly in private. They rarely contradicted what men said, but in our private conversations they were generally more outspoken and expressed a growing sense of impatience that the movement had not produced concrete results for the Tai-Ahom. The women prioritized the demand for ST status as their primary objective because they saw in that classification the possibility of employment and benefits for their sons. They also suggested several strategies for achieving the goal of becoming an ST group, but they were very reluctant to take leadership initiatives even at the village level. Whenever I probed into the reasons, they said it was a man's role to lead the community, while their role as women was to take care of the home front and support the men. This response was not at all unusual because women in Assam, as in the rest of India, are hardly encouraged to become leaders. The so-called Tai-Ahom women of Assam, while they wanted to be outside the identitarian framework of the label Indian, had internalized the social constructs of Indian womanhood and were complacent in this position.

Although I have not arranged the conversations with the different groups in a chronological order, a vague pattern is somewhat noticeable. The variety of responses makes us aware of the constitutive nature of the movement that brought heterogeneous groups together in a precarious arrangement for a temporary period of time. At different stages, different purposes and goals motivated people to join. Compiling an inventory of these reasons does not help us to formulate an explanation of why some people in Ujani Aham were looking at the Tai-Ahom movement for identity and history. But it does make us aware that these people were agents in the movement. They were there because they wanted to be participants in the construction of an identity and to create belonging within a framework that was acceptable to them. The politics of local identity thrived in 1990s Assam because there was a constituency—active and engaged—to give it meaning, however various it was.

Urban professionals were the most vocal group. For most, the identity movement was a struggle to forge economic and social benefits, mostly for their class group. They were less concerned with the political demand for an independent homeland and abstract concepts of "finding" a Tai-Ahom self. These pragmatic professionals envisioned the movement to be a quick way to make significant financial progress. Their quest for economic and social improvement was complicated by the issues of heritage and genealogy. Within the group there was a noticeable class division. There was a small group who claimed royal heritage, as progeny of the swargadeos. But the dominant group in the class of urban professionals was formed by the descendants of title holders, the so-called Ahom nobles, who now saw and represented themselves as "true Ahoms." The extended family of the royalty, mostly unknown and uninvolved in the movement, looked on those who were representing themselves as "true" Ahoms as being below their class and refused to mix with them.

Raj Kumar, an architect and scion of the "Ahom" royal family, talked about the confusion of the exroyals and his disdain toward those who claimed to be "true Ahoms" during our extended conversations over several days. Although he was very supportive of my research project and even expressed an interest in visiting "the villages to experience firsthand how Ahom people lived," he told me that he was "ashamed with what is going on." In reply to my question about his evaluation of the identity movement, he stated: "Why claim an Ahom identity when there is nothing to regain? The entire world is moving to a twenty-first-century culture. Here we want to be Ahoms! What they mean I do not know or understand. You see, the entire game is of politics. Hence, I try to keep away from all this." When I probed further and asked him to explain to me the politics of Ahom, he said:

> In Assam we have all kinds of people. We have Koch, Kachari, Muslims, Ahoms, Chutias—you name it. Do the people really care for these community identities? Is there any real feeling for the labels? Why are people today looking to be Ahoms now? This resurgence is taking place in the tenure of Hiteshwar Saikia. It is now convenient and politically expedient to be Ahom. Many people are taking advantage of this situation. You cannot imagine how much money is poured into this enterprise. The money is not for public good. The same people who are involved in the various Ahom organizations are actually getting a lot of personal benefits. It suits Hiteshwar Saikia. He has been made a

swargadeo, and he is happy. Everybody is looking to make gains. People are going to laugh at us. Ahoms want to be Tai. They do not even know what it is. The Ahom language can belong to anything. It can be classified under any Tibeto-Burman language family. These days, we call ourselves Tai-Ahoms. It is hard to believe how things are shaping. The people here have found that Thailand is a prosperous place. They want to be part of that world. You see, the whole thing is one of convenience.[4]

I was not very surprised by what I heard or how Raj Kumar framed his argument against the movement. In Raj Kumar's opinion certain entitlements were his family's heirloom and he had to maintain his claims over these for they were the only things left to the exroyals. According to him, the term "Ahom" was one of the ornaments of the royal household, which, without a doubt, was quite contrary to what his predecessors, the swargadeos, believed. He opined that if the honor of being Ahom was relinquished to the low and sundry, differences between the exroyalty and general people would be erased. For Raj Kumar, Hiteshwar Saikia's claim to be Ahom was unacceptable—more so because Saikia used it as a way to bolster his political and financial power. Despite his vehement criticism of the movement and Saikia's role in it, when I asked Raj Kumar how he identified himself, he immediately replied, "I am an Ahom." He was not completely detached from the movement either, although he was critical of it. Raj Kumar had designed and built the Ahom Seng Reng at Jorhat, and he proudly gave me a tour of the building.

While Raj Kumar's position can be read as one of ambivalence, Ajay Singh, another member of the defunct royal household, was clear that he felt the Tai-Ahom movement was a political strategy and he did not want to be involved in it. He told me in a sad voice:

You are the first person who has approached the Rajabari [the household of the royal family] to discuss about Ahoms. We are not consulted by anyone. In 1989, when the Tai delegates visited Assam, we were asked to host them. The Ban Ok wanted to show them Ahom royalty, but since then we had no more exchanges . . . The visit of the Thai delegates cost us thousands of rupees. We cannot afford that. We are salaried people. I don't work, but my wife teaches in Guwahati. We have been left very little land since the Land Ceiling Act. But we cannot ask the government for money to host our guests. I would much prefer that they do not burden us with these events. . . . I believe that their next plan is to host a two-hundred-year anniversary celebration to commemorate the shift of the Ahom capital from Sibsagar to Jorhat during the colonial administration. Nobody has talked to us about it. I prefer that they keep us out of this; it is only a platform for political dealings. What do we in the Rajabari have to do with it?[5]

Both Raj Kumar and Ajay Singh, members of the old royalty, were quite bitter about the present Tai-Ahom movement. Their cynicism was not unnatural; the days of their ancestor's rule were long over, and now they had nothing to gain by claiming Ahomness. Even if they did, the leadership was not going to be in their hands. The new terrain of Ahom identity was the playground of politicians, like Hiteshwar Saikia, who was, in their eyes, a descendant of "low officials" who served their family. How could they now serve Saikia or the likes of him without losing their pride and position?

The group of urban professionals who now called themselves "true Ahoms" did not agree with the views of the exroyals. On the contrary, many of them were enthusiastic about the movement and saw it as a site where they could assert their position and gain power. Jiba Gogoi, Hiteshwar Saikia's former finance minister, identified himself to me "as a full-blooded Hindu Ahom." In defense of the Tai-Ahom movement he said:

> There is Nagaland, Meghalaya, and many more such states for ethnic groups . . . Why should Ahoms not get Ahomland? . . . Ahomland does not mean Thailand. We, Ahoms, should not think of ourselves as anything else but real Assamese. We should be the ones to set the standards of culture and customs in Assam, like our swargadeos did in the past. Surely, this will allow us to have better relations with Thailand because we share the same past. But now we live here, and we have to claim our true rights. We forgot our language and accepted Assamese language and culture. We forgot Thailand, from where we had come. Assam became our homeland. That pride needs to be revived. We cannot settle for compromising treaties to demarcate the Ahomland as an isolated pocket from others.

Gogoi claimed that the glorious history of buranjis, which was the true legacy of the Ahom people of Ujani Aham, had been denied to them. He justified the reasons for their demand for identity as a way to overcome the tyranny of their hopeless present. As he explained: "The demand for Ahom is for various reasons. The entire rural population of Ujani Aham is terribly deprived and very poor. Hence, they are finding every excuse to rise in revolt. Probably the noise of being Ahom is more than other ethnic movements in Assam. Ahoms are a very straightforward, outspoken, big hearted, proud people. Hence, they cannot tolerate injustice."[6]

While Jiba Gogoi was positive about the movement and did not hesitate to identify with it even though he was an elected representative, there were others who were far more critical. For example, Hiren Gohain, a professor at Guwahati University, was politically active in the movement of Ahamia Jatigathan. He was somewhat self-conscious of his identity as an "Assamese Ahom," but he did not think it was an issue. For him the Ahom were not a separate community from the Assamese. Also, as an avowed Marxist, he was more concerned with the abject poverty of the Assamese people at large. In his estimation the Tai-Ahom movement was a distraction, splintering the community and alienating people from each other rather than raising the consciousness of their shared history of exploitation. Ultimately, a movement like the Tai-Ahom, he thought, benefited few at the cost of the majority in Assam. His analytical approach to the movement was both political and historical. In his view one had to go back to colonialism to trace the origin of such an identity movement. In his estimation "the question of identity arose in the nineteenth century, and suddenly everyone was looking for homelands. All this happened when the question of who is a pure caste Hindu became important. The Ahoms who were also looking for some sort of acceptance and recognition circulated the idea of migration, because they could not be part of caste Hindu society." He further suggested that a true understanding of this movement must take into account the politics of the region: "There are a variety of people within the Ahom community. Some people do not want to be Ahoms. They are within the Hindu society and want to remain there, while there are the die-hard Ahoms, on the other side. As well, there are people who are neither here nor there. They have their feet on two boats. But all this about Ahom identity will make sense only if they can articulate what is their aim. What will they do with this Ahom identity if they manage to construct one?"[7]

Because Gohain was aware that the present leaders did not have a plan beyond the basic demand of becoming an ST group, he dismissed the movement as a game beguiling the people of Assam. Moreover, he feared that "for most people there will be few achievements, many failures, and much frustration." Ultimately, he predicted that creating "enchantment for the past that is dead and gone will be more agonizing than hopeful, and it will break Assamese people into pieces."

Hiren Gohain's view that Ahoms were a part of Assamese society and their break from the parent community would prove to be counterproductive was not accepted by Numal Gogoi, a professor at Dibrugarh University and an active member of the Ban Ok. He explained why he thought Gohain was wrong in these words:

He [Gohain] cannot understand Ahom needs because he is an intellectual living in Guwahati. He should go back to his parental village in Ujani Aham, he will see a different picture there . . . Ahoms are the most neglected community. They have ruled for six hundred years, but now they are totally deprived. We have never got any benefits. Only now that we have Hiteshwar Saikia as the chief minister, we are getting some benefits. After that, there will be no more benefits to be had. So we are saying make us a scheduled tribe, [and] that will assure us some privileges. But we are facing a great deal of criticism. We are part of Assamese society, but we are surviving as a separate jati [community] because caste Hindu groups do not care about us. They want to say that after 1979, since the AASU movement, we have divided further to create a separate movement. They are not aware that there was an International Tai Seminar where we faced great embarrassment, for we did not know our own history and culture. We have to learn it all over again, and many in Assam do not want us to. Is this right, a just expectation?[8]

In defending the Tai-Ahom movement and articulating the reasons why Ahoms wanted to claim the past, most middle-class professionals seemed to view the movement as a way to combine political interests with demands for economic improvement by becoming an ST group. When pressed further to explain why they were claiming a royal heritage alongside a tribal identity, most people were extremely reluctant to discuss the issue. However, Kiran Gogoi, a high school teacher, expressed her opinion quite clearly. She did not know what were the different criteria required by the government to classify a community as an ST group, although she was certain that there would be a lot of room for negotiation. She did not see why Ahoms could not be in the ST category as well as be accepted as descendants of swargadeos. In her words:

We [Ahoms] think of ourselves as tribal. We were always considered a tribal community by caste Hindus. They do not eat with us or mix with us. They do not marry our daughters. When we were growing up we were called all sorts of names. Even in the areas of Sibsagar and Nazira, where our ancestors ruled and we were a majority group, caste Hindus had more power, social prestige, and clout compared to us. Our forefathers ruled them, but when the forefathers were ousted from power, their progeny were pushed to the bottom of the social pile. Socially, the Hindus look down at us. But, at the same time, they do not want to officially recognize us as a tribal community. That will give Ahoms many privileges and benefits, like easy access to the Indian Administrative Service, appointments in many national government offices with less competition, relaxation of the age barrier in competitive exams, and many other benefits that the government of India provides to backward or scheduled tribes. I believe the plan to change the present status of Ahoms from Hindus to that of a scheduled tribe is supported by Hiteshwar Saikia. Otherwise, he is likely to suffer the most. His electoral constituency in Nazira will become a labor constituency, since tea laborers are the largest voting group there, as elsewhere in Ujani Aham, and they will demand to reserve the seats for their community.[9]

Kiran Gogoi and many others who were involved in the movement in Guwahati, unlike Hiren Gohain, were not critical of the government's involvement in their cause. They did not see it as polarizing them from other communities in Assam. On the other hand, they viewed the government of Hiteshwar Saikia as an aid for mobilizing people directly, so that they would be able to achieve some concrete and beneficial results. From the discussions I had with several more people, it became evident that they saw the Tai-Ahom movement as a viable oppositional politics which let them play the stakes of ethnicity, past history, and lack of opportunities in the present to achieve tangible and long-lasting rewards in the end. Their view was expressed by Numal Gogoi, when he stated "Why should not the government of Hiteshwar Saikia, who is an Ahom, help the movement to ensure a better economic future for Tai-Ahoms?"[10]

The second group I identified consisted of religious leaders such as deodhais, mohans, and bailungs. These men had lived obscure and often marginal lives, and were now on the brink of destitution. They owned little or no paddy land, their children were poorly educated, and, in the case of deodhais, had no say in the Hindu religious system and practices. On the whole, they were emblematic of a terrible cycle of poverty and social deprivation. This group, confined mostly to Patsako, Bokata, and villages in the surrounding areas of Sibsagar and Dhemaji, had latched onto the Ahom movement to reclaim spiritual rights, gain social acceptance, and ensure their children's future. Through the Tai-Ahom movement they expected to replace the "corrupt" Brahmins, who had used religion to gain an elevated social position and economic benefits in the past and to continue to exercise power in Assam.

In contrast to the openness of urban professionals, the deodhais were not comfortable with discussing their participation and the kind of activities they were involved in. They complained vehemently about the Brahmins and their methods of exploitation, and spoke about their own attempts to undo these. They did not see themselves as part of the Tai-Ahom political movement, for their struggle, they claimed, had a longer history than the present Ban Ok organization. To an extent this claim is true because in the early 1960s they had organized their own society to deal with the problems of Ahom religion. Evidently, they were unsuccessful and their movement died. Once again, under the leadership of Ban Ok, they were making a comeback and they expected that this time they would be successful.

For the deodhais the generic name of the enemy was "Hindu," and they pinned all of their problems on this group. Within this group they included their exploiters—landowners, government officials, merchants, and political officials. The identification of a singular enemy allowed them to create identity boundaries and a sense of belonging to a social order that they connected with. In mapping themselves as a particular group different from Hindus, they adopted some emblems, objects, and artifacts as their identification tools. Phra Lung religion became the mainstay in their claim to be Ahom. As such, they have been actively propagating this religion and encouraging conversion from Hinduism among the supporters of Tai-Ahom in order to claim their place of importance within the movement. In the deodhais' view a return to Phra Lung religion is the only way to avoid the backwardness and confusion of identity in the present and to gain economic and political power in the future.[11]

Mostly confined to the villages of Ujani Aham, deodhais had strong linkages with the ULFA cadres in the area and they often showed their support for the ULFA, sometimes bypassing Ban Ok's directive to remain confined to religious and cultural issues only. In the ULFA's struggle deodhais saw the possibility of a decline in the power of caste Hindus in Assam and a way to open up a space for low-caste and tribal groups to rise up. Ritual events of the new religion of Phra Lung and the ULFA's recruitment campaign in villages brought the two groups together, sometimes in the same courtyard in villages.[12] Hence, the interaction between the deodhais and Ban Ok sometimes became hostile and reproachful, with the deodhais siding with the aggressive group, the ALDC, who had strong linkages to the ULFA. Generally, it could be said that deodhais cohered with the ALDC's ethos to make Ujani Aham an Ahom homeland by getting rid of the Brahmins and Hindus. They saw in this possible transformation the hope of becoming the primary beneficiaries of the resources and development schemes that would follow as a consequence.

Deodhais have benefited the most from the "noise" made about Tai-Ahomness. Many were appointed as Tai language teachers, some were licensed as government contractors for the Public Works and Development Department, still others gained prominence in local politics. The economic boom that they experienced from the frequent visits of Thai scholars to their villages brought significant changes in their material conditions. However, they were not at all comfortable discussing this with me. Instead, they expressed only their religious concerns and justified their reasons for supporting the Tai-Ahom movement. Ahom, in their explanation, was a religious identity different from Assamese Hindu and Indian, although they could not explain the exact nature of the differences. On several occasions they summed it up by saying, "We are not like them [Hindus]. Our religion is different." They had no words to articulate what was different, only in their hearts they felt different, they said.

Tilu Hatibarua is a deodhai's daughter from Patsako. She is employed in the jadughar as a research officer. During our initial meetings in the village, she was unwilling to discuss the Tai-Ahom movement. Rather, she spoke about the "deodhai religion and customs," and even distanced herself from the label Ahom. She stated that "Ahom is a concocted term in Assam," and she explained, "We do not call ourselves Ahoms. When we meet, we introduce ourselves as a member of so-and-so *thal* [kinship group]. That is our identity." Clearly, she saw herself as being outside of the Ban Ok's Ahom movement, or at least that was the impression she conveyed to me during our initial meeting. It is hard to analyze her reasons. Maybe she had initially adopted this strategy to discourage probing on my part. Over time, however, she cautiously engaged in conversations with me, and as we got to know each other she spoke more freely about her role in the Tai-Ahom movement. Her faith in the religion and culture of deodhais was unwavering and, as she claimed, "without it we might as well cease to call ourselves Ahoms." She further explained: "We are deodhais. Only the deodhais maintain the *riti-niti* [traditions and customs] of Ahom culture. The others have become so assimilated with Hindu people that they have lost all that our forefathers held dear. Ahoms no longer have Ahom riti-niti. Ahoms want to be recognized as Ahoms so that we can speak our language and practice our religion. Only when we do so will we be able to claim our connection with the glorious past of the swargadeos and our ancestors. Religion is the most important element in the revival."[13]

Tareswar Barua seconded Tilu Hatibarua's criticism of caste Hindus, as well as of Ahoms who had lost their religion. Tareswar Barua, also a resident of Patsako village, proudly told me in our very first meeting, in April 1994, that he belonged to an "original deodhai family." According to him, a return to "deodhai religion" was the only cure for the present maladies, for without the support of a firm religious foundation, identity was not meaningful. He explained the close connection between religion and identity in these words:

> The Ahom culture went into hiding for a long time, since people were ashamed to call themselves Ahom. The Ahoms, particularly the de-odhais, were looked down upon by the caste Hindus. Our father, Jay-aswer Barua [who is about eighty years of age] is totally lost. He refuses to give up Hinduism. But we are trying. We have realized that we have been cheated by the caste Hindus. . . . In the past, some of our people had accepted Hinduism and even Vaishnavism. They have now re-turned to their forefathers' religion. There is a growing consciousness about being Ahom. We now call ourselves Chow so and so. We no longer refer to ourselves by the prefix Shri or Mister that the Hindus and British had taught us. To be able to claim a cultural position is a new thing and it indicates that people want to be seen as Ahoms and not as Hindus anymore. Also, our women refer to themselves by the honorific term, Nang, although it is less common among them. . . . In the last few years, a lot of bad luck has befallen our community. We believe that the disasters were due to our rejection of the old religion. . . . We want to be Ahoms to regain our glory and fortune. The days of our ancestors (swargadeos) were grand. We too can make it glorious if we recognize our heritage and offer worship to our ancestors. Our puthis have all the information we need. We are learning to read them and will be able to reclaim our language, religion, and culture from these puthis.[14]

It was not surprising that men like Tareswar Barua emphasized the importance of religion in the newly found Tai-Ahom identity movement. This was a way for them to ensure their position of power, which their fathers had lost by becoming Hindu. To regain a following, Tareswar

Barua and other deodhais were using the emotions of fear and superstition by claiming that the miserable and pecuniary condition of the village people was a punishment of the Ahom gods for forsaking the original religion. They were now taking on the responsibility of calling the misguided people to return to Phra Lung religion, which they presented as the only solution for ensuring the community's well being. The message was compelling. Many believed the deodhais' explanation, and the growing popularity of Phra Lung religion in villages like Patsako and Jahasuk was a testimony to the rapid rate of conversion. Particularly those who wanted to participate in the Ban Ok events converted to the new religion. Phra Lung, as the deodhais expected, became a tool for identifying oneself as Ahom, or so it seemed on the surface in the villages of Ujani Aham where the movement had taken hold.

A very similar assertion of the intimate connection between Phra Lung religion and Tai-Ahom identity was made by Nabin Borgohain, the deodhai of Jahasuk village, Dhemaji, who claimed he had converted "several thousand Hindus and made them true Ahoms." He became angry when I once asked him, "Why do you insist that the Ahoms are different from Assamese Hindus? What difference does it make whether you adopt the Phra Lung religion or not?" He retorted:

> Ahoms had become Hindus sometime in the fourteenth century. The swargadeos founded the kingdom, then invited the Brahmins and gave them land in perpetuity with copper plate edicts. The Hindus established twenty-two satras [Vaishnava monastic establishments] and made the Ahoms Hindus. But this did not happen to the Muslims. They kept their religion. We kept them near Dikhou, where they set up their village. When the gossains [Vaishnava priests] were made supreme, and Rudra Singha became king [1696–1716], he lost the swargabani [sacred right of Ahom rulers]. The Hindus made us take saran [initiation under the gossains]. But Ahoms never bow before others . . . When our swargadeos tried to bring the variety of people together, they lost the original language and culture. We have four vedas of our own—Pha Lai Veda, Pha Pin Veda, Lik Lai Veda, and Khek Lai Veda. But the swargadeos discarded them. The Hindus destroyed us. We lost our land, religion, and culture. Others became important in our home. We had our own language, culture, and religion, yet we had taken the culture and religion of Hindus. Now we do not need it any longer, because they did not think of us as one of them.[15]

Nabin Borgohain and Tareshwar Barua, although they derided the caste Hindus for sycophancy and ungratefulness and for amassing power through various means from the swargadeos, did not suggest a radical transformation or a reconceptualization of Ahom society in new terms. Instead, they understood religion in the same terms as Hindus, using words like Vedas for Ahom books, puja for worship, and so on. They merely translated the terms that they deemed necessary. They also continued to engage in the same discourses of power and hierarchy. The change that they were recommending within the Phra Lung religion was that Ahoms should not accept Brahmin priests, but rather entrust the priestly class of deodhais with power so that they could revive the old religion. In the new space of Ahom religion, deodhais imagined they would be elevated and made to benefit from economic and political gains. The most important issue for them was land redistribution, and they expected that revivalism would reward them with new land grants so that they could overcome their pecuniary condition. Thus they imagined that they would be made wealthy and happy, once again.

However, the internal perception of deodhais was fraught with several problems. How one would qualify as a priest and thus have power to represent the community was a major issue. Particularly in the villages of Patsako, Bokota, and Jahasuk, where the entire community claimed their origin in deodhai families, it was impossible to decide on this matter. Leadership of the community guaranteed possible gains that were not assured to followers. Hence, no one in these villages was willing to give up their claim—and with it the possibility of concrete rewards. The position of Tilu Hatibaruah, a woman who was trained in the deodhai rituals by her father, was even more precarious. As a woman, could she be a deodhai? Besides the complications that were brought to the fore by issues of gender and leadership, another simple problem was the illiteracy in the community at large.

The aspirations of leadership by deodhais could not be realized because they were unable to guide the community, even in the religious matters that they claimed were their forte. Being illiterate in the Ahom language, they never read the puthis and could not translate the scriptural principles into religious practice. They memorized some of the prayers that were written by Domboru Deodhai, but beyond that constructed repertoire they could not engage in religious discourses and challenge the authority of the Brahmins and Vaishnava gossains of Hindus. As such, they were severely handicapped in their efforts to suggest and enact the distinctive changes that would clearly mark the boundaries of Ahom religion and identity. In this condition, the talk about religious revival as a "way out of Hindu hegemony" was less likely to become a reality.

The third group of people I have identified were the most heterogeneous, but they had one common factor: they were all young and hopeful high school and college students. These young men and women showed no interest in the politics of the leaders, but they expressed a romantic interest in learning about "their" past—the "Ahom past." They enthusiastically attended almost all public meetings, rallies, and conventions, and they were inspired by the Thai delegates' appeal to unite the Tai people of Assam under the banner of Ahom. In response, they started organizing several student groups: the Man-Tai Students Association (Great Tai), the Tai Students Association, and the Tai-Ahom Students Association were products of their efforts. They hoped through these organizations to bring together, in a common venue, various groups of Tai people from Assam. These lofty hopes could hardly be realized, however, for within the student body was a clear demarcation dividing urban and rural students.

The urban students showed very little interest in the everyday and political issues of Ujani Aham and had little or no knowledge about the ALDC and the ULFA. Their counterparts in the villages, on the other hand, were deeply influenced by the ULFA and the ALDC. On the whole, despite the different degrees of association with Ban Ok, the ALDC, and the ULFA, the space created by these organizations allowed the students to form associations to discuss issues that were important to them.

What were these issues that were important to students? Evidently, it was not economic benefits or religious identity that motivated them, although many admitted that if these gains were made they "would benefit in the long run." A major factor that drew them to the Tai-Ahom movement was the possibility of travel—of visiting and studying in foreign places—and Thailand was a very attractive option for realizing this dream. They expected that besides the novelty of traveling to a new country, Thailand was a place where they could learn about "the Tai past." Some of them hoped to stay in Thailand, because, they stated, "we originally came from there." Relatively speaking Thailand is not far from Assam; in fact, it is closer than Delhi, and the airfare for a flight from Assam to Thailand is cheaper than the airfare for flying to Delhi. Despite the proximity, Thailand, for these young men, promised the possibility of new experiences that could not be had in Assam. They imagined these experiences would be qualitatively different because, in the eyes of these young people, "Thailand is a modern place." Their interest in Thailand was not misplaced, for they were witnessing the keen interest held by Thai scholars in the history and culture of their forefathers, about which they knew nothing until the Thais made it evident.

Santanu Buragohain, an undergraduate student in a local college in Guwahati, admitted that he was "keen to study the past so that we could present ourselves to the world, on our own terms, in our own words, and define who we are as Tai-Ahoms." To be able to do this, Santanu joined me in studying the Tai-Ahom language with Nabin Syam. He also encouraged his sister to travel to Thailand and enroll in a business institute. Their father, a wealthy engineer, encouraged his children to "find the Ahom past." However, after two months of intense language coaching, Santanu decided to stop attending the class, because he had to prepare for an exam. Thereafter, I met Santanu several times and noticed that over time his interest in studying Ahom history and culture had waned considerably. His explanation was that "the movement is getting too political. Its life and achievements are contingent on the continued goodwill of the government. I do not want to involve myself with politics."[16] Later I learned that his father was a political opponent of Hiteshwar Saikia, and, naturally, his son was not keen to meddle in a venture of Tai-Ahom identity supported by Saikia.

Khunlung and Majoni Gogoi are siblings who were attending Guwahati University when I met them. Neither was interested in the Tai-Ahom movement, although their parents were actively involved. They had little to say about Tai-Ahom identity, although they agreed that it was "necessary to assert our difference from the general Assamese people." Khunlung liked to paint stilllife pictures, and he had recently painted several pictures of Ahom swargadeos based on his imagination of them. When I asked his opinion about the Tai-Ahom movement, he said, "I don't know much about it. . . . I paint these pictures because I like painting. Also, my father asked me to paint them. For me painting is a hobby." He was not certain if or how his paintings would impact the Tai-Ahom movement, but he essentially dismissed the possibility by saying, "Well, I don't expect people to believe these are lifelike representations of swargadeos. [They are] fictional. My paintings are based on personal imagination. Why should anyone see it otherwise?" When I reminded him that people often failed to make that distinction and offered him the example of Pushpa Gogoi's imaginative painting of Sukapha that was used as an icon during a

Sukapha Divah celebration, Khunlung simply shrugged his shoulders and said, "but the painting is not of Sukapha. We don't know what he looked like in real life. If people cannot understand that this is a fictional representation I don't know what to say."[17] It was very intriguing to me that Khunlung was so certain that he knew what was a fact and what was not. Yet, like everyone else, he had accepted without question that Tai-Ahom is an ethnic community, although there is no historical evidence to back this claim.

Khunlung's sister, Majoni, married an engineer. I attended their Chaklang ceremony (the Ahom religious wedding that was once performed only by royalty).[18] When I asked her if she had chosen to have a Chaklang ceremony to emphasize her Ahom background, she was confounded by my question. She said, "I never thought about it that way." The reason she had this ceremony, she stated, was because her "father could afford a Chaklang wedding. That was a more important reason." She identified herself as an Ahom, but told me she was "not too keen to study it as an academic subject or become involved in the politics of Tai-Ahom."[19]

Jintu Saikia, Hiteshwar Saikia's son, was more than willing to discuss the Ahom need for identity when I met him at his father's official residence. However, he did not see any difference between Ahoms and Assamese Hindus, which he explained was due to his secular upbringing. He said, "My grandfather was a tea plantation employee. Hence, we were exposed to a lot of different influences even in early childhood. We offered worship to Durga, Shiva, and had Me-dam-me-phi celebrations. We are not stuck to one kind of belief. We are not orthodox. In any case, nowadays Ahoms have incorporated all of the gods and goddesses of the Hindu pantheon in their worship. So there is nothing exclusive about Ahoms." In turn, he posed a question to me: "You have been living in villages, attending Ahom religious functions and academic conventions. Have you found any difference between Ahoms and Assamese Hindus?" "What differences do you think I should have found?" I asked. To this he replied, "We are Assamese-Ahom-Hindus. There is no need for some of us to think exclusively as Ahom. There is no difference. That is what I wanted to emphasize to you."[20] This was almost an echo of his father's words. Several months later, when I met Hiteshwar Saikia in his office, he adamantly expressed that Ahoms were Assamese Hindus. However, in a skewed way he admitted that Ahoms needed to be acknowledged as a Scheduled Tribe to ensure certain benefits not available to them as Assamese. In his words, "Ahoms are Assamese. One who speaks, lives, and loves Assam and will work for the interest of Assam is an Assamese. Ahoms have been serving Assam for over six hundred years. I am an Assamese-Ahom-Hindu. Ahoms will always be Assamese, but tribal for constitutional purposes. . . . Nothing is certain at this time."[21]

In the villages of Patsako and Jahasuk, the young men saw the Tai-Ahom movement as their opportunity to make a difference. They were not as sophisticated in their assumptions as were the students in Guwahati, although, like them, they were also interested in traveling to Thailand. For many, though, the more immediate concern was dodging the military raids in their villages. Hence, opportunities to engage them in conversations were very few. Many of them had temporarily left their homes for colleges or had taken petty jobs in the city to support their families. Those who joined the ULFA movement, no doubt, left their homes for good. In the villages I lived in and visited, there were more occasions for me to meet and speak with young women than there were for meeting with young men. Almost all the young women showed no interest in the larger issues of identity raised by the Tai-Ahom movement, and they never investigated what gains they could expect in the future. Some of them told me they had attended the Ban Ok's annual conferences with their parents and also participated in the cultural events. These had been momentary pleasures for them; that was what they remembered and clung to. They identified themselves as Ahom because they felt that everyone else in the village is Ahom. If I asked if this was seen as a new development, almost all of them would say that they didn't know, and that I should ask their fathers. Whether this was apathy or a lack of knowledge was hard to tell.

The young women, however, were most helpful and often showed me different "Tai-Ahom artifacts," such as clothing and jewelry, that the family possessed. They also accompanied me when I had to walk long distances to someone else's home for an interview. From them I learned about the visits of Thai scholars and the performances of religious rituals that the village elders had put up on those occasions. They had witnessed them firsthand but were not certain what they said because only the men were allowed to deliberate on them. The Tai-Ahom identity, at least from their viewpoint, as I understood, was a gender-divided movement where the space for women's participation and involvement was very limited. Hence, they had very little to say about it.

Besides the Tai-Ahom villages in Ujani Aham, there are several Tai villages. The residents of these villages claim they are Tai people but not Tai-Ahom. I visited several of these villages and from my conversations with elders I learned that they trace back their migration to Assam to the late eighteenth and early nineteenth centuries, during the Anglo-Burmese wars. These Tai people, such as the Phakey, Aiton, Khamyang, Turung, and Khamti, were ambivalent about the Tai-Ahom movement. Their interest, or lack thereof, was very much dependent on two factors: their level of association with Tai-Ahom leaders and the physical proximity of their village to a Tai-Ahom village. For example, the Khamyang Goan in Salapathar (which is not far from Patsako) was interested in the Phra Lung movement. Being a Buddhist village, they wanted to assist the deodhais in their return to the religion of their forefathers, which they believed was Buddhism. In other villages, like the remote Tai-Turung village in the Titabor subdivision in Jorhat district, the people were very uneasy about discussing the Tai-Ahom movement. Likewise, the Phakey village in Jeypore, the Chaudang village in Mariani, and many others showed no interest in the Tai-Ahoms.

The young men in these villages, in contrast to the elders, were somewhat more curious about the Tai-Ahom identity movement. They also had several concerns, the most important of which was the label Tai-Ahom. They feared that if this label were to be recognized in the future, it would become the generic identity for all Tai people, because the Tai-Ahom group would dominate and they, the different Tai groups, ultimately would lose their particular identities as a result. But like the Tai-Ahom students at Guwahati, these young men in the villages shared a desire for new experiences, and they looked forward to traveling to Thailand so that they could live a different and more challenging kind of life than did their fathers and grandfathers in Assam.

P. Syam of Rohan Syam Khamyang Gaon articulated this hope. Syam attended school in Dibrugarh where he was training to be a medical technician. I first met him in his village and then several times in Guwahati. He wanted to tell me "all about the Khamyang history and people, who are not Ahom, but Tai." He showed me several handwritten manuscripts written in a Tai script. These were Buddhist religious texts donated to the *vihara* (temple) by Thai and Burmese patrons to earn merit. As he became more comfortable with me, Syam willingly discussed the politics among Tai groups in Assam. He told me that "the Ahom people are not really Tai. But they have taken up the cause of Tai communities. They are powerful, especially because they have the support of Hiteshwar Saikia. . . . Due to the Ahom movement, we are getting several visitors from Thailand, who also visited our village. They have invited us to Thailand."[22] He expressed hope that when he finished his education in Assam, he could travel to Thailand where he expected to find a lucrative job.

Syam's views were not popular with other Tai young men, who were far more skeptical. They doubted that the Ahoms would include them when they achieved their goals. Therefore, they said they were working for a general Tai movement, rather than confining themselves to the Tai-Ahom agenda. P. Turung of Tai-Turung Gaon in Titabar (an active member of the Man Tai Students organization) stated: "I hope they [Ahoms] will broaden their goals, and speak for all Tai people living in Assam and Arunachal Pradesh. . . . The Turung, Aiton, Khamyang and other Tai groups are already recognized as Scheduled Tribes in the Indian constitution. The Ahoms are not. They now want to claim tribal rights. But how can royalty be tribal? We will support them if they include our grievances too. The Tai group could be a formidable force if we unite. But the move has to come from the Ahom leadership."[23] He never explained to me what were the "grievances" of the different Tai groups that he wanted Tai-Ahom leaders to address.

In a similar vein, several young people expressed the need for Tai communities to join together in order to formulate a separate Tai identity, so that they could set themselves apart from the other Assamese groups. If I asked if that new identity would be Ahom, they did not know if they would settle for it. They wanted a movement that would claim the "Mongoloid people" under one banner, so that they could open themselves to various possibilities. To be recognized in India was only one of the options. As one of them summed up: "When Ahoms talk about their links with Thailand, we do not object. Besides creating a market for nostalgia, it is economically beneficial for us. If emotional bonding with Thailand will open up markets of opportunity, we will wholeheartedly support it. Also, we are not petty or parochial."[24]

The entry of these different groups of young men into the Tai-Ahom movement was very beneficial to organizations like Ban Ok, the ALDC, and the ULFA. These young men provided them with immediate and intimate connections to several different groups of youth—rural and urban, Ahom and non-Ahom—and increased the visibility of their causes manifold. In addition, the participation of young people changed the demography of the identity struggle. It also created several layers of discrepancies, because the young men and women were not particularly interested in the politics of Tai-Ahom identity yet looked forward to the promise of benefits that might significantly change their lives. They brought to the movement a forward-looking vision rather than a preoccupation with the past. For them the movement was a way out of the drab and isolated life they lived in Assam. Because the Tai-Ahom movement spoke to their quest for change (in the form of increased and viable connections with Thailand, as well as possibilities of better education and exposure), it was attractive to the heterogeneous Tai student groups. It is difficult, however, to gauge how long the Tai-Ahom movement will hold young people's imaginations and continue to motivate them to fill the empty spaces in public gatherings, join the protest marches in the state capital, and organize militant opposition.

The documentation of a variety of people's voices—the followers, not leaders, of Tai-Ahom—that I have provided in this chapter establishes the multiplicity of actions, expectations, and demands. We have to recognize that what enlightens us about Tai-Ahom is not only a set of ideas that encapsulates their history, culture, and society, but the experiences of people today who claim to be Tai-Ahom. Identity and culture are the focal points of their assertion, but they do not share homogenous imaginations. There are clear divides between the classes and their respective expectations. The urban class saw the movement as a political and professional tool for empowerment, and they narrowly focused on the issue of job allocations and economic improvements that would be facilitated by becoming an ST group. They were not concerned about the social implications such a move would have; Ahoms were already considered by caste Hindu as low and polluted people, and becoming an ST group would put them even lower in the social class system defined by caste Hindus. In a very pragmatic way the professional class rationalized that they were suffering more losses in their present condition. Becoming an ST group was a way out of the lack of opportunities as well as the dominance of the caste Hindu groups who controlled economic power in Assam. They believed that an improved economic condition would make them far more acceptable to caste Hindus, who despised them because they were powerless and poor. In other words, they realized that caste Hindus would always dislike and look down on them, no matter their official or social position. The professional class seemed to feel that it would be better to make some gains by becoming an ST group than to continue on with the status quo prevalent now.

On the other hand, for the depressed groups of deodhais—the subalterns in the movement, so to speak—the issues were quite different. For them the movement was an arena of resistance against the exploitative institutions that they identified as being within the domain of Hindus. Without undertaking any dramatic and independent action, deodhais were constructing, as well as inventing, small and big religious traditions in their homes and villages, organizing discussion sessions in sabhas, and even telling slanderous stories about Hindus. These men were writing a new narrative of resistance in their own locales. The Tai-Ahom movement, they expected, would deliver them from an ignominious and powerless condition, and place them, once again, in positions of social and religious leadership so that they could actively outline the course of the identity movement.

We have also seen that within the variety of Tai-Ahom worldviews, the position and involvement of men and women were very different. Urban and middle-class women had little say in the movement, like their counterparts in the villages. This is not to say that the women lacked interest in or ideas about the Tai-Ahom identity. We have seen their spirited versions in preceding paragraphs. However, because women were not included as equal players and agents, they were still struggling to find a language to articulate their expectations, and a narrative of women's demands had not yet come to the fore. Likewise, the spaces that the urban youths occupied were quite different from those of the young men in the villages, and consequently their aspirations differed as well. Urban youths wanted adventure and experience of a new kind in the form of travel and education in Thailand. In the globalized world dominated by capitalism, it is not surprising that these young men of Assam considered a new level of consumerism in another place and culture as a way to create a difference that would set them apart from those "back home" in Assam—the Assamese. But the young men in the villages who were engaged in a life-and-death struggle to change their identities by supporting ULFA activities could not afford such luxurious dreams. As such, they were mostly absent from the dialogues of Tai-Ahom identity construction and could not articulate the gains they hoped to achieve. These men were actively engaged in the movement, but they were the absent subaltern who were made invisible by the forces of circumstance.

In spite of the gaps that were evident between the gender and class divides (as well as those between young and old, urban and rural) a variety of people were definitely engaged in the movement and were facilitating and sustaining change. I am not suggesting here that these people were autonomous architects of their world; I believe these agents were also subjects of the history and society that they inhabited. They made and were made by circumstances internal and external to their world. The people who participated in this identity movement have verified in their own words that rather than there being one Tai-Ahom people, there are many Tai-Ahom peoples within the movement. The variety was present to register their reactions and responses to the rejection and exploitation meted out by the institutions and people in power. The bottom line was that the variety of peoples in the Tai-Ahom movement were able to put up a precarious frontier of sameness by constructing "an enemy" to resist. By joining the movement to create change—cultural, political, and economic—they were consciously acting on as well as being acted on by forces of history and identity both within and outside Assam.

The demands of the people, like the people themselves, were various. Some demands had concrete goals, such as redistribution of land rights, recognition as a Scheduled Tribe community, better opportunities in education and professional development, and so on. Many expectations were also quite vague—for example, the revival of culture. We know that culture is not a static concept but is a living institution always in the making. (Wolf 1992; Fox 1985). The Tai-Ahom claimants, however, may not agree with this outlook in evaluating their culture. For them Tai-Ahom culture is a homogenous, monolithic essence that was always there and that remained unchanged over time. According to them, the buranjis emblematize this culture. They believe that the movement for identity will enable them to retrieve from obscurity and Hindu oppression their original culture. Thus, they would, once again, become their "true Ahom selves." Whether they accept culture as fluid and evolving or static and permanent is not of great importance; rather, it is the process through which isolated, fragmented, and local demands have been transformed to make up a collective agenda that is my primary concern in this book.

There was no a priori societal logic before 1981 that determined the construction of Tai-Ahom culture and politics. Yet, very quickly after the first international Thai studies meeting a group of leaders emerged and spread the discourse of a lost Tai-Ahom identity and encouraged people in Ujani Aham to join in the struggle to find that identity. Many different communities of people in villages and towns responded to this rhetoric. To say that the people who rallied around this movement were conscious of themselves as agents (anticipating their participation) or were merely subjects acted on by manipulating leaders would be an exaggeration in either case. Rhetoric and memory, leaders and audiences, worked together to make up new issues, and in the emerging political process and culture of Tai-Ahom they were also transformed.

The people involved in the movement, from the very beginning, represented a wide variety, as we know. Despite their obvious differences, they shared one common emotion: they all brought to the movement a deep sense of longing for something that was not there, an absence that needed to be filled. This they called Tai-Ahom and interpreted it variously. No common ground developed to make up one solid foundation of Ahomness for them, but the variety of perspectives allowed Tai-Ahom to be several things to the people and kept them involved and hopeful for change. They did not seem to care whether the history and identity they were espousing were accepted as true or false by researchers like me. In their hearts, they said, they were Ahoms, and that is all that mattered to them. They wanted the government to accept this simple logic so that they could be officially recognized as Tai-Ahoms. They claimed that by recognizing them as Ahoms, the government could undo the historical, religious, and cultural wrongs meted out to them by neglect, denial, and silence.

When I finally left Assam in December 1996, the movement was still active, but the tempo had slowed considerably after Hiteshwar Saikia passed away on April 26, 1996. That year in December Sukapha Divah was celebrated, but it was not the grand celebration that I had witnessed in 1995. Although I was asked by many activists and leaders of Ban Ok to stay and witness the resurgence of Ahom over the next few months, I decided to leave. My fellowship period was over, and I had plans to return to Wisconsin to start writing my dissertation. Even as I was leaving, I knew that despite the claims of their leaders, Tai-Ahom would never be the vigorous movement it was two years ago. Predictably, it limped along for a few more years, but as of this writing it is history—a past that people talk about. It is no longer the stuff that shapes politics and draws thousands together under one banner to discuss, dream, and strategize. Tai-Ahom identity never became anything that various people wanted it to be. Once again, in Assam, like many movements before it, Tai-Ahom became a failed political rhetoric. Why is it that movements like this can be so attractive to people in Assam, and what were the real issues behind the Tai-Ahom movement? I will address these questions in the conclusion.

*The Past and Present: Connecting Memory,*

*History, and Identity*

At the beginning of the twenty-first century, identity in Assam is, as elsewhere in many parts of the world, a highly contested issue. The number and type of the various groups that are making divergent claims to identities without success is, for the observer, baffling. The point that has been clarified here after examining the history, culture, and politics of Tai-Ahom is that it is a multipurpose label renewed, time and again, in the colonial and postcolonial periods to fulfill political, cultural, and emotional needs without strictly defining the community that uses it. This has led me to conclude that Tai-Ahom is a name in circulation but does not mean a fixed people. Whether we approach Tai-Ahom identity as a conceptual issue (like all identities, it is impermanent) or as a historical problem (the failure of institutions to create an identity that could penetrate and stabilize community), we will conclude that identity is a process in Assam.

A problem that has become evident and is connected to this perspective is the question of the political location of people within the Indian nation-state. For a variety of reasons, the people of Assam today feel denied of their rights as citizens in India. In the past, during the period of anticolonial struggle (early twentieth century), this important problem was held in check because a single "enemy" (British colonial rule) was identified to unify the diverse people within one platform. The people of Assam were encouraged to join the movement as one of the many colonized and aggrieved people of India. In the mid-twentieth century, emancipated from the "enemy," the nation-state emerged and selectively constructed the notion of a citizen, as we saw in chapter 1. Over time, the concept of an Indian citizen was attached to particularistic identities, initially to a civilizational location of the Gangetic plain, and, thereafter, to a religious identity of caste Hinduism. The Indian "nation" dissolved into many dominant and subject positions; the people in the northeast became the most distant and voiceless subjects within the national framework.

I have argued in this book that the lack of a common and shared history and memory between the peoples of Assam and the rest of India emerged as a specific problem on both sides. The people of Assam could not accept the label Indian easily because it erased the past as they understood it and also imposed on them a historical memory that was alien to them. This was explained in political and cultural terms as "victimization" or "colonization." In turn, the Indian state saw this rejection as a subversive attempt at the frontiers to undermine the process of nation-state building, and the state responded to it with force and antagonism. Without finding a lasting solution in Assam, identities emerged such as Assamese, Bodo, Tai-Ahom, and the like. These labels and the boundaries that have been constructed between them are new and artificial. The imaginary space that coheres the variety in Assam to struggle against the label Indian depends on an awareness of the lack of social, economic, and political justice. The denial of rights of citizenship drives identity movements in Assam. Tai-Ahom is one of the most recent labels that gained prominence and acts as an imaginary horizon through which societal and political demands of recognition and rights are made in Ujani Aham.

### FORMS OF TAI-AHOM: PRECOLONIAL, COLONIAL, AND POSTCOLONIAL PERSPECTIVES

I have argued based on the buranji literature that in precolonial Assam, Ahom was an elusive label used for a class of high officers and nobility, but it did not denote an ethnic community. This does not mean that community identity was totally unknown and unrecognized in precolonial Assam. The writers of buranjis remind us on many occasions that a "kun-how" or "us" group was the dominant social formation in the swargadeos' domain. Conceptually, "us" was both a conglomerate of different groups of "us-selves," as well as a space within which the multiplex groups interacted and communicated. The position of the swargadeos' domain at the junction of India, Burma, and Tibet served as a crossroads and made the space and experience of the "kun how" or "us" group into a dynamic, fluid, ongoing formation without fixed boundaries and frontiers of identity. "Us" was loosely cohered into a body politic by the institution of the swargadeo, which served as a common identifier for everyone.

The trajectory of the inclusive crossroads society was somewhat changed in the late seventeenth century with the introduction of Brahmins. The loosely configured society of "us" was Hinduized, as the court became more favorable to the high Hinduism of Brahmins. This shift did not radically transform the identity of groups that made up "us," although the qualification of those who did not belong to the "us" community—the Bangalis—became more evident over time. Religion was not the main attribute of identification, for we know that Muslims continued to be an integral part of the "us" group. The antagonistic "Bangali" represented an "enemy" polity that threatened the swargadeo's administration. Hostility toward the Bangali was based on this awareness. The formation of a political frontier of identity did not translate into individuated identities with different labels in precolonial Assam. The fluid and ambivalent "us" community was the location and identity of people.

The "us" community continued to be a loose, heterogeneous, formative service group under the rule of the swargadeo. His administration was managed by an elite class of Ahom officers. Ahoms, however, were not outside the "us" community of subjects. They hailed from different societies and class groups within it. The labels of identity that they upheld were not ethnic, religious, or language based, but were derived from place names. Even these were not permanent, however; a person or group could change his or their label voluntarily or involuntarily by moving to another place within the swargadeo's domain. Men became Ahom officers by favor of the swargadeo. This favor could be revoked when the swargadeo deemed it necessary. It was a royal prerogative that was often exercised. Being Ahom, it is obvious from the buranjis, was not permanent. Identity in this sense was not singular, but rather was changing, fluid, and potentially pluralistic. The swargadeo's domain, until its annexation to British India in the nineteenth century, continued to be a kind of place wherein identities were indeterminate. The social formation of hierarchies and class divided the subject communities, but the shared experiences of particular groups or classes did not constitute a recognizable, demarcated identity.

The chain of events that followed during the colonial administration transformed the class of Ahom officers from a loose network of a privileged group representing different places into a collective ethnic identity. In the colonial administrative parlance Ahom was made into something quite different from what it was in the buranjis. Writing the history of "natives," or making one up for those without it (in this case the Ahoms), was guided by British colonial interest and enterprise. The colonial administrators understood very well that dominating subject populations required not just political and administrative control, but cultural control as well. Hence, the logic of colonial rulership was reinforced with anthropological and racial assumptions that were current in nineteenth-century England. Complicated tabulations of castes and tribes—their customs and beliefs, histories and polities—in short, an overview of the political and moral world of subjects, allowed the colonial state to codify them and create rules of governance. In Assam, among the "governable" communities, the Ahom group was designated as an ethnic nobility of Shan who had migrated and settled in Assam and founded a kingdom that they ruled for six hundred years. The "aristocratic plot" of the identity of the Ahoms created by colonials served multiple purposes. It created a family of rulers from which to inherit power and distinguished them from other subjects, both "governable" and "ungovernable" groups. The British projected their own future in Assam onto this venture. Thereafter, by means of invoking the languishing climate of Assam and the effect of Hinduism on the aristocratic Ahom warrior tribe, the colonials explained the death of the Ahom community and erased them from administrative memory. Ahoms were dispensed with and British agents became the masters of the soil and people. A subject group of "governable" peasants called the Assamese was created to replace the "dead Ahom," and they served as the bulwark of colonial administration in the frontiers. The Assamese were reduced to an impoverished economic category through the development of colonial capital, and they remained so until the end of colonialism. Groups that resisted this makeover were neglected, forgotten, and, over time, silenced in the records of colonial history.

I have analyzed the anticolonial movements of the late nineteenth and early twentieth centuries and the rhetoric of "foreign rule" that was created to end British colonialism in India. Confronted with the alien "them," the leaders of the anticolonial movements, I have argued, felt compelled to forge a sense of unity to construct a political society from among the diverse peoples of India. The creation of a political frontier was accompanied by claiming the colonial administrative category—Indian—as the identity of people. I have shown that the myth of the Indian in its moment of inception could not become hegemonic, for different myths also occupied the same space. In Assam, the tension between the competing myths expressed itself in the formation of a new Ahom politics. The Congress party, the main champions, who opposed the "other" (British) rule, was deemed in Assam to be representative of upper-caste

Hindus, a label that was not very appealing to many groups. Ahom politics emerged in opposition to the Hindu Assamese. Characteristic of this politics of Ahom was a call to return to the days of the swargadeos. The subsequent historical literature that followed reduced the past to an artifact of Ahom rulers. The local narratives, instead of debunking the colonial version of their history, appropriated it without critically analyzing the myths that had been created. Rhetorical reminders of Ahom rule were formulated with the expectation that they would allow leaders of Ahom politics to carve an independent Upper Assam state in the postcolonial period.

It appears from the historical records that the outgoing colonial government was not totally averse to this assumption. Governor Reid backed the demand in these words: "Throughout the hills [of Assam] the Indian of the plains is despised for his effeminacy but feared for his cunning. . . . The people of Assam are as eager to work out their salvation free from Indian domination as are the people of Burma, and for the same reasons." In the same document, J. P. Mills, secretary to Governor Reid, suggested: "I would go so far as to make a gesture of *offering* to restore the old Ahom kingdom as a State—needless to say on very strict conditions. The chief condition would be that the new State would be deprived of none of the democratic institutions Assam now enjoys; the entire power would be in the hands of Ministers responsible to the legislature. The Raja would be nothing more than a figurehead. But, as a figurehead he might well arouse sentiment, and we should get a modicum of praise for restoring past prestige, instead of universal abuse for reducing Assam to an insignificant fragment."[1] The Congress leaders showed no interest in reinstating local institutions in Assam, which they viewed as another attempt of colonials to "divide and leave." Based on the claim that independent India should include all of the provinces of British India (barring the Muslim-majority areas that later became Pakistan), the Congress refused to let go of Assam. The small group of Ahom supporters termed this "Indian colonization" and persisted in emphasizing their differences from Congress politics.

In the early twentieth century the amalgam opposing "Indian colonization" in Ujani Aham was not sufficient to construct a community identity called Ahom. Instead, they developed an isolationist discourse of Luitpaar as the homeland of Ahoms and claimed the culture of Ujani Aham as their platform for gaining power and defying the growing power of the INC there. The Ahom politicians did not achieve a great deal locally, but the distance between Assam and rest of India kept widening. On August 15,

1947, along with the rest of the country, the tribal groups in Assam, as well as Christians, Muslims, caste and noncaste Hindus were transformed into Indians. For this variety, Indian identity was a nominal category. Over time, it became the site for exacerbating tension between Indians and local groups in Assam.

The postcolonial Congress government headed by Nehru promised to make India an inclusive nation-state for all within it. The accent of the Nehruvian vision was secularizing civil society and establishing a socialist economy. In pursuance of these goals, linguistic states were created and a planned economy was launched.[2] The structuring of linguistic states and a public sector economy, instead of creating a variety of horizontal regional states, divided them vertically. Economic development in the public sector became the monopoly of one region—north India. This region was a majority area for Hindus and Hindi-speaking people. The reductionism of India's future to north Indian issues meant that large portions of the rest of the country and population were neglected at the cost of north Indian development. Assam was one of the casualties in this lopsided economic scheme. Instead of heavily investing in money and resources to create an environment of inclusion within the new nation-state, Nehru's government made a policy of keeping investment out of the northeast, because the frontier was exposed to possible foreign invasion. After the 1962 debacle of "Chinese aggression," the northeast was shut off from the rest of India through various restrictive measures that later became codified as "Restricted Areas Policy." In the meantime, the overemphasis on the development of only one region—north India—created a two-tier society of states: north India at the top, and all other groups of states and regions below it. The national government overlooked this breeding ground of problems and assumed that the electoral rights of adult franchise could effectively handle grievances and the ballot box would uphold the will of the majority in a parliamentary democracy.

It is true that at the inception of the Indian state, adult suffrage was also established in India. Technically everyone had an equal voice in the electoral democracy. But was it the reality in India? North India had the largest population and was represented by the most strident leaders of the Congress party. As such, it became the dominant voice in the parliamentary democracy. The "tyranny of majority" discouraged the development of a national state.[3] Regions with small populations immediately lost their voice in the cacophony of the majority in the national parliament. The center of gravity became north India, and other regions and states became clients of north Indian power. The dominant groups of north India (citizens) and the suppressed communities from all other regions (subjects) became the pattern of the political landscape of India, which was reinforced as Indian identity became more and more aligned to the Hindi/Hindu local identities of the north Indian Gangetic belt. Instead of rethinking and reformulating the electoral process and distributing some power among the neglected regions, a powerful central state was promoted. The more the government under Nehru tried to create a unitary administration for all of India, the more fissures began to appear.

In addition to the class and regional divides that were entrenched, cultural and "ethnic" demarcations began to show. The government sought to cement the diverse population by presenting to them one version of national history under the slogan "unity in diversity." The single history of India, once again, like the experiments in planned economy and secularism, was an imposition from above and was conceived in terms of north India. The national history of India became the narration of the powerful dynasties of the Gangetic plain. The superficial common ground of Indian history became an explosive site of dissension and division. The south and northeast became the earliest causalities of north Indian historical hegemony. Local identity movements based on separate linguistic identities emerged in these regions and engulfed the people in an endless struggle with the central authorities in Delhi.

The gap between Delhi and Assam became evident in the event of the 1962 "Chinese aggression." Instead of Delhi sending reassurances and reinforcements, the authorities abandoned the people. The result was that the isolated and fragmented individuals and groups in Assam turned their feelings of desperation and anger against the Indian state into action and were radicalized. In chapters 4–6 I discussed the processes, agents, and aspirations of the political and social movements that experimented with new identities such as Assamese and Ahom in their anti-India/anti-Hindu campaigns. I have shown how the cultural movement led by Ban Ok and the political agenda of Juva Chatra Parishad organization in Ujani Aham developed into a more radical movement under the leadership of the ULFA, which resulted in a direct confrontation of the peasant-soldiers with the Indian army. Initially, few recognized the torrential populist idiom of the movement. In fact, Delhi misread the movement as a militant uprising and deployed armed forces against the ULFA. In the meantime the ULFA had already entrenched itself in the villages of Ujani Aham, facilitated by their supporters within the Tai-Ahom, the AASU, and the

Juva Chatra Parishad organizations. For a while in the village Assam, the ULFA movement became everyone's movement. Over time the increasingly violent activities of the ULFA and the reaction of Delhi toward them transformed Assam into a war zone.

To be able to carry on the battle in Assam, leaders and supporters of the ULFA realized that they had to find a home ground to embed their vision of an identity that was clearly different from that of Indians, and create a group that was recognizable, distinct, and cohesive. With the support of the ULFA, the Tai-Ahom identity movement raised its pitch and demanded a separate and autonomous identity for Ujani Aham. This identity movement in Assam was not simply the creation of a demarcation between "us" and "them." It was not merely a cultural identity movement, but a political and social movement as well.[4] Backed by the ULFA, Tai-Ahom leaders raised important questions about the representation, voices, and rights of people who had been silenced in the national domain. The language of identity was a language of demand for citizenship in the Indian democracy. Curiously, for realizing the objectives of achieving full citizenship in India, Tai-Ahom and ULFA leaders linked up with Thai scholars and Shan rebels. The alliances generated a "transcendence" of a greater collectivity linking local with transnational agents in a common discourse of interests against the state.[5] On the one hand this was an explosive development, and, on the other, for many a liberating politics.

Within the vocabulary of modern nation-state politics, the Tai-Ahom movement falls in the category called subnational. I argued earlier that the category subnational is not a very handy term to evaluate social and political movements that question the Indian union. The accent on "sub" automatically privileges the artificial construct, India, and makes the nation-state the primary location of identity. The narrative of Indian national history was created by claiming, coercing, co-opting, and often erasing the histories of the many peoples living within its territories. The official narrative of Indian history is no one's history but rather circulates and gains legitimacy as the history of people backed by the force of the state. It is precisely this imposition and artificiality that many groups are fighting. Also, the term subnational implicitly signifies secondariness of the movements: in the chronology of birth, they are perceived as following the nation-state. Hence they are deemed inferior in rank, and often their claims to existence and legitimacy are discounted. Further, they are viewed as threats to the proper functioning of the state apparatus. Taking the case of Assam, and the Tai-Ahom movement more specifically, I have argued that local movements are not derivative discourses but are rooted to memory in a place that enables the people to construct the boundaries of community identity to mark their difference from others. In other words, memory, history, and identity combined together make a distinct political claim for a group in a specific place. This makes them local movements with nationalistic aspirations.

The Indian state's claim that it can and will root out these aberrant local movements is presumptive. These movements demanded that the potential for the democratization of political and cultural institutions, such as identity, should be realized. They have highlighted how the present centralized, unitary structure of the state has failed to realize this potential. The national government's unwillingness to acknowledge demands for heterogeneity, and its inability to recognize what these movements represent, could have highly detrimental effects on the nation. People in Assam, as elsewhere in India, are not lacking an understanding of the importance of national identity. Their demand for local, fragmented labels of identity, such as Tai-Ahom, is rather an exercise of their political right to an identity within a space they consider to be home—the place of Ujani Aham where Ahom, and later Assamese, developed. They are organizing on an issue to draw attention to the lack of power and the economic marginalization and political peripheralization that the central government imposes on them.

I have argued that it would be more helpful to view and analyze the Tai-Ahom movement as an expression of "local nationalism." I hesitate to call it ethnic nationalism because Tai-Ahom is not an ethnic group. Neither is it a completely elite-driven politics, as many have argued for other instances of ethnic nationalist movements in India (Brass 1991; Phadnis 1989). We have seen that multiple agents are part of the Tai-Ahom movement, and they represent the rich and poor in Luitpaar. Urban elites are no doubt a noticeable group within the variety, and they try to forge their agendas as best as they can. But to reduce the movement to an engineering feat of elites to which the poor and dispossessed have been co-opted is a misreading of the Tai-Ahom movement. Nor is it a resistance movement that is driven by mere politics without a stable understanding of the connection between people and place. Tai-Ahom identity continues to be variously discoursed and interpreted in several different sites, no doubt, between motley groups of reformists, politicians, revolutionaries, peasants, and religious leaders. However, there is an ideological and emotional cementing factor that binds various groups of peasants and elites in Ujani Aham. Ultimately, the aim of these proponents is one thing: to find their location of identity in the place called Ujani Aham. The foundation of local historical memories and the experiences of marginality enable them to think and cohere into one group, a nation of Tai-Ahom, and thus encourage them to continue the struggle.

The Tai Ahom identity struggle is the representative banner that was created and organized to pursue general concerns that matter to the communities of Ujani Aham. They want the national government to address these concerns and provide some kind of a satisfactory solution. In so doing, leaders of Tai-Ahom do not pretend they can dismantle and root out the influence of the national state in their locale. Rather, their effort is to create a situation that would allow them to associate as a group, not reduced to a separatist, fictional community but rather as powerful members who represent a specific society that is democratic and inclusive in Ujani Aham. We have to evaluate the Tai-Ahom identity movement, along with other local nationalist movements, against this background that involves a dual process of including the national in local terms and the local seeking to be part and parcel of the national, while maintaining both cultural and social diversities within a territorially demarcated place. The juxtaposition of the local and national by Tai-Ahom leaders is made evident in their demands. They want recognition of their identity; they want to have access to the national public resources for development and progress in their communities; and they want opportunities to make contributions to the social policies and decision-making process in economic, political, and cultural matters. I read the movement as a voice of people who are seeking admission and rights to the nation as citizens and who know where they belong in Assam.

Can their demands be achieved? Like many other regional/local identity movements ongoing in India, the Tai-Ahom movement also envisages that democracy should establish mechanisms through which power can be shared and the "oppressed" allowed to voice their concerns as a group. Disputes over the labels of identity draw attention to this concern of the right to organize and be represented as a specific group—that is, to maintain heterogeneity while they continue to be part of a composite national community. The people who want to identify as Tai-Ahom do not want to be simply identified as Assamese for the convenience of Delhi. They rightly interpret Assamese as a historic label of disempowerment and marginalization. To overcome the condition of "oppression" and create presence, they are insisting on bringing back the "dead" history of the Ahoms into living memory. By becoming and being recognized as Tai-

Ahom, they posit the claim to self-identity and, by that token, exercise the right as citizens to representation within the Indian nation. The language of identity is a political demand for the redistribution of power and the right to certain freedoms and guarantees that are denied to groups of people in Assam. As Stuart Hall and David Held (1989, 177) argue, the demand for such a citizenship is far more encompassing than a demand for mere political rights, for it aims to restructure the social along with individual aspects of identification, which is both political and social in the final outcome.

Unfortunately, within the modern nation-state of India there is very little space to accommodate such demands. Hence, movements like Tai-Ahom never make the national headlines, and few people outside the region ever hear about them. Although for a while Tai-Ahom looked like it was gaining in power within Assam (as it continued to receive financial support from Hiteshwar Saikia's ministry), it never became a state-sponsored or a statewide movement like the AASU and AGP movements that spearheaded the Assamese nationalist movements. Throughout its duration it was caught in the peculiar position of being a people's movement in Ujani Aham, but it could not subvert the Assamese movement. Also, its unclear association with the ULFA made it marginal within certain circles. The Assamese Hindu community in particular found the anti-Hindu stance of Ahoms—their use of alcohol and beef—distasteful and unacceptable. The Assamese Muslims never made much connection with the movement, although many continue to claim that they were the "king's men" as Boras, Saikias, and Hazarikas. This makes them insiders in Assam, and they are Assamese but don't claim to be Ahom. The peculiar Muslim position in this regard is confusing, but I suppose minorities have little choice but to embed themselves within majority groups, and becoming Assamese ensures that possibility. On the whole, the valley-dwelling Assamese—Hindus and Muslims—rarely showed sympathy or interest in the Ahom demands. The effort to create Ahom remained confined to Ujani Aham with occasional celebrations showcased in Guwahati. Scholarship on Ahom did not develop, although almost everyone in Assam, even today, invokes the autonomous history of the swargadeos as their inheritance. As far as I know, I am the first person to write a history of the Ahom struggle for identity within Assam. The indifference of Assamese societies, scholarly neglect, and the lack of state support have all combined to submerge Tai-Ahom. Delhi has paid no attention to this movement; Tai-Ahom today is almost dead.

I have emphasized in this book that India and Indian are not fixed categories, nor do they have a narrative of sequential events to connect the diverse population into one singular entity and institution. Instead multiple histories and memories occupy and compete in the same space of the nation-state and splinter identity into many labels. The lack of a central "core" is often exemplified in the various identity movements ongoing in India. By taking the case of the Tai-Ahom identity movement in Assam, I have tried to show the multiple and various imaginings of the past and the future at the frontiers of the nation-state. Through the consolidation of historical, mythic, as well as fictional materials mediated at various levels, the label Tai-Ahom emerged in Ujani Aham. These people in Assam were seeking to overcome their subject position and were looking for acknowledgment in several different quarters. I read the Tai-Ahom movement as a symbol of a fragile moment of happening and remembrance of those who have not been allowed to investigate and remember a different kind of history outside the national historical narrative, within which they have been made visibly absent. Although Tai-Ahom is a vague concept and a confusing label, it evokes a deep-seated emotion for something concrete—a place to call home, an identity, and recognition. It is an attempt by marginal people to write history from their standpoint. To me, Tai-Ahom is not a fiction but a quest that is as yet unfulfilled.

Can the nation-state accommodate this demand? The record of the Indian state has been mixed. The postcolonial governments at Delhi have followed a carrot and stick policy toward the northeast. From the period of Indira Gandhi's role as prime minister to the bjp regime (1968–2003), Delhi has never addressed the identity issues raised by various local movements in the northeast. Instead, the government has adopted the policy of bribing people into silence. This started with financial concessions such as subsidized tax and aid money. Although Assam has received very little relative to Nagaland and Arunachal Pradesh, the central government has on several occasions dangled lucrative financial cards for the Assamese to grab. With these also came the increasing presence of military units. The Assam Valley, since the rise of the AASU in the late 1970s, has been transformed into a military garrison. Since 1996, the bjp government has made some overt gestures to bring Assam back into the fold of India. They started by repealing the Restricted Areas Policy in 1997. Several economic packages were also delivered in the form of creating new national educational institutions, as well as the development of gas refineries and power plants. Along with this, the BJP has devised long-term strategies to draw Assam into the cultural orbit of the Hindutva family. Through pujas and yatras they are reminding the valley people of their Hindu heritage. In areas such as Guwahati, a new discourse claiming Assam as part of the Mahabharata family has emerged as a consequence.[6]

Will the BJP policy for the northeast, particularly its policy in Assam, produce long-term benefits for the people and economy? The ubiquitous BJP plan throughout India is to create bonds between different groups of caste Hindus, a strategy they have adopted to firm their claim to power. The slogan Hindutva has become very handy for this purpose. Those who reject that appeal in Assam, such as the ULFA organization and the Tai-Ahom movement, are neglected and punished. To undermine these groups, the BJP has adopted a policy of rewarding only some groups of Assamese. This is particularly evident as the BJP has drawn the Assamese Hindu community within its political fold and has distanced the Assamese further from other groups, both the plains and hills peoples. Tai-Ahoms, because they deny their Hindu past, are seen as troublemakers in Assam and are totally neglected by the BJP. The policies of the BJP that encourage the creation of Hindu enclaves within Assam can only exacerbate tensions.[7]

Scholars of Assam have suggested different strategies as to how to reform the impasse between Assam and the Indian nation for meaningful progress in the region. Sanjay Hazarika, a journalist and author, has suggested a political solution focused on stopping the illegal immigration from Bangladesh into Assam. He argues that the outmigration of Bangladeshi people to Assam should be stopped and the fluctuation of demographic patterns stabilized so that the local Assamese people can involve themselves in development schemes with guidance from Delhi (Hazarika 1995 and 2000). The suggestion that Delhi should come to the rescue of Assam to make an Assamese identity is quite perplexing. For over one hundred years, the Assamese have been resisting impositions from the outside to make them one thing or another. Hazarika's suggestion is far more insidious, because in one stroke of his pen he is trying to make the struggle of Assam and Delhi one and the same. The identification of the "others" as Bangladeshi Muslim does not solve Assam's problems, nor does it enable the outline of a defined Assamese identity. Asking Delhi to interfere and set the record straight for local identity could set a dangerous precedent. Backed by legal and armed power, Delhi would be empowered to call on regional groups to identify "outsiders" in their midst, people to be punished and evicted as part of the effort to create a monolithic Indian identity. Just such punishment and eviction is an emerging reality in other areas, a fact to which Godhra bears witness.

Negating Hazarika's hasty call for rescue and support from Deli to save Assam, Sanjib Baruah, a political scientist, suggests a different arrangement for creating a more fruitful relationship between the center, Delhi, and Assam, a regional state. Baruah is in favor of a greater distribution of power to the northeast region and recommends that a federated structure should be created and be put into place "which ultimately is the only way to bring subnationalism and pan-Indianism closer together" (1999, 213). I agree with Baruah that Assam, after all, is a part of India, and that Delhi has to recognize its place within the union. A federated polity is an important step in this direction. The devolution of power would allow the federated states to have a greater say in the administration of their own units. This, no doubt, would create new possibilities for political and economic development. But in itself a federated India is not a solution. The restructuring has to be accompanied by substantive and total democratization, otherwise majority groups in different states will continue to wrest power and control and marginalize smaller groups. The citizenship rights of all have to be recognized and upheld. Political federation is a beginning. But the real change has to be in the psyche and language of interaction. This means that Delhi has to make several alterations in its approach to the northeast in general and Assam in particular. It has to begin by remedying the language of interaction with Assam. Pejorative classifications made in caste Hindu civilizational terms, such as mlecchas, asuras, and antarjya, and political terms, such as rebels, insurgents, and terrorists (all of which Delhi has used to degrade the people and make them into second-class citizens), have to be eliminated. The political and mental boundaries of the government's language have to change if it is to build trust across the frontier. India has to be more than a place where people are forced to live as second-class citizens. For the people of Assam, as we have seen, the idea of an Indian identity is more a threat of the erasure of their local selves than a promise of improvement. The government has to change this attitude by prioritizing the people, and this must be made evident to them through various ways and means.

More important, Delhi has to come to terms with the plural pasts that are littered in the landscape of modern India. It is misleading for the political regimes in Delhi to assume that the constructed Indian history and identity is deeply rooted and is immutable, unchangeable, and simple. Indian national history and identity are both contingent, and the central government has to acknowledge the limits of their application and know that they can be subverted. Indian identity and national history have to learn to live and share the space with many other labels and narratives. Recognizing the multiple pasts of Indian peoples without politicizing and silencing them as instruments of adversaries can help to mitigate the continuing mistrusts and grievances of neglected and marginalized groups.

Rewriting a new, composite national history is crucial in this enterprise.[8] History has to be reverted to the people, not simply as a token symbol to acknowledge present and absent communities but as a shared space where communities can learn about each other and be given a voice to represent their multiple memories and what these mean to them. People have to find themselves in history because, as Dipesh Chakrabarty notes, "history speaks to the figure of the citizen" (1992, 57). An inclusive Indian history could create a sense of inclusion within the nation-state. National history, therefore, has to be everyone's history, not an artificial construct given to the people as a directive from above.

Indian history must be plural and acknowledge plurality, which is its reality. Toward this end, an alternative history that emphasizes pluralism and diversity should be written and widely disseminated. Religion cannot be the central theme of this kind of history (as it is now). Instead, cultural and regional diversities, as well as different tellings of history from various regions, must be introduced and reinforced in multiple ways. History textbooks circulating in north India must have detailed, extensive information on the peoples, cultures, societies, and economies of south India, as well as east and west India. Likewise, every part of India should introduce, through the voices of local scholars and everyday people, the histories of other units. The national educational system must encourage students to engage in depth with the materials and knowledge presented by different groups and communities. These kinds of histories must be written and presented by the local people of a region, coordinated by a central board, but not manufactured by a national history textbook board in New Delhi (as it is done now). National history has to become local, and local histories must be made national. If this is achieved—that is, if a real democracy of historical knowledge is developed, encouraged, and taught—the plural communities in India will be able to find themselves and others on a horizontal plane. This would foster a sense of connection to the nation and make the state trustworthy, and the existence of the "other" would be acknowledged as part and parcel of what constitutes the citizen communities of India. One could then move beyond diversity and build an Indian nationality that people accept as legitimate and desirable.

# Epilogue

On April 3, 2002, a new airport was opened in Guwahati—the Loko-priya Gopinath Bordoloi International Airport. The first flight (with a fourteen-member crew and 221 passengers) was destined for Bangkok, Thailand. The government hoped that the international airport would facilitate travel and commerce between India and Thailand and other Southeast Asian countries via Assam. On April 4, 2002, the *Times of India* reported that BJP civil aviation minister, Shahnawaz Hussain, on the occasion of the inaugural ceremony, stated: "This flight has assumed added importance in view of the fact that many people in the NE region had ancestral roots in Thailand." Tai-Ahom groups were ecstatic that the government at long last was acknowledging their history, their past. They convened once again in Guwahati. This time it was a larger composite unit that called itself Ahom Sabha. The leaders and followers of Ahom Sabha hoped that the government would now notice them and give them their due now that Assam's connection with Thailand was established. The airport was to be their landing site (in both a literal and figurative way).

Within the government circles, however, nobody talked about Tai-Ahom or recognizing Tai-Ahom identity. It was a forgotten story. The government discourse was centered on the profit that could be generated through the business and trade facilitated by the international airport. For this to happen, the business communities had to be encouraged to invest in the enterprise. After six months of limping along without being able to attract businesses to invest in trade and travel to Southeast Asia, the Assam government recently declared that it would not be able to maintain the flight to Thailand. The flight was grounded for an "indeterminate period" and the international airport is no longer international. A few national flights come and leave the airport daily.

For a moment it appeared as though what was said in the buranjis to have happened in 1228 would actually happen in 2002, that Assam would be connected to Thailand. But, the idea still has not yet taken off.

# *Notes*

PREFACE

1  The term Tai designates a linguistic community (Thai, on the other hand, is the name of the people of Thailand). Lao, Shan, as well as minor languages of southern China, Upper Burma (Myanmar), Laos, Thailand, and Vietnam are included in the Tai language family to which Tai-Ahom belongs. Geographically Tai-Ahom is located within India, but its linguistic root is in Southeast Asia. The community that is today claiming to be Tai-Ahom wants to reconnect to this Southeast Asian past.

2  Deodhais are the high priests of the Tai-Ahoms. In the precolonial Assam kingdom deodhais were highly respected because of their esoteric powers and knowledge of the scared texts called *buranjis*. Even today many hold them in great reverence. They are considered the original scribes of the Ahom buranjis. The deodhais lost their privileged position after the influx of Brahmins, which started in the seventeenth century.

3  I am borrowing this term from Sanjib Barua (1999). In chapters 1 and 2, I discuss the category "Assamese" to argue that no such community existed before British colonialism. The term Assamese was created by the British for revenue purposes and was used to differentiate the people of the Assam Valley from their neighbors, the Bengalis. Today the term Assamese is used to qualify the inhabitants of Assam who claim Assamese as their first language.

4  Buranjis were written both in the Assamese and Ahom languages. Because Ahom is considered a "dead" language in Assam, the buranjis written in Ahom have not been studied. For a discussion on buranjis and their contents, see chapter 3.

5  In the 1970s, the Maruti car was launched by Sanjeev Gandhi (youngest son of the late prime minister, Indira Gandhi) as a middle-class option for car ownership, which until then was a luxury in India. Since the 1980s, ownership of a Maruti car along with a passionate interest in the game of cricket became symbolic of middle-class Indian identity.

6  When Tai-Ahoms refer to *puthi* they mean religious books, whereas for them the buranjis are history books that record mundane, day-to-day affairs. Puthis include the stories and details about their kings, who were gods on earth, and hence they are sacred. In Tai-Ahom belief ancestors are gods.

7  My conversations with Domboru Deodhai and others in Assam, unless otherwise stated, were in Assamese. The English translations of these conversations are mine, and I have tried to retain the original flavor and spirit of these exchanges. But bear in mind that translation, although it conveys meaning, also erases and creates new meanings that may differ from that intended by the speaker.

8  Bihu is the spring festival that is celebrated all over Assam. Those who claim Tai-Ahom identity today also claim that their ancestors started the celebration of Bihu in Assam.

9  This has been communicated to me through several letters and e-mails from Assam.

10 This is the main organization of the Tai-Ahom identity movement. From now on I will refer to it as Ban Ok. The history and activities of the organization are discussed in detail in chapter 5.

11 Dampata is the worship of ancestors and is the most important religious ritual of Tai-Ahoms. A detailed description of dampata worship is provided in chapter 5.


**INTRODUCTION**

1  For a detailed description of the term Assam, see K. Barua 1923; and S. Barua 1928.

2  See also *Home Miscellaneous Series*, no. 765, 20-1-1868, Oriental and India Office Collection, British Library, London.

3  Robert Reid, "A Note on the Future of the Present Excluded, Partially Excluded and Tribal Areas of Assam," 7.4.1941, Confidential, Mss Eur, E. 278/4 (g), Oriental and India Office Collection, British Library, London.

4  The Brahmaputra Valley is divided into Upper and Lower Assam. These were administrative units that were devised by colonials for revenue purposes. The division was also cultural. People of Upper Assam were deemed different from those of Lower Assam, and the language, traditions, customary practices, and so on were emphasized to maintain the difference. The British demarcation worked largely because internally the people of Upper and Lower Assam also thought they were different. The reasons for the internal division are many, but most important is that the two areas had different rulers and, as a result, the histories of the kingdoms developed separately. The lack of a shared past makes the peoples of Upper and Lower Assam believe that there are some unbridgeable differences. In the rest of the book I will use the

term Upper Assam to refer to the British administrative unit. The term Ujani Aham, on the other hand, is the local term of Assam that refers to both the culture and place of Upper Assam and is upheld by local people as their mark of identification. The history of Ujani Aham is discussed in chapter 4.

5 For lack of a better term I use "animist" to explain the religious beliefs of communities that do not fall into the other categories listed.

6 I use the letter "h" to mark the local pronunciation rather than the velar fricative "x" that some scholars prefer (Baruah 1999). The letter "h" is the closest phonetic sound to the velar fricative that local people use. In Assam people refer to themselves as Ahamiya, and not Assamese. Likewise, my name locally is Yasmin Hoikia, not Yasmin Saikia, which is the Anglo version of the name.

7 For a political history of the kingdom of Kamrupa, see Chaudhury (1966 [1959]).

8 The anti-Bangledeshi rhetoric in India has taken a new and aggressive turn. Recently, Deputy Prime Minister L. K. Advani made a public statement that twenty million Bangladeshis were living in India, many of them in the northeast, and that they should be expelled. There is no evidence that such huge numbers of Bangladeshis are living in India, but rhetoric can easily create reality. The term Bangladeshi many think is an euphemism for Muslim, and the real target of BJP politics is the Muslim community. At an international level the hunt for Bangladeshis can easily lead to a breakdown in the relationship between India and Bangladesh.

9 Hereafter I will use the name Luit instead of Brahmaputra so as to emphasize the particular section of the river that flows through Upper Assam/Ujani Aham. Although Luit is not a commonly used term for the Brahmaputra River today, I use it here because it is a concept that is peculiarly internal to Upper Assam, which is the area of the Ahom movement. In general terms, Luit is a site of nostalgia for the past: the memory of Luit and the past come together in the images and emotions constructed and circulated by those involved in the identity movement. I will discuss these images of Luit and their connection to Tai-Ahom in chapter 4.

10 The figures vary a little. However, from the various sources it is evident that Assam's per capita in current prices is significantly less than the all-India average (see the Web site www.orissagov.com).

11 The ethnic population in Assam has changed a great deal in the last few decades. Over 40 percent are immigrants, of which over 26 percent are Bengali speakers. Ethnic Assamese think of themselves as a minority group in the state today, although this fact is not statistically proven.

12 Here I am following Nora's argument that emphasizes that subjects as well as evidence, although diverse, could be brought together under the same category of analysis and interpretation (1989).

13  I discuss history writing as a local enterprise in detail in chapter 1.

14  See my reading of buranjis in my *In the Meadows of Gold* (1997).

15  The *Ahom Buranji* was translated and edited by G. C. Barua in 1930. The original manuscript is not available in the archive or the DHAS, which was confirmed by Nabin Syam, the bibliographer for Tai buranjis at the DHAS and my language teacher. I thus consulted the published edition for translation. While the English translation of *Ahom Buranji* repeatedly uses the term Ahom in the text, in the Tai version the term Ahom does not occur. One therefore has to conclude that the term Ahom used in the translation is a development of later times when the buranji was commissioned for translation by colonial agents in the early twentieth century.

16  For a detailed reading of the Gujarat carnage, see indianthinkersnet@yahoo .com, digest no. 578.

17  I will discuss the demand for Scheduled Tribe status in subsequent chapters in some detail.

18  I will discuss the reasons for Thai interest in Tai-Ahoms in chapter 5.

19  In modern India the official count is Aryan 72 percent, Dravidian 15 percent, and Mongoloid 3 percent.

20  I use the term unthinkable as Pierre Bourdieu (1980, 14) has defined it—that for which there is no way to conceptualize.

21  Michel-Rolph Trouillot's study (1995) on the colonial silence concerning the Haitian Revolution is thought provoking. History, he argues, is both knowledge and narrative. The construction of history is more than a simple exercise of power; it also behooves us to ask who exercises this power, in what sites and locales, and with what consequences.

22  The Subaltern collective's claim that they are writing history from below, histories of local people, histories of the unspoken, and so on is what I am questioning. The experiences of the marginal embedded in the documents of the powerful (such as the colonial archive) often reveal new historical evidence as the Subaltern collective claims, but the traditional modes and perspectives of established Western history of the "conscious agents" have not yet been undone by the collective. Much of history simply happens and people participate in it not because they are exercising agency but because they become a part of that landscape in which history plays itself out. Moreover, the collective has emphasized the dramatic moments of "insurgent consciousness" by forgetting the everyday forms of resistance by marginal groups. As a consequence, what is missing in the narratives of the Subaltern collective is the voice of the voiceless, unheard mass. The project was inaugurated to solve the problem of the elite-centered political history of institutions by bringing people back into the story. But it has created a new problem of making only some kinds of stories of subordination and the subordinated worthy of retelling. I find R. O'Hanlan's (1988) criticism of the Subaltern

collective's project very helpful for understanding what has been left out of Subaltern narratives.

23 The co-option of the south within the national narrative is discussed in chapter 1.

24 Two other books that come to mind on Assam are Sanjib Baruah's *India against Itself* (1999) and Audrey Cantile's *The Assamese* (1984). Even so, both of these books predictably argue for acknowledging the connections of India and Indian culture and politics with the province and people of Assam, rather than provide a different set of possibilities for interpreting Assam's culture and history that transcends beyond the national.

25 Decentering the national narrative has also been taken up by scholars both of Dalit history and of women's history in South Asia.

26 A theoretical argument on the study of the fragment has been made by Gyan Pandey (1992 and 1995).

### I. IDENTIFICATION IN INDIA

1 For accounts of the events surrounding partition, see Butalia 2000; Bhasin 2000; and Pandey 2001.

2 For a theoretical discussion on the politics of nationalism in Assam see chapter 6 and the conclusion.

3 Michael Billig (1995) has argued that national identity and the nation-state are intimately tied together by the use of political rhetoric, symbols, and collective memory, and all are constructs. The link between people and soil, he argues, which was once articulated in mystical terms, has now become banal. The banality of nationalism needs to be investigated to understand how ideology is constructed and used so as to render the construction beyond controversy. The theme of a united India was constructed to combat colonial rule, but today the ideology of India is a sacred theme that is beyond question and challenge.

4 For further reading on the history of these languages, see King 1986.

5 Hindu society in India is divided into four castes—brahmin, khastriya, vaishya, and shudra. The first three castes are considered twice born, or unpolluted, while the last group, the shudra, is deemed the polluted caste. Of the four castes the brahmins are considered supreme, and they control the knowledge of the ancient religious texts and implement dharma (caste duty). For further readings on caste in India, see Thapar 1993, 95–123; Habib 1996, 161–79; *Manusmriti* 1999; and Hays 1988, 211–30.

6 Alongside the INC, in 1925 the right-wing Hindu organization Hindu Mahasabha was formed by Keshav Balaram Hegdewar. Hindu Mahasabha was largely responsible for representing the Hindu community in preindependent India as the core community of Indians, thereby forcing the INC to adapt its

politics to Hindu majoritarian views. The Hindu conservatives within the INC welcomed the move. The present-day BJP party is the inheritor of the ideology of the Hindu Mahasabha.

7   For further reading on the Nehruvian project on nation building, see Khilnani 1998.

8   It is interesting to note that what appears on the map is not the lived reality. For example, in the northwest both Gilgit and Hunza are mapped within India but are actually administered as part of Azad Kashmir and politically controlled by Pakistan. Likewise, there are several villages in the northeast that are mapped within the province of Arunachal Pradesh and are thus claimed as part of Indian territory, but in reality the Chinese government controls those areas.

9   Regarding Punyabhumi, see G. Carter, "Journal and Scrapbook," *Mss. Eur. E262,* Oriental and India Office Collection, British Library, London. Rama is one among the 360 million gods of the Hindu pantheon. He is represented as an ideal king who ruled the province of Ayodhya, in modern Uttar Pradesh. Rama Rajya was the idyllic domain where everything was perfect and tranquil, and modern Indians want to imagine that it is possible to re-create such a utopia. In the twentieth century, Gandhi brought back the concept of Rama Rajya into Indian politics. Since then the longing for the perfect past has motivated many to act on it, to the extent of creating policies at the highest level of the national administration to drive out all non-Hindus from India, so that the re-creation of Rama Rajya would once again be possible.

10  The etymological origin of Bharat is variously argued. Some believe the name is derived from the legendary king Bharat and his sons. Others say that the term Bharat is derived from the epic poem Mahabharata. Another version is that the place got its name from Bharat Muni, an important sage who is mentioned in the Mahabharata.

11  Here I lump together several historians. R. C. Majumdar and Jadunath Sarkar were more conservative in their views and promoted a "Hindu" national history. Marxist scholars such as D. D. Kosambi, Romila Thapar, Muhammad Habib, and Irfan Habib endorsed a national history that would not privilege one group and that emphasized the role of economic and social structures in engendering change. Among contemporary nationalist historians, Bipin Chandra, Ashish Nandy, Mushirul Hasan, and K. N. Pannikar are strong advocates of a single Indian history. No doubt their representations are all quite different. This creates the impression that they are writing different versions of Indian history; however, they all continue to write about Indian history as if it can be told as one narrative.

12  For a further discussion of the Baburi Masjid/Ram Janam Bhumi controversy and the politics of religious identity in India, see Ludden 1996.

13  Savarkar explained that "the ideas and ideals, the systems and societies, the

thoughts and sentiments which have centered round this name are so varied and rich, so powerful and so subtle, so elusive and yet so vivid that the term Hindutva defies all attempts at analysis" (1923, 3). Although Savarkar is credited as the founder of Hindutva, recent studies on the subject show that he borrowed the concept from the writings of Anne Beasant, an active member of the Theosophical Society founded by Madam Blavatsky in 1886 to promote Hinduness and create a national awakening. See "How Original was Savarkar?" at www.Indiathinkersnet@yahoo.com, digest no. 573.

14  The homogenization of Indians and Hindus in historical representations were initiated by the Bharatiya Vidya Bhavan scholars. In 1977–1978, the project of rewriting Indian history was seriously taken up under the aegis of the Janata government. For a detailed study of the politics of production of a communal history, see Powell 1996. A newer version of Indian history has been written during the BJP administration and is currently in circulation.

15  Personal transcription Televised speech, Doordarshan, India, May 27, 1996.

16  The textbook controversy ongoing in India since the BJP took power in 1997 has brought this to the fore.

17  "Reid's Collection," *Mss. Eur. F236/79*, Oriental and India Office Collection, British Library, London.

18  Ambika Giri's poem here is taken from Barua's *Assamese Literature* (1941, 77–79).

19  See Rajkhowa 1995. See also *The Assamese Nation*, United Liberation Front of Assam (ULFA), manifesto submitted to the United Nations General Assembly, 1992; and the Document of Indigenous Peoples' Rights, www.geocities .com/capitalhill/congress/7734/. This Web site is updated every two weeks and has links to many other sites on self-determination movements ongoing in Assam.

20  When Mir Jumla, the Mughal commander of Aurangzeb, entered the capital of Garhgaon in 1661 he wrote to the emperor boasting that he had opened the way to reach China (see Robinson 1841, 165).

21  The chronicle was discovered by Jadunath Sarkar and brought to the notice of historians in 1921 through occasional articles published in the *Journal of Bihar* and by the Orissa Research Society. The original manuscript is in the Bibliotheque Nationale in Paris. The original Persian text was translated into English by M. I. Bora and was published in 1936 by the DHAS at Guwahati (the second edition was published in 1992).

22  The original manuscript is in the Bodelian Library at Oxford University. An abstract of the work was published in 1872 by H. Blochman in the *Journal of the Bengal Asiatic Society*, and Jadunath Sarkar published a summary in the same journal between 1901 and 1902. An unpublished translation of the first six chapters by Mrs. E. Higgins is available in the S. K. Bhuyan Library in Guwahati. The quotes in this section are from the Higgins translation (pp. 44, 51–53).

23 Giga Singh of the Mughal account is no other than Jayadhvaj Singha (1648–1663).

24 Generally, the symbol of the cow is sacred to Hindus. In Assam, a secret sect of neo-Vaishnavites constructs a cow with rice paste that is to be eaten by the assembly of men. We can assume that Glanius's reference to the images of gold and silver cows is in reference to the Nandin, the bull, which is generally seen in the Shiva temples of Assam, particularly in the heartland of Sibsagar.

25 J. P. Wade, "Geographical Sketch of Assam," X/2145/1 Map Collections, Oriental and India Office Collection, British Library, London.

26 Regarding the "uninhabitable tracts," see map HV8:X/2142, Oriental and India Office Collection, British Library, London. Comments by colonial administrators are in the Curzon Collection, *Mss Eur F 111/247a*, Oriental and India Office Collection, British Library, London.

27 Mallite, Bailey, and Carter produced several albums and scrapbooks on Assam. There are 850 pictures and prints available under the heading "Assam" in the Oriental and India Office Collection.

28 These captions are provided by colonial photographers who sum up assumptions about the people in Assam and the colonial interest there. See pictures in album 10, Oriental and India Office Collection, British Library, London.

29 For a history of tea cultivation in Assam, see chapter 2.

30 Letter by John Brodrick to the Governor General, Lord Curzon, India Office, London, June 9, 1905, Public No. 75, *Mss Eur F111/247a*. Oriental and India Office Collection, British Library, London.

31 The information here from Dewan is given in Mills 1854, in the appendix "Translation of a Petition Presented in Person by Moniram Dutt Borwah Dewan, on account of Ghunnokanth Singh Joobaraj and Others."

32 See Udayon Misra, *The Periphery Strikes Back: Challenges to Nation-state in Assam and Nagaland* (Simla: Indian Institute of Advanced Study, 2000), pp. 68–71.

33 "Letters Issued to Government," Series II, vol. 46, no. 725, May–June 1872; vol. 47, no. 1318, July–September 1872; vol. 50, no. 306, 1873; vol. 51, nos. 236, 240, 276, 443, 615, November 1873–January 1874, Assam State Archive, Guwahati.

34 Mills 1854; see the appendix "Observations of the Administration of the Province of Assam by Baboo Anundaram Dekeal Phukan," p. x.

35 Many social movements follow the same trajectory. Initially, the middle-class elite constructs an agenda, and then to achieve success the lower classes are drawn into the enterprise. The composite enterprise dissipates once the leaders achieve a measure of success. The "democratization" process is always unequal and incomplete. See Rubin 1997; and Eckstein 2001.

36 For an excellent study of the political rhetoric of Bhupen Hazarika's songs, see Baruah 1999, particularly chapter 6.

37 Robert Reid, "A Note on the Future of the Present Excluded, Partially Ex-

cluded and Tribal Areas of Assam," April 7, 1941, "Confidential," *Mss Eur, E. 278/4 (g)* Oriental and India Office Collection, British Library, London.

38  Personal conversation with the late Parag Das, 1995, Guwahati, Assam.

39  Recently a new political alliance was made between leaders of the Bodo movement (fighting to break away from the Assamese) and the United Liberation Front of Assam (which claims to speak for the Assamese people). The temporary alliance seeks to garner support and strengthen the opposition base against their common enemy, the Indian government. How long the alliance between the two groups will last remains to be seen.

40  "Letters Issued to Government," Series II, vol. 50, no. 1873, Assam State Archive, Guwahati.

41  "The Ahom Association," File no. 362, 1940, Assam State Archive, Guwahati.

42  Personal interviews conducted in Patsako Gaon, Sibsagar, and Pathar Syam Gaon, Titabar, Assam, 1994–1995.

43  Note by Thanuram Gogoi in "Ripunjaya Smriti Movement," File no. 362, 1940, Assam State Archive, Guwahati.

44  In seventeenth-century Assam, Shankardeva, a reformist leader, preached a new creed of *bhakti* (devotional) worship to counter the expensive rituals and worship system of Brahmanic Hinduism. Over time the teachings were instituted, the devotees became known as Shankarias, and a class of priests called *gossains* took over the control of the newly converted. Several centers of Shankaria religion were established and the office bearers of these centers became Satradhikaris. It did not take too long for this group of priests to move away from the teachings of Shankardeva's devotional religion and become steeped in rituals and hierarchy. This paved the way for new levels of exploitation of the masses.

45  "Asamiya," File no. 3, 1924, Assam State Archive, Guwahati.

46  Ibid.

47  For a similar narrative account, see Borooah Bahadur 1900.

48  "Sibsagar Zila Ahom Sabhar Karya Vivarani," File no. 362, December 7, 1940, p. 14, Assam State Archive, Guwahati.

49  Staff Report, *Assam Tribune*, April 25, 1941.

50  "Ahom Association," File no. 362, Assam State Archive, Guwahati.

### 2. COLONIAL ORIGINS OF AHOM

1  Masonry structures developed in Assam in the course of interactions with the Mughals. According to buranjis, the Mughal copies became so popular as a royal building style that commoners were prohibited from building similar structures. However, the copied buildings of Assam departed from the original Mughal structures in dimensions, styles, and form to develop into a unique Assam style of architecture. Almost intentionally the buildings of

Assam integrated the *chou chala* roof style of Bengal and the cone-shaped *mastaka* of Buddhist stupas, which were blended with the arch and octagonal floor plan of Islamic architecture. Animal and flower motifs were borrowed from local kingdoms in the region such as the Kacharis, and the art of stone buildings were also copied from them. Building activities in Assam, however, predate the late seventeenth and early eighteenth centuries. In the previous periods too many structures were built of bamboo and wood. These are mentioned in buranjis. In the Assam kingdom, certain places were considered "important" and "powerful," and once they were recognized for their auspicious qualities the site was continuously built on. The architectural relic of the Kareng-ghar that stands today is one of a long line of buildings that stood on that very spot. According to buranjis, *singori ghars* for the coronation of swargadeos were built on the compound where the Kareng-ghar stands today. The earlier structures made of bamboo did not survive the ravages of time. The multilayered past of these places and the monuments are rarely understood by passing viewers. The present effort to homogenize and appropriate the monuments as Tai-Ahom building is an oversimplification of a complex architectural history of both time and place.

2   According to a British observation in 1826: "The sovereign and his nobility in Assam live[d] in thatched huts with walls of bamboo mat, supported by saul posts, and built in the fashion of Bengal with arched ridges and mud floors, each apartment being a separate hut" (Hamilton 1828, 1: 72). Certainly, this description does not fit the Kareng-ghar. The "thatched huts" of the royalty and nobility and the Kareng-ghar clearly were different and served different purposes.

3   In buranjis the term Bengali is used to denote all groups of people who lived or came from outside the western limits of the Assam kingdom. Its specific use was for Muslims, including within this category the invaders from Bengal and the Mughals of Delhi. In this case, the reference to Ghansyam, a Bengali, is to a Mughal soldier who either stayed back in the Assam kingdom or was taken a prisoner of war when Mir Jumla gave up the siege of Garhgaon after collecting a huge tribute from the Assam king.

4   "Jenkins' Report of Upper Assam" entries from January 20 to March 11, 1838, *Mss Eur F257*, Oriental and India Office Collection, British Library, London.

5   Ibid.

6   "Wade's Geography," *A2/43/N-28*, p. 5. S. K. Bhuyan Library, Guwahati.

7   Ibid., p. ii. See also IOR x/2145/1, "Geographical Sketch of Assam," Oriental and India Office Collection, British Library, London.

8   This refers to the small range of hills that form a ring around the city of Guwahati. The mention of Odoigeer connected to the myth of Ahom origin leads me to suspect that this myth of origin developed toward the end of the

late seventeenth century when the outpost of Guwahati was claimed by the swargadeo as the western limit of the Assam kingdom. This arrangement was made after Mir Jumla's invasion (1661–1662). From then on, the Bar Phukan, one of the five important nobles of the kingdom, was permanently posted in Guwahati to provide defense in the westerly quarter, and thus Guwahati became an integral part of the swargadeo's kingdom.

9   J. P. Wade, "Account of Assam," *Mss Eur D 103*, Oriental and India Office Collection, British Library, London, lv–lxv.

10  Walter Hamilton reports that Wade believed that the Naras were a Buddhist tribe living in the neighborhood of Assam. In this initial stage of collecting stories concerning the Ahoms, it appears that British agents made several mistakes that they later revised. In 1828, Hamilton summed up the problem in these words: "Nothing satisfactory has as yet been ascertained respecting the ancient history and religion of Assam, the national traditions have a strong tinge of the fabulous" (1928 1: 74).

11  J. P. Wade. Account of Assam, *Mss Eur D103*, Oriental and India Office Collection, British Library, London, 1–6.

12  This myth is probably part of a formula of narratives of kings and heroes. It is not unique to Assam or even to India, but similar stories of the foreign origin of heroes occur in a variety of narratives (Segal 1990). An interesting point to note here is that foreign warriors are transformed into legitimate rulers, in Assam as elsewhere, through marriage with local women. "Ahoms" were indigenized in this manner as we will see in the narratives of buranjis that I discuss in chapter 3.

13  I have borrowed the term "mythic-history" from Hill (1988) to describe the period and narratives that connect the world of gods with the kingdom created by men: in this case Tai-Ahom swargadeos.

14  The Shans, today, live in Upper Burma. They are considered a minority group, and to assert their identity they have been engaged in a long, drawn-out fight with the Burmese government. For a description of the connections between Ahom and Shan history, see Gurdon 1913, 282–87. For a description of Shan history and culture, see Milne 1910.

15  Walter Hamilton, "Commerce of Assam: A Desultory Notice of Assam," appended to *The Survey of Rungpoor*, B1/R8/A-D, S. K. Bhuyan Library, Guwahati.

16  The narrative of Ahom as migrants from somewhere in Upper Burma or Southern China became established after Edward Gait wrote his history of Assam in 1921. His assertion was based on early administrative accounts of the British, where Ahoms were presented as a "foreign" group who had migrated and settled in Assam in the thirteenth century. Interestingly, although local chronicles record the story of migration and settlement, buranjis do not tell us in precise terms the location of their original home nor do

they call the migrants by the name Ahom. The story of migration and the label Ahom were both fixed by the colonial agents.

17 For a detailed account of the migration of Brahmins to Assam and their impact on precolonial society, see 1989.

18 The *kakotis* were representatives of the swargadeos in foreign courts. Swargadeo Pratap Singha (1603–1649) introduced the office of kakoti, and the initial kakotis were brahmins imported from the Koch kingdom—the rivals of the swargadeo on the western limit of the Brahmaputra Valley. In the reigns of successive swargadeos several different kinds of kakotis from different clans and "tribal" groups were appointed. However, the office of the Tamuli Phukan continued to be manned by Brahmins (see *Tungkhungia Buranji* [Bhuyan 1932, 183]).

19 Traces of this manuscript have not yet been found. Although I made several requests to the Directorate of Historical and Antiquarian Studies (DHAS) for the *Ahom Buranji*, I never saw it. Nabin Syam, my Ahom language teacher and a research officer of Tai manuscripts at the DHAS, admitted that they did not have this buranji in their collection. Nor has his attempts to find it among private collectors yielded any results. Further, my search for this buranji in the British Library did not produce a positive result. What *Ahom Buranji* did Gunabhiram translate and what happened to that manuscript?

20 Mungkang is probably Muang Kiang, which was an autonomous Mao principality in upper Irrawaddy. After its integration into the large Mao empire, it was designated, for a short time, as the capital (see Elias 1876).

21 Some believe this icon was a precious gem. Others think it was a *salgram* (idol) of Shiva, who is also referred to in the Hindu tradition as Soma-deva.

22 In the Yogini Tantra, the area of modern northeast India, including Bhutan, is divided into four *piths* (zones). They are Ratna, Kama, Swarna, and Saumar. The area of Saumar pith corresponds roughly to the region of present-day Arunachal Pradesh, where the famous Parasuramkund, the watery cave of the Hindu god Parasuram, is said to exist.

23 The Assam pandits maintained different methods for reckoning time. One is the Tao Singha—the sixty-year cycle. Within the Tao, each year is called *lakli* and is named but not numbered. After every sixty years a new cycle begins, and the lakli names are recycled in the new Tao. Although the sexagesimal system of the Assam kingdom is believed to be a carryover from the original Ahom homeland, presumed to be in Upper Burma, in other parts of India, particularly south India, the same system was also in use. Hence it is difficult to say with certainty how the Assam kingdom established this system.

24 These are not names of specific people but rather are titles that are rendered both in an archaic Tai language as well as in Assamese. Tai-Ahoms, today, assume that Thaomung is a name of a person. Likewise, they assert that Sukapha is the name of the original founder of the Tai-Ahoms. In all proba-

bility Sukapha is a rendition of Chow Ka Pha, the title for princes in the confederated Mao empire.

25 This story of the origin of Ahom is recorded in the *Assam Buranji, Ms. 59*, folios 2b-5a (translation mine). See also Tamuli-Phukan 1906. Several versions of the story with minor changes and certain additions are available in several other buranjis.

26 The problem of dating and authorship of buranjis will be addressed in chapter 3. Suffice to say here that the published edition of this manuscript dates the original buranji to the nineteenth century. Kashinath Tamuli-Phukan was the compiler. This is the only buranji we have so far that is both dated and signed by the compiler.

27 See also Cochrane 1911, 1132–42.

28 This is the Burmese name for the Lauhitya Valley. It bears resemblance to Vaisali, the famous Buddhist site in Bihar. Could this be an attempt by the Burmese court to map Assam within the sacred Buddhist landscape?

29 Wade suggests that Roo-poot is an Ahom term meaning a "document of knowledge," where "roo" means knowledge and "poot" means document (J. P. Wade, "Account of Assam," *Mss Eur D* 103, p. i–ii, Oriental and India Office, British Library, London).

30 "Extract Bengal Political Consultations," July 29, 1820, *Board's Collection*, vol. 770, Oriental and India Office Collection, British Library, London.

31 Ibid.

32 Ibid.

33 For a discussion on the establishment of these households, see *Tungkhungia Buranji* (Bhuyan 1932, xvi).

34 "Letter from the Raja of Burma to Assam," "Letters to the British Government," Series II, vol. 7, May 31, 1838, Assam State Archive, Guwahati.

35 *Board's Collection*, 1833–1834, vol. 1443, Oriental and India Office Collection, British Library, London.

36 Walter Hamilton, "Commerce of Assam: A Desultory Notice of Assam," unpublished report, B1/R8/A-D, S. K. Bhuyan Library Guwhati.

37 Hamilton, 1928, 66–77. See also Mills 1854; and *Board's Collection*, 1835–1836, vol. 1505, no. 59025, Oriental and India Office Collection, British Library, London.

38 "Letters to the British Government," Series II, vol. 7, 1838, Assam State Archive, Guwahati; emphasis mine.

39 As late as 1941, Robert Reid, governor of Assam, argued that it was not necessary to isolate Assam and link it to India. He reasoned that "the people on the Assam side of the present boundary are much nearer to the Burmese than they are to the Indians. Their languages are exactly the same in some cases as those on the Burman side, and there is no difference of race at all, and there is constant communication, so far as there is any communication at all,

it runs across the Hukong Valley into the Naga Hills on the Assam side" ("A Note on the Future of the Present Excluded, Partially Excluded and Tribal Areas of Assam," 7.4. 1941, Confidential, *Mss. Eur E. 278/4* [g], pp. 16–17, Oriental and India Office Collection, British Library, London).

40 "Letter to Mills from A. H. Danforth" (missionary), Guwahati, July 19, 1853, appendix 1A, in Mills 1854, xxx.

41 Letters from Andrew and John Carnegie, *Mss Eur C 682*, 1865–66, Oriental and India Office Collection, British Library, London.

42 "Letter from J. P. Wade to F. Fowke," November 16, 1792, Goalpara, in "Wade's Geography," A2/43//N-28, p. 22, S. K. Bhuyan Library, Guwahati.

43 The Christian missionary A. H. Danforth, in Mills 1854, xxviii.

44 "Extract Political Letter to India," December 3, 1834, *Board's Collection*, vol. 1505, no. 14, Oriental and India Office Collection, British Library, London.

45 "Letters to the British Government," Series II, vol. 7 1838, Assam State Archive, Guwahati.

46 Ibid., 23.

47 Ibid., 26–27.

48 See Mills 1854, 27–34. Butler, in *Travels in Assam* (1855, 239–42), occasionally refers to the inferior abilities of the Assamese.

49 "Letter from Lt. Col. Jenkins to Moffat Mills," May 23, 1853, in Mills 1854, Appendix B. No. 275 of 1853, pp. iv–vi.

50 "Translation of a petition presented in person by Moneeram Dutt Borwah Dewan on account of Ghunnokanth Singh Joobraj and others," cited in Mills 1854, xvii.

51 "Assam Congress Opium Enquiry Report," September 1925, compiled by R. K. Hatibarua, Jorhat, Assam, Oriental and India Office Collection, British Library, London, p. 20.

52 Ibid., p. 22.

53 This was Clayton's argument on behalf of the British Government of India at the Geneva Conference on Opium Use (1920). Quoted in Assam Congress Opium Enquiry Report, p. 46.

54 The initial accounts on Assam written by Robinson and Butler set the pattern of this representation. Mills established it as an official description for Assamese.

55 "Description of Assamese," "Letters to the British Government," Series II, no. 118, August 1864–April 1865, Assam State Archive, Guwahati; emphasis mine.

56 This became evident to me when I did a quick survey of the *vamsavalis* (genealogical accounts) of several families who claim to be Tai-Ahom. While their narratives often start in the heartland of Sibsagar, for the period of colonial administration they locate their family stories in far-flung areas such as Dhemaji in the northern bank, Moran, and Sadiya, and some even farther

away toward Arunachal Pradesh, where the British administration could not reach them. The "inner line" jurisdiction operated in those areas. The primary reason for out-migration was to escape the harsh revenue demands made by colonial authorities.

57 "About Archaeological Remains," "Letters to British Government," Series 11, vol. 9, no. 67, 1840, Assam State Archive, Guwahati.

58 For a detailed description of the maidams of Sibsagar, see Clayton 1848. Also, *Changrung Phukanar Buranji* (Bhuyan, 1990 [1932]) details the construction procedure of royal maidams.

59 Robert Reid, "Assam and the Northeast Frontier of India," *Mss Eur E 278/19*, p. 1, Oriental and India Office Collection, British Library, London.

60 *Mss Eur R.70/1-6*, Oral Archives, Oriental and India Office Collection, British Library, London.

61 *Oil and Gas Journal*, June 6, 1924, L/E/&1175/15(ii), Oriental and India Office Collection, British Library, London.

62 "Petroleum Situation," *Quarterly Reports by the Petroleum Department*, L/E/7/1866/File no. 21242, Oriental and India Office Collection, British Library, London.

63 *Mss Eur C 300*, Oriental and Indian Office Collection, British Library, London.

64 Ibid.

65 *Mss Eur R.70/1-6*, Oriental and India Office Collection, British Library, London.

66 Veronica Westmacott, "We Were Survivors," *Mss Eur C.394*, p. 193. Oriental and India Office Collection, British Library, London.

### 3. THE MEMORY OF THE LOCAL: THE STORIES THE BURANJIS TELL

1 Yuga is the cycle of time. The "Time of Origin" (or Sacred or Great Time) is the "receptacle" for a new creation after an end or *pralaya*. Time is represented as a wheel or *chakra*—the perfect circle with the focal point of the universe situated at its center in mysterious stillness. The Bhagavad Gita explains this concept of time in a conversation between Lord Krishna and his friend Arjuna in the battlefield of Kurukshetra.

2 I am not able to trace this figure in any Hindu mythology. Presumably this deity proliferated and became many entities. They became the devotees of Indra. This tale seems to borrow from Vedic myths as well as other traditions of east India and Burma, as well as Tibet.

3 This story bears some similarity with the Bon-Po account of the genesis of their first kings and with Buddhist myths of origin prevalent in Myanmar and Thailand. According to the Bon-Po tradition of Tibet, Gri-gum-brstan-

po, the first ruler, descended from heaven on a golden rope (see Haarh 1969, 145–46; and Hoffman 1969, 137–45). The Bon-Po religion was dominant in the fifth and sixth centuries in Tibet, and coincides with the time that Khunlung and Khunlai are said to have descended to earth and established their capital at Mung-ri-mung-ram. In the Bon-Po accounts a similar story is told of the god-kings descent to the mountain called Dran-mo-dran-chun, which Hoffman thinks is Mount Meru (Hoffman 1969, 140).

4   In the chronicles of Burma, Mung-ri-mung-ram is represented as three cities: Mung La, Mung Hi, and Mung Ham. They were the chief cities of the mighty Mungmao kingdom. P. R. Gurdon (1913, 282–87) identified the region of Chiang-Mai or Zimme in northern Thailand as the area of Mung-ri-mung-ram, although this is not proven.

5   The Ahoms claim the Noras as their parent community. No such kingdom or group is referred to in the annals of Burma. The lack of corroborating evidence makes it almost impossible to determine the history of Noras. Oral tradition in Assam locates the Nora kingdom in the Hukoong Valley in Upper Burma.

6   The Namkiu Lake was a bone of contention between British India and the court of Burma when the border between Assam and Burma had to be determined (see "Governor's Secretariat Confidential File," no. 283, Political A, Sept. 1929, nos. 1–11, Assam State Archive, Guwahati).

7   The Chutias and the Kacharis were two important group who controlled the hill passes to and from Assam before the advent of the swargadeo rule. Suhungmung annexed the Chutia kingdom in the fifteenth century. Today, Chutias are divided into four groups: Ahom-Chutia, Hindu-Chutia, Deuri-Chutia, and Barahi-Chutia. The Morans were an autochthonous group, who were sometimes classified by colonial agents as a subgroup of the Bodos/Kacharis. Local people in Upper Assam say that they were a Tai group who had migrated several centuries before the Ahom and mingled with the people in the area and became part of the society. The Barahis, which in Assamese means "eaters of pigs," were an autochthonous group.

8   All of these places are within the present-day district of Sibsagar.

9   The Kacharis trace their origin from the mythical demon-goddess Hirimba. Their king was thus referred to as Hirimbeshwar. The capital of the Kacharis in ancient times was called Hirambapur, which today is called Dimapur and is mapped within Nagaland.

10  J. P. Wade "Account of Assam," *Mss Eur D 103*, Oriental and India Office Collection, British Library, London. Also, see transcript copy, A1/Vol. 2 at the S. K. Bhuyan Library, Guwahati. Wade assumed that the tradition of buranji writing in Assam was somehow connected to the writing cultures of the East. Hence, he connected the tradition of buranji writing to the Japanese royal culture of writing. A cursory investigation of Japanese history reveals

that the tradition of "boronji" writing probably developed as a Brahmanic Sanskrit tradition that was carried over from India.

11  For a similar view, see Nath 1948, 125.

12  This is from the *Satsari Buranji*, Bhuyan 1960. The first chronicle called *Assam Buranji from Khunlung to Khunlai*, was probably originally compiled in the late seventeenth century. This chronicle covers the periods from A.D. 569 to A.D. 1677 and was commissioned by Atan Buragohain, the famous minister who fought the Mughals in the late seventeenth century. The *Assam Buranji* opens with these lines: "Ovations to the Lord Sri Krishna. Ovations to Lord Shiva. This is an exposition of the lineage of the Swargarajas. The Mahapatra Bura Gohain in the service of the swargadeo has commissioned the writing of this manuscript in *Rupit*."

13  This process started during the reign of Susenpha, or Pratap Singha (1603–1641), and the tradition was maintained by his successors. For a historical study of Brahmins migrating to different courts across the Indic subcontinent, see Datta.

14  See, for example, the *Tripura Buranji* (Bhuyan 1938).

15  Time is calculated in many different ways in buranjis. In the Indic system, the Saka rulers, starting from A.D. 78 created a calendar named after their rule. In Assam, besides the Saka calendar, a sixty-year cycle called Taosingha also was in use. Besides Assam, the sexagesimal system was used in South India for astrological calculations. The interactions, both commercial and religious, between Southeast Asia and peninsular South Asia are well known. The dates that I provide for different swargadeos' rule are based on the Gregorian calendar. I have taken the Saka dates of the buranjis and added seventy-eight years to it, thus all dates are calculated in the Western style.

16  The best known of the Koch manuscripts is the *Vamsavali of the Darrang Rajas* (see Gait 1963, viii, 47; and Gait 1917). The manuscript of the *Vamsavali* is now at the DHAS, Guwahati. Several undated Kachari buranjis have been found. A recent addition to the collection in the DHAS is *Ms 149*. It is a comprehensive text covering the periods from the fifteenth century until 1832, when the British annexed the Kachari kingdom. That the Kacharis had a script culture is also evidenced in their copper plates and stone inscriptions. Gait (1963) used a Jaiantia historical manuscript; the original manuscript is not available.

17  Sen 1927, vols 2, 3, 4; Rajamala n.d. In 1724, two envoys of the Assam Kingdom, Ratna Kandali and Arjun Das, traveled to the court of Tripura. During their stay there they were greatly influenced by the tradition of writing in the Tripura court.

18  When Gait undertook the project of translating the buranjis, very few people in Assam knew the language. He writes, "The old tribal language . . . is similar to that of other Shan tribes, and is written in a character derived from the Pali. The knowledge of it is now confined to a few old men of the deodhai or

priestly caste. . . . To rescue from oblivion the records written in it, I selected an educated Assamese, Babu Golap Chandra Barua, now a clerk in the office of the Deputy Commissioner, Lakhimpur, and gave him a committee of five deodhais to teach him Ahom and to assist him in translating their manuscripts. The work was by no means easy, the deodhais themselves proved far from proficient, and it was nearly three years before all the manuscripts that could be traced were translated. Having no knowledge of the Ahom language myself, I have had to rely entirely on the translations made by the Assamese gentlemen" (1963, x–xi).

19  The debate on whether the Puranas are Brahmanic or Khastriya literature is ongoing (see Rao 1993).

20  I know this from my conversations with many deodhai families in Assam.

21  The number given for the DHAS buranji count is the official one provided by the research officer at the institution. Most of these buranjis are in Assamese. Most of the religious texts are in Tai language.

22  Legend has it that Sukapha was accompanied by two gohains, the Bar Gohain and the Bura Gohain. The office of Bar Patra Gohain was created in the reign of Suhan (1488–1493). The first Bar Patra Gohain was a Naga named Kanseng (Bhuyan 1960, 1: 12).

23  Initially there were no divisions between skilled and unskilled paiks. However, with expansion and inclusion of various kinds of subject groups, paiks became categorized as *karhi, somuwa,* and *bahiya*. The karhi paiks were those skilled in archery; the somuwa paiks were the skilled artisans—goldsmiths, musicians, dancers, etc; and the bahiya paiks were the general paiks such as cultivators and seasonal foot soldiers who filled in for all kinds of tasks as required.

24  This was probably not the first census taken in the swargadeo's domain. In the reign of Suhungmung or Dihingiya Raja (1497–1539), a census of the population was completed after the defeat of the Chutias in A.D. 1523 or so. We have references in the buranjis that after the conquest of the Chutia capital of Sadiya, the Morans, Barahis, and captive Chutias were grouped together, and a Naga, called Kangseng, was appointed as Tyao Konwar (Bar Patra Gohain) to administer them (Bhuyan 1960, 1:40).

25  "Assam Buranji Puthi," *Ms 59*, folio 4a, DHAS, Guwahati, hereafter abbreviated as *Ms 59*. Tamuli-Phukan (1906, 106) in his *Assam Buranji* also makes similar reference to Mungkungia.

26  Captain Jenkins, *Mss Eur F257/5*, Oriental and India Office Collection, British Library, London.

27  It is said that the Raha (in present-day Nowgong district) and Janji (in present-day Jorhat district) passes were the outposts of the swargadeo's domain. No one could pass through them without making payment. This was one way to collect a toll and to determine the nature of the traffic of people

through the outposts. Any unwarranted travel was severely punished (see Bhuyan 1990, 170: 108, 227: 132, 255: 143). Similar references are also available in other buranjis.

28 "Agar Din, Etiyar Din," B3, *MS 15*, S. K. Bhuyan Library, Guwahati.

29 "Historical Notes: Assam Buranji Obtained from the Family of Sukumar Mahanta," B1/R6/A, S. K. Bhuyan Library, Guwahati. Hereafter referred to as "Historical Notes."

30 Maniram Dewan, "Assam Buranji Bibek Ratna," *Transcript 108*, 1878, DHAS, Guwahati; "Historical Notes," p. 164.

31 A thuriya is a two-faced earring. It is considered a unique artifact of the Upper Assam Valley. The Kacharis were well known for the art of making thuriyas in gold, silver, and wood.

32 "Historical Notes," p. 174.

33 "Historical Notes," pp. 175–76; *MS 59*, folio no. 20a.

34 "Historical Notes," pp. 184–90.

35 For a history of the Namati Saikia family, see Hussain 1979.

36 *Ms 59*, folio nos. 21a, 21b; "Historical Notes," p. 189.

37 *Ms 59*, folio no. 14b.

38 *Ms 59*, folio no. 15b; "Historical Notes," p. 168.

39 *Ms 59*, folio no. 18b; "Historical Notes," pp. 173–74.

40 *Ms 59*, folio nos. 16b, 17a; "Historical Notes," pp. 169–70.

41 *Ms 59*, folio nos. 14b, 15a.

42 *Ms 59*, folio no. 20a; "Historical Notes," p. 176.

43 Mumai Tamuli became famous in history as the general who single-handedly repelled the Muslim invasion of Bengal. The Tai-Ahom revivalists have made Mumai Tamuli into "an Ahom hero," and they are demanding that major institutions, such as the Study Centre for the All-India Services in Assam, be renamed after him.

44 In Assam, the term jat is used loosely. It does not stand for caste, as it does in the rest of India, but rather refers to an occupational group. One's affiliation to an occupational group was not fixed, but was easily changeable according to aptitude and skill.

45 Dipesh Chakraborty (1992) argues that in the case of South Asia, through various practices and policies of early and late capitalism, history was made into a compilation of evidence collected by officials and state agents. Local histories were reduced to "myths" of natives.

### 4. RATIONALIZING A HISTORY

1 These songs are my translation. For an extended reading on the politics and poetics of Bhupen Hazarika's songs in general, see Baruah's 1999.

2 I had several conversations with my parents about this topic. The sentiment

quoted here was repeated several times; in a nutshell, it neatly sums up the place and time called Luitpaar.

3 Hazarika used the term "Luitporia" in his song *Luitporia Dekabondhu Tomar Tulana Nai* (My dear friends from the banks of the Luit, no one compares with you), which was recorded in 1992.

4 For an extensive reading on the postcolonial migration pattern into Assam and the structure and impact of different "others" there, see Barua 1999.

5 This is not confined to the Tai-Ahom movement. In many parts of Assam, similar grievances about "suffering" have emerged. The principal demand is economic. The people want the state to rectify the arrangements of land distribution and the control of the local economy (see Barbora 2002, 1285–92).

6 While the people of Ujani Aham call it Luit, outsiders refer to it as Lohit, which is a Sanskritized version that means "red river." According to Hindu legend the source of the Luit is Parashuramkund, the well of fratricidal crime where the mythic figure Parashuram slew his iconoclastic father to revive faith and morality in the community. Ujani Aham people cannot tell you what Luit stands for: it is a colloquial term and is seemingly not connected to any religious belief.

7 On the banks of the Brahmaputra the history of Assam records several battles: the Kacharis and the army of the swargadeos fought incessantly for occupation of its fertile floodplains. The Mughals—Bangalis—rowed upstream, over and over again. They battled with the flotilla of the swargadeos in the hopes of furthering the trade linkages with East and Inner Asia. Several kingdoms rose and fell on its banks. Merchant boats of the British colonials traveled its waters in search of potential economic opportunities along its course.

8 See Walter Buchannan's hand-drawn map, *Eur Mss D106*, Oriental and India Office Collection, British Library, London.

9 A similar story of connection between home and self-identity is revealed in the nostalgic reminiscences of the refugees from East Bengal (modern Bangladesh). Long after they left East Bengal (due to the partition in 1947) the refugees continued to tell stories of their home villages and locate themselves in the homes they left behind (see Chakrabarty 1996, 2143–51).

10 There is a lot of debate on the issue of whether vedekhi and Assambakhi are the same. Nowadays, everyone who resides in Assam and speaks Assamese is considered an Assambakhi. They are distinguished from videkhis—those who do not adopt the local language and customs of Assam. Despite this clear distinction between the two groups, taken as a whole both communities are considered "outsiders." Within this category of "outsiders" there are several degrees of separation. Some groups like Nepalis and Sikhs are considered to be "outsiders" but not so much as are the Bengalis, particularly

Muslim Bengalis, and Marwaris. At the heart of this distinction are economic and religious issues. Because Marwaris control the commercial and trading economy, the Assamese are very averse to them. Among the Bangladeshis who have moved to Assam and live there, the Muslim population is targeted. Most of them are sharecroppers and wage laborers. These groups threaten to occupy land and displace the Assamese from menial jobs. The rising tide of the BJP politics of Hindutva have made the Bangladeshi Muslims the most distant "other." The two groups—the Marwaris who are at the top of the economic chain, and the Bengali Muslims who are at the bottom of it and profess a different religious faith, other than Hinduism—are targeted for discrimination.

11 All the buranjis I have read confirm the story of settlement along the river. For a detailed description of the process of settlement, see Saikia 1997, 4–7.

12 The remarkable importance of natural images in shaping, forming, and creating cultural traditions in Western Europe is wonderfully enumerated by Simon Schama in *Landscape and Memory* (1995).

13 The best-known example that is often cited is the claim that Jewish identity and Israel are inseparably interlinked through time and space.

14 In Mali the snake is seen as such a symbol. It is called Dugu Dasiri, the "village snake" that according to legend wraps itself around the village and protects it from outsiders. In this case, the snake embodies the boundary of "us" versus "them" and maintains that separation (personal conversation with Cherif Keita, professor of Francophone studies at Carleton College, Northfield, Minnesota, December 25, 1998).

15 Ohnuki-Tierney has argued that "rice is the metaphor of self. . . . Rice paddies are *our* ancestral land, *our* village, *our* region, and ultimately, *our* land, Japan" (1994, 10).

16 Both Numal Gogoi and Nirma Gohain confirmed this opinion on different occasions during personal conversations.

17 I am withholding the names of these villages because I prefer not to expose my hosts to the disdain and contempt of the urban Assamese, who do not investigate the reasons for such dietary practices but hastily conclude they are "dreadful" and "uncivilized."

18 Regarding this food selection, see also Gogoi and Gogoi 1984, 174–77, 438–46.

19 In areas of Assam where Brahmanic Hinduism has taken root, "unusual" food habits such as those described are not tolerated because they are considered impure or polluted. Assamese Brahmins are not vegetarians, but they are very judgmental about other peoples' food and eating habits. Brahmins elsewhere in India consider the Assamese Brahmins polluted and impure. No doubt, standards of purity and impurity of "self" and "other" are determined to exclude and discriminate. In India, vegetarianism and concepts of pure and impure food developed later, in and around the early modern period (the

fifteenth and sixteenth centuries) when various books of Hindu religious thought and philosophy were compiled and written down. This can be gleaned from reading the Rigveda and early Brahmanic literature, where we find several mentions of sacrifice and partaking of meat in ritual settings (see also Jha 2002).

20 In India during the anticolonial struggle Gandhi capitalized on the idea of village self-sufficiency based on weaving what he called the khadi program. He urged every household to produce their own clothes to break away from the cycle of dependency on British textiles and thus the British government. Ultimately, this program became remarkably successful and brought together all kinds of people from all over India to form a revolutionary mass demanding independence for India and the end of British colonialism.

21 Rohan Syam Village, Sapekhati, April 17, 1994.

22 Dipthongs as well as paired words are common in Ujani Aham. For example, in Ujani Aham people use the term *mit-mat* ("speak to each other") whereas in the rest of Assam the Sanskrit word *katha* is commonly use. Likewise, "to hide" is *dhuk-dhak*, elsewhere referred to as *lukuwa*; *phat-phatuwa* is "to study" or "be learned," but elsewhere one uses the word *parha*, from the Sanskrit *parhoe/parhna*. Kinship terms peculiar to the Tai villages of Ujani Aham include *pu* for father, *mae* for mother, *nisaw* for uncle, *apadeo* for aunt, *pu-thau* for fraternal grandfather, *pu-nai* for maternal grandfather, *anai-deo* for grandmother, *kai* for older brother, *pu* for son, *ji* for daughter, and the newly incorporated terms *chow* for Mr. and *nang* for Mrs. or Ms. Examples like these abound, making Ujani Aham speech markedly different from that spoken in the rest of Assam. The speakers view Ujani Aham's language and vocabulary as "pure" Assamese.

23 Catherine Lutz and Lila Abu-Lughod have drawn our attention to the connection between language and emotion. See their preface in the edited collection *Language and the Politics of Emotion* (1990).

24 Personal conversation with Nabin Borgohain, March 27, 1995, Jahasuk village, Dhemaji, Assam.

25 Personal conversation, March 3, 1995, Jahasuk village, Dhemaji, Assam.

26 On "Separate Electorate" and "Minority Status" by the same author, see the *Assam Tribune*, April 25, 1941.

27 See "President Chou En-Lai's Letter to Leaders of Asian and African Countries," *Peking Review*, November 30, 1962, p. 10.

28 Personal conversation, May 25, 1995, Moran, Assam.

29 Personal conversation, April 8, 1996, Moran, Assam.

#### 5. PERFORMANCE AND POLITICS OF TAI AHOM

1 The Sonapur district is located thirty miles northeast of Guwahati. Although not too far from the capital city, deemed a "tribal area," Sonapur is largely

neglected. The administration is a tribal council that mediates issues and problems for villages with state administration. The state government's attitude is to leave these villages as they are—in other words, isolated, backward and marginal—and use them as "vote banks" during elections. Sonapur College, where the conference was held, included a couple of dilapidated buildings made of stucco and bricks. To accommodate the conference attendees, a pavilion was set up in the grassy compound and a few chairs were provided for guests. We were bused to the meeting by Ban Ok. Interestingly, the village people were not invited to the meeting, nor did they show interest in it. "Tribal dances," which were the highlight of the convention, were performed by college students, many of whom came from nearby villages.

2   The Thai economist Pasuk Pongpaichit spoke at length about developing different strategies to increase local bargaining by the villages with the state in matters such as education, employment, and livelihood. Her speech was both political and academic, but the subtle message that Tai-Ahoms must resist the "capitalist" enterprises of the state was not lost on anyone. All of the Thai delegates emphasized this strategy and assured their help in the cause of the Tai-Ahom movement. Curiously, after the meeting we were bused to a local tea plantation for lunch. No one seemed to be able to resist the wonderful spread in the sprawling compound of the owner's bungalow.

3   By "discourse communities" I mean, as Foucault has argued, that which is contingent and knowable through language and rules determined by power. Discourse is an intensely political act that creates frontiers between "us" and "them." A discourse community is structured on this theoretical framework and draws on past history, myths, and symbols and transforms them into "facts" to provide a basis for action in the present. Such a community is structured around specific goals such as repossession of land and territory, culture, and means of production, as well as the restoration of rights, status, and power. To reach these goals a set of leaders is necessary to mobilize feelings of solidarity, support, and duty as well as an audience that can relate to the issues and translate the ideas of the leaders into action. In other words, the leaders and groups form a "discourse community" of shared objectives and agendas.

4   Following David Held (1991) I hold that citizenship depends on the right to enjoy entitlements and liberties in both the state and civil society.

5   In Assam local nationalism is a continuous phenomenon. The rhetoric has its appeal even today. See "Protect Sanctity of Assamese Language," *Assam Tribune* (online version www.assamtribune.com), September 11, 2002.

6   There is an attempt among scholars studying the contemporary communal history of India to read the ULFA movement as a separatist Vaishnavite struggle. According to these scholars, the ULFA movement showcases the lack of integration and establishment of a homogenous Hindu identity that the BJP

claims as its success. It is true that ULFA is an antinational movement, but the use of religious politics to evaluate the ULFA is misplaced. The BJP has falsely accused Christian missionaries of generating and sustaining a psychology of difference among the people of the northeast. Rather, Hindu communities in Assam and the rest of the northeast have been historically suspicious of Indian/Hindu communities and have always seen themselves as different. This was very clearly articulated to me by Parag Das when I asked him why ULFA, which was organized and controlled mainly by young Hindu men, wanted Assam to break away from India. He replied, "We may be Hindus, but we are a different kind of Hindus from Indians. They don't seem to get it, despite our telling them so in so many different ways throughout our history" (personal conversation in Guwahati, March 17, 1995). For a recent write up on the ULFA movement, see moderator's note, Indiathinkersnet@ yahoogroups.com, digest no. 533, July 7, 2002. See also "ULFA Used Hindu Ashram as Head Quarters," *New Indian Express*, August 2000.

7 Personal conversation (location and dates for which have been withheld to maintain the anonymity of the people who helped me establish contact with some of the ULFA leaders).

8 I am making this statement based on my private conversations with late Parag Das, the well-known investigative journalist and editor of the Assamese weekly *Hat Din*. Parag was shot and killed on April 26, 1996, at a busy intersection in Guwahati. His assassination was not thoroughly investigated and his killers were never found. The silencing of a voice such as Parag's has to be taken seriously for this, once again, has a double-edged consequence. At one level, the lack of government interest in investigating the case has strengthened belief among the people of Assam that no one cares about them or their condition. At another level, it fuels passions for political dissent. Besides ULFA, many believe that Assam has been transformed into a militarized zone in order to silence dissent against the Indian state.

9 I believe many other ancestors have been found by the pan-Thai ideologues. Some of them locate their genealogical past in South China, others in northern Vietnam, and still others in Laos. In other words, the past is up for grabs for Thais to claim.

10 Thai economist Chatthip Nartsupha is an ardent supporter of Tai-Ahom (I will discuss his contributions and agenda later in this chapter). On two occasions—the international Tai-Ahom studies conference held February 1995 in Guwahati, Assam, and the international Thai studies conference held October 1996 in ChiangMai, Thailand—I had the opportunity to hear Chatthip claim a historic connection between the Tai-Ahom and Thai people. On these occasions he also publicly endorsed ULFA and claimed them as supporters of Tai-Ahom, adding that they were enabling Ahoms to assert a new identity.

11 I have been asked to explain if my family is related to Hiteshwar Saikia. I have to answer this question in a roundabout way using an anecdote to illuminate the nature of our relationship. While I was trying to leave India at the end of my research in 1995, the security officer on duty at the airport decided to grill me about the reasons for my long stay in Assam. His questions became more and more probing, and for a moment I was afraid I would be charged for some offence. Suddenly, he noticed that my last name is Saikia. Hiteshwar Saikia was then the chief minister of Assam. "Madam," he asked me, "How are you related to the chief minister of Assam?" I was about to say that we are not relatives, but then I recalled an incident in 1992 at the same airport and the rejection I suffered for being unable to convince the officer that I was an Indian—an insider so to speak. This time I was not going to let them decide on my behalf, so I stated, "We are from the same clan." It was a vague answer but not a lie. The security officer, who I think knew next to nothing about Assam, was impressed that I was connected to an important person like Hiteshwar Saikia. He profusely apologized and let me go. The Saikias of Nazira are from the same clan, and both Hiteshwar Saikia and my family claim Nazira as their home.

12 Terwiel 1994, 1–21. During a meeting with Terwiel on June 25, 1995, in Hamburg, Germany, he told me that he no longer accepted the Tai-Ahom rituals as ancient.

13 Personal conversation, December 26, 1992, Patsako Gaon, Assam.

14 "Saw Naru Saw Ai Kai—I am invoking my ancestors, the gods, to be with us on this occasion. My ancestors came from Mung-Mao. It is in Upper Burma, near the province of Yunnan in present-day Southern China. Sukapha, the mighty ruler of Mung-Mao, led his men to Mung-dun-sung-kham [Assam]. He defeated the Nagas and Kacharis and became the ruler of the Assam Valley. Here the group was given the name Ahom meaning 'unequal,' 'unique.' Sukapha was the first swargadeo of the Ahom kingdom in Assam. The Ahom swargadoes ruled for six hundred years without a break until the British occupation. I have come here today to represent the problems of my people, the Tai-Ahoms, to this body of scholars." This speech was recalled for me by Domboru Deodhai during our meeting on December 26, 1992 (the translation here from Assamese is mine). What struck me about this speech was that the story was directly borrowed from the colonial accounts. The colonial myth-making process was so successful that it had erased other versions (if they existed) of the past, and there was no other way of telling about Ahom that was counter to the colonial narrative. People in Assam did not see it as a problem. Rather, they upheld the colonial version as "authentic" history and believed that the British agents had a claim to knowledge of history because they were the rulers. For a good theoretical study of the colonizing of consciousness in India, see Nandy 1983.

15  Terwiel related this story to me.

16  A public declaration to this effect was made during the Me-dam-me-phi celebration on January 31, 1992, in Guwahati, Assam. I discuss the ceremony and the politics of religion later in this chapter.

17  Because of their large numbers, the Assamese Ahom is the predominant group in the Tai-Ahom movement.

18  Personal conversation with Ni Chailung Gohain of Nam Phakiyal village, Jeypore, Assam, on April 16, 1994. Saimit Wailung of Rohan Syam Gaon, Sapekhati, Assam, expressed the same view the next day, April 17.

19  Since 1981 the Ban Ok convened its annual meetings in small villages and towns in Upper Assam.

20  "Now He Is a Swargadeo!" *Sentinel*, December 3, 1992.

21  Pushpa Gogoi, the artist of this portrait, admitted that the image of Sukapha was based on his personal imagination. In his words, he needed to project "Sukapha's Mongol ancestry so that Tai-Ahoms would identify with Mongoloid races of Assam" and not caste Hindus (personal conversation, March 27, 1995, Dhemaji, Assam).

22  "Sukapha Divah Celebration," Ajir Assam, December 4, 1994. Similar reports were published in several dailies in Assam.

23  These are Hindu goddesses who are publicly worshiped on designated days of the year.

24  Many communities in Assam, both rural and urban and Hindu and Tai-Ahom, are followers of Shankaria Vaishnavism. Some Tai-Ahoms are abandoning the religion to protest against the ill treatment they have suffered at the hands of the gossains who have always considered them *antarjya* (polluted people). I discuss the anxiety leading to the breakaway of these groups in chapter 6.

25  Generally, offerings were also made to the deceased women in the family. Because Mr. Gogoi's mother was alive, the ritual was confined to the worship of deceased male members. I am not certain if such elaborate rituals of worship were also performed in the Gogoi household to honor the deceased members of Mrs. Gogoi's family. Throughout my stay in Assam, I noticed that the patrilineal connections were those upheld.

26  Personal conversation, February 1995, Sibsagar, Assam.

27  The function of this organization unsurprisingly was restricted to the annual celebration of Jaymati Divas, which commemorates the semimythical legendary princess, Jaymati. The character Jaymati is absent in the buranjis, but the story of her marriage to the first Tungkhungia prince, Gadapani, and her subsequent torture at the hands of his rivals has become a popular oral tradition. I do not know when this tradition started. The celebration of Jaymati glorified Tai-Ahom women for their victimhood and unflinching devotion to wifely duties, which is reminiscent of the *sati* tradition in India.

Taking into account the established idiom of male dominance in the Tai-Ahom movement, one can interpret the valorization of women not as a strategy of empowerment but as an effort to make them docile objects to be acted on.

28 The first Hu-pat ceremony was performed in North Lakhimpur (personal conversation with Nagen Hazarika, June 15, 1995, Guwahati, Assam).

29 Memorandum to the prime minister, from the Society of Phralung Buddhist Culture and the Ahom Religious and Cultural Council, Sibsagar, Assam, August 9, 1995.

30 Draft constitution of the Ahom Land Demand Committee, April 1995. Ratneshwar Borgohain gave me a copy. Although it is printed, it is circulated only among the so-called Tai-Ahom people and is not available outside.

31 When I raised this issue at the international Thai studies conference in 1996, many Ahom and Thai scholars took strong objection. The complaint was not about bad scholarship but about my role as conduit.

32 Personal conversation, May 27, 1995, Moran, Assam.

33 For further discussion, see Baruah 1994; Hazarika 1994; and Dasgupta 1997.

34 Questions concerning ULFA were politically sensitive and were considered "dangerous," hence not many people in Assam wanted to discuss them. The intelligence files on ULFA were not open to the public. However, I had the opportunity to meet several people who guardedly discussed the issues. The text in this section is based on firsthand interviews with people directly and indirectly connected with the ULFA (but their identities are withheld from the text).

35 "Memorandum Demanding a Separate Autonomous Unit of Upper Assam Districts of Lakhimpur and Sibsagar," All Assam Ahom Association, May 28, 1967, pp. 1–2.

36 The translation of Jatiyatabadi as "racial/ethnic awareness" is my own, loose one. Lacking a more precise definition I use it as a working phrase, and I am aware that other translations could be equally valid.

37 According to Buddheshwar Gogoi: "We were not satisfied with what the AASU were doing." To explain, he added, "I might like and trust the Mahatma (Gandhi), but I am not going to endorse each and every policy of his . . . We did not see any meaning in the AASU movement. We wanted a more definite, precise agenda for the people of Assam, and we were ready for an armed struggle" (personal conversation, May 27, 1995). In the course of the interview it became clear that what Gogoi meant by Assam was a narrow, territorial definition of Upper Assam, to which the area of Lower Assam had a tenuous attachment that could be done away with, if necessary.

38 Local gossip in Assam identified Rang Ghar as the birthplace of ULFA. According to Buddheshwar Gogoi, "The Rang Ghar story has gained currency. They have even fixed a date, April 7, 1979, as the birth of the ULFA. All

this is conjecture, but I prefer to leave the story as it is. Maybe that is necessary for the public" (personal conversation, May 25, 1995, Moran, Assam).

39  Personal conversation, Buddheshwar Gogoi, May 25, 1995, Moran, Assam.

40  An essential part of the installation ceremony of swargadeos involved a sacrifice made to the gods. Initially, human beings were sacrificed on such an occasion. Later, they were replaced by the sacrifice of animals, generally a white bull (for details, see Saikia 1997, 29, 217).

41  The Motoks are probably descendants of the groups called Morans and Barahis in the buranjis, the earliest supporters of Sukapha, who assisted in the founding of the rule of swargadeos.

42  Gogoi could not produce a copy of the constitution because it was confiscated several years ago by the army during one of their many raids on his house. According to him, a few more copies existed but they were hard to find. Particularly, in 1995, since the Terrorist Arms Detention Act (TADA) was in place, many people decided to destroy subversive literature in the fear that they would be apprehended by the authorities and imprisoned. I did not pursue its search too carefully for the same reasons. Personal conversation, March 16, 1995, Moran, Assam.

43  Personal conversation, Buddheshwar Gogoi, March 10, 1996, Moran, Assam.

44  Personal interview with Sunil Nath, surrendered member and former publicity secretary of ULFA, November 7, 1994, Guwahati, Assam.

45  Personal conversation, date and place witheld to protect informant.

46  Personal conversation, April 2, 1994, Guwahati, Assam.

47  Personal conversation with Chatthip Nartsupha, February 7, 1995, Guwahati, Assam.

48  Both Romesh Buragohain and Pushpa Gogoi admitted Nartsupha's influence on their lives and political careers.

49  Pasuk Pongpaichit, professor of economics at Chulalongkorn University in Thailand is a leading critic of the Western capitalist development of Thailand. See also Nartsupha 1991a and 1991b.

50  For reference, see Coedés 1963, 119–21.

51  See also Wichasin 1996, 13–14.

52  Since 1996, two international Thai studies conferences were held, in Amsterdam and in Thailand. I do not know how many Tai-Ahom leaders attended these conferences. The passing away of Hiteshwar Saikia in 1996 meant the end of much of the financial assistance for Tai-Ahom leaders to travel abroad to solicit support for their movement. Whether their absence at the conferences and subsequent meetings also affected international interest in Tai-Ahoms needs to be investigated.

53  For an analytical reading of the economic phases and tensions leading to the unraveling of the Thai economy, see Pongpaichit and Baker 1998 and 2000.

54  Pushpa Gogoi, general secretary of Ban Ok, explained to me these details and
the reasons for pursuing them during our conversations in Dhemaji in March
1995.

### 6. THERE WAS NO PLOT IN THE PEOPLE'S STRUGGLE

1  This is a seventeenth-century chronicle, as I previously mentioned. According to Bidya Phukan, Domboru Deodhai's son, the buranji is a royal chronicle
and is not a history of the Ahom community.

2  I attended several sabhas during my stay in various villages. Not all of them
were formal discussion sessions. Sometimes, a gathering of elders was convened for my benefit so that I could ask about Ahom history and culture,
something the "elders knew all about." Most of these sabhas were convened
in the local school or in the courtyard of the village temple, if there was one.
Very rarely was anything outside the buranjis discussed in these gatherings.
Repeating the stories of the buranjis was considered essential for disseminat-
ing knowledge of the Tai past. This had become very popular even in non-
Ahom, Tai villages. In Pathar Syam Gaon in Titabar, a Turung village that
claimed to be Tai but not Tai-Ahom, I was told, "We meet to discuss various
issues. This helps in spreading the knowledge about our history and culture.
Although we do not read the buranjis because we are not Ahoms, we tell our
children the stories of Ahom swargadeos and our long history of association
with them. We have to maintain our culture and religion. How can we continue to have an identity if we forget and lose it?" (personal conversation with
Lakshmi Syam of Tai Turung village, April 27, 1994, Titabar, Assam).

3  This reminded me of Matsuda's (1996) reading of memory in French history.

4  Personal conversation, April 24, 1994, Jorhat, Assam.

5  Personal conversation, February 28, 1994, Jorhat, Assam.

6  Interview by author, May 31, 1995, Dispur Office, Guwahati, Assam.

7  Personal conversation, May 19, 1995, Guwahati, Assam.

8  Personal conversation, March 20, 1995, Guwahati, Assam.

9  Personal conversation, March 30, 1994, Guwahati, Assam. I met with Kiran
Gogoi's wife several times thereafter and she expressed a similar opinion
during our conversations about Tai-Ahom identity.

10  Although I quote Numal Gogoi here, Nagen Hazarika, Pushpa Gogoi, Ra-
meshwar Buragohain, and many other leaders and followers of Ban Ok
expressed similar opinions.

11  The protest movements in Peru and in Juchitán depict a similar pattern. The
rebellious rhetoric of return to the past is not meant to be a return to primi-
tivism or a backward state of life. Rather, nostalgia is a package expected to
create pathways for economic progress for the adherents (see Nugent 1997;
and Rubin 1997).

12 Buddheshwar Gogoi narrated to me the story of the first public meeting conducted by the ULFA leaders in a small village (name withheld) in Sibsagar district. He ended the narration with these words: "I was amazed. At the end of the meeting all the assembled people told us, 'you have our support.'" March 10, 1995, Moran, Assam.

13 Personal conversation, March 8, 1995, Sibsagar, Assam.

14 Personal conversation, April 12–14, 1994, Patsako village, Sibsagar, Assam.

15 Interview by author, March 24, 1995, Jahasuk village, Dhemaji, Assam.

16 Personal conversation, April 3, 1995, Guwahati, Assam.

17 Personal conversation, June 1, 1995, Guwahati, Assam.

18 For more information on the Chaklang, see Bhuyan 1990, 258–63: 146–49.

19 Based on personal conversations, April 1994 to May 1995.

20 Personal conversation, November 15, 1994.

21 Personal conversation, May 31, 1995, Guwahati, Assam.

22 Personal conversation, June 5, 1995, Guwahati, Assam.

23 Personal conversation, May 28, 1995, Guwahati, Assam.

24 Personal conversation, October 11, 1994, Guwahati, Assam.

### CONCLUSION

1 Robert Reid, "A Note on the Future of the Present Excluded, Partially Excluded and Tribal Areas of Assam," 7.4.1941, Confidential, *Mss Eur E. 278/4* (*g*), pp. 16, 21–22, Oriental and Indian Office Collection, British Library, London.

2 For a further reading on Nehruvian economics and secularism, see Khilnani 1998; and Nanda 1995.

3 Democratic regimes are supposed to make room for recognition and representation of constituent elements—big and small. The question of numbers has confused the working of pluralistic democracies, where larger groups assume they have the right to be authoritative. In India, instead of following a path of conflict resolution that can transform antagonism among adversaries into a tolerant system of give and take, the majority groups have ruled and forced their will on the small groups. The problematic functioning of democracy in India has taken a new turn with the development of what is now called "religious democracy"—the rights of Hindu groups are upheld at the cost of all other religious communities.

4 Beppe Karlson (2000) has identified the emergence of the Rabha identity in the borderland area of the Duars situated between Assam and Bengal as a cultural movement without political developments.

5 "Transcendence" here is from Phillips 1991, 81.

6 See the report, "Lost Treasures of Assam," *Assam Tribune* (online version www.assamtribune.com), August 13, 2002.

7 In 2002, a new organization called United Muslim Front of Assam was created. This development was very disturbing, because it was the first time Muslims in Assam have taken a religious stand of separation and identity. Heretofore, Assam Muslims and Hindus have taken pride in their "secular" society, which seems to be eroding under the BJP's religio-political tutelage.

8 Unfortunately, the BJP has adopted an opposite policy. In 1999, a "master narrative" of Hindu history for India was written, and recently textbooks promoting a BJP version of history were released. The effort of the government is focused on fashioning a history that will singularly glorify the contributions to Indian history of Brahmanic Hindu civilization. In the BJP government's view, history has to be an instrument for socializing children in India to be good, obedient citizens (read subjects) of the nation by taking pride in Hindu culture and religion. This policy disregards the impact that such a narrative would have on minority communities throughout the nation-state. The government is creating a breeding ground of dissension and future tension with full realization of its role, and their callousness in doing so is utterly disgraceful and unacceptable. Although several voices of protest have been raised, the government is continuing with its plan to manufacture a history that suits its agenda of parochial, centralized Hindu politics and identity for India.

# References

Abu-Lughod, Leila. 1993. *Writing Women's Worlds: Bedouin Stories*. Berkeley: University of California Press.

Acharyya, N. N. 1966. *The History of Medieval Assam*. Guwahati: Dutta Baruah.

Ahsan, Aitzaz. 1996. *The Indus Saga and the Making of Pakistan*. Karachi: Oxford University Press.

Alam, Javeed, and S. Sharma. 1998. "Remembering Partition," *Seminar* 461 (January): 98–103.

Al-Idrisi. 1960. *India and the Neighbouring Territories in the Kitab Nuzhat Al Musht q fi 'Khtiráq al-'afq*. Trans. M. S. Ahmed. Leiden: E. J. Brill.

All Assam Ahom Association. 1967. "Memorandum Demanding a Separate Autonomous Unit of Upper Assam Districts of Lakhimpur and Sibsagar." Sibsagar: All Assam.

Altorki, S., and C. El-Solh, eds. 1988. *Arab Women in the Field: Studying Your Own Society*. New York: Syracuse University Press.

Anadaya, A. 1978. "Statecraft in the Reign of Lu Tai of Sukhodaya (ca. 1347–1374)." In *Religion and Legitimation in Thailand*, ed. Bardwell Smith. Pennsylvania: Anima Books.

Anderson, Benedict. 1991. *Imagined Communities: Reflections on the Origin and Spread of Nationalism*. 2nd ed. London: Verso.

Andrews, Geoff, ed. 1991. *Citizenship*. London: Lawrence and Wishart Limited.

Annanta, K. K., ed. 1973. *Raghuvamsha of Kalidasa*. Madras: Ramayana Publishing House.

Antrobus, H. A. 1957. *A History of the Assam Company, 1839–1953*. Edinburgh: n.p.

Appadurai, Arjun. 1981. "The Past as a Scarce Resource." *Man* 16:201–19.

Auerbach, E. 1953. *Mimesis: The Representation of Reality in Western Literature*. Trans. W. Trask. Princeton: Princeton University Press.

Babur. 1996 [1483–1530]. *Babur Namah; or, Memories of Babur, Prince and Emperor*. Ed. and trans. Wheeler Thackston. Washington, D.C.: Freer Gallery of Art; New York: Oxford University Press.

Bailey, A. 1985. "The Making of History: Dialectics of Temporality and Structure in Modern French Social Theory." *Critique of Anthropology* 5, no. 1: 7–31.

Bajpai, K. D., ed. 1967. *The Geographical Encyclopedia of Ancient India*. Part 1. Varansi: Indic Academy.

Baron, Salo. 1960. *Modern Nationalism and Religion*. New York: Meridian Books.

Barth, Fredrik. 1969. *Ethnic Groups and Boundaries*. Boston: Little, Brown.

Barthes, Ronald. 1985. *Mythologies*. New York: Hill and Wang.

Barua, Birinchi. 1941. *Assamese Literature*. Bombay: P.E.N. All India-Centre.

Barua, B., and Nandalal Deodhai Phukan. 1964. *Ahom Lexicon*. Guwahati: Directorate of Historical and Antiquarian Studies of Assam.

Barua, Golap Chandra, ed. 1930. *Ahom Buranji*. 1st ed. Calcutta: Baptist Mission Press.

Barua, Hem. 1954. *The Red River and the Blue Hill*. Guwahati: Lawyer's Book Stall.

Barua, Keshav Kanta. 1923. *Asamar Athutajatir Uttpattir Bibaran*. Assam: Dhanaraj Gogoi Publication.

Barua, Saniram. 1928. *Assam Buranji, Mulak Man-Citra*. Guwahati: T. K. Bandhyapadhyay.

Barua, S. L. 1985. *A Comprehensive History of Assam*. Delhi: Munshiram Manoharlal Publication.

Baruah, Khirod. 1995. "The Tai, Thai, and the Khamti Language." Paper presented at the Second International Conference on Tai Studies, Guwahati, February 7–10.

Baruah, Padmanath. 1906. *Asamar Buranji, or the History of Assam*. Tezpur: Lila Agency.

Baruah, Padmanath. 1922. *Buranjibodh; or Lessons on the History of Assam*. 2nd ed. Tezpur: Lila Agency.

Baruah, Sanjib. 1994a. "Conflict as State-Society Struggle: The Poetics and Politics of Assamese Micronationalism." *Modern Asian Studies* 28, no. 3: 649–71.

——. 1994b. "The State and Separatist Militancy in Assam: Winning a Battle but Losing the War?" *Asian Survey* 34, no. 10: 863–77.

——. 1999. *India against Itself: Assam and the Politics of Nationality*. Philadelphia: University of Pennsylvania Press.

Basso, Keith. 1992. "Speaking with Names: Language and Landscape among the Western Apache." In *Reading Cultural Anthropology*, ed. George Marcus. Durham: Duke University Press.

Basu, Amrita. 1992. *Two Faces of Protest: Contrasting Modes of Women's Activism in India*. Berkeley: University of California Press.

Benson, S., and R. Roy, eds. 1986. *Presenting the Past: Essays on History and the Public*. Philadelphia: Temple University Press.

Berger, P., and T. Luckman, eds. 1967. *The Social Construction of Reality*. New York: Doubleday.

Bhattacharjee, Chandana. 1996. *Ethnicity and Autonomy Movement: Case of Bodo-Kacharis of Assam*. New Delhi: Vikas Publication.

Bhuyan, Suryya Kumar. 1931. "Aham Abidan Sastra." *Abahan* 3, no. 3: 257–63.

——. ed. 1932. *Tungkhungia Buranji; or, A History of Assam, 1681–1826 A.D.* 1st ed. Guwahati: Directorate of Historical and Antiquarian Studies of Assam.

——. ed. 1938. *Tripura Buranji*. 1st ed. Guwahati: Directorate of Historical and Antiquarian Studies of Assam.

——. ed. 1960. *Satsari Assam Buranji*. Guwahati: Guwahati University Press.

——. ed. 1990. [1932] *Deodhai Assam Buranji*. 3rd ed. Guwahati: Directorate of Historical and Antiquarian Studies of Assam.

Billig, Michael. 1995. *Banal Nationalism*. London: Sage Publications.

Blackmore, Mathew. 1960. "The Rise of Nan-Chao in Yunan." *Journal of South East Asian History* 1, no. 2: 47–61.

Blatti, J. 1987. *Past Meets Present: Essays about Historic Interpretation and Public Audiences*. Washington, D.C.: Smithsonian Institution Press.

Blochman, H. 1872. "Fathiyah-i-Ibriyah." *Journal of the Bengal Asiatic Society*.

Bourdieu, Pierre. 1980. *Le sens pratique*. Paris: Editions de Minuit.

Bora, M. I., ed. 1992. *Baharistan-i-Ghaybi*. 2nd ed. Guwahati: Directorate of Historical and Antiquarian Studies of Assam.

Bora, Jnanaath. 1938. "Asom Desh Bharatuarshar Bhitarat Thakiba Kia?" In Dinanath Sarmah, ed. *Awahon*. Calcutta: n.p.

Borbora, Sanjay. 2002. "Ethnic Politics and Land Use: Genesis of Conflicts in India's North-East." *Economic and Political Weekly* 37, no. 13 (March 30): 1285–92.

Borooah, Padmanath. 1906. *Assamar Buranji; or, The History of Assam*. 2nd ed. Tezpur: Lila Agency.

Borooah Bahadur, Goonabhiram. 1900. *Assam Buranji, or the History of Assam Including the History of the Ancient Kingdom of Kamrup from the Earliest Time and Containing a Brief Note of the Castes, Language, Religion, Commerce, Agriculture, Arts and Social Customs of the People and the Internal Government of the Province*. 4th ed. Calcutta: Monica Press.

Bose, Sugata, and Ayesha Jalal. 1997. *Modern South Asia: History, Culture, Political Economy*. London: Oxford University Press.

Bradley, C. B. 1904. "The Oldest Known Writing in Siamese." *Journal of the Siam Society* 6, no. 1: 1–64.

Brass, Paul. 1985. "Ethnic Groups and the State." In *Ethnic Groups and Ethnic States*, ed. Paul Brass. London: Croom Helm.

——. 1991. *Ethnicity and Nationalism: Theory and Comparison*. New Delhi: Sage Publications.

Braudel, Fernand. 1973. *Capitalism and Material Life, 1400–1800*. London: Weidenfeld and Nicolson.

——. 1980. *On History*. Chicago: University of Chicago Press.

Breckenridge, Carol. 1989. "The Aesthetics and Politics of Collecting." *Comparative Studies in Society and History* 31: 195–216.

Briggs, L. P. 1949. "The Appearance and Historical Usage of the Terms Tai, Thai, Siamese, and Lao." *Journal of American Oriental Society* 59, no. 2: 60–73.

Broman, B. M. 1968. "Early Political Institutions of the Thai: Synthesis and Symbiosis." Master's thesis, University of Washington.

Buragohain, Purnakanta. 1946. *Ahamar Adi Buranji*. Jorhat: n.p.

Burke, Peter, ed. 1991. *New Perspectives on Historical Writing*. Philadelphia: University of Pennsylvania Press.

Burrad, S. G. 1914. *Records of the Survey of India: Explorations on the North-East Frontier. Vol. IV.* Calcutta: Superintendent of Government Printing.

Butalia, Urvashi. 2000. *The Other Side of Silence: Voices from the Partition of India*. Durham: Duke University Press.

Butler, J. 1847. *A Sketch of Assam with Some Account of the Hill Tribes*. London: Smith, Elder and Co.

———. 1855. *Travels and Adventures in the Province of Assam during the Residence of Fourteen Years*. London: Smith, Elder and Co.

Cantile, Audrey. 1984. *The Assamese: Religion, Caste, and Sect in an Indian Village*. London: Curzon.

Cantor, Norman. 1991. *Inventing the Middle Ages*. New York: William Morrow.

Carter, Paul. 1987. *The Road to Botany Bay: An Essay in Spatial History*. Cambridge, England: Polity Press.

Carthew, Mathew. 1942. "The History of the Thai in Yunan." *Journal of the Siam Society* 40, no. 1: 1–39.

Casson, Lionel, ed. 1989. *Periplus Maris Erythraei. . . .* Princeton: Princeton University Press.

Chakrabarty, Dipesh. 1992a. "Death of History, Historical Consciousness, and the Culture of Late Capitalism." *Public Culture* 4, no. 2 (spring): 47–66.

———. 1992b. "Postcoloniality and the Artifice of History: Who Speaks for the "Indian" Pasts?" *Representations* 32, no. 1 (winter): 1–26.

———. 1996. "Remembered Villages: Representation of Hindu-Bengali Memories in the Aftermath of the Partition." *Economic and Political Weekly*, August 10: (1996): 2143–51.

Chatterjee, Bankim Chandra. 1914. "Letters." *Bengal: Past and Present* 8, no. 2: 273–74.

Chatterjee, Partha. 1992. "History and the Nationalization of Hinduism." *Social Research* 59, no. 1: 111–49.

———. 1993a. *The Nation and Its Fragments: Colonial and Postcolonial Histories*. Princeton: Princeton University Press.

———. 1993b. *Nationalist Thought and the Colonial World: A Derivative Discourse*. Minneapolis: University of Minnesota Press.

Chatterji, S. K. 1955. *The Place of Assam in the History and Civilization of India*. Guwahati: University of Guwahati.

Chaudhuri, Nirad. 1976. *Culture in the Vanity Bag*. Bombay: Jaico.

Chernela, Janet. 1998. "Death, Memory, and Language: New Approaches to History in Lowland South American Anthropology." *Latin American Research Review* 33, no. 1: 167–91.

Choudhury, D. P. 1970. "The North East Frontier of India." *Modern Asian Studies* 4, no. 4: 359–65.

———. 1977. "British Quest for Trade Routes from Assam to Eastern Tibet." *Asian Affairs* 56, no. 2: 180–84.

Choudhury, Pratap. 1994. "The D.H.A.S.: It's Inception." In *Dr. Suryya Kumar Bhuyan: A Centenary Volume 1894–1994*, ed. S. Thakuria. Guwahati: Suryya Kumar Bhuyan Birth Centenary Celebration Committee.

Choudhury, P. C. 1966 (1959). *The History of Civilization of the People of Assam to the Twelfth Century A.D.* Guwahati: Directorate of Historical and Antiquarian Studies of Assam.

———, ed. 1976. *Hastividyarnava*. Guwahati: Publication Board of Assam.

Clayton, C. 1848. "Description of the Tomb of an Ahom Noble." *Journal of the Asiatic Society of Bengal* (June): n.p.

Clifford, James, and George Marcus, eds. 1986. *Writing Culture: The Poetics and Politics of Ethnography*. Berkeley: University of California Press.

Cochrane, W. W. 1911. "An Ahom Legend of Creation." *Journal of the Royal Asiatic Society*, 1132–42.

Coedés, George. 1921. "The Origins of the Sukhodaya Dynasty." *Journal of the Siam Society* 16, no. 1: 1–11.

———. 1968. *The Indianized States of Southeast Asia*. Trans. Susan Brown Cowing. Honolulu: University of Hawaii Press.

Cohn, Bernard. 1971. "The Pasts of an Indian Village." *Comparative Studies in Society and History* 3: 241–49.

———. 1980. "History and Anthropology: The State of Play." *Comparative Studies in Society and History* 12: 198–221.

Collingwood, R. G. 1946. *The Idea of History*. Oxford: Clarendon Press.

Comaroff, Jean, and John Comaroff. 1992. *Ethnography and the Historical Imagination*. Boulder: Westview Press.

Connerton, P. 1989. *How Societies Remember*. Cambridge: Cambridge University Press.

Connor, Walker. 1992. "The Nation and Its Myth." *International Journal of Comparative Sociology* 33: 48–57.

———. 1994. *Ethnonationalism: The Quest for Understanding*. Princeton: Princeton University Press.

Cook, Nigel, ed. 1996. *The Transmission of Knowledge in South Asia*. Delhi: Oxford University Press.

Corfield, Penelope, ed. 1992. *Language, History, and Class*. Oxford: Basil Blackwell.

Crane, Susan. 1997. "Writing the Individual Back into Collective Memory." *American Historical Review* 1025: 1372–85.

Credner, W. 1935. *Cultural and Geographical Observations Made in the Tali (Yunnan) Region with Special Regard to the Nan-Chao Problem*. Bangkok: Siam Society.

Dahbour, Omar, and Micheline Ishay, eds. 1999. *The Nationalism Reader*. New York: Humanity Books.

Dalton, E. T. 1872. *Descriptive Ethnology of Bengal*. Calcutta: Government Printing Office.

Dasgupta, Jyotindra. 1997. "Community, Authenticity, and Autonomy: Insurgence and Institutional Development in India's Northeast." *Journal of Asian Studies* 56, no. 2: 345–70.

Dasgupta, R. 1982. *The Art of Medieval Assam*. New Delhi: Cosmo Publication.

Datta, S. 1989. *Migrant Brahmans in North India*. Delhi: Motilal Banarsidass.

David, Selborne. 1980. "On the Methods of History Workshop." *History Workshop Journal* 9: 150–61.

Davies, H. R. 1970. *Yunnan: The Link between India and the Yangtze*. 2nd ed. Taipei: Chieng Wen Publication Co.

Department of Archeology and State Museum, Government of Assam. n.d. *The Hand-Book of the Assam State Museum*. Guwahati: Saraighat Printers.

Devi, L. 1965–66. "Ahom and Assamese Buranjis." *Quarterly Review of Historical Studies* 2: 97–100.

Devi, Nalini Bala. 1962. *Sandhya Sur*. Guwahati: Bani Prakashan.

Deyell, John. 1990. *Living without Silver: The Monetary History of Early Medieval North India*. New Delhi: Oxford University Press.

Digby, S. 1971. *War-Horse and Elephant: A Study of Military Supplies*. Lahore: Oxford University Press.

Dikshit, K. N. 1924–25. "A Note on the Ahom Stone Pillar Inscription." Dehra Dun: Archeological Survey of India.

Dodd, W. 1923. *The Thai Race: Elder Brother of the Chinese*. Iowa: Torch Press.

Doniger, Wendy. 1993. *Reciprocity and Transformation in Hindu and Jaina Texts*. Ed. Purana Perennis. Albany: State University of New York Press.

Duara, Prasenjit. 1995. *Rescuing History from the Nation*. Chicago: University of Chicago Press.

Eaton, R. 1990. *Islamic History as Global History*. Washington, D.C.: American Historical Association.

Eckstein, Susan. ed. 2001. *Power and Popular Protest: Latin American Social Movements*. Berkeley: University of California Press.

Eisenstadt, S. 1978. *Revolution and Transformation of Societies: A Comparative Study of Civilizations*. New York: Free Press.

Eliade, M. 1963. *Myth and Reality*. Trans. Willard Trask. New York: Harper and Row.

Elias, Ney. 1876. *Introductory Sketch of the History of the Shans in Upper Burma and Western Yunnan*. Calcutta: Foreign Department Press.

Elliot, H. M. and J. Dawson. 1981 [1966]. *History of India as told by her own Historians*. Delhi: Idarah-i-Adabiyat-i-Delli.

Elwin, Verrier. 1969. *The Nagas in the Nineteenth Century*. London: Oxford University Press.

Erikson, Erik. 1950. *Childhood and Society*. New York: Norton.

Fabian, J. T. 1983. *Time and the Other: How Anthropology Makes Its Object*. New York: Columbia University Press.

Feely-Harnik, G. 1978. "Divine Kingship and the Meaning of History among the Sakalava of Madagascar." *Man* 13: 402–17.

Fentress, James, and Chris Wickham. 1992. *Social Memory*. Oxford: Blackwell.

Fernandez, J., ed. 1991. *Beyond Metaphor: The Theory of Tropes in Anthropology*. Stanford: Stanford University Press.

Finley, M. 1965. "Myth, Memory, and History." *History and Theory* 4, no. 3: 281–302.

Fisher, M. A. 1990. *Shared Authority: Essays on the Craft and Meeting of Oral and Public History*. Albany: State University of New York Press.

Fleet, J. F. 1963. *Corpus Inscription Indicarum*. 2nd ed. Vol. 3. Varansi: Indological Book House.

Foucault, Michel. 1972. *Archaeology of Knowledge and Discourse on Language*. Trans. A. M. Sheridan Smith. New York: Pantheon Books.

Fox, R. G. 1985. *The Lions of Punjab: Culture in the Making*. Berkeley: University of California Press.

Gait, Edward. 1895. "Notes on Some Ahom Coins." *Journal of Asiatic Society* 44: 286.

——. 1917. *Vamsavali*. Calcutta: Baptist Mission Press.

——. 1963. *The History of Assam*. 3rd ed. Calcutta: Thacker Spink and Co.

Gallagher, Winifred. 1993. *The Power of Place: How Our Surroundings Shape Our Emotions, Thought, and Action*. New York: Poseidon Press.

Geertz, Clifford. 1963. "The Integrative Revolution: Primordial Sentiments and Civil Politics in the New States." In *Old Societies and New States*, ed. Clifford Geertz. Glencoe, Ill.: Free Press, 1963.

——. 1973. *The Interpretation of Cultures*. New York: Basic Books.

——. 1980. *Negara: The Theater State in Nineteenth-Century Bali*. Princeton: Princeton University Press.

——. 1983. *Local Knowledge*. New York: Basic Books.

Gellner, Ernest. 1983. *Nation and Nationalism*. Ithaca: Cornell University Press.

Gillis, John. ed. 1994. *Commemorations: The Politics of National Identity*. Princeton: Princeton University Press.

Glanius. 1682 [1673]. *A Relation of an Unfortunate Voyage to the Kingdom of Bengala*. London: n.p.

Gleason, Philip. 1983. "Identifying Identity: A Semantic History." *Journal of American History* 69, no. 4: 910–31.

Gogoi, Lila. 1986. *The Buranjis: Historical Literature of Assam*. Guwahati: Omsons Publications.

————, ed. 1990. *The Thai Khamtis of North East India*. 2nd ed. Delhi: Omsons Publications.

Gogoi, N. 1987. *The Assamese-Tai-English Dictionary*. Tinsukia: Nang Nirada Gogoi.

Gogoi, Padmeshwar. 1968. *The Tai and the Tai-Ahom Kingdom of the Brahmaputra Valley*. Guwahati: Guwahati University Press.

————. 1976. *Tai-Ahom Religion and Customs*. Guwahati: Guwahati University Press.

Gogoi, Pushpa. 1993. *Descriptive Catalogue of Tai Manuscripts*. Dhemaji: Purbanchal Tai Sahitya Sabha.

Gogoi, Pushpa, and Bogen Gogoi. 1984. *Tai-Ahom Dharma*. Dhemaji: Purbanchal Tai Sahitya Sabha.

————, eds. 1994. *Tai Sanskriti*. Dhemaji: Purbanchal Tai Sahitya Sabha.

Gogoi, Thanuram. n.d. "Ripunjaya Smriti Movement." Guwahati: Assam State Archives.

Gohain, B. 1977. *Sacrifice and Head Hunting in North East India*. Guwahati: Lawyer's Book Stall.

Goody, Jack. 1968. *Literacy in Traditional Societies*. Cambridge: Cambridge University Press.

————. 1986. *The Logic of Writing and the Organization of Society*. Cambridge: Cambridge University Press.

————. 1987. *The Interface between the Written and the Oral*. Cambridge: Cambridge University Press.

Gordon, Daniel. 1995. "Review Essay." *History and Theory* 34, no. 4: 340–54.

Gosling, B. 1991. *Sukhothai, Its History, Culture and Art*. Singapore: Oxford University Press.

Goswami, Tirtha Nath. 1915. *Mular Para Haral Bhongoni Ripunjay Smriti Ba Prayachitta Bebhasthabidhan*. Calcutta: n.p.

Goswami, Upendranath. 1998. *Ahamia Lipi*. Guwahati: Publication Board of Assam.

Gowalkar, S. 1939. *We and Our Nationhood Defined*. Nagpur: India Prakashan.

Grierson, G. E. 1904. *Linguistic Survey of India*, vol. 2. Calcutta: Office of the Superintendent of Government Printing.

Guha, Amalendu. 1977. *Planter Raj to Swaraj: Freedom Struggle and Electoral Politics in Assam, 1826–1947*. New Delhi: People's Publishing House.

Guha, Amalendu. 1991. *Medieval and Early Colonial Assam*. New Delhi: K. P. Bagchi and Company.

Guha, Ranajit. 1997. *Dominance without Hegemony*. Cambridge: Harvard University Press.

Haar, E. 1969. *The Yar-Lun Dynasty*. Copenhagen: G. E. E. and Forlag.

Habib, Irfan. 1982. *The Atlas of the Mughal Empire*. Delhi: Oxford University Press.

————. 1996. *Essays in Indian History: Towards a Marxist Interpretation*. Delhi: Oxford University Press.

Haimendorf, C. von. 1939. *Naked Nagas*. London: Methuen.

Hall, D. G. E. 1955. *A History of South East Asia*. New York: St. Martin's Press.

Hall, Stuart, and David Held. 1989. "Citizens and Citizenship." ed. *New Times*, ed. Stuart Hall and Martin Jacques. London: Lawrence and Wishart.

Hamilton, Walter. 1828. *The East India Gazetteer, Containing Particular Description of the Empires, Kingdoms, Principalities, Provinces, Cities, Towns, Districts, Fortresses, Harbours, Rivers, Lakes, etc. of Hindoostan and the Adjacent Countries; India Beyond the Ganges and the Eastern Archipelago together with Sketches of the Manners, Customs, Institutions, Agriculture, Commerce, Manufactures, Revenue, Population, Castes, Religion, History and Culture of the Various Inhabitants*. London: Panbury, Allen & Co.

Handique, Bhuban. 1994. *Changrung Phukanar Buranji*. Dhemaji: Purbanchal Tai Sahitya Sabha.

Handique, Radha. 1924. *Mula Gabhoru*. Jorhat: Sarat Chandra Press.

Handler, Richard. 1988. *Nationalism and the Politics of Culture in Quebec*. Madison: University of Wisconsin Press.

Harootunian, H. 1988. *Things Seen and Unseen: Discourse and Ideology in Tokugawa Nativism*. Chicago: University of Chicago Press.

Harper, Ralph. 1966. *Nostalgia: An Existential Exploration of Longing and Fulfilment in the Modern Age*. Ohio: Case Western Reserve University Press.

Harvey, David. 1997 (1996). *Justice, Nature, and the Geography of Difference*. Oxford: Blackwell Publishers.

Hays, Stephen, ed. 1988. *Sources of Indian Tradition*. Vol. 1. New York: Columbia University Press.

Hazarika, Nagen. 1994. *Moron Sangeet*. Mangaldai: Suman Printers.

Hazarika, Sanjoy. 1994. *Strangers of the Mist: Tales of War and Peace in India's Northeast*. New Delhi: Viking.

———. 2000. *Rites of Passage: Border Crossings, Imagined Homelands, India's East and Bangladesh*. Delhi: Penguin.

Held, David. 1991. "Between State and Civil Society: Citizenship." In *Citizenship*, ed. Geoff Andrews. London: Lawrence and Wishart.

Hellman-Rayanayagam, Dagmar. 1995. "Is There a Tamil Race?" In *The Concept of Race in South Asia*, ed. Peter Robb. Delhi: Oxford University Press.

Herzfeld, M. 1987. *Anthropology through the Looking-Glass*. Cambridge: Cambridge University Press.

Higham, Charles. 1989. *The Archeology of Mainland South East Asia*. Cambridge: Cambridge University Press.

Hill, J., ed. 1988. *Rethinking History and Myth: Indigenous South American Perspectives on the Past*. Urbana: University of Illinois Press.

Hobsbawm, E., and T. Ranger, eds. 1986. *The Invention of Tradition*. Cambridge: Cambridge University Press.

Hocart, A. 1969. *Kingship*. Oxford: Oxford University Press.

——. 1970. *Kings and Councillors: An Essay in the Comparative Anatomy of Human Society*. Chicago: University of Chicago Press.

Hodson, T. C. 1987 [1937]. *India Census Ethnography, 1901–1931*. Delhi: USHA.

Hoffman, H. H. R. 1969. "An Account of the Bon Religion in Gilgit." *Central Asiatic Journal* 13, no. 2: 137–45.

Horne, D. 1984. *The Great Museum: The Representation of History*. London: Pluto Press.

Horowitz, Donald. 1985. *Ethnic Groups in Conflict*. Berkeley: University of California Press.

Howell, David. 1998. "Territoriality and Collective Identity in Tokugawa Japan." *Daedalus* 127, no. 3: 105–31.

Howarth, David, Aletta Norval, and Yannis Stavrakakis. 2000. *Discourse Theory and Political Analysis: Identities, Hegemonies, and Social Change*. Manchester: Manchester University Press.

Hunter, W. W. 1879. *Statistical Account of Assam*. London: Trubner and Co.

Huntington, Samuel. 1990. *Leaves from the Bodhi Tree*. Seattle: University of Washington Press.

Hussain, Manirul. 1993. *The Assam Movement: Class, Ideology, and Identity*. Delhi: Manik Publication.

Hussain, Mohibul. 1979. *Ahamat Mussalman*. Sibsagar: Mohibul Hussain.

Hutton, Patrick. 1994. "Book Review. *History and Memory* and *Assassins of Memory: Essays on the Denial of the Holocaust*." *History and Theory* 33, no. 1: 95–107.

——. 1997. "Mnemonic Schemes in the New History of Memory." *History and Theory* 36, no. 3: 378–91.

Jalal, Ayesha. 1994 [1985]. *The Sole Spokesman: Jinnah, the Muslim League, and the Demand for Pakistan*. Cambridge: Cambridge University Press.

Jardanova, Ludmilla. 1987. "The Interpretation of Nature." *Comparative Studies in Society and History* 29: 195–200.

Jenkins, Francis. 1838. "Jenkins' Report on Upper Assam." London: India Office Library.

Jha, D. N. 2002. *The Myth of the Holy Cow*. London: Verso.

Kakati, B. K. 1978. *The Mother Goddess Kamakhya*. Guwahati: Lawyer's Book Stall.

Kakati, Sarbeshwar. 1939. "Hatimura Devalayar Dhangha Ba Sesh." *Abahan* 1, no. 4:416–18.

Kapferer, Bruce. 1988. *Legends of People, Myths of States: Violence, Intolerance, and Political Culture in Sri Lanka and Australia*. Washington, D.C.: Smithsonian Institution Press.

Kapur, Rajiv. 1986. *Sikh Separatism: The Politics of Faith*. London: Allen and Unwin.

Karlsson, B. G. 2000. *Contested Belonging: An Indigenous People's Struggle for Forest and Identity in Sub-Himalayan Bengal*. London: Curzon.

Kaul, B. M. 1967. *An Untold Story*. New Delhi: Allied Publishers.

Kaviraj, Sudipta. 1992. "The Imaginary Institution of India." In *Subaltern Studies:*

*Writing on South Asian History and Society*, Vol. 7, ed. Partha Chatterjee and Gyan Pandey. Delhi: Oxford University Press.

Kedourie, Elie. 1960. *Nationalism*. London: Hutchinson.

———. 1971. *Nationalism in Asia and Africa*. London: Weidenfeld and Nicolson.

Keyes, Charles. 1981. "The Dialectics of Ethnic Change." In *Ethnic Change*, ed. Charles Keyes. Seattle: University of Washington Press.

Khilnani, Sunil. 1998. *The Idea of India*. New York: Farrar, Straus and Giroux.

Khordadbhih, Ibn. 1889. *Kitab al Masalik wa'l Mamalik*. Trans. M. D. De Goeje. Leiden: E. J. Brill.

King, Christopher. 1986. *One Language, Two Scripts: The History of Hindi and Urdu*. Delhi: Oxford University Press.

Kondo, D. 1990. *Crafting Selves: Power, Gender, and the Disourse of Identity in a Japanese Workplace*. Chicago: University of Chicago Press.

Kosambi, D. D. 1990 [1956]. *An Introduction to the Study of Indian History*. Bombay: Popular Prakashan.

Kulke, H., and D. Rothermund. 1986. *A History of India*. Totowa, N.J.: Barnes and Noble.

Laclau, E., and C. Mouffe. 1985. *Hegemony and Socialist Strategy*. London: Verso.

Lahiri, Nayanjyoti. 1991. *Pre-Ahom Assam*. Delhi: Munshiram Manoharlal Publishers.

Lambert, Eric. 1942. "A Short Note on the Ahoms." *Journal of the Siam Society* 40, no. 1: 39–64.

Leach, E. R. 1981 [1965]. *Political Systems of Highland Burma*. London: Athlone Press.

Le Goff, Jacques. 1992. *History and Memory*. Trans. Steven Rendall and Elizabeth Claman. New York: Columbia University Press.

Levi-Strauss, C. 1979. *Myth and Meaning*. New York: Schocken Books.

Lightbrown, R. J. 1982. "British Views of India." *History Today* 32 ( July): 23–27.

Litzinger, Ralph. 1998. "Memory Work: Reconstituting the Ethnic in Post-Mao China." *Cultural Anthropology* 13, no. 2: 224–55.

Lowenthal, David. 1985. *The Past Is a Foreign Country*. Cambridge: Cambridge University Press.

———. "Identity, Heritage, and History." In *Commemorations: The Politics of National Identity*, ed. John Gillis. Princeton: Princeton University Press.

Luce, G. H. 1958. "The Early Syam in Burma's History." *Journal of the Siam Society* 56, no. 2: 123–72.

Ludden, David, ed. 1996. *Contesting the Nation: Religion, Community, and the Politics of Democracy in India*. Philadelphia: University of Pennsylvania Press.

Lutz, Catherine, and Lila Abu-Lughod, eds. 1990. *Language and the Politics of Emotion*. Cambridge: Cambridge University Press.

Malinowski, B. 1984. "The Role of Myth in Life." In *Magic, Science, and Religion, and Other Essays*. Westport, Conn.: Greenwood Press.

Mani, Lata. 1990. "Contentious Traditions: The Debate on Sati in Colonial India." In *Recasting Women: Essays in Indian Colonial History*, ed. Kumkum Sangari and Suresh Vaid. New Brunswick: Rutgers University Press.

*Manusmriti*. 1999. (English) Delhi: Penguin.

Marbariang, I. 1970. *Assam in a Nutshell*. 2nd ed. Shillong: Chapala Book Stall.

Marr, D., and A. Milner, eds. 1986. *Southeast Asia in the Ninth to Fourteenth Centuries*. Singapore: Institute of Southeast Asian Studies.

Matsuda, Matt. 1996. *The Memory of the Modern*. New York: Oxford University Press.

Mattingly, Cheryl. 1998. "Time, Narrative, and Cultural Action." *American Anthropologist* 100, no. 1: 184–86.

McLeod, W. H. 1989. *Who Is a Sikh? The Problem of Sikh Identity*. Oxford: Clarendon Press.

Medhi, Kaliram. 1998. *Assamese Grammar and the Origin of the Assamese Language*. Guwahati: Publication Board of Assam.

Menon, K. D., ed. 1975. *Tripura District Gazetteers*. Agartala: Tripura Government.

Menon, Ritu, and Kamla Bhasin. 2000. *Borders and Boundaries*. New Brunswick: Rutgers University Press.

Metcalf, Barbara, and Tom Metcalf. 2000. *Concise History of India*. Cambridge: Cambridge University Press.

Miller, J., ed. 1980. *The African Past Speaks*. Hamden, Conn.: Archon.

Mills, Moffat. 1854. *Report on the Province of Assam*. Calcutta: Calcutta Gazette Office.

Milne, Leslie. 1910. *Shans at Home*. London: John Murray.

Miri, S., ed. 1978. *Religion and Society of North East India*. New Delhi: Vikas Publishing House.

Misra, Udayon. 2000. *The Periphery Strikes Back: Challenges to the Nation-State in Assam and Nagaland*. Simla: Indian Institute of Advanced Study.

Mitchell, J. F. 1883. *Report, Topographical and Military, on the North-East Frontier of India*. Calcutta: Superintendent of Government Printing.

Mitra, R. C. 1951. "The Decline of Buddhism in India." *Visva Bharati Annals* 6: 1–92.

Mitra, Subrata, and R. Lewis, eds. 1996. *Subnational Movements in South Asia*. Boulder: Westview Press.

Moore, S. 1986. *Social Facts and Fabrications: "Customary" Law on Kilimanjaro, 1880–1980*. Cambridge: Cambridge University Press.

Naipaul, V. S. 1979. *Bend in the River*. New York: Knopf.

Nanda, B. R. 1995. *Jawaharlal Nehru: Rebel and Stateman*. New Delhi: Oxford University Press.

Nandy, Ashish. 1983. *The Intimate Enemy: Loss and Recovery of Self Under Colonialism*. New Delhi: Oxford University Press.

Narayan, Kirin. 1989. *Storytellers, Saints, and Scoundrels: Folk Narrative in Hindu Religious Teaching*. Philadelphia: University of Pennsylvania Press.

Nartsupha, Chatthip. 1991. "The 'Community Culture' School of Thought." In *Thai Constructions of Knowledge*, ed. Manas Chitakasem and Andrew Turton. London: School of Oriental and African Studies.

——. 1996a. "On the Study of Tai Cultural History." *Thai-Yunnan Project Newsletter* 32 (June): 14–15.

——. 1996b. "Research Experience in Thai History." *Thai-Yunnan Project Newsletter* 32 (June): 21–22.

Nath, R. M. 1948. *The Background of Assamese Culture*. 2nd ed. Guwahati: Dutta Barua and Sons.

Nehru, Jawaharlal. 1946. *The Discovery of India*. Calcutta: Signet Press.

——. 1947. *An Autobiography*. London: n.p.

Neog, Maheshwar. 1974. *Asamiya Sahityar Ruprekha*. Guwahati: Assam Publication Board.

——. 1979. *Annals of the Assam Sahitya Sabha*. Jorhat: Assam Sahitya Sabha.

Nora, Pierre. 1989. "Between Memory and History: Les lieux de memoire." Trans. Marc Roudebush. *Representations* 26: 7–25.

Nugent, David. 1997. *Modernity at the Edge of Empire: State, Individual, and Nation in the Northern Peruvian Andes, 1885–1935*. Stanford: Stanford University Press.

Ohnuki-Tierney, Emiko. 1987. *The Monkey as Mirror: Symbolic Transformations in Japanese History*. Princeton: Princeton University Press.

——. 1990. "Introduction: The Historicization of Anthropology." In *Culture through Time*, ed. Emiko Ohnuki-Tierney. Stanford: Stanford University Press.

——. 1991. "The Emperor of Japan as Deity (Kami): An Anthropology of the Emperial System in Historical Perspective." *Ethnology* 30, no. 3: 199–215.

——. 1994. *Rice as Self: Japanese Identities through Time*. Princeton: Princeton University Press.

O'Hanlan, R. 1988. "Recovering the Subject: Subaltern Studies and Histories of Resistance in Colonial South Asia." *Modern Asian Studies* 22, no. 1: 189–224.

Ong, W. 1967. *The Presence of the Word: Some Prolegomena for Cultural and Religious History*. New Haven: Yale University Press.

——. 1982. *Orality and Literacy: The Technologizing of the Word*. New York: Methuen.

Padnis, Urmilla. 1989. *Ethnicity and Nation Building in South Asia*. New Delhi: Sage Publications.

Pandey, Gyan. 1992. "In Defence of the Fragment: Writing about Hindu-Muslim Riots in India Today." *Representations* 37 (winter): 27–55.

——. 1995. "Voices from the Edge: The Struggle to Write Subaltern Histories." *Ethnos* 60, nos. 3–4: 223.

——. 2001. *Remembering Partition*. Cambridge: Cambridge University Press.

Panikar, K. N. 1995. *Culture, Ideology, and Hegemony: Intellectuals and Social Consciousness in Colonial India*. New Delhi: Tulika.

Parel, Anthony, ed. 1997. *Hind Swaraj and Other Writings*. Cambridge: Cambridge University Press.

Paul, P. L. 1939. *The Early History of Bengal*. Vols. 1 and 2. Calcutta: Indian Research Institute.

Pettigrew, Joyce. 1995. *The Sikh of the Punjab: Unheard Voices of State and Guerilla Violence*. Zed Press.

Phillimore, R. H., comp. 1945. *Historical Records of the Survey of India*. Dehra Dun: Surveyor General of India.

Phillips, Anne. 1991. "Citizenship and Feminist Theory." In *Citizenship*, ed. Goeff Andrews. London: Lawrence and Wishart.

Phukan, J. N. 1981. "Sources of the History of Assam: The Inscriptions in Ahom (Tai) Language." Paper presented at the Assam Research Society, Guwahati, February 21–22.

———. 1994. "Some Aspects of the Buranjis." Presentation in honor of Dr. Suryya Kumar Bhuyan Centenary Celebration, Guwahati University, May 4.

Phukan, T. 1994. "Ahom Hakalar Muga Kheti." In *Tai Sanskriti*, ed. Gogoi and Gogoi. Dhemaji: Purbanchal Tai Sahitya Sabha.

Polo, Marco. 1939. *The Travels of Ser Marco Polo*. Vol. 2. Revised by H. Yule. Edinburgh: Edinburgh University Press.

Pongpaichit, Pasuk, and Chris Baker. 1998. *Thailand's Boom and Bust*. Chiang Mai: Silkworm Press.

———. 2000. *Thailand's Crisis*. Chiangmai: Silkworm Press.

Powell, Arvil. 1996. "Perceptions of the South Asian Past: Ideology, Nationalism, and School History Textbooks." In *The Transmission of Knowledge in South Asia*, ed. Nigel Cook. Delhi: Oxford University Press.

Price, R. 1983. *First Time: The Historical Vision of an Afro-American People*. Baltimore: Johns Hopkins University Press.

Pye, L. 1985. *Asian Power and Politics: The Cultural Dimensions of Authority*. Cambridge: Harvard University Press.

Rajani, Mom Chao Chand Chirayu. 1976. *Guide through the Inscriptions of Sukhothai*. Honolulu: University of Hawaii Press.

Rajkhowa, Arobindo. 1995. *Ahamar Sadhinatar Nyajyata*. Assam: Sadhinata Prakashan.

Rao, V. N. 1993. "Purana as Brahmanic Ideology." In *Purana Perennis: Reciprocity and Transformation in Hindu and Jaina Text*, ed. Wendy Dongler. Albany: SUNY.

Ray, B. 1991. *Myth, Ritual, and Kingship in Buganda*. Oxford: Oxford University Press.

Ray, H. C. 1985. *The Dynastic History of Northern India*. 2nd ed. Vol. 1. Delhi: Munshiram Manoharlal Publication.

Raychoudhuri, Ambika Giri. 1929. *Asamiya*. Guwahati: Assam State Archives.

Redfield, R. 1953. *The Primitive World and Its Transformation*. New York: Cornell University Press.

Reid, Anthony, and David Marr, eds. 1979. *Perceptions of the Past in Southeast Asia*. Hong Kong: Heinemann Educational Books.

Reid, Robert. 1966. *Years of Change in Bengal and Assam*. London: Ernest Bern.

Renan, Ernest. 1999 [1882]. "What is a Nation?" In *The Nationalism Reader*, ed. Omar Dahbour and Micheline Ishay. New York: Humanity Press.

Richards, John F. 1974. "The Islamic Frontier in the East: Expansion into South Asia." *South Asia* 4: 91–109.

———, ed. 1983. *Precious Metals in Later Medieval and Early Modern Worlds*. Durham: Carolina Academic Press.

Ricouer, Paul. 1980. *Contribution of French Historiography to the Theory of History*. Oxford: Clarendon Press.

———. 1991. *From Text to Action*. Evanston, Ill.: Northwestern University Press.

Risely, H. H. 1891. *The Tribes and Castes of Bengal*. Calcutta: Bengal Secretariat Press.

Robb, Peter. 1995. *The Concept of Race in South Asia*. Delhi: Oxford University Press.

Robinson, W. 1841. *A Descriptive Account of Assam with a Sketch of the Local Geography and a Concise History of the Tea-Plant to which is Added a Short Account of the Neighbouring Tribes Exhibiting their History, Manners and Customs*. London: Ostell and Lepage.

Rosaldo, R. 1989. *Culture and Truth: The Remaking of Social Analysis*. Boston: Beacon Press.

Royce, Anya Peterson. 1982. *Ethnic Identity: Strategies of Diversity*. Bloomington: Indiana University Press.

Rubin, Jeffrey. 1997. *Decentering the Regime: Ethnicity, Radicalism, and Democracy in Juchitán, Mexico*. Durham: Duke University Press.

Rushdie, Salman. 1996. *East, West*. New York: Vintage.

Rybezynski, Witold. 1986. *Home: A Short History of an Idea*. New York: Viking.

Sahlins, Marshall. 1985. *Islands of History*. Chicago: Chicago University Press.

Said, Edward. 1979. *Orientalism*. New York: Vintage.

Saikia, Yasmin. 1995. "The Making of the Assamese Frontier: Whose Frontier Is It Anyway?" Paper presented at the 24th Annual South Asia Conference, University of Wisconsin, Madison, October 17–19.

———. 1997. *In the Meadows of Gold: Telling Tales of the Swargadeos in the Crossroads of Assam*. Guwahati: Spectrum Publications.

Sarkar, Jadu Nath. 1984. *The Art of War in Medieval India*. Delhi: Munshiram Manoharlal Publication.

Sattar, Abdus. 1965. *Sangmrisranat Aahamia Sanskriti*. Khowang: Art Press.

Sarvarkar, V. 1923. *Hindutva: Who Is a Hindu?* Poona: Veer Sarvarker Praashan.

Schafer, Roy. 1992. *Retelling a Life: Narration and Dialogue in Psychoanalysis*. New York: Basic Books.

Schama, Simon. 1995. *Landscape and Memory*. New York: Knopf.

Schreiner, P., and R. Söhner. 1987. *Sanskrit Indices and Text of the Brahmapurana*. Vol. 1. Wiesbaden: Otto Hanrassowitz.

Schwartzberg, Joseph. 1978. *A Historical Atlas of South Asia*. Chicago: University of Chicago Press.

Scott, David. 1832. *A Memoir of Late David Scott*. Calcutta: Baptist Mission Press.

Scott, James. 1985. *Weapons of the Weak: Everyday Forms of Peasant Resistance*. New Haven: Yale University Press.

Segal, Robert, ed. 1990. *In Quest of the Hero*. Princeton: Princeton University Press.

Seidenfaden, Eric. 1958. *The Thai Peoples*. Bangkok: Siam Society.

Sen, K., ed. 1927. *Rajamala*. Agartala: n.p.

Shahid, Amin. 1995. *Event, Metaphor, Memory: Chauri Chaura (1922–1992)*. Delhi: Oxford University Press.

Sharma, D. 1981. *Kamarupasasanavali*. Guwahati: Publication Board of Assam.

Sharma, M. M., ed. 1977. *Inscriptions of Ancient Assam*. Guwahati: Directorate of Historical and Antiquarian Studies.

Sharma, P. C. 1988. *Architecture of Assam*. Delhi: Agam Kala Prakashan.

Shastri, G. 1984. *The Arthashastra of Kautilya*. Vol. 1. Delhi: Bharatiya Vidya Prakash.

Smith, Anthony. 1986. *The Ethnic Origins of Nations*. Oxford: Basil Blackwell.

——. 1992. "Ethnicity and Nationalism." *International Journal of Comparative Sociology* 33: 1–4.

Smith, R. B. *Siam; or, the History of Thais from Earliest Times to 1569 A.D.* Baltimore: Decatur Press, 1966.

Spence, Donald. 1982. *Narrative Truth and Historical Truth*. New York: Norton.

Society of Phralung Buddhist Culture and the Ahom Religious and Cultural Council. 1995. "Memorandum to the Prime Minister."

Stein, M. A., ed. 1961. *Kalhana's Rajatarangini*. Vol. 1, book 2. Delhi: Motilal Banarsidass.

Stock, B. 1983. *The Implications of Literacy: Written Language and Models of Interpretation in the Eleventh and Twelfth Centuries*. Princeton: Princeton University Press.

——. 1990. *Listening for the Text: On the Uses of the Past*. Baltimore: Johns Hopkins University Press.

Subramanian, Narendra. 1999. *Ethnicity and Populist Mobilization: Political Parties and Democracy in South India*. New York: Oxford University Press.

Sukhabanij, K. 1956. "Was Nam Thom the First King of Sukhothai?" *Journal of the Siam Society* 44: 139–44.

Talbot, Cynthia. 2001. *Precolonial India in Practice: Society, Region, and Identity in Medieval Andhra*. New York: Oxford University Press.

Tamuli-Phukan, Kashinath. 1906. *Assam Buranji*. 1st ed. Calcutta: Majumdar Press.

Tarlo, Emma. 1996. *Clothing Matters: Dress and Identity in India*. Chicago: University of Chicago Press.

Tatlam Darshan Singh. 1999. *The Sikh Diaspora: The Search for Statehood*. Seattle: University of Washington Press.

Terwiel, B. J. 1983a. "Ahom and the Study of Early Tai Society." *Journal of the Siam Society* 81, no. 2: 42–62.

———. 1983b. *The Tai of Assam and Ancient Tai Ritual.* 2 vols. Gaya: Review Office of South East Asian Studies.

Terwiel, B. J. 1994. "Ahom Ritual: A Brand-New Ancient Tradition." Paper presented at the Conference on Myth and Social Life in Southeast Asia, University of Leyden.

Terwiel, B. J., and Ranoo Wichasin. 1992. *Tai Ahoms and the Stars: Three Ritual Texts to Ward Off Danger.* Ithaca: Southeast Asia Program, Cornell University.

Thapar, Romila. 1978. *Ancient Indian Social History: Some Interpretations.* New Delhi: Oxford University Press.

———. 1993. *Indian History: Historical Probings.* Delhi: Oxford University Press.

———. 1986. "Society and Historical Consciousness: The Itihasa–Purana Tradition." In *Situating Indian History,* ed. R. Thapar and S. Bhattakcharya. Delhi: Oxford University Press.

Thompson, E. P. 1978. *The Poverty of Theory.* London: Merlin.

Tilak, B. G. 1938. *The Artic Home in the Vedas.* Nagpur: Tilak Bros.

Tillotson, Giles. 1994. "Orientalizing the Raj." *Marg* 46, no. 1: 15–66.

Toland, Judith. 1993. "Introduction. Dialogue of Self and Other: Ethnicity and Statehood Building." In *Ethnicity and the State,* ed. Judith Toland. New Brunswick: Transaction Publishers.

Trouillot, Michel-Rolph. 1995. *Silencing the Past: Power and the Production of History.* Boston: Beacon Press.

Turner, Victor. 1967. *The Forest of Symbols: Aspects of Ndembu Ritual.* Ithaca: Cornell University Press.

United Liberation Front of Assam. 1992. "The Assamese Nation." n.p.

———. 1978. *The Children of Woot: A History of the Kuba Peoples.* Madison: University of Wisconsin Press.

Vansina, Jan. 1985. *Oral Tradition as History.* Madison: University of Wisconsin Press.

Vansittart, Henry, ed. 1785. *The History of the First Ten Years of the Reign of Alamgeer.* Calcutta: Daniel Stuart.

Verma, T. P. 1976. *Development of Script in Ancient Kamrupa.* Guwahati: Assam Sahitya Sabha.

Washbrook, David. 1997a. "After the Mutiny: From Queen to Queen Empress." *History Today* 47: 10–15.

———. 1997b. "India and the British." *History Today* 47: 3–15.

Watson, Forbes, J., and John W. Kaye. 1868. *Peoples of India: With Descriptive Letterpress of the Races and Tribes of Hindustan.* Vol. 1. London: Indian Museum.

Weiner, Myron. 1978. *Sons of the Soil: Migration and Ethnic Conflict in India.* Princeton: Princeton University Press.

White, Hayden. 1987. *The Content of the Form: Narrative Discourse and Historical Representation.* Baltimore: Johns Hopkins University Press.

Wichasin, Ranoo. 1991. "Ahom Revivalism in Assam," *Lik Tai Khwam Tai* 9 (1991).

———. 1996. "The Ahom Buranji Project." *Thai-Yunnan Project Newsletter* 32 (June): 13–14.

Widlund, Ingrid. 2000. *Paths of Power and Patterns of Influence: The Dravidian Partities in South India*. Uppsala: Uppsala Universitet.

Wilson, Adrian, ed. 1993. *Rethinking Social History*. Manchester: Manchester University Press.

Winichakul, Thongchai. 1994. *Siam Mapped: A History of the Geo-Body of a Nation*. Honolulu: University of Hawaii Press.

———. 1982. *Europe and the People without History*. Berkeley: University of California Press.

Wolf, Eric. 1988. "Inventing Society." *American Ethnologist* 15: 752–61.

Wurgaft, Lewis. 1995. "Identity in World History: A Postmodern Perspective." *History and Theory* 34: 67–85.

Wyatt, David. 1982. *Thailand: A Short History*. New Haven: Yale University Press.

Zeigler, Norman. 1976. "Marvari Historical Chronicles: Sources for the Social and Cultural History of Rajasthan." *Indian Economic and Social History Review* 13, no. 2 (April–June): 219–50.

Zertal, Idith. 2000. "From the People's Hall to the Wailing Wall: A Study of Memory, Fear, and War." *Representations*, no. 69 (winter): 96–126.

Zerubavel, Yael. 1994. *Recovered Roots: Collective Memory and the Making of the Israeli National Tradition*. Chicago: University of Chicago Press.

*Index*

Borgohain, Homen, 197

Borgohain, Nabin, 162, 199, 239, 240

Borgohain, Ratneshwar, 202

Borgohain. *See* Swargadeo's
administration

Borooah, Padmanath Gohain, 70–72

Brahmaputra River, 8–10, 109, 148,
153

Brahmaputra Valley, 59. *See also*
Assam: geo-political history of

Brahmins: in precolonial Assam, 120,
123–124, 253

British colonial administration of
Assam, 57–75, 94–101; and census
making, 41, 64, 74, 93, 110, 127,
142; and commissioning of buranjis, 121; and construction of
Ahom ethnicity, 142–143, 253–255;
and construction of Assamese subjects, 80; and construction of the
concept of India, 41–51; and construction of a regional history, 17,
20, 30–32, 101–102, 110, 124–125;
and depictions of Assamese people,
56–58, 95–97, 102, 109; and division of subjects into castes and
tribes, 41–42, 50–51, 74; and economic exploitation of Assam, 95–
111, 254; and erasure of Ahoms, 80,
93–97, 100–102, 143, 254 (*see also*
Swargadeo's administration: British
colonial administration's relationship with); and importation of
labor, 106–109, 155; and introduction of cash crops into Assam, 97–
99; land distribution and revenue
policy of, 97–101; opium policies
of, 95–107; and petroleum exploitation in Assam, 108–110

Bruce, Robert, 104

Buddhism, Tai-Ahom relationship
with, 221, 245

Buragohain, Romesh, 217

Buragohain, Siva, 168

Buragohain, Santanu, 242

Buranjis, xii-xvi, 16, 20–33, 59, 83–89,
111–140, 154, 163, 164, 196; contents of, 114–116, 119–142, 253;
general description of, 113–114,
121–124, 137; origin of, 118–120;
utilization of, by Tai-Ahom identity
movement, 226, 232

Burma: British colonial relationship
with, 9, 92–94; historical relationship of, with Assam, 8, 73, 86, 87,
116, 124, 190; modern relationship
with Assam, 180

Burmese rebel groups: relationship
with Tai-Ahom, 220; relationship
with ULFA, 212

Butler, John, 93, 95

Calcutta, 29, 58, 60, 105, 202

Caste Hinduism: dominance of, in
Indian national narratives, 47, 251–
255

Caste Hindus: in Assam, 85–86;
national privileging of, 41–51, 256–
257, 264; Tai-Ahom relationship
with, 159–164, 187–202, 228, 234–
248. *See also* Anti-caste Hindu sentiment in Assam; Indian national
government: relationship with
Assam

Chakarepheti Buranji, 137

Changrai, 52

Charaideo, 104, 154, 170, 209

Chatra Parishad movement, 170–171

Chetia, Anup, 179, 214

Chetia, Purandar, 164

Chetia, Umesh, 28, 29

China: relationship with India and
Assam, 37, 165–167, 256

Cholas, 47

Yasmin Saikia is an assistant professor of history at the
University of North Carolina, Chapel Hill.

Library of Congress Cataloging-in-Publication Data
Saikia, Yasmin.
Fragmented memories : struggling to be Tai-Ahom in
India / Yasmin Saikia.
p. cm.
Includes bibliographical references and index.
ISBN 0-8223-3425-9 (cloth : alk. paper)
ISBN 0-8223-3373-2 (pbk. : alk. paper)
1. Ahoms (Indic people)—Ethnic identity. 2. Assam
(India)—Ethnic relations. I. Title: Struggling to be
Tai-Ahom in India. II. Title.
DS432.A39S25  2004
954'.16200495919—dc22
2004007046